Designing Systems
for
Internet Commerce

G. Winfield Treese
Lawrence C. Stewart

ADDISON-WESLEY

An Imprint of Addison Wesley Longman, Inc.
Reading, Massachusetts • Harlow, England • Menlo Park, California
Berkeley, California • Don Mills, Ontario • Sydney
Bonn • Amsterdam • Tokyo • Mexico City

Many of the designations used by manufacturers and sellers to distinguish their products are claimed as trademarks. Where those designations appear in this book and Addison-Wesley was aware of a trademark claim, the designations have been printed in initial caps or all caps.

The authors and publisher have taken care in the preparation of this book, but make no expressed or implied warranty of any kind and assume no responsibility for errors or omissions. No liability is assumed for incidental or consequential damages in connection with or arising out of the use of the information or programs contained herein.

The publisher offers discounts on this book when ordered in quantity for special sales. For more information, please contact:

Computer & Engineering Publishing Group
Addison Wesley Longman, Inc.
One Jacob Way
Reading, Massachusetts 01867

Library of Congress Cataloging-in-Publication Data

Treese, G. Winfield.
   Designing systems for Internet commerce / G. Winfield Treese,
Lawrence C. Stewart.
      p.   cm.
   Includes bibliographical references and index.
   ISBN 0-201-57167-6
   1. System design. 2. Internet commerce. I. Stewart, Lawrence C.
II. Title.
QA76.9.S88T74 1998
658.8'00285'4678--dc21   98-11176
                                                    CIP

ISBN 0-201-57167-6
Text printed on recycled and acid-free paper.
1 2 3 4 5 6 7 8 9 10–MA–0201009998

First printing, April 1998

For Erica and Samantha

Contents

Preface   xi

CHAPTER 1 *Introduction*   1

Why the Internet and Why Now?   2
Strategic Issues   4
What Do We Mean by "Internet Commerce"?   5
Business Issues in Internet Commerce   6
Technology Issues in Internet Commerce   7
Who Owns Internet Commerce in an Organization?   8
Structure of the Book   9

Part One   **The Business of Internet Commerce**

CHAPTER 2 *The Commerce Value Chain*   15

Introducing the Commerce Value Chain   15
Components of the Commerce Value Chain   17
Who Is the Customer?   21
Marketing on the Internet   22
Doing Business Internationally   25
The Legal Environment   27
Summary   30

CHAPTER 3 *Internet Business Strategy*   31

    Commerce and Technology Revolutions   31
    An Historical Analogy   32
    The Internet Value Proposition   34
    Four Strategies   35
    New Competitive Threats   38
    New Competitive Opportunities   39
    Summary   40

CHAPTER 4 *Business Models—Some Case Studies*   41

    Introduction to Business Segments   41
    Consumer Retail   43
    Business-to-Business Cataloging   53
    Information Commerce   59
    Summary   67

CHAPTER 5 *Conflicting Goals and Requirements*   69

    Goals of the Participants   69
    The Role of Standards   74
    Privacy versus Merchandising   76
    Secure Electronic Transactions   79
    Summary   82

CHAPTER 6 *Functional Architecture*   83

    What Is Architecture?   83
    Core Architectural Ideas   84
    Roles   86
    Components   90
    Examples of System Architecture   92
    Summary   101

CHAPTER 7 *Implementation Strategies*   103

    Planning the Implementation   103
    Outsourcing   104
    Custom Development   106
    Packaged Applications   107

The Role of Internet Service Providers   108
Commerce Service Providers   111
Project Management   112
Staying Up to Date   113
The Role of Standards   115
Round-the-Clock Operation   116
Security Design   118
Multiorganization Operation   118
Summary   119

Part Two   The Technology of Internet Commerce

CHAPTER 8   *The Internet and the World Wide Web*   123

The Technology of the Internet   123
Development of the Internet   124
Design Principles of the Internet   125
Core Network Protocols   127
The World Wide Web   132
Agents   136
Intranets   137
Extranets   137
Consumer Devices and Network Computers   138
The Future of the Internet: Protocol Evolution   138
Summary   139

CHAPTER 9   *Building Blocks for Internet Commerce*   141

Components in an Internet Commerce System   141
Content Transport   141
Server Components   148
Programming Clients   151
Sessions and Cookies   153
Object Technology   156
Commerce Client Technology   160
Technology for Fulfillment of Digital Goods   163
Summary   168

CHAPTER 10 *System Design*   169

    The Problem of Design   169
    Our Philosophy of Design   170
    An Architectural Approach   171
    Security   177
    Design Principles versus "Technology of the Day"   179
    Summary   180

CHAPTER 11 *Creating and Managing Content*   181

    What the Customers See   181
    Basic Content   182
    Tools for Creating Content   189
    Managing Content   195
    Multimedia Presentation   198
    Different Faces for Different Users   199
    Integration with Other Media   206
    Summary   207

CHAPTER 12 *Cryptography*   209

    Keeping Secrets   209
    Types of Cryptography   210
    How to Evaluate Cryptography   212
    Operational Choices   214
    One-Time Pad   215
    Secret Key (Symmetric) Cryptography   216
    Public Key (Asymmetric) Cryptography   219
    Protocols   223
    Key Management   228
    Summary   233

CHAPTER 13 *Security*   235

    Concerns about Security   235
    Why We Worry about Security for Internet Commerce   236
    Thinking about Security   239
    Security Design   241
    Analyzing Risk   243

Basic Computer Security   247
Basic Internet Security   249
Client Security Issues   249
Server Security Issues   253
Achieving Application Security   255
Authentication   257
Summary   263

CHAPTER 14 *Payment Systems*   265

The Role of Payment   265
A Word about Money   266
Real-World Payment Systems   266
Smart Cards   279
Internet Payment Systems   282
Online Credit Card Payment   284
Electronic Cash   287
Micropayments   288
Payment in the Abstract   293
Summary   294

CHAPTER 15 *Auxiliary Systems*   295

The Details Behind the Scenes   295
Taxes   296
Shipping and Handling   299
Inventory Management   303
Summary   306

CHAPTER 16 *Transaction Processing*   307

Transactions and Internet Commerce   307
Overview of Transaction Processing   308
Transaction Processing in Internet Commerce   310
Client Software   311
Integrating Existing Systems   312
Keeping Business Records   313
Audit   317
Backup and Disaster Recovery   318
High-Availability Systems   318

Replication and Scaling   320
Implementing Transaction Processing Systems   321
Summary   324

Part Three   Systems for Internet Commerce

CHAPTER 17 *Putting It All Together*   327

Building a Complete System   327
System Architecture   330
SecureLink   334
Transact   337
Summary   349

CHAPTER 18 *The Future of Internet Commerce*   351

Trends   352
Discontinuities   355
Staying Up to Date   356
Strategic Imperatives   356
Closing Remarks   357

Resources and Further Reading   359

Index   365

Preface

In 1994, *The Economist* ranked the Internet between the telephone and the printing press in its long-term impact on the world. Just as those inventions transformed society, so the Internet has already begun a transformation—one that is happening much faster than the earlier revolutions. Commerce, of course, is one arena already feeling the effects of the Internet. In the past few years, we have seen dramatic changes in some businesses, the creation of new businesses, and significant effects on others.

In the nineteenth century, fast transportation—the railroad—fundamentally changed commerce. At the end of the twentieth century, the Internet is making fundamental changes to commerce for the next century. We are just at the beginning of the revolution. It is a revolution made possible by technology, offering a tremendous variety of new business opportunities. The technology will continue to change, and change at a rapid pace. New markets will appear and old ones will be transformed or disappear entirely. The short-term changes in technology and markets are important, but the reaction to them must be balanced with a long-term business vision. The challenge is using the technology effectively to achieve business goals.

The audience for this book is what we call the "Internet commerce team." This team includes people responsible for business and those responsible for technology. It includes those who develop the strategic vision for a company and those who put the strategy into action. In other words, the Internet commerce team is the group of people who work to make Internet commerce happen, from vision to implementation.

Our focus is on making Internet commerce happen and making it successful over the long term. In some ways, Internet commerce seems deceptively simple: companies think, "Let's put up a Web site and watch the money roll in." A year later they're wondering what happened and why it wasn't successful. As anyone involved in running a business knows, nothing is ever that easy. The basic rules of business haven't changed, but the Internet does change the playing field. It offers new markets, new ways to get close to customers, and new ways to work with partners.

For some, the excitement over Internet commerce has created a "credibility gap" between grand visions of change and the day-to-day problems of running computer systems for a business. It is easy to paint an exciting vision of the future, yet often difficult to figure out how to get there. This book aims to help bridge this gap, grounding the vision of change with what is possible for businesses to achieve with the changing technology.

Throughout the book, we emphasize both *practice* and *principles*—the what and the why. Practices are the actions—the specific ideas for specific circumstances. Principles are the general rules—the elements on which practices are built. As technology changes (or, for that matter, as business models change), the practices will need to change. The principles, in contrast, change more slowly and can be applied in a wide variety of circumstances. When a team understands the principles underlying what they do, they can adapt to changing circumstances and develop new practices for it. Without that understanding, they can become incapacitated when the situation changes and different practices are needed to be successful.

What the technology brings is a combination of new opportunities, changing cost structures, new customers, and faster response times. The technology opportunities must be combined with and tempered by the business goals. This book is about that combination—designing computer systems for doing business on open networks.

When we say this book is about design, we mean that it is intended to help with the design process. It doesn't give all the answers; the actual design for your business requirements is likely to be very different from someone else's. Nonetheless, we can explore some of the common issues and critical questions to ask when planning any system for Internet commerce. In the process, we look at some of the key technologies of today and apply those technologies in several examples.

A word of warning: at times it may seem that we are overly concerned with potential problems—the things that can go wrong. These are not reasons to avoid Internet commerce. Rather, we think it is important to approach Internet commerce as you would any other business proposition, understanding the downside as well as the upside, the risks as well as the benefits. On balance, using the Internet for commerce can be a tremendous asset for businesses. Doing everything possible to maximize the chances for success is merely good business.

We have created a Web site for this book at http://www.treese.org/Commerce/.

Acknowledgments

This book is an attempt to write down what we have learned about Internet commerce so far. Much of our experience in this area is drawn from our association with Open Market, which began operations in April 1994, but we have applied many of the lessons learned about the Internet and about systems design during our earlier careers at Xerox, Digital Equipment, and MIT, as well as from our academic associations with MIT, Harvard, and Stanford University.

We would first like to acknowledge the great contributions and support we have received in this endeavor from Shikhar Ghosh, Gary Eichhorn, Andrew Payne, Peter Woon, and the rest of our colleagues at Open Market. In one way or another, everyone at Open Market has contributed to this work.

The editorial team at Addison-Wesley has been outstanding, with our editor Karen Gettman, assistant editor Mary Harrington, production coordinator Jacquelyn Young, and the editor who inspired this work, Carol Long.

We have been fortunate to have many insightful reviewers for early drafts of our manuscript. Our thanks to Russell Nelson, Nathaniel Borenstein, Marcus Ranum, Richard Smith, Brian Reistad, Dave Crocker, Ray Kaplan, Bruce Schneier, John Adams, John Romkey, Fred Avolio, Kurt Friedrich, Alex Mehlman, Paul Baier, Ian Reid, Jeff Bussgang, Kevin Kuechler, and the anonymous reviewers.

Writing a book is a challenge not only for the authors, but for our families as well. To our wives, Marie Briasco and Cathy Briasco, and our daughters, Erica Briasco Treese and Samantha Marie Briasco-Stewart, go our thanks and our love. We are truly blessed.

Win Treese
Newton, MA
treese@acm.org

Larry Stewart
Burlington, MA
lstewart@acm.org

CHAPTER 1   *Introduction*

> For I dipped into the future, far as human eye could see,
> Saw the Vision of the world, and all the wonders that would be;
> Saw the heavens fill with commerce, argosies of magic sails
> —Alfred, Lord Tennyson[1]

Internet commerce has become the new frontier for businesses around the world. Though what is now the Internet began over 25 years ago, only in the past few years have we seen significant use of the Internet for commerce. The explosion of the Internet has been accompanied by claims of business revolution, ways to "make money fast working out of your home," and even the end of the nation-state. But what is the substance behind the sizzle?

We believe that the convergence of the global Internet with commerce will fundamentally change the way business is done, and this book is about making Internet commerce successful. Internet commerce brings some new technology and new capabilities to business, but the fundamental business problems are those that merchants have faced for hundreds—even thousands—of years: you must have something to sell, make it known to potential buyers, accept payment, deliver the goods or services, and provide appropriate service after the sale. Most of the time, you want to build a relationship with the customer that will bring repeat business.

---

1. Alfred, Lord Tennyson. *Locksley Hall,* 1842.

Why the Internet and Why Now?

In the short term, there are two reasons for a company to get involved in Internet commerce:[2]

- The top line: the ability to reach new customers and create more intimate relationships with all customers.

  On the Internet, every business has a global presence. Even small and medium-sized companies can now easily reach customers around the world. The technology of computing and communications enables a business to know more about its customers, share more of its information with customers, and apply that information to improving relationships and creating sales.

- The bottom line: drastic cost reductions for distribution and customer service.

  The Internet dramatically lowers the distribution costs for information, and dramatically improves the ability to keep information current. In a world where customers of all kinds are demanding more information about the products and services they purchase, the ability to deliver that information (and do it cheaply) becomes an important part of making the sale. And on the Internet, information may *be* the product.

Over the long term, the Internet may well change the structure of the competitive landscape. Instant communications will transform the relationship between businesses and their customers and the conversion from physical to digital will displace the source of business value. In many cases we cannot yet see the nature of the changes. For example, will the network lead to great consolidation of suppliers or to a flowering of thousands of small merchants each newly capable of global distribution? There are powerful arguments for both. Even more fundamentally, businesses will face competition from companies in completely different industries, requiring fundamental reassessment of their value propositions for the customer.

These considerations follow almost naturally from the technical and economic nature of the Internet. Following are some of the key properties of the Internet.

- The Internet is interoperable.

  Almost by definition, a computer is connected to the Internet if it can communicate with any other computer connected to the Internet. There are two factors that make this possible: the use of standardized protocols and the availability of universal naming, addressing, and routing. The standards of the Internet make this communication possible, without requiring prearranged agreements about how computers will communicate.

---

2. An alternate view is that the two reasons for a company to get involved in Internet commerce are the same as those for many areas of business: fear and greed.

- The Internet is global.

  Because the Internet structure is based on standardized and universal connectivity, it has rapidly become a global network. Since the network itself is used to distribute software, there is a readily available worldwide base of users with a common set of software, forming a foundation for business systems with a broad base of potential users.

- The Web makes it easy.

  The World Wide Web[3] has made highly functional multimedia content easily available to users worldwide. People with little or no computer experience can get connected to the Internet and use Web browsers very successfully.

- The costs of the network are shared across multiple applications and borne by the end users.

  Most businesses and consumers connected to the Internet pay for their own connections, and they are then free to use the network for any number of purposes. In consequence, a provider of information does not need to pay for a distribution system, other than its own connection to the network. The users of the service pay for the distribution. Because the network is shared among many users, the cost of this essential infrastructure is amortized across a wide variety of applications.

Access to a Global Market

"Globalization" is a common word these days, as advances in communication and transportation make it possible for businesses to operate worldwide. Suppliers and customers may be located anywhere. In many cases, countries are lowering or removing barriers to trade, encouraging more and more international commerce.

The Internet is accelerating this trend. By providing worldwide, high-bandwidth communications, the Internet makes it possible to work more effectively with customers, partners, and suppliers around the world. But it also does more than that. Because the cost of the communication is essentially the same whether the parties are down the street or halfway around the world, the Internet makes such collaboration and commerce much more efficient.

In effect, everyone on the Internet can have a global presence. More to the point, everyone on the Internet actually does have a global presence, whether they think of it that way or not. Anyone on the Internet can view your Web page, for example, and you don't have to do anything special to enable him or her to do so.

---

3. Like many technologies, the Internet comes in layers. The base layer of the Internet includes the fundamental naming, addressing, routing, and communications machinery. Above that, the World Wide Web is a particular, extremely popular, application that uses the Internet for communications. In turn, business applications can run layered on top of Web technologies.

This is not to say that the Internet makes international trade worry free. As we shall see, there are still issues of payment, currencies, shipping, and differing national, regional, and local regulations. But for many businesses, the experience may well be like any number of small bookstores who put up Web sites and suddenly received orders from Indonesia or Nepal. That the Internet is already making the world smaller is not an overstatement—it's the daily experience of millions of Internet users.

Dramatic Reduction in Distribution Costs

In the U.S., sending a printed brochure or catalog in bulk through the postal service can cost several dollars for each recipient. Sending the equivalent in electronic mail, or simply providing the same "brochureware" on a Web site, requires some up-front investment to be on the network, but the per-recipient cost is nearly zero.

One of the most intriguing possibilities of the low distribution costs is the ability to provide even more information at lower cost and to have that information be up-to-the-minute accurate and searchable. Customers of all kinds are demanding more and accurate information about what they buy. Electronics engineers are interested in detailed specifications, sample schematics, and design notes for components that they might use for a new product. Consumers want to know how the product works, how it compares to others, even its environmental impact. The low cost of providing such information over the Internet makes it possible to do so—any other way would be prohibitively expensive.

Of course, the same ideas hold for selling information or software online. These "digital goods" can be delivered over the network cheaply and efficiently. For some products, that can mean eliminating expensive packaging (boxes, CD-ROMs, packing material, etc.) entirely. For others, it is a new distribution channel that complements the channels already in place. The cost, low to begin with, is the same for customers all over the world.

Strategic Issues

We believe the advent of the Internet brings with it two strategic issues: concentration versus empowerment, and new competitive challenges.

Concentration versus Empowerment

The Internet permits direct access from creators of value to consumers, and greatly reduces the costs associated with distribution. This could lead to great concentration of suppliers or to the opposite—the creation of tens of thousands of small and medium-sized suppliers to global niche markets. It seems likely that both will happen. On the one hand, there may be a handful of music supersites combining excellent prices, great customer service, and worldwide distribution, but there won't be hundreds. On the other hand, easy access to a global community can enable marginal niche markets to reach a critical size capable of supporting a profitable business. For example, an electronic store serving the global market for antique buggy whips could be a viable business.

New Competitive Challenges

The Internet short circuits traditional distribution chains in a way that can change the nature of competition. The most obvious changes are those of geography and cost structure. Because it is not necessary to create an expensive distribution channel to enter a new territory, the Internet can bring formerly disjoint enterprises into direct competition. For the consumer these lowered barriers of entry can create advantages, but for the producer costs and efficiencies must become competitive worldwide.

More interesting things start to happen when competition crosses between whole industries. Consider the example of selling financial instruments. Traditionally, banks and brokerages have provided trading services, whereas publishers have provided comparative information. On the Internet, these lines become blurred and may disappear entirely. Because content can be linked directly to transaction, a user who links to a financial information site could place an order on the spot. Is the publisher in the trading business or is the brokerage now a publisher? Sometimes the situation defies analysis, but thinking through who owns the customer relationship is a good place to start. As always, keep a very clear view of the value provided by your business to your customers.

What Do We Mean by "Internet Commerce"?

So far, we have used the term *Internet commerce* generally, without being specific about what it means. Internet commerce means many things to many different people, so we want to be precise about what it means in this book. By Internet commerce, we mean the use of the global Internet for purchase and sale of goods and services, including service and support after the sale. The Internet may be an efficient mechanism for advertising and distributing product information (sometimes called *brochureware* in the trade), but our focus is on enabling complete business transactions.

Other Types of Electronic Commerce

Internet commerce is but one type of the more general "electronic commerce." Electronic commerce has a much longer history, though much of it was behind the scenes, typically linking suppliers to large manufacturers or service organizations. Speaking broadly, electronic commerce includes the use of computing and communication technologies in the financial business, online airline reservation systems, order processing, inventory management, and so on.

Historically speaking, the best known idea in electronic commerce has been Electronic Data Interchange (EDI). Originally created for linking together the participants in the transportation industry, it has become common for many organizations working with their suppliers and partners. EDI is really an umbrella term for many different kinds of activities, each specialized for a particular trading relationship. Creating an EDI relationship is often a long process, requiring detailed negotiation over message types and data formats (unless, of course, one party is powerful enough to dictate the terms to the other). EDI has been tremendously useful for many organizations who have created EDI systems and could afford to make the investment in them.

It is worth noting that EDI and the Internet do not exclude one another. Indeed, EDI, which specifies certain kinds of messages, can be used with the Internet, which is a way of moving data. Already many companies are using the Internet as the communications substrate for EDI applications, and there are specialized products on the market for creating EDI-Internet applications.

Internet commerce, in contrast, transcends many of the restrictions of EDI. The communication can take place over a shared public network, rather than building a specialized network or contracting for expensive Value-Added Network (VAN) services. More important, the Web enables spontaneous business transactions between buyers and sellers with no prior relationship. That first step may be the beginning of a long-term relationship, and in some cases it will make sense for the trading partners to negotiate specialized messages, EDI or otherwise, to enable them to work together more effectively.

Business Issues in Internet Commerce

First and foremost, Internet commerce is about business: using the network effectively to achieve business goals. The technology, including changes in both computing and communication, provides many tools to be used in reaching those goals. If we do not have a clear idea of our business goals in using the network, then technology cannot help us achieve them.

This is not to say that business goals cannot change to take advantage of the technology. It is entirely appropriate, for example, to choose a new focus on closer customer relationships using the Internet to communicate with customers. Without the network, such a goal may have been too expensive or difficult to achieve. The Internet might enable a company to achieve that goal in a way that it could not before. But the business goal, including how to measure success, is the key, not just an idea like, "Hey, we could send e-mail to our customers!"

Business issues for Internet commerce cross the entire range of business activities, from attracting customers to fulfilling their orders, and from sales to accounting. They include questions that businesses ask of any new idea.

- How does it fit with our strategy? Should our strategy change?
- What does this mean to our competitive situation?
- Do we expect return in the short term, or is this a long-term investment?
- How much will it cost? What do we expect to accomplish?
- How will we measure the success?
- How does this affect our sales channels, our partners, our suppliers?

Every company has many other questions used in evaluating new activities, and the Internet should not be exempted from such thinking.

One thing to watch out for in Internet commerce: the costs of getting started may seem very low, but over time a project may grow to significant size. There is always something new to add: some new technology twist to throw in or a seemingly small extension to a Web site. Setting up a Web site seems easy: a few HTML pages, hosting on a local Internet Service Provider (ISP), and maybe handling some electronic mail. Contrast such a system with one that allows real-time catalog updates, keeps and uses customer profiles, takes payment in various ways, links to inventory and fulfillment systems, and provides customer support functions. One approach is to allow such functions to accrete willy-nilly onto an initial Web site over time; a second approach is to plan the site to evolve, learning from each step and modifying the plan as appropriate. Although a company might succeed with the first approach, it will likely have little idea of what it cost, and may not have any way to figure out if it has succeeded or not. The second approach may not provide the instant gratification of getting a Web site running as soon as possible (though that might be a goal of the more careful process), but it does allow a company to focus on what it is doing and what it is getting for its investment. We don't recommend a third alternative—designing and building the perfect system all at once. This will take a long time, and whatever is done will need to change as circumstances and technologies change, as they inevitably will.

In large part, this book is about the issues involved in following the second strategy. Different companies will, of course, have different business issues and goals. In this book, we have set out to explore many that are common across businesses. Even when the issues are not directly on target for a particular business, we hope they will inspire others that are, leading to a successful plan for Internet commerce.

Technology Issues in Internet Commerce

Technology is, of course, what makes Internet commerce possible. The invention and subsequent spread of the World Wide Web, in particular, provided the technical foundation for many different applications, including those for business. Since its introduction, the Web has changed rapidly, with both rapid growth in usage and dramatic evolution in protocols, systems, and applications. For commerce systems, there are two key technology issues: what technology to use and the fast pace of technological change.

This book is mostly about that first issue: how to apply Internet technology to business problems. Commerce applications bring together many technology components: the Web, databases, high-speed networking, cryptographic algorithms, multimedia, and others. Putting them together to form a secure, high-performance, integrated system can be challenging, but the principles and ideas presented here should provide some useful guidance. The earliest Internet commerce systems were custom software. More recently, it has become possible to assemble a commerce system by using toolkits to integrate software modules and applications from different suppliers. We are now seeing the emergence of packaged application software for Internet commerce, in which a complete or nearly complete system is available from a single supplier, perhaps needing integration only to connect it to existing business systems.

The second technology issue, the pace of change, is a fact of life on the Internet today, and there is no end in sight. To be successful, therefore, any commerce system must be prepared to accommodate and incorporate new technologies as they become available. The key to such adaptability is a coherent system architecture, which lays out what is to be accomplished and why. By focusing on the ends and the fundamental principles, we can adopt new technologies that help us achieve those ends, while avoiding new technologies that may seem exciting, but in reality do not fit in with our goals or the system. The rise of toolkits, modules, and application software help a great deal in coping with technology change, since the costs of adapting and using new technologies can be amortized over many customers.

Who Owns Internet Commerce in an Organization?

Who owns Internet commerce in an organization? Who operates the system? Is it sales and marketing? Or the MIS group? Or, if transactions are involved, the accounts receivable department? At first glance, this may seem an odd question to ask, especially since for any particular group the answer may appear obvious. In fact, the experiences of many companies suggest that a clear understanding of the answer is a critical factor in success. The problem is that it is far too easy to have more than one group think that it is driving Internet commerce for an organization, leading to confusion within, as well as for customers. To compound the problem, fragmented attempts at Internet commerce will often result in money being spent on the same or similar basics: hardware, core software components, network connections, and so on.

In reality, successful Internet commerce is almost always a combined effort, drawing on the strengths of many different groups within a company: sales and marketing for effectively presenting products or services on the Net, MIS for operating or outsourcing the round-the-clock commerce systems, links to the accounting systems for transactions, and so on. An Internet presence may begin as a fringe operation—often appropriately so, thereby avoiding the slowness and stodginess of a corporate bureaucracy. But effective Internet commerce is an extension of a company's business, and so should draw on the resources of the company. Internal bickering over ownership can easily lead a project (or projects) to failure, leaving a company unable to move quickly enough to adapt to the rapid pace of change in commerce applications. Because of the perceived critical importance of the Internet, an Internet commerce project may attract the attention of, or even be initiated by, senior management.

Structure of the Book

This book is organized into three parts. In the first part, we analyze the business requirements for Internet commerce and raise a number of fundamental design issues in the context of commerce systems for business-to-business applications, retail, and the information industry. In the second part, we describe some of the fundamental technologies used for commerce on open networks. We pay special attention to Internet and Web technologies, system design, cryptography and security, payment systems, and transaction processing. Finally, in the third part, we "put it all together" into a complete system, and conclude with an assessment of the challenges ahead.

Part One—The Business of Internet Commerce

Chapter 2 examines the commerce value chain. Part of the design of business systems is to develop a clear and accurate view of all the elements necessary for the system to be successful. An engine does not make an automobile, and an entire car is useless without roads, gas stations, and passengers. The commerce value chain helps us identify all the elements necessary for success.

Chapter 3 is devoted to Internet business strategy. The degree of change that the Internet makes in the economic landscape has not been seen since the development of the railroads 150 years ago. The consequent changes in economies of scale and scope require new strategic thinking.

In Chapter 4, we introduce business requirements and issues for Internet commerce systems by looking at examples aimed at consumer retail, business-to-business cataloging, and the publishing and sale of information goods.

A successful commerce system requires alignment among many constituencies, including consumers, merchants, financial processors, governments, and technologists. These groups have different priorities, and social, legal, and technological constraints can affect the viability of the business. Chapter 5 examines some of these issues in the context of Internet commerce. Many of the difficulties and problems with Internet commerce arise when these different groups are (or appear to be) in conflict.

Successful businesses must navigate these shoals in working effectively with customers, partners, and suppliers.

In Chapter 6, we discuss the components, roles, and architectural approaches to Internet commerce, and introduce the notions of decomposition of function and of trust models. Approaching the design of a system with a high-level architecture can enable a system that evolves and adapts over the long term as technologies and business requirements change.

There are many ways to design, develop, install, and operate information technology systems, from in-house development to packaged software operated by a service bureau. Chapter 7 addresses the planning and project management issues that go far beyond the features and functionality of software.

Part Two—The Technology of Internet Commerce

The second part of the book focuses on technology issues, with an eye toward understanding the key ideas underlying the technology.

As an introduction, Chapter 8 surveys the technology underpinnings of the Internet and the World Wide Web. In Chapter 9, we go beyond the basics to look at how the technology can be applied to systems for Internet commerce.

In Chapter 10, we discuss a philosophy of design, architectural principles, and the making of design decisions. These decisions are often independent of implementation technology, which enables an implementation to *swap in* new technological components as they are developed.

Chapter 11 discusses the creation and management of *content* for Internet commerce. Loosely speaking, content is whatever people look at on the Net. We survey the means for creating, managing, and commerce-enabling content.

One of the biggest issues for Internet commerce systems is security. Modern cryptography is the foundation of security systems for commerce, and Chapter 12 provides a quick overview of the field. Simply using cryptography (in some unspecified way) rarely creates a secure system, so we discuss how to think about the application of cryptography to applications. In Chapter 13, we go beyond the foundation of cryptography to the design of secure systems. We advocate a systemic design approach to the security of Internet commerce systems. Proper use of cryptography is a key part, but careful design of security policies, mechanisms, characteristics of the application, and containment procedures all play important roles.

Payment systems are often seen as the core of Internet commerce systems, and they clearly play an important role. In Chapter 14, we discuss a variety of payment systems and their application to Internet commerce. Beyond the technical aspects of payment systems, we discuss their trust models and cost structures.

Enterprises require complete business solutions, and Chapter 15 examines some of the auxiliary systems necessary for dealing with taxes, shipping, and inventory.

Commerce is an exchange of goods for value received. Transaction processing is the part of the system that ensures that a business transaction is completed once the parties agree to it. In computer systems, especially those distributed across a network, this is often not as easy as it seems, especially when something goes wrong. Chapter 16 introduces this complex topic, including a discussion of issues such as scaling, performance, reliability, and business record keeping.

Part Three—Systems for Internet Commerce

Now that we have created a plan and surveyed available technology components, how can we assemble a working system? Chapter 17 describes one approach to packaged application software for Internet commerce.

Over time, Internet commerce will change rapidly. Once your system is up and running, how do you keep up to date in this rapidly changing world? We discuss how to stay on track when buffeted by the evolution of technology, and Chapter 18 lays out some paths for the future.

Part One

The Business of Internet Commerce

CHAPTER 2

The Commerce Value Chain

He chose to include the things
That in each other are included, the whole,
The complicate, the amassing harmony.
—Wallace Stevens[1]

Introducing the Commerce Value Chain

When a consumer buys a manufactured item in a store, it is merely one step in a complex process that began with the raw materials used in creating the item. At each step in that process, something of value was added along the way. That value may have been refining the raw materials, molding them into a useful shape, transporting them for further processing, or selling the item to the final consumer. We sometimes refer to this as the "value chain" for a product—the chain of adding value in creating and delivering a product.

Even though this idea of a value chain is most clearly exemplified by a manufactured product, we can use it to describe many kinds of business activities, including more focused components of the very broad chain just described. For example, we can look at the value chain of a retail store, which includes selecting products that will be sold, purchasing them from a wholesaler or manufacturer, arranging an attractive display, advertising to attract customers, assisting customers with their selections, taking payment for the product, and delivering it to the customer. Each of these links in the chain

---

1. Wallace Stevens, "It Must Give Pleasure," *Notes Toward a Supreme Fiction*, 1947.

is important to the business, and if any of them break down, the whole business is affected.

Similarly, we can look at developing a system for Internet commerce in terms of the value chain needed by the business. In part, the value chain will be related to that of the underlying business (for example, selling books). Another part comes from looking at the value chain required by doing business online. Understanding these two pieces and how they fit together is an important part of creating a successful business in Internet commerce. We will look at the value chain from a third perspective, in terms of all the customer-facing activities of a business.

In this chapter, we look at a very general value chain for Internet commerce, as shown in Figure 2-1. This value chain is focused on a business' interactions with its customers. The details will certainly be different for different businesses (and for some different business models), but we have found this general approach to be very effective in organizing an approach to business online. The components of this general value chain are the following:

1. Attract customers

   Marketing—get and keep customer interest

2. Interact with customers

   Sales—turn interest into orders (generally *content*)

3. Act on customer instructions

   Order management—order capture, payment, fulfillment

4. React to customer requests

   Customer service, technical support.

We look at these in more detail below.

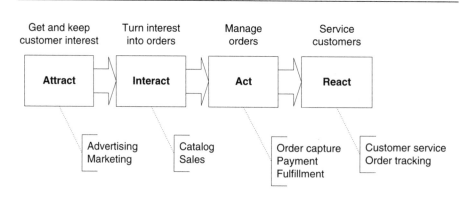

FIGURE 2-1. **The Commerce Value Chain**

Looking at the value chain for a business helps to define areas of focus—what the business is best at, or where the most emphasis should be given. Even in businesses that may appear to be very similar, differences in emphasis can have major effects, both for Internet commerce and for more traditional forms.

For example, consider two bookstores, one that emphasizes large selection and one that emphasizes personal service. In the physical world, such a difference is reflected in many decisions: where to locate the store, the size of the store, the kind of employees that might be hired, the kinds of computer systems needed to support the business. Similarly, on the Internet such bookstores would develop their businesses quite differently. A focus on large selection might require a comprehensive database and tools for searching for books in different ways (by title, author, publisher, ISBN, etc.), whereas a focus on personalized service might result in forums for discussions among customers, interaction between customers and employees, and other kinds of services.

Thinking carefully about the value chain can help one select the most important ideas from a long list of possible activities in Internet commerce. The large bookstore, for example, may want to provide all of the services of the smaller one, but if it does not focus first on its core abilities—providing easy access to a large number of books—it is much less likely to succeed. When moving a business onto the Internet, it is tempting to try to do everything, because it seems easy or simply because it seems possible. It is necessary to have an overt strategy for each part of the value chain, not merely those in which your business is differentiated; however, it is not really necessary to do everything yourself. Many companies use partnering to fill out the value chain, so that each link is strong.

Components of the Commerce Value Chain

The key components of the value chain can be very different for different industries, and even among different businesses within a particular industry, such as in the following example. In this section, we look at a generic value chain for Internet commerce. In part, it serves as an example of how one might break down a value chain to analyze it more closely, and in part it exemplifies some of the most important components for business on the Internet. Throughout this section, we use catalogs for consumer retail purchases as examples. In the next chapter, we look at several different kinds of businesses and how the commerce value chain applies to them.

Attract Customers

The first component of the generic Internet commerce value chain is *attract*. By this we mean whatever steps we take to draw customers into the primary site, whether by paid advertising on other Web sites, electronic mail, television, print, or other forms of advertising and marketing. The point of this phase is to make an impression on customers and draw them in to the detailed catalog or other information about products and services for sale.[2]

Interact with Customers

The second component is *interact*. By this we mean turning customer interest into orders. This phase is generally content oriented and includes the catalog, publication, or other information available to the customer over the Internet. The content may be distributed by many different mechanisms, such as the World Wide Web or electronic mail. In some cases, there may be links between Internet commerce and content distributed by other media, such as CD-ROMs.

Editorially, content may change infrequently or frequently. Technically, content may be *static* or *dynamic*. Static content typically consists of prepared pages, such as those from a catalog, that are sent to a client upon request. These pages must be recreated whenever the information on them changes. Dynamic content, on the other hand, is generated at the time of the request, drawing upon one or more information sources to produce an appropriate page of information for the client. Some sources of information for dynamic content include databases, such as a parts database with pricing information; the capabilities of client software, such as what graphic formats can be used; or even who the clients are, or what organizations they are with. Dynamic content is often used when the editorial content changes frequently, or when the natural storage medium for the information is a database, or when the information is used for multiple purposes.

We discuss the creation and presentation of content in more detail in Chapter 11.

Act on Customer Instructions

The next component in the commerce value chain is *act*. Once a buyer has searched through a catalog and wishes to make a purchase, there must be a way to capture the order, process payment, handle fulfillment, and other aspects of order management.

Order Processing

Often a buyer wishes to purchase several items at the same time, so the order processing must include the ability to group items together for later purchase. This capability, sometimes called a *shopping cart* in the case of retail transactions, usually includes the ability to modify the contents of the shopping cart at any time. Thus, the buyer is able to discard items, add new ones, change the quantities, and so on.

---

2. With the advent of active advertisements with built-in transactional capability, the lines between the phases of the value chain are becoming blurred.

When the buyer is ready to complete the purchase, it is often necessary to compute additional charges, such as sales tax and shipping costs. The order processing system then presents the buyer with an itemized order form, including all charges, so the buyer can pay for the items.

Payment

Depending on the terms of the order, the buyer may pay for it (or provide payment instructions) as part of the order capture. Once an order is final, the buyer can pay for it. As in the real world, there may be many ways to pay for an item. Some of the methods may be online analogs of those found in the real world: credit cards, purchase orders, etc. Other methods of payment may exist only for Internet commerce, using new technologies developed especially for a networked system. For example, in an online publishing system, it may be feasible to charge a small amount for a single magazine article, rather than requiring someone to purchase the entire magazine.

The single most important property of an online payment system is that the seller can use it to collect payment from the buyer. That is, no matter which payment mechanisms each one may be capable of, there must be at least one they can agree on. This property has several implications. First, the seller's system must be able to handle the kinds of payment important to the seller's business. For example, credit cards are commonly used for consumer retail transactions, but businesses often buy from each other using purchase orders. There may also be nontechnical constraints on what payment methods can be used. To accept credit cards, a merchant must have an account with an acquiring bank that handles the transactions. Without such an account, creating the technical infrastructure to allow for credit card payment is useless.

Second, the seller must be careful about imposing requirements on the buyer's system. If the buyer must have a particular software package to handle a particular kind of payment system, the universe of possible buyers is likely to be much smaller than it would be otherwise. In some cases, of course, all of the desired customers will have such software, or be willing to obtain it. Again, the key point is to keep the customer and the business in mind when selecting the technology.

Note also that completing this stage does not necessarily mean that funds have been transferred into the seller's bank account. Some payment instruments, including both credit cards and purchase orders, extend credit to the buyer, who will make the actual payment later. In such cases, it is common for the seller's system to authorize the transaction, whether by requesting such authorization from a third party (such as the bank that issued a credit card) or its own internal rules (such as whether a purchase order relationship has been established). As we shall see later, final settlement of a transaction may not take place until the item has been shipped.

We discuss payment systems and how they can be used in Chapter 14.

Fulfillment

Now the order has been placed and the payment made (or at least a satisfactory promise of payment). The next step is fulfilling the order. How that happens depends on the type of thing purchased. If the item ordered is a *physical good* (sometimes called a *hard good*) that will be delivered to the buyer, then the order is usually forwarded to a traditional order processing system, with the result that someone picks up the object, packs it, and ships it. In this case, the online commerce system must have a method for forwarding orders. This step could be as simple as printing out or faxing an order form for a person to handle, or it may use a more complicated interface, such as EDI, to another computer system. The precise mechanism, of course, depends on how orders are handled by the rest of the business.

A second kind of order is a request for a service to be performed in the real world. For example, one might order a singing telegram online. Although the fulfillment happens in the physical world, this is a service, not a physical good. For our purposes, however, we can think of these as being handled like physical goods. The order is passed to a system or person who causes it to be fulfilled.

The third kind of order is more closely tied to the Internet commerce system. We call this category *digital goods*.[3] Digital goods include a wide variety of online delivery, including software that is delivered online, magazine or news articles, reports, access to a database for a period of time, and so on. Fulfillment of digital goods can be quite complex, as we shall see.

We discuss the integration of systems for fulfillment of physical goods in Chapter 15, and some aspects of systems for fulfilling orders for digital goods in "Information Commerce" on page 59.

React to Customer Inquiries

Finally, after a sale is complete, the customer may have some questions or difficulties that require service. Although many questions require a person to answer, others can be answered with the appropriate information system. For example, a transaction system that keeps track of all of a customer's purchases can generate a statement summarizing them. Customers who are wondering whether or not their orders have been shipped might check back with the system. A more complicated example is how the system handles a failure when delivering a digital good.

Suppose that a customer buys a software package online. While the software is being downloaded to the customer's computer, an error in the network causes the download to fail. What can the customer do? Clearly they should not buy the item again, so they

---

3. Digital goods are sometimes called "soft goods" to contrast them with "hard goods," or to remind one of software. This can cause confusion with the traditional meaning of "soft goods" to mean apparel, so we prefer the term "digital goods."

need some "proof of purchase"—such as a receipt—that the fulfillment server will accept in order to allow the customer to attempt another download.

Using people to answer customer service calls can be very expensive, so it is worth investing in systems that eliminate questions that do not require the capabilities of a person. As noted previously, these systems often provide routine (or even exceptional) information in response to simple queries. But at least as important is designing the system to remove the need for the customer to ask the question. In the preceding software example, the use of the receipt allows the customer to solve the problem easily, without having to call anyone for assistance.

Who Is the Customer?

One of the most important questions for any business is "Who is the customer?" It may seem to be an obvious question, but often businesses (or other organizations) do not have a clear understanding of the answer. And sometimes the answer is subtler than it appears at first. For example, consider a company selling electronic components used in personal computers. In one sense, the customer is the organization that assembles the computers, which buys components in large quantities. It is the organization that places the orders, negotiates terms, takes delivery, and pays for the components. But perhaps a more important group of customers are the specifying engineers—the people who decide which parts go in the computer. Once that decision is made, much of the rest follows more or less automatically, as long as a satisfactory contract can be negotiated.

To sell effectively to these two customers, one would probably adopt very different strategies. Similarly, in designing an online commerce system to work with these customers, one would create very different systems. The specifying engineers, for example, must be able to find the parts they need in the catalog quickly. They must also have access to detailed information, specifications, and sample schematics illustrating how a part can be used, and a way to order sample parts for building prototypes.

The other kind of customer, those who manufacture computers using the parts, have a very different set of problems to solve. They order parts in large quantities, need to ensure timely delivery, and arrange payment based on a complex contract. Although both kinds of customer can benefit from using the Internet, it would be impossible to create a successful system without understanding in detail who the customers are and what problems they have to solve.

Developing Customer Relationships with Internet Commerce

Good relationships with customers are often one sign of a successful business. Customers with good relationships tend to buy from the same vendors again and again, and it is almost always easier to keep a customer than to find a new one. As with the question "Who is the customer?" this may seem obvious, but it is frequently treated as a secondary concern. From the perspective of Internet commerce, we can look at two particular aspects of customer relationships: improving the existing service for customers and finding ways to apply new technologies to deliver better or different service.

One of the best ways to build strong relationships is with communication. Customers want to know where a vendor is going, what it can do, why there is a problem, whether or not there are problems on the horizon, and so on. They also want this communication to be efficient and focused on their interests. Any particular customer of AT&T, for example, is probably not interested in knowing about everything that AT&T does. Some customers are interested in how to lower their personal long-distance bills, whereas others want to know how to create a global telecommunications infrastructure.

The Internet enables vendors to communicate with customers in ways that are efficient for both parties. It is efficient for vendors because the incremental costs of communicating are small, and because the messages can be specific to individual customers or groups of customers. It is efficient for customers precisely because it can be focused on their needs and interests. Conversely, if the vendor does not make efficient use of the communication, customers may object and the relationship can be soured.

This communications capability can also be used to provide new services, particularly up-to-date status information about an order or service. For example, many logistics companies (such as Federal Express and United Parcel Service) have created ways to check on the status of a delivery. The Internet made it possible to connect these companies with their customers more closely, thereby improving their customer relationships.

Marketing on the Internet

Many people are attracted to Internet commerce because the Internet offers a new way of marketing. Although this book is not about marketing on the Internet, this section describes a few of the relevant concepts and issues. Over the past few years, the hype about marketing on the Internet has swung between two extremes: the Internet is a completely new and different medium for marketing, or it's just another medium like print or television. Another aspect of marketing on the Internet is the combination of communications with other recent applications of technology to marketing, such as the use of very large databases with extensive information about demographics and transactions.

The Internet Is Different from Other Media

One of the most important properties of the Internet is that everyone can be a publisher, reaching the same worldwide audiences as giant media conglomerates. More than anything else, this property defines how the Internet is different from other media. The telephone allows one to call one person at a time, limiting (in time) the number of people one can reach. Using a telephone also requires both people to be available to talk at the same time. Traditional mass media, such as newspapers, magazines, and television, reach large audiences, but the ability to do so is limited, either by the availability of scarce resources such as available television channels, or simply by the investment required to create and distribute the medium.

These limitations do not apply to the Internet. For most communications, using tools such as electronic mail or the Web, the sender and receiver do not need to be present at the same time to communicate with each other (as long as their computers can do so, of course). On the Internet, there is very little that distinguishes the computer system of a single person from that of a large corporation. The differences may be in available bandwidth and server capacity, but not in the possibility of reaching a large audience.

What are the implications of these differences? One is obvious: small merchants can reach customers on the Internet very effectively. A second one is that the communications technology, combined with databases of customer information, preferences, and so on, makes it easier to reach customers as individuals. These properties can be the basis of new marketing campaigns that build on the core capabilities of the network.

The Internet Is the Same as Other Media

Faced with the differences of the Internet as a marketing medium, many people thought, "This is so different that I don't need to know anything about traditional marketing." Few of the businesses begun on that principle in 1994 are still around, but this reaction remains common as more people discover the Internet.

As with some of the other topics we have discussed, the classic business and marketing questions are still relevant.

- Who is the customer?
- What does the customer need?
- What does the customer want?
- What message do you want the customer to remember?
- How can information be presented to the customer most effectively?

Technology is no substitute for a good understanding of the basic principles of marketing and knowledge of the customer. What it can provide is the ability to reach the customer in more interesting and sophisticated ways.

Understanding the Demographics

Of course, one of the key questions in marketing is the demographics of the universe of possible customers. As the Internet has grown, the demographics have changed substantially. The network began in the research community, then grew to widespread use in academia. Technology companies were attracted, followed by other businesses, and now a large number of consumers. Because of this rapid change, which continues to occur, we do not discuss the details of Internet demographics here. Rather, we believe that there are a few important principles to remember for including Internet demographics in a marketing plan.

1. The demographics are changing rapidly. What is true today may not be true tomorrow, so it is important to watch the trends, and how they might affect the marketing plan.

2. Focus on the demographics of target customers, rather than searching Internet demographics for interesting possible customers. Then look for ways to take advantage of their Internet use to reach them, whether that is with the Web, electronic mail, or another application.

One-to-One Marketing

A current hot topic in marketing of all kinds is "one-to-one marketing."[4] Rather than targeting a mass audience, one can make a very direct pitch to individual customers by tailoring the messages to their known interests, likes, dislikes, and buying history. This requires the collection and processing of large amounts of information about customers, their buying habits, and other relevant demographic information. In many cases, the market is a small group of similar customers. One-to-one marketing is being used in such areas as direct mail, carefully focused television advertising, and providing selected coupons to individuals at point-of-sale terminals.

The Internet is an ideal medium for one-to-one marketing, because the communication technology immediately provides the direct channel. A Web site can identify customers before they browse a catalog, and then use that identity to customize the presentation. This customization can take many forms, such as selecting which items to display, providing targeted special offers, or inserting advertisements of likely interest. Even when a customer is anonymous, his behavior may provide some clues that are useful in tailoring a message. A search engine, for example, may select advertisements to display based on the customer's apparent area of interest.

As another example, an airline may have special fares to advertise. In general, customers are only interested in flights originating from their home city, so that most information in a mass advertisement would be irrelevant to most customers. Simply by

---

4. See Don Peppers, *The One-To-One Future: Building Relationships One Customer at a Time* (Doubleday, 1993).

keeping track of a customer's home city, the airline can send an electronic mail notice of the special fares that is almost certainly of more interest to the customer than a complete listing of specials.

Advertising

Advertising on the Internet takes many forms. One of the simplest is a Web site describing products or services for sale. Of course, just having a Web site is no guarantee that potential customers will visit, so ads are placed in many other locations. Many companies purchase ad space on other Web sites, hoping to lure customers who visit those sites. Internet search engines are a common location for ads, because of the volume they attract, but any popular site may be a good location. Keeping in mind issues of demographics, a good site for advertising need only be popular with potential customers, not necessarily popular with the Internet at large. Increasingly, advertisements in print or on radio and television quote universal resource locators (URLs) to link those media to the Internet.

Another form of advertising is placing links to a Web site in places that potential customers may visit. Such sites may include search engines, general or specialized directories, reference materials describing the kinds of products or services being sold, and so on.

Advertising on the Internet should be done with care, however. Because the network began in an academic and research setting, there is considerable resentment toward intrusive advertising. Sending unsolicited advertising to Internet mailing lists (a practice sometimes called *spamming*) is widely disliked, as well as being inappropriate for most lists.

Doing Business Internationally

One of the most revolutionary things about the Internet is the way it brings people and organizations together around the world. For someone in Cambridge, Massachusetts, there is very little apparent difference between communicating with someone in New York City and with someone in Bombay, India, except possibly the available network bandwidth and a slight difference in latency. This ability gives any online business the potential to reach customers around the world and to become a true international business.

International business issues, however, are not so simple. From the relatively straightforward problems of currency conversion, to the problems of presenting one's message in several languages, to the complexities of import/export laws and tariffs, there are a host of new problems to address.

In this section and the next, we discuss some of the most important issues in creating an effective international online business. Many of these issues concern reaching customers effectively, such as using local languages. Others are concerned with legal and regulatory questions that must be addressed before a business is permitted to operate at all.

International Software

The most important aspect of software for use in different countries is that the presentation, such as the user interface, can be adapted to local conventions. In many cases, that means translating all of the displayed information to local languages. To do that, the software must be able to display whatever character set is required (a stringent requirement, since some languages require multibyte characters but most software stores each character in a single byte). The software must also be capable of using the translated messages, which is not always the case.

In addition, the software must be able to handle the local currency (and, for some locales, multiple currencies at the same time).

International Content

Internet commerce may be the first exposure a business has to the complexities of the international environment. Beyond mere translation of text, true internationalization of content requires extensive work. We list here just a few issues.

- References to local objects, geographies, people, and news events do not translate well.
- Humor doesn't translate well.
- Sometimes words, particularly product names, have very different interpretations in different countries.
- Trademarks work differently in different countries.
- Colors, particularly as used in corporate color schemes and logos, give different impressions in different cultures.

These sorts of issues are well understood by multinational companies, but represent serious problems for smaller companies wanting a global presence.

Privacy

Many countries, especially in Europe, have strict laws governing the collection and use of personal information about consumers. Although the details of those laws are beyond the scope of this book, any online business operating in such countries must be sure that its systems comply with local law.

In any case, it is good business practice to inform customers of what kinds of data are being collected and how this data is being used (for one-to-one marketing by the same business, sold to others for marketing purposes, etc.). Most consumers on the Internet know very little about issues of privacy online, so they may have unrealistic expectations. By explaining the relevant privacy issues up front, a business can avoid later problems if customers feel their privacy has been compromised.

The Legal Environment

The rapid development of computer and communications technology has presented many challenges for legal systems around the world. For example, the ability to gather, correlate, and search large volumes of information about individuals and organizations raises questions of privacy that simply did not arise before the technology was developed. The challenges are magnified by the pace of technology's evolution, which moves much more quickly than the legal system. Some experts and other observers are calling for wholesale changes in the law to adjust to a technology revolution.

In this book, we take a practical view of the legal situation for Internet commerce. Business operates in a legal environment, and many business practices are codified or enforced by the legal system. Contracts, for example, are governed by law, but this law arose out of the needs of businesses. Legal systems will not change overnight, but they may certainly adapt to new business practices and requirements that arise from Internet commerce. Many of the key questions that arise for online businesses are not settled, and new laws and court decisions will change the rules. The important point is that the legal environment is an integral part of the world that Internet commerce systems live in, and we must be sure to take it into account in developing a strategy for Internet commerce.

This section outlines many of the important legal issues and problems to consider in planning systems for Internet commerce. The authors are not lawyers, and our discussion is not intended to replace the advice of a competent attorney. We do suggest that it would be wise to consult an attorney who understands and appreciates the effects technology is having on business and the law.

Taxation

One of the most immediate legal questions that arises is taxation, especially sales tax. Since businesses are legally obligated to pay the taxes, it is important for software systems to compute taxes where appropriate and to keep the records necessary to prove that the business is complying with the law. Unfortunately, computing tax can be very complicated, depending upon many factors, such as the type of good or service for sale, the parties involved, the locations at which the seller does business, and the location of the buyer. In the U.S., sales taxes are imposed by states, counties, and municipalities, so the tax rules are different for many different jurisdictions. It is beyond the scope of this book to explore these issues in depth, but anyone doing business online should be sure to understand the obligations regarding taxation and implement a system capable of complying with the law.

Of course, the rules for taxation differ from country to country, so any system that will be selling products or services on an international basis may need to reflect this requirement.

Many governments, both national and regional, have considered imposing new taxes for online businesses. There is at present a strong feeling among many that such taxes will hamper the development and adoption of Internet commerce systems, so it is unclear at this time what new taxes, if any, may affect online businesses. In any case, it is important for online business to be alert for changes that may affect their operations.

Digital Signatures

In the real world, personal handwritten signatures are used on many business documents to indicate that the business agrees to the statements in the document or to authorize the actions described. We generally assume that a signature is unique to an individual and that it is not forged. Electronic documents cannot be signed by hand, but cryptography has given us a tool to accomplish the same purpose: digital signatures. We discuss the technology of digital signatures in Chapter 12. For the moment, it suffices to understand that a digital signature on an electronic document can be used in many respects just like a signature. An electronic contract, for example, might be digitally signed by the parties to it, just as they sign contracts by hand today.

Several states in the U.S. have passed, or are considering passing, legislation that recognizes digital signatures as legally binding under certain circumstances. At the present time, none of the laws are the same, and there is no federal law governing the use of digital signatures nationwide. For the moment, then, digital signatures should be used carefully in situations that require binding signatures, although they can easily be used for other purposes in online commerce. Although there are some efforts underway to extend and harmonize the state legislation, this remains an area of rapid change. In addition, there is by no means any international consensus on digital signatures, so international businesses must be especially careful in using them.

Copyright

Protection of intellectual property, via patents and copyrights, has been a matter for national law. Although there has been a gradual rationalizing of disparate national positions, the arrival of the Internet has made it imperative. Copyright is of particular interest to many content providers on the Internet. Since information is provided in digital form, it can easily be copied, modified, and disseminated without permission or payment to its owner.

The use and protection of intellectual property distributed on the network has both a legal and a technical aspect. We examine some of the technical issues in Chapter 4. For the legal issues, we recommend the World Intellectual Property Organization (WIPO: http://www.wipo.org) for a proposed framework for protection of intellectual property on the network, and the International Digital Object Identifier Foundation (DOI: http://www.doi.org) for a proposed means of uniform identification of documents on the Internet.

Regulation of Cryptography

The use of cryptography is fundamental to providing the security required for Internet commerce. Cryptography encompasses encrypting data for privacy, providing reliable means of verifying identity, recording a digital signature, and ensuring that messages and other documents have not been tampered with. The technical details of cryptography are described in Chapter 12.

Governments have long taken an interest in cryptography because of its role in protecting information. In some cases, the use or sale of cryptographic technology is regulated (and, of course, the regulations differ from country to country). The United States, in particular, restricts the export of strong cryptography in mass-market software, which makes it difficult for American companies to sell products with strong security outside the country. Because of the military uses of cryptography, cryptographic systems are treated as munitions. While the U.S. currently has no restrictions on the use of cryptography by its citizens within the country, other countries, such as France, regulate the import and use of cryptographic systems.

The U.S. does make exceptions to these export controls under certain circumstances. In particular, it is usually possible to export systems that are used solely for encrypting information about financial transactions, although each product must be specifically approved for export.

For online businesses in the U.S., these issues are usually not relevant, unless the business is creating and selling software for encryption. However, such regulations affect the security of Internet commerce systems around the world, and they may specifically affect transactions between foreign customers and U.S. businesses. If the customer's system has weak security, then the overall security of the transaction is also weak. In addition, the lack of uniformity means that it is much harder to build confidence in the security of the global Internet commerce infrastructure.

The Problem of Uncertainty

A significant risk for online commerce is that so many legal questions remain unanswered. In the United States it is clear that the legal system must evolve, at least somewhat, to meet these challenges. Some of that evolution will happen in Congress and in state legislatures, but many of the most important changes will come from the courts as they apply existing laws and precedents to cases involving online businesses. Because many of the technology questions are complex, it is difficult to predict how the courts will rule in many situations.

We believe that the benefits of Internet commerce more than justify taking the risk. But as companies proceed, they should be mindful of the legal issues involved and be careful to ensure that they understand the implications and risks inherent in their actions.

A related problem for the developers of software is that of patents. Internet software is expanding rapidly and many companies are seeking patent protection for their intellectual property. Without substantial expense in searching, it may be difficult to know whether some new idea has already been invented and requires licensing. In addition, the technology is changing so rapidly that the two to three year delay from patent filing to issue is a matter of real concern.

Summary

The commerce value chain gives us a useful way to think about Internet commerce projects. By focusing on the value delivered to the customer, rather than the technology, we can more readily understand what pieces we need to assemble for the application. Then, with an idea of the customer value firmly in mind, we can develop the business strategy, which is the subject of the next chapter.

CHAPTER 3 *Internet Business Strategy*

> The best ideas are common property.
> —Lucius Annaeus Seneca[1]

Commerce and Technology Revolutions

This chapter presents some ideas about Internet business strategy that represent the thinking of Shikhar Ghosh and others at Open Market, rather than the creative efforts of the authors—we are technologists, not business visionaries—but we have recast them in our own words.

It may seem odd to have a chapter about broad-brush business strategy in a book about the design of systems for Internet commerce. We think it makes sense, because the Internet changes so many of the facts underlying the basic assumptions of business. Jeff Bezos of Amazon.com has noted that changes in technology or infrastructure affect commerce in two phases, or waves. In the first wave, companies use the new technology to improve old processes and business models. In the second, more important, wave, companies use the new technology to completely reinvent their business. As we will see, the last time something as important as the Internet happened to business was in the middle of the nineteenth century when the railroad changed the world. That transition took 50 years. The Internet transition is happening much faster.

---

1. Lucius Annaeus Seneca, *Epistles.*

Because of the speed and scope of the changes introduced by the Internet, designers of Internet commerce systems cannot focus merely on the technology, but must also understand their companies' fundamental business strategy. Business leaders must also appreciate the technology enough to think through their strategy in terms of both new competitive opportunities and new competitive threats.

An Historical Analogy

Few innovations have the capability to change the entire competitive business environment. During our lifetimes, only the Internet has the potential to affect commerce as much as the nineteenth-century railroad. "The impact of the rail network was like nothing the United States had ever seen before or indeed has seen since."[2] To understand the business potential of the Internet, it is necessary to first understand the railroad.

The railroad was first introduced in 1825 and became the dominant mode of transportation in the United States by 1890. Consider some of the changes wrought during this period, as shown in Table 3-1.

Before the railroad	After the railroad
Travel between New York and Boston in four days	Travel between New York and Boston in less than one day
Transportation depends on weather and location of waterways	Transportation depends on the ability to lay rails
Dispersed work force (92% of population in 1830 is rural)	Concentrated work force (50% of population in 1920 is urban)
8,000 U.S. time zones	4 U.S. time zones
Vacation (if at all) near home	Vacation away from home
Transport a ton of goods for 5–15 cents per mile (wagon or steamboat in 1825)	Transport a ton of goods for 1 cent per mile (by rail in 1884)

TABLE 3-1. **Changes Wrought by Rail Transportation**

Today's Internet is remarkably similar to the nineteenth century's railroad infrastructure development, except that the Internet is happening much faster. Consider some of the factors shown in Table 3-2. The last entry in the table is particularly important—both the railroad and the Internet accelerated a fundamental economic change that was already underway. In the case of the railroad, cheap transportation accelerated the industrial revolution whose key enabler was the steam engine. In the case of the Internet, cheap communication is accelerating the information age whose key enabler is

---

2. Alfred D. Chandler and Richard S. Tedlow, *The Coming of Managerial Capitalism: A Casebook on the History of American Economic Institutions* (Richard D. Irwin, 1985).

	Railroad (1825–1890)	**Internet (1969–1997)**
New infrastructure	First water-independent transportation infrastructure	First global public information infrastructure
Original purpose (not commerce)	Passenger traffic; military	Military and civil defense; research
Importance of standards	Width of tracks (gauge)	Network and communications protocols (TCP/IP)
New security challenges	Railway police hired to manage new crimes	Security protocols and standards
Source of innovation	Steel production, accounting, logistics	Software, networking, fiber optics
Accelerate fundamental economic trends	Industrial age (key enabler: steam engine)	Information age (key enabler: computer)

TABLE 3-2. Comparison of Railroad and Internet Infrastructure

the computer. Bob Metcalfe, one of the inventors of the Ethernet computer network, explains this effect through Metcalfe's law: *The utility of a network increases as the square of the number of nodes connected.* The ability to route goods by rail between arbitrary factories accelerated the industrial revolution. Likewise, the ability to route information between arbitrary computers is accelerating the information age.

In terms of their impact on commerce, today's Internet is also remarkably similar to the nineteenth century's railroad. Consider these factors:

- Economies of scale

  Railroads made large mining and agricultural operations practical. The Internet makes it possible to offer large numbers of titles in one store such as Amazon.com or CDNow.

- Source of competitive advantage

  Transportation enabled a regional competitive advantage, such as that possessed by the vineyards of France to dominate the wine market. The Internet can enable a single site like Travelocity to offer full services.

- Inventory needs

  Just-in-time delivery of coal enabled factories to run with little energy inventory. Because the Internet can deliver perfect copies of information goods immediately, digital goods commerce sites may need no inventory at all.

- Variety, choice, and availability

  Rapid transportation made perishable goods such as fish and fruit more widely available. The Internet can eliminate distribution bottlenecks that limit the market for information.

- New opportunities

  By capitalizing on the economies of scale, the railroads, in effect, created large-scale corporations. Indeed, some of the earliest large corporations of the industrial age were themselves railroads. Similarly, the opportunities of the Internet enabled Netscape, CNet, and Yahoo! to grow to substantial size very rapidly.

The Internet Value Proposition

Internet commerce needs to start with a strategy. The analysis of strategy starts with value—what are the sources of Internet value? We believe the ability of the Internet to change the landscape of commerce comes from two key ideas: the Internet can be used to transform customer relationships and it can displace traditional sources of business value. These two ideas lead in turn to four basic strategies for a business to consider both in exploiting the Internet and in defending itself from competitors.

Transform Customer Relationships

By exploiting the Internet, many aspects of traditional commerce can evolve from being supplier-centered to being customer-centered, as shown in Table 3-3. This idea leads to two business strategies: a customer-centered business organized around a product or organized around meeting all the needs of a particular group of customers. We call the first approach the *channel master* strategy and the second the *customer magnet* strategy.

Displace the Source of Value

The Internet, by moving commerce from the physical world to the information world, enables commerce to shift from dealing with atoms to dealing with bits. The effect of this conversion is shown in Table 3-4. A focus on the supply chain leads to the strategy we call the *value chain pirate*; a focus on distribution—reaching the customer—leads to the strategy we call the *digital distributor*.

Supplier-centered	Customer-centered
Supplier chooses hours of operation	Supplier always available, customer chooses hours
Supplier chooses locations of service	Service delivered at customer location
Supplier delivers services	Customer serves himself
Focus on supply chain	Focus on customer needs
One to many	One to one

TABLE 3-3. **Transforming Customer Relationships**

Physical world	Information world
Atoms	Bits
Physical value	Digital value
Economies of scale	Economies of scope
Mass produced	Mass customized
Information value	Knowledge value
Distribution as a constraint	Distribution as an enabler
Local	Global

TABLE 3-4. Transforming the Sources of Value

Four Strategies

The two key ideas, using the Internet to transform customer relationships and to displace traditional sources of value, lead to our four Internet business strategies: channel master, customer magnet, value chain pirate, and digital distributor. In many situations, mixed strategies may also be useful.

Channel Master

The channel master strategy works by using the Internet to build deeper relationships with customers in order to sell one's traditional goods and services. The channel master is organized around products, concentrating on the best possible delivery of those products and their related services. A company using the channel master strategy reengineers all of its customer-facing activities—channel masters must integrate the commerce value chain with their existing operations.

Example—Cisco

Cisco Systems is a $7 billion provider of Internet software, hardware, and services. Cisco uses its Web site as a sales channel to its customers and partners. By the fall of 1997, its Internet channel was operating at a $3 billion annual run rate.

- Attract—get and keep customer interest

  Cisco offers a full online catalog and demonstration of its ordering process. Customers are notified of pricing changes for prespecified products.

- Interact—turn interest into orders

  The online catalog enables searching, browsing, and configuration of purchases. Intelligent agents suggest alternatives (such as software upgrades) and identify errors.

- Act—coordinate order fulfillment

  Orders link to procurement and order management databases. Customers can monitor or receive notifications about order status and check lead times.

- React—provide after-sales service

  Customers can access comprehensive documentation and self-help intelligent agents. A Bug Alert mechanism automatically notifies customers of bugs.

The results for Cisco have been spectacular: 70 percent of all product support is delivered through the Internet, and a very large fraction of orders now arrive through the Internet channel.

Customer Magnet

The customer magnet strategy works by using the Internet to attract a customer group by meeting their broadly shared needs with a knowledge-sharing environment and aggregated supplier access. The customer magnet is organized around a group of customers, delivering a broad range of products and services to those customers. A company using the customer magnet strategy seeks to be the destination of choice for a whole category of customers. Customer magnets must integrate the value chains of multiple suppliers into one customer-facing whole.

Example—Tripod

Tripod is an electronic community for Generation X'ers. It targets people between the ages of 18 and 34 who are seeking advice on money, health, and careers. In addition to providing information, Tripod encourages and helps members to build their own Web sites.

- Attract—get and keep customer interest

  Tripod offers free information with links to many sites. Members participate in discussion groups, surveys, and real-time conferences about current topics.

- Interact—turn interest into orders

  Tripod partners with Security First Network Bank (SFNB) to provide a customized interface to SFNB's home banking service.

- Act—coordinate order fulfillment

  SFNB provides home banking over the Internet, including round-the-clock access to account information.

- React—provide after-sales service

  SFNB offers round-the-clock customer service. Tripod also offers online forums for advice on money management.

By May 1997, Tripod had grown to 320,000 members and expected annual revenues of $1 million.

Value Chain Pirate

The value chain pirate strategy works by capturing someone else's margins by displacing them from their value chains. The value chain pirate is organized around the value chain, seeking to leapfrog both upstream and downstream providers in an effort to more directly connect suppliers with customers. A business using the value chain pirate strategy seeks the positions on the value chain which offer the greatest leverage. Value chain pirates must use the commerce value chain to support a new, direct buyer/supplier relationship.

Example—ONSALE

ONSALE sells computers and consumer electronics on the Web through an interactive, 24-hour online auction that displaces traditional retail channels.

- Attract—get and keep customer interest

    ONSALE notifies customers of upcoming auctions that would be of interest to them based on their individual profiles.

- Interact—turn interest into orders

    Auctions are open 24 hours a day. Bidders can track counterbids in real time.

- Act—coordinate order fulfillment

    ONSALE has automated billing, shipping, and tracking via the Internet.

- React—provide after-sales service

    Customer inquiries are managed by e-mail and an online tracking system. Profiles are maintained for repeat customers.

ONSALE has been profitable since the first quarter of 1996 and acquired 60,000 customers in its first 18 months of operation.

Digital Distributor

The digital distributor strategy works by eating away at traditional value propositions by focusing on pieces of the value that can be delivered better through the Internet. A company using the digital distributor strategy is organized around disaggregating traditional bundles of products and reaggregating products and services which can be efficiently delivered through the Internet. Digital distributors must create a new customer value chain from scratch.

Example—Classifieds2000

Classifieds2000 provides Web-based classified advertising across many categories. It competes with newspapers in this industry and generates revenue solely through corporate advertising.

- Attract—get and keep customer interest

  Classifieds2000 offers free links to sites related to purchases (such as the Kelley Blue Book site for interested car buyers).

- Interact—turn interest into orders

  Through their "Cool Notify" service, Classifieds2000 sends e-mail to customers to alert them about new postings matching the profile of their desired goods.

- Act—coordinate order fulfillment

  Classifieds2000 is linked to Trade-direct, which acts as an intermediary to the transaction. They accept credit cards and enable order tracking online.

- React—provide after-sales service

  Classifieds2000 offers campaign reports to its advertisers, enabling them to measure the effectiveness of their advertising.

Classifieds2000 lists over $500 million in goods and services every week.

New Competitive Threats

Each of the four Internet business strategies can be used alone or in combination by competitors, and each forms a different kind of threat to a business.

- Channel master

  Can competitors create superior channels to your customers? Your customers could be attracted, by better prices, better service, and more convenience, to a competitor who takes a holistic view of the channel.

- Customer magnet

  Can competitors attract your customers and sell them your products? You could lose your customer base to someone offering a broader range of services, and be forced to survive as a commodity wholesale supplier to your competitor.

- Value chain pirate

  Can competitors hijack your position in the value chain? Your supplier could leapfrog your position in the value chain and sell directly to your customers. Your distributor could obtain parts directly from your suppliers.

- Digital Distributor

  Can competitors disaggregate your value proposition? If your value proposition is based on an aggregation of goods and services, it is possible for a niche competitor to excel at some part of the overall offering.

These questions can only be answered in the context of a concrete business situation, but an example may be instructive. Consider the case of a traditional full-service brokerage faced with the need to analyze its competitive position in light of the Internet.

The value proposition of the full-service brokerage is one-stop shopping for the sale of analysis and trading services. What happens when competitors adopt each of the four Internet business strategies?

- Channel master

  Another brokerage, say Merrill Lynch, goes online with consumer brokerage services, providing some of your customers with a more convenient and full-featured channel to essentially the same products and services.

- Customer magnet

  Motley Fool forms a community of avid investors and could potentially offer commoditized brokerage services under their brand.

- Value chain pirate

  E*Trade, a new online broker, is bumping traditional brokers out of the value chain.

- Digital distributor

  Wall Street City is selling analysis without trading services from their Web site.

New Competitive Opportunities

The dualism of competitive threats is that they are also new competitive opportunities. Again, each of our four business strategies must be analyzed for its applicability to your business.

- Channel master

  Can you improve your customers' buying experience by improving your cost, convenience, or ability to customize?

- Customer magnet

  Do your customers share broad needs that lend themselves to new bundles of products and services?

- Value chain pirate

  Can you jump over your direct suppliers or customers and capture their margins?

- Digital distributor

  What parts of other companies' value propositions could you improve by offering them on the Internet? What offerings can be added to your own package to make it more attractive?

Summary

We advocate a three-step approach to selecting and implementing a business strategy for the Internet: select a strategy, design the commerce value chain, and implement an evolving solution.

In the first phase, think through the overall strategy from both the point of view of potential competitive opportunity and from the point of view of the potential competitive threats from others. Will you be a channel master, customer magnet, value chain pirate, or digital distributor? Or is a combination the correct strategy? This process should lead to your "virtual value proposition."

Next, consider each stage of the commerce value chain and your preferred approach to attracting customers, interacting with them, acting on orders, and reacting to customer service requests. We suggest an "outside-in" approach, focused on the relationship of customers to each aspect of the business.

Finally, plan an iterative implementation, so as not to be caught by surprise by a technology shift or change in market conditions.

CHAPTER 4

Business Models—Some Case Studies

From things that differ comes the fairest attunement.
—Heraclitus[1]

Introduction to Business Segments

For this book, we have selected three business segments for detailed consideration of system requirements and design options:

- Consumer retail

  Businesses selling physical goods direct to an individual end consumer. We will further separate retail businesses into large businesses with complex requirements and small and medium enterprises with more basic needs (and smaller budgets) for Internet commerce.

- Business-to-business cataloging

  Businesses with online catalogs selling products to other businesses. We focus on MRO (maintenance, repair, and operations) goods rather than COGS (cost of goods and services) ordering. COGS generally implies large production orders for manufacturing, and although online systems and technologies such as EDI (Electronic Data Interchange) are used for this category of commerce, by the time a product is in production, catalogs of components are not the issue. We do specifically include the use of online catalogs for designers wishing to select components for later use in products.

---

1. Heraclitus, *On the Universe.*

- Information commerce

  This is a broad category, but we include businesses which plan to distribute digital goods (information products and services) online with fulfillment right over the network. Publishers of online magazines and the online distribution of software, although quite different businesses, would both be included. The essential feature is online fulfillment.

In a marketing sense, a business segment is a collection of companies in the same business area, such as passenger car manufacturers or newspaper publishers, who would have similar requirements for products and services. We are doing something slightly different; we are using the word *segment* to describe collections of businesses with similar requirements for Internet commerce, whether or not they are in the same business area.

Segment Granularity, Market Size, and Timing

Segmentation can occur at any level of granularity. For example, newspaper publishers might be further segmented into chains, large market dailies, and community weeklies. For Internet commerce, a segment like information commerce would break down into publishing, software distribution, and information services. Information services might break down into information search and retrieval, reservations, and financial services.

There are many reasons for segmenting a market or an area of technology, but they boil down to focus. Focus means concentrating on exactly those elements that are essential to the application or market, and not diverting effort toward those elements that are either not needed or not appreciated by the customer.

Segment granularity is a difficult issue. If the segment is too broad, then development resources may not stretch across all the necessary features. If the segment is too narrow, the market may not be large enough to support the business.

Segment Similarities and Differences

There are great similarities in the requirements of our three chosen segments. All have the need to attract customers, present products, assemble orders, do transactions, accomplish fulfillment, and deliver customer service. We will focus on these common elements, but also describe the areas in which the segments have very different requirements. As an illustration, the retail segment has a great need for merchandising capability, whereas business-to-business applications may have unusual requirements for payment by purchase order and for approval workflow.

The information commerce segment may be the most distinct of the three, since information businesses may not need physical delivery of products and the corresponding customer service mechanisms, but will have very complex requirements for online fulfillment.

Commerce Value Chain

In keeping with the structure of the previous chapter, we will examine our chosen segments using the structure of the commerce value chain shown in Figure 2-1 on page 16:

- Attract—advertising and marketing
- Interact—content
- Act—order processing, payment, fulfillment
- React—customer service

In keeping with the systems design structure of this book, we break up the transaction processing phase of the value chain into separate sections—order processing, payment, and fulfillment.

Consumer Retail

This section discusses the commerce value chain for businesses selling goods directly to an individual end consumer.

Value Proposition

The consumer retail segment has probably the least certain value proposition of the three. There are several ways to look at it, but the ability to inexpensively deliver a precise message to a worldwide audience creates a number of opportunities.

- Ability to reach a global market

  Because the Internet reaches consumers worldwide, a small local or regional business can suddenly reach a global audience. This can result in increased sales with minimal costs for distribution. An alternative view is that the worldwide audience can enable a niche market to gain a critical mass of customers, which may create a whole new class of retailers.

- Reduced marketing and selling expenses

  The creation and distribution of catalogs for direct marketing represents a substantial cost of sales. Although content creation costs for an online catalog may be higher than for a traditional catalog, the Internet enables a great reduction of printing and mailing costs.

- Increased efficiency of operation

  In traditional catalog order businesses, orders are processed over the telephone or by mail. These are labor-intensive processes. On the Internet, the consumer does much more of the work of creating a complete order, which can then be automatically entered into the order processing system. In addition, the network can be used for customer self-service and inquiries which would otherwise tie up operators.

- Ability to target consumers more precisely

  Online and interactive sites permit marketing "narrowcasting" to target customers. With paper catalogs it is impractical to print a different catalog targeted to each potential customer, but on the Internet, such *one-to-one* marketing is entirely possible, if not straightforward.

- Ability to convey more accurate product and availability information

  Because the content of an online catalog of goods is easily changed compared to printed materials, it can be both accurate and timely. The catalog can accurately reflect inventory, and can also be used to sell small lots of products whose quantity available would not justify space in a printed catalog.

System Functionality

Retail business occurs at many scales, from small shop to large multinational. The larger enterprise will naturally have more complex requirements for Internet commerce than the smaller.

- Small shop

  A small ongoing business may have a relatively static catalog, and simple requirements for record keeping and order entry. The store catalog would be created using a commerce-enabled desktop publishing application, and operated by an outsourcing company offering Web site hosting services. Orders would be collected by a commerce service provider[2] and sent to the shop by fax. Online payment would be by credit card or not required at all. Customer service would be most easily handled by telephone. Typical merchandising techniques would be coupons or occasional sales.

- Medium-size direct marketing

  Depending on the number of items (SKUs or *stock keeping units*) in the catalog, the online catalog would be produced either by a product database together with display templates to generate catalog pages on the fly, or by a desktop catalog authoring system generating product pages. Online orders would require shopping cart features, tax and shipping charge calculation, and credit card payment, and

---

2. A commerce service provider is a company offering Internet transaction services on an outsourced basis.

would be delivered to the store electronically. Given sufficient size, a customer registration database and online customer service would be included. Merchandising techniques would include coupons, promotions, sales, and perhaps membership discounts.

- Large retailer

  The most demanding retailer would require a highly dynamic Web site with the capability to handle frequent product and pricing changes. Product display would be linked to inventory on hand. Order taking could include private label as well as traditional credit cards, as well as on-account purchasing. Orders would be routed electronically to the retailer's ERP (*enterprise resource planning*[3]) system. Merchandising techniques could be highly complex, including one-to-one marketing and cross selling (suggesting accessory or complementary products). For international sales, support of multiple languages and currencies would be important.

With these general outlines of functionality, let's take a more detailed look at the various parts of these systems.

Attract—Advertising and Marketing

Attracting customers includes such diverse activities as advertising, coupons, promotions, sales, frequent buyer programs, and similar mechanisms. We call these activities *merchandising*. They are intended to build brand awareness, attract customers, and make them more likely to buy. To some extent, these activities fall into multiple elements of the commerce value chain. For example, one may receive a coupon as the result of making a purchase.

- Advertising

  Advertising puts the merchant or product in front of consumer eyes, either in store, such as "visit our housewares department," or out of store, such as on the side of a bus. On the Internet, advertising takes many forms, including banners on popular sites, e-mail newsletters, or simply listings on widely used search engines. Advertising is typically an expense for a retailer, but advertising can be revenue to a vendor in the information commerce segment.

- Coupons

  Possession of a retailer's coupon typically confers a lower price for the consumer. A coupon may appear as part of an advertisement, or may be given out at the checkout stand, triggered by purchasing activity. Coupons are used to build awareness of a product and to induce consumers to try a new brand, with the hope of switching. Internet-based digital coupons may directly link to a transaction service.

---

3. An enterprise resource planning system is a general term encompassing accounting systems, manufacturing planning, and other mission-critical business applications.

- Sales

  A sale means special prices for products for a limited period, perhaps with limits on the number of units available to a buyer. Sales are used as general promotions to build a customer base and increase awareness (in conjunction with advertising), and also as a way to clear built-up inventory, such as after a major holiday.

- Promotions

  Sales and coupons are examples of promotions, but a promotion can be quite complex. For example, a promotion might include a special price on a bundle of products even from different retailers, such as tuxedos, cake, and honeymoon arrangements as a complete wedding package.

- Frequent buyer programs

  Frequent buyer and other types of customer loyalty programs offer promotions to frequent customers. For example, purchases create frequent buyer points which can be redeemed for goods and services. Since points are not useful at other retailers, the consumer has an incentive to concentrate purchases with one or a few retailers.

- One-to-one marketing

  Retailers try to learn as much about their customers as possible. When more or less the same products are available from a number of sources, retailers compete on the basis of convenience, price, and quality of service. The Internet removes the geographic basis of convenience, and price is always a difficult basis for competition, leaving quality of service. Knowing a lot about a customer can help a retailer provide high-quality service.

  One-to-one marketing generally means the customization of a system to the level of the individual consumer. It includes such things as the creation of individual customer profiles and the generation of content specific to the user.

Interact—Content

The simplest view of retail Internet commerce content is as the online equivalent of a direct marketing catalog. This is probably accurate for the broad middle of the market, but the Internet is a platform that can offer commerce services to the millions of small merchants around the world. For these organizations, simple desktop publishing of commerce-enabled catalogs is appropriate. For stores with up to a few hundred items, the catalog could be created or modified by marketing personnel or anyone familiar with desktop publishing.

Farther upscale, frequent price changes and product changes make a simple desktop publishing model untenable. In this segment, a desktop database, coupled to an authoring tool up to an online database creating Web content on the fly, would be used.

At the most complex end of the market, dynamic catalogs, perhaps driven by real-time inventory information, would be used. The complexity of the technology would require ongoing information systems support.

In any of these cases, it is necessary to attract customers to the Web site or online catalog. A number of techniques are available:

- Registration with Internet search engines

- Printed hypertext links on traditional menus, catalogs, and advertising

- Internet advertising on popular or related sites

Act—Order Processing

Order processing functions appropriate for retail purchases include the following kinds of activities:

- Shopping cart or order aggregation function

  On the Internet, a shopping cart is not a physical cart, but a logical database of items being considered for purchase. The shopping cart may include the capability for the buyer to change the quantity or other attributes of an item, and can contain hypertext links back to the catalog page from which the item originated.

  An electronic shopping cart may also be able to accumulate coupons and contain items from multiple vendors to facilitate comparison shopping.

- Order validation

  It may be appropriate to validate an order based on a variety of business rules. For example, a PAL television receiver would not work in North America, or a collection of computer system components might not be complete without a necessary cable. A merchant might not forbid such a suspect order from going through, but calling the matter to the buyer's attention could reduce downstream returns and customer service costs.

- Application of coupons or other discounts

  Coupons and other forms of merchandising such as affinity programs and quantity discounts are logically applied to the whole order. The order aggregation function in principle could recognize sets of items which together have a package price, whether the items are selected together or separately.

- Cross selling

  It may be appropriate to offer the buyer additional merchandise, depending on the current contents of the shopping cart or previous shopping and purchase behavior. (The latter capabilities are relevant only if the identity of the buyer is known, since a shopping cart might be anonymous or registered.) For example, a purchase of a flashlight might trigger an offer of batteries.

- Calculation of sales and other taxes

  Sales taxes require complex rule sets involving the tax classification of the product, the location and tax status of the buyer, and the location and tax status of the seller. In the United States there are more than 6,000 tax jurisdictions at the city, county, and state government levels. Elsewhere, Canada has provincial sales taxes (PST) and a national goods and services tax (GST) and Europe has a complex set of value-added taxes (VAT). An Internet commerce system must correctly handle this complexity.

- Calculation of shipping and delivery charges

  In the case of physical goods ordered online, most orders will be delivered rather than picked up. Shipping charges may be bundled into the price, but frequently they are extra. Several different forms of delivery may be available (overnight, 2-day, ground), and the charges may depend on the quantity of items, their weight, and their value.

- Presentation of the rolled-up order to the buyer

  It is important for the buyer to know what is being purchased at what prices. This can help build consumer acceptance of a new medium, as well as reducing downstream customer service, returns, and dispute handling costs.

Once a final validated order is available, the buyer will select a payment mechanism. It may happen that the price depends on the payment mechanism, in which case the selection of the mechanism should be viewed as part of order processing.

Act—Payment

In real-world retail settings, the majority of payments occur by cash, credit, check, or payment card. Payment cards may be further divided into credit cards, charge cards, and debit cards. As we will discuss in the chapter on payment technology, each of these has electronic analogs; but for our purposes now, we are interested in a quick outline of the business properties of these mechanisms.

Cash

- Cash is a bearer instrument.

  The seller does not need to trust the buyer when cash is used—assuming counterfeiting is not a problem! The value is inherent in the instrument and is transferred immediately from buyer to seller. The buyer, on the other hand, has to trust the seller to deliver the product once cash has been delivered.

- Cash is anonymous.

  The seller does not have to know the identity of the buyer in order to accept cash. Cash is also suitable for transactions of which the buyer does not require a transaction record. On the Internet, other means of tracing buyers, including the shipping address for physical delivery, may limit the utility of this property of cash.

- Cash is suitable for small-value transactions.

  Because cash can have very small transaction costs, it is suitable for small-value purchases. The total system costs of handling cash, including counting, storage, security, mistakes, theft, and so forth can be quite high, however, so this property of cash should be analyzed carefully.

Credit

It was once common for retail establishments to extend credit to their customers. This is still common for services (electricity, telephone), but rather less so for retail businesses. Many companies have branded credit cards, but these are considered elsewhere. Credit may have a larger role on the Internet as a means of efficiently handling small-value transactions, but this will be considered in the section on information commerce.

Check

A check is an order from the buyer to her bank to pay the seller so much money.

- Checks are not guaranteed.

  The redemption of a check is not really assured until the check is deposited and cleared through the banking system, and value is actually moved from the buyer's account to the seller's account. Funds may not be available to back the check, or the buyer may stop payment.

- Checks require authentication.

  A seller does not know for sure that the buyer has the authority to write a check on a given account. In addition to the risks of nonpayment due to the lack of a guarantee, a check may be invalid if it is forged. Another way to say this is there is no obvious connection between the check and the person writing it. This is why sellers ask for other forms of identification and why check guarantee services exist.

- A check is a contract.

  Even if payment of a check is halted, a signed check may represent a contract between buyer and seller, and therefore be capable of collection.

In accepting checks, the seller accepts a certain amount of risk of nonpayment. On the other hand, the seller is not paying someone else to assume the risk.

Debit Cards

A debit card is a kind of payment card that directly transfers funds from the buyer's bank account to the seller. These cards are widely used in Europe and the Far East, and less widely used in North America. Debit cards benefit the seller, because payment is guaranteed and immediate, and transaction costs are lower than for credit cards. Debit cards may be less advantageous to the buyer because (in the United States) debit cards do not provide the consumer protections of the Consumer Credit Protection Act.

Credit and Charge Cards

Credit cards are so ubiquitous that few people appreciate their complexity. Incidentally, a charge card is a purchasing card which does not extend credit; the full amount of the charges are due when the monthly bill arrives. The operating framework for credit cards is provided by the card association regulations (Visa, MasterCard, American Express, etc.) and, in the United States, by the Consumer Credit Protection Act.

From the seller's perspective, the salient facts are these.

- Credit cards may or may not guarantee payment.

  When a credit card is presented in person, and the retail clerk complies with all the steps of the process, such as requiring and checking the cardholder's signature and obtaining a real-time authorization, then the card association will guarantee payment. In other situations, such as mail or telephone order (MOTO) or other card-not-present transactions, the merchant may have to assume more risk of nonpayment.

- Credit cards have substantial transaction fees.

  The seller typically pays a fee of several percent of transaction value for a credit card purchase. The fee is generally composed of two parts: a flat fee to the various parties who handle the mechanics of authorization messages and so forth, and a percentage to the acquirer (typically the seller's bank) and issuer (typically the buyer's bank) for assuming various risks. The overall rate might be something like 25 cents plus 2 percent. This fee structure means that the effective percentage fee grows as the transaction value shrinks, so that using a credit card for a 25-cent purchase would result in a net loss to the seller. With typical transaction values in the physical world, this is not usually a problem since the average Visa transaction is something like $70.

From the consumer's perspective, credit cards provide a number of protections.

- Protections against theft or misuse.

  The Consumer Credit Protection Act (in the United States) provides that a cardholder is not liable for any unauthorized charges once the issuer has been notified of loss or theft, and in any event, the cardholder is not liable for more than $50 of unauthorized charges. The principle in effect here is that the issuers and credit card system operators should be responsible for assuring adequate system security.

- Merchants are validated.

  Consumers have some assurance of the bona fides of the seller by virtue of the seller's acceptance of the card. The card issuers hold the buyer harmless if it turns out that the merchant is fraudulent. This is a substantial benefit for commerce over the Internet, where the buyer does not have access to traditional means of inquiry about the status of a merchant.

- Card issuer provides customer service.

  Generally speaking, if a consumer buys something with a credit card, the card issuer offers a single point of contact for disputes. In cases of nonperformance by the seller, or even of poor-quality goods, the seller can dispute the resulting charge with the benefit of substantial clout. Some cards extend consumer warranties and offer various kinds of insurance.

Summary

To the extent that the closest existing analog of Internet commerce is provided by mail-order catalogs, it seems likely that for the near-term future most online retail commerce will be conducted by credit card.

Act—Fulfillment

Fulfillment refers to the process of delivering the goods ordered to their destination, and includes a number of steps:

- Transmission of order information from point of sale to warehouse

- Packing and order assembly for shipping

- Shipping and delivery

For physical goods, except for the first step, Internet commerce has the same fulfillment issues as other sorts of retail commerce. Order entry, however, may occur in various ways within Internet commerce.

- Small business

  The Web presence of a small business may be maintained by a hosting service at a separate location from the business. As orders come in, they must be conveyed back to the business' fulfillment function. This can be accomplished by fax, by regular or encrypted e-mail, or by polling an online list of pending orders.

- Medium business

  A mid-sized business, particularly one already equipped for mail-order business, may wish to integrate orders originating on the Internet with others. This integration can be manual or automatic, depending on the volume of orders expected.

- Large business

  A large business engaging in Internet commerce will most certainly wish to integrate the order stream originating on the Net with other order streams. This integration may take the form of a direct link between the Internet transaction machinery and the business' existing order management or ERP system.

Relationship between Payment and Fulfillment

Generally, payment is not due until the seller is ready to deliver goods. When a credit card is used for payment, the card association rules generally require that although authorization can occur at the point and time of sale, settlement, which actually transfers funds, can only occur upon shipment. This implies that either there must be notification from the fulfillment service back to the payment function, or that the settlement part of payment can be handled by the fulfillment service.

React—Customer Service

The Internet presents many opportunities for either improving the value of customer service delivered or reducing its cost. The key observation is that in most settings, customer service representatives are acting as *human modems*. For example, in telephone customer service, the operator listens to information coming in by telephone and keys it into a customer service application terminal. Then the operator reads some amount of information off the screen back into the telephone. Because the Internet puts a screen right in front of the customer, there is an opportunity for *customer self-service* and a reduced cost structure.

Opportunities for Improved Service

- Greater service capacity

  With Internet service, the system is available 24 hours a day, 7 days a week with no need to schedule a flexible work force according to peak hours and seasons. With communications routed over a global network, *follow the sun* support can switch from one support center to another as daylight hours move around the globe.

- Reduced error rates

  Errors associated with the human-modem functions can be eliminated, and the screens seen by the customer can be backed by immediate feedback and automatic step-by-step validation of input. With online forms, users can check choice boxes to indicate their intentions, and calculations can be done immediately by computer, further reducing errors.

- Richer information available

  There is no need to restrict the information available to voice, so tables, text, images, and graphics can all be used.

- Self-help or community help

  Frequently Asked Questions is a great format for customer self-help. In customer service the same questions arise all the time. These can be addressed in a searchable knowledge base.

- Direct linkage to status information

  Inquiries about order status can directly link over the network to sites maintained by all the parties involved, such as shipping and delivery companies.

- Proactive information delivery

  Information about product features, shipping delays, and recalls can be "pushed" to customers by e-mail, or posted to their online personalized statement pages.

- Multiple-language support

  Separate sets of Web pages can be maintained for all languages used by the customer base.

Opportunities for Reduced Costs

There are obvious economies for electronic customer self-service.

- Reduced personnel costs

  Since customers have direct access to relevant information, an organization may need fewer customer service representatives, or it may reallocate their time for other tasks.

- Reduced physical plant costs

  The traditional call center can be smaller, saving on real estate, buildings, equipment, and operating costs.

- Reduced telecommunications costs

  Because Internet protocols are packet switched, rather than circuit switched, a larger number of "calls" can be handled on similar telecommunications facilities.

Business-to-Business Cataloging

In this section, we discuss catalogs for maintenance, repair, and operations, and for component sourcing for products. MRO goods are such things as office supplies, physical plant repair parts, and consumables such as cleaning supplies. These areas of commerce are characterized by high-volume, low-value purchases; repeat business from the same customers; and high order processing costs for both buyers and sellers.

Value Proposition

The key benefits of putting a business-to-business catalog online are immediate cost savings and an ability to provide better service.

- Reduce cost of selling

  In addition to the cost benefit of an online catalog over the printing and distribution expenses of paper, many business applications require a depth of information difficult to represent on paper. For example, engineers use catalogs to select components for new product designs. Once a part is selected, other services such as faxback are often used to obtain detailed drawings and schematics. These functions are largely information based and can be conducted online.

- Reduce order processing costs

  MRO purchasing tends to involve large numbers of low-value orders. As such, the order processing costs can be significant. By automating the ordering process flow, these costs can be substantially reduced. (Handling a purchase order costs between $50 and $300, split between buyer and seller.)

- Improve service levels for low-volume customers

  Business-to-business catalog companies frequently provide special services for their largest customers. These services, such as custom catalogs, special negotiated prices, and order aggregation, are typically economic only for large customers when they are provided by traditional means. The Internet can bring these value-added features within reach of smaller-volume customers.

- Provide higher-quality information for customers

  The electronic medium of an online catalog permits it to be searchable, and to contain a much greater depth of product information than would be possible on paper. Searching makes the catalog easier to use, and can be a competitive advantage simply because it is faster. Depth of information is possible because the hypertext capabilities of the World Wide Web permit the user to click through a catalog item to reach detailed product information and application information *underneath*.

- Accurate information

  Unlike paper catalogs, an online catalog can always be up to date, with accurate product information, availability, and prices updated in real time.

Differences from Consumer Retail

With substantial background from the consumer retail segment in mind, this section discusses business requirements for business-to-business cataloging in terms of the differences from consumer retail.

Attract—Advertising and Marketing

Many of the merchandising techniques of retail also apply to business-to-business commerce. The key problems for a seller are to attract the attention of a recommender on the buy side and to become a qualified, or ideally a preferred, vendor.

Interact—Content

Our model for the use of Internet commerce for selling MRO products is an online catalog. At a high level, business catalogs are very much like consumer catalogs, but there are a number of differences.

Searching Is Essential

Business catalogs can be very large; it is not uncommon for a catalog to contain 50,000 or 100,000 different parts. For this reason, searching capability is essential. For industrial parts, the searching mechanism should not have a predefined hierarchy. If the customer is looking for two-inch, brass, 90-degree pipe fittings, there is no obvious reason to search for these attributes in any particular order. One solution to this problem is a technique known as *parametric search*.

In this example, the requisitioner may be faced with a catalog of thousands of pipe fittings. After selecting "brass," the catalog might inform the requisitioner that there are 3,200 types of brass fittings. Selecting "90-degree elbow" may reduce the number to 300; selecting 2 inch may further reduce the number to 10, representing various couplings. Once the number of hits is reduced enough, it makes sense to scroll through an exhaustive list of the 10 possible parts.

Custom Catalogs

Businesses that do repeat business with other businesses often evolve special agreements, special pricing, and even design special components not available to other customers.

- Special part numbers

  The electronic nature of an Internet catalog makes it feasible to publish a different version for each significant customer. The part numbers displayed can be the customer's part numbers, instead of or in addition to the supplier's part numbers.

- Special pricing

  Pricing by special agreement or according to volume schedules can be reflected directly in an online catalog.

- Security requirements

  In order to keep one customer's activity secret from another, business-to-business catalogs have higher authentication and security requirements than is typical for retail. For example, if the catalog shows special pricing due to corporate agreement with a specific customer, only employees of that customer should be allowed to access the catalog.

Act—Order Processing

Business-to-business order processing can be substantially more complex than retail order processing. On the seller's side, real-time checks of inventory availability and order consistency are likely, as are the order processing components of business-oriented payment mechanisms. On the buyer side, the order processing can be much more complex.

Approvals and Workflow

In business ordering, there are a variety of roles:

- Requisitioner—individual who wants something purchased
- Approver—individual who authorizes the funding for the purchase
- Purchaser—individual who does the purchasing

In consumer purchasing, these roles are usually held by a single individual, whereas in business, they may be separate and never in the same place at the same time. To the extent that a purchasing agent has a clerical role, the automation of Internet commerce may reduce the need for the role, permitting it to be combined with that of the requisitioner.

The major order processing function essential for business-to-business applications is an approval workflow mechanism that permits an order, once composed, to be routed through the appropriate process. Additional issues include requirements for line-item-level detail, cost allocation, and fine-grained control over shipping and delivery.

Delegation

An important capability in systems intended for business-to-business use is the ability for an authorized user to delegate authority to another user. In the consumer model, parents may have some control over the online purchasing abilities of their children, but the requirements are much more complex in the business context.

- A department administrator delegates authority to department members to log in to and search supplier catalogs.
- A manager delegates authority to a subordinate to approve purchases while the manager is on vacation.

Act—Payment

Several additional means of payment are appropriate for business-to-business commerce.

Purchase Orders

A purchase order is not really a payment mechanism itself, but rather a means to create billing records for later settlement by a direct payment instrument. At the point of sale, the purchase order connects the order, typically via a reference number, to the order tracking system of the buying organization.

In Internet commerce, a purchase order would be an acceptable means of payment only if the buying organization has arranged credit with the seller and the buyer is appropriately authenticated and authorized by the buying organization to make purchases.

Procurement Cards

Procurement cards work the same way as credit cards, but have a number of features specialized for business commerce. The idea of procurement cards is to delegate purchasing authority to the lowest levels possible within an organization, but to provide high-quality reporting to enable proper financial controls.

- Goods category restriction

  When a procurement card is used to make a purchase, the authorization decision is made not only on the remaining credit available, but also on the Selected Industry Code of the store, the purchase history of the buyer, and perhaps on information about the product being sold (if the authorization system has that information available). The buying organization sets up proper profiles for each buyer, which might permit the purchase of $100 per month of office supplies, but not hardware or food.

  Procurement card support in an Internet commerce system implies that the system will transmit detailed information on purchases to the card authorization network, in addition to amounts.

- Reporting

  Standard credit cards provide information on purchasing as items on the paper monthly bill. Procurement cards provide detailed purchase reports to the buying organization, often in near real time, in an electronic form.

Electronic Funds Transfer

Electronic funds transfers are somewhat akin to checks, in that they are instructions to transfer funds from one account to another. Like checks, EFT has a fixed overhead cost unrelated to the amount of the transfer, and also like checks, the funds transfer networks do not assume liabilities for customer service. Unlike other payment mechanisms, electronic funds transfers are fast—overnight or immediate—and provide both parties with immediate acknowledgment of their execution.

In the United States, there are really two EFT networks: the Automated Clearinghouse (ACH) network which is used for automatic payroll deposits, investment funds transfers, and bill payment; and the various Automated Teller Machine (ATM) networks which are used for obtaining cash and for using debit cards at gas stations and grocery stores.[4] The ACH network typically works overnight, whereas the ATM networks work in real time.

For Internet commerce, EFT payments offer more immediate effect and a reduced requirement for trust between parties compared to checks, and a lower cost structure than credit or procurement cards. However, the ACH networks were really intended for repetitive payments, and they have fairly complex technical and administrative procedures for setting up a transfer; the ATM networks work for individual payments, but usually require a complex infrastructure to handle PIN numbers securely.

Act—Fulfillment

Business-to-business needs add some additional requirements for fulfillment systems:

- Predefined ship-to addresses

  When requisitioners can order small to medium-sized items without review, and when the volume of orders makes any after-the-fact review unlikely, fulfillment systems can provide some additional protection against abuse of the system by permitting only predefined ship-to addresses to be used. This capability will typically be part of the order management phase, but linked to fulfillment. When business purchasing is set up, a set of predetermined legitimate shipping addresses are loaded. Requisitioners can select from them, but not alter them.

- Order aggregation

  When a business sends a large volume of small orders to a supplier, aggregating the orders in a single shipment on a daily or weekly basis can save shipping and overhead costs. Traditionally, this order aggregation is done by hand, but electronic systems make it easier. Even if orders are entered by individual requisitioners, the fulfillment stage of the commerce system can recognize a common buying organization and shipping address, and combine orders.

---

4. There are also institutional large-dollar-transaction networks like CHIPS and Fedwire.

- Multiple ship-to addresses, scheduled deliveries

  In business, it frequently happens that a central purchasing organization buys a large quantity of supplies for the benefit of multiple locations. In this case, the fulfillment system has to handle multiple shipping addresses, perhaps on a line-item basis. When orders are aggregated, even for a single location, then the fulfillment system must designate the final destination of each part of the order.

React—Customer Service

For business-to-business commerce, we broaden the definition of customer service to include all services delivered after the point of sale—training, technical support, and software maintenance, for example, in addition to traditional customer service.

- Training

  For many products, online training may be an effective means of customer education. Unlike paper training manuals, but like computer-based training, Internet-based training can be highly interactive. Not only can the training system include simulations or access to the real product (for software products, anyway), but instructors can communicate with students online.

- Software maintenance

  Software maintenance refers to the practice of delivering patches and version upgrades to a software product for a fixed annual fee, in effect a subscription, following the purchase of an initial version. The Internet is a nearly ideal channel for distribution of software, and it is equally suited to the delivery of upgrades. With a software purchase, a vendor might supply a subscription enabling the customer to download new versions as they are released.

- Technical support

  After the sale, many companies sell technical support. This term includes answering questions about the product and its application and assisting with working around bugs and other sorts of product problems. For high-technology equipment and software, the network can be used for remote diagnosis and even repair.

  One additional opportunity for vendors is to set up an electronic community for their customers. Online forums and files of frequently asked questions can be effective means of customer self-help.

Information Commerce

In this section we discuss the use of the Internet for commerce in *digital goods*, which can be fulfilled right over the network.

Value Proposition

The essential features of online information commerce are the collapse of the traditional distribution chain and the ability to explore new business models.

- Collapse of the distribution chain

  On the Internet, information providers have direct access to information consumers, without an intervening distribution channel. For the first time, the marginal cost of delivering a product to an incremental consumer is very near zero. In addition, there is no *shelf space* or *channel bandwidth* limitation to artificially boost distribution costs.

- Business models

  Because the medium is ultimately flexible, information providers, be they publishers or authors of software, can easily experiment with new business models such as software rental, pay-per-view documents, and microtransactions, as well as traditional models such as advertising and subscriptions. In effect, the efficiency of the medium and reduction of transaction costs enables the unit of information commerce to be much smaller.

Business Models

One of the challenges of information commerce is how does one make money? We review some of the revenue models for information commerce.

Advertiser Supported

A content provider can generate revenue through advertising. Advertisers pay for impressions, a set of eyes looking at their advertisement. A site that has interesting and compelling content attracts lots of visitors, and the advertisers will pay for that. If the site can also collect registration information from visitors that includes demographic information such as age, sex, or zip code, then advertisers will pay more.

On the World Wide Web, there is also the technical opportunity to gauge the effectiveness of an advertisement by the numbers of users who click on it.

Subscription Services

Subscriptions are a traditional model for print, and can also work online. In a subscription model, the consumer pays a recurring fee for ongoing access to information.

Bundling Arrangements

In order to achieve a sufficient critical mass of information to attract visitors, content owners may sell access rights to each other's constituencies, or a service provider who is not directly in the content business may license access to content for their users.

Document Sales

This is a broad category, encompassing, for example, the sale of research reports or individual articles, or the online sale and delivery of software.

Usage-based Charging

In this business model, users pay according to usage. Usage can include many attributes, such as connect time, search queries, or number of pages viewed. Both information products, such as an online newspaper, and information services, such as search engines or online games, are amenable to usage-based charging.

Information Marketplace

Because the Internet greatly reduces transaction costs, it could lead to a world in which the ultimate providers of information sell directly to the ultimate consumers in a vast information marketplace. Perhaps the most intriguing set of questions is what role there will be for middlemen, distributors, and aggregators of information.

For an information marketplace to evolve, the following components are necessary:

- Rights management

  For authors and publishers to distribute their information online, they must be able to specify the permitted uses of the information in a standard format.

- Containers

  A container is an envelope that protects information in transit and before sale. Containers can be freely distributed on the network, on CD-ROM, or via broadcast. When the contents of a container are purchased, the container unlocks to reveal the content. Frequently, different fees apply for viewing, printing, and other forms of access. Containers can also be used to prevent an authorized user of information from distributing it to unauthorized users.

- Superdistribution

  The concept of superdistribution encompasses the encoding of distribution rights along with information in a secure container. An information aggregator can purchase rights to redistribute the content in a container, and pass a modified container along. When the end user eventually pays for access, parts of the fee go to the distribution chain and parts to the original author.

- Clearinghouses

  Clearinghouses for both intellectual property rights (copyright management) and for payment are necessary components for the information marketplace. Clearinghouses collect fees from end users and distribute them according to the rules in the secure containers.

Differences from Consumer Retail and Business-to-Business

This section discusses the business requirements for information commerce in terms of the differences between it and consumer retail and business-to-business cataloging.

Requirements for Customer Systems

Although the segments discussed previously may have quite complex requirements for the purchaser, in terms of Web browser capabilities or platform capabilities to run client applets, information commerce may put more stringent requirements on the buyer simply to handle the information content itself.

Interact—Content

In information commerce, the content is itself the product. We will discuss under "fulfillment" some of the problems of online delivery. In this section we discuss the varieties of online products and services being sold.

*   Software

    The Internet is a natural medium for online distribution of software. Except for printed manuals and recording media, software is entirely information. Online software distribution includes selling the right to download a distribution kit, accepting payment for shareware, free download of distribution kits combined with sale of a license key, and subscriptions to software for network computers.

*   Searchable databases

    Content providers can charge for access to databases, including search facilities. The information in such a database can be of high value, and sometimes the value is really in the organization of the information. Charging can be usage-based or subscription oriented.

*   Dynamic information

    The Internet is a great medium for distribution of newsfeeds, financial quotes, sports news, and other rapidly changing information. So-called *push* distribution can deliver dynamic information direct to the desktop.

*   Online magazines and newspapers

    This sort of content is essentially the same as the content delivered on paper, but made more valuable by timeliness and an ability to search. Online magazines can also be personalized to the individual, and even composed from a variety of sources.

*   Reports and documents

    Online repositories of reports and documents save a great deal of duplicate effort over paper. With paper, manual filing is very expensive and adds little value. Electronic filing makes sure documents are never lost or misfiled, multiple copies are available for checkout, and searching and indexing make the content accessible.

- Multimedia objects

  Given adequate bandwidth (wait a few years!), it is perfectly feasible to deliver full-fidelity movies and television on the network. Images and audio are already widely used on the Web.

- Interactive services

  Online forums, chat rooms, telephone calls, virtual worlds (multiuser dungeons), and games can all be delivered online.

- Information services

  Stock brokerages, banks, travel agencies, and ticket agencies are all examples of information services where no physical objects need change hands. All these sorts of businesses can be carried out online.

Act—Order Processing

The primary differences of order processing for information commerce from the other segments are that the user experience may need to be much simpler, and authentication plays a more central role.

Because information commerce may be carried out in microtransactions, there is a need for an individual purchase event to be very fast and nonintrusive to the user experience.

Authentication is especially relevant because of the need for online fulfillment. For example, in the case of an ongoing subscription, the system needs to authenticate (identify) the user at the time of purchase, and make appropriate database entries, so that the same user can be authenticated and authorized at the time of information delivery.

Act—Payment

Several additional payment systems seem appropriate for information commerce. Naturally, heavyweight payment systems such as purchase orders or credit cards are completely appropriate for large-value purchases such as long-term subscriptions or downloaded software.

Sometimes the choice of a payment system is made for business reasons, such as the approval process or risk management, and sometimes for economic reasons. When economics are important, the size of the transaction is the key factor. Each payment mechanism has a typical transaction cost, ranging from $.25 for a credit card transaction to perhaps $50 to $100 for processing a purchase order. Obviously a purchase order is uneconomical for a $10 purchase, but what happens when the purchase is $.10 or less? The necessary answer is to use a payment mechanism with an appropriately small transaction cost.

Electronic Cash

Electronic cash systems have several cash-like properties, such as anonymity, but the relevant characteristic for us is a typically low transaction cost. An electronic cash transaction may be viable in the five-to-ten-cents range. Systems that require a real-time link to a clearinghouse will have higher transaction costs than systems which work in disconnected environments.

Microtransactions and Tokens

Microtransactions are very similar in structure to electronic cash, but have transaction costs that can make them useful for transactions of fractions of a penny. Token systems are those in which larger amounts of money are traded for tokens or credits (a private currency, really) which can only be used at a particular service. Several microtransaction systems have been proposed; the basic idea is to modify the basic client-server protocol of the World Wide Web so that individual interactions debit the buyer and credit the seller. Tokens can be implemented more simply, by keeping the user's credit balance at the server.

Transaction Aggregation

Without extra technology, the seller has the option to collect multiple billable events and to charge for them by the batch. This process can amortize the transaction overhead over a large number of transactions, hopefully bringing the exchange of value into an economical range for the given payment system. Aggregation can be either of two types:

- Taxi meter, or charge up

  In this system, the meter accumulates usage charges, and the buyer pays for them all at a later date. The difficulty is that the seller is extending credit to the buyer, which may be problematic when the buyer is unknown or anonymous. With credit cards, it is possible to obtain an authorization (guarantee of credit availability) in advance of settlement (funds transfer), so that the credit risk can be transferred to the card issuer.

- Parking meter, or pay down

  In this system, the buyer prepays a lump sum, perhaps $10, and then uses the credit balance during the course of some time period. The difficulty here is the seller's stance toward refunds (typically none) and the seller's responsibility to not lose credit balance records.

In both models of transaction aggregation, there are many technical details and questions of business policy. For example, should the necessary authorizations be immediate or can they be deferred?

Act—Fulfillment

For Internet commerce in physical goods, fulfillment is through traditional channels.[5] For digital goods managed by information commerce, fulfillment is online. For different kinds of content, different mechanisms of fulfillment are appropriate.

Downloading

The simplest forms of digital goods are those downloaded to the client computer once. Online purchases of software or reports fit this category. Typical mechanisms are to charge for the download itself, charge for access rights to the download area, or charge for a license key. The differences are subtle but important—what happens when the download fails? Disks can fill up, modems can be cut off, or the power can fail. For these reasons, it is prudent to plan for download failures and to automatically recover from them.

- Charge for download

  This method is appropriate for small downloads, which are unlikely to fail. If the download does fail, either the user will pay again, or a customer service call will result, with a request for a refund. Charging for download may be the best choice for microtransactions, where the theory is "optimize the common case." Most downloads will succeed, so they should proceed with no user intervention. The user will not worry about the occasional double charge for retrying a failed connection attempt because they are so inexpensive anyway.

- Charge for license key

  Charging for the license key to unlock the download permits the download area to be publicly accessible, since the download is useless without the key. If the locking technology is such that a given key works only on a particular computer, then once created, the key can be distributed freely as well, because it is useless anywhere else than its intended destination. Delivering the key and content separately is complex and perhaps suitable only for higher-value purchases (unless the whole procedure is automated).

- Charge for access

  Charging for access to the download area is an interesting hybrid design. In this case, access to the fulfillment area is granted for a reasonable period of time, deemed sufficient for all users to successfully download the product. For example, download access might be granted for eight hours—long enough for several attempts to download the product, including a trip to the store for more blank diskettes.

---

5. At least until the advent of the matter restorer PC peripheral, which will create the physical object given its description. For example, see Neal Stephenson, *The Diamond Age (Bantam Books, 1996),* or George O. Smith, *The Complete Venus Equilateral (Ballantine, 1976).*

Subscriptions

We distinguish a subscription from a download by the notion that a subscription carries with it some sort of ongoing access to a service, which essentially means that the user who bought the subscription must be able to authenticate himself to the service, and that the service grant authorization for access going forward. There has to be a subscription database which says who is to be granted access (authorization), and there has to be a way for a user to prove he is who he claims to be (authentication).

There are several ways to solve these problems, but any solution must allow for such complexities as renewals, grace periods, refunds, access to multiple fulfillment servers, and user access from multiple computers.

Push Content

Fulfillment of push content, which is actively delivered by the content service rather than downloaded by the user, is managed either by creating a database record at the server to enable delivery (point-to-point delivery), or by delivering to the end user credentials which permit the content to be tuned in and decoded (broadcast delivery).

React—Customer Service

The key customer service issues for information commerce are the same as for other segments.

- I didn't buy that (or I don't remember buying that).
- I didn't receive the delivery (or it arrived here broken).
- I didn't like what I received.
- I was charged the wrong amount.

The difference is that in information commerce, there is every possibility of using technology to assure delivery, to the point that "I didn't receive the delivery" is a very rare complaint.

Copy Protection and Rights Management

One other problem with digital content is that it can be copied. The difference between information delivered physically (books, magazines) and information delivered online is not that copying is impossible offline, but that copying is incredibly cheap online. The content owner has a number of choices:

- Don't worry about it

  Doing nothing about rights management may be the best choice. If the information is already available for free in the library, for example, there is not much point in spending money or causing customer inconvenience to prevent occasional copying. In this case, however, there is some value to helping set the social context that copying without paying is wrong, and in managing one's exposure. Similarly, it may be appropriate to do nothing if the content itself is not what is valuable about the online service. For example, if the ability to search is what is valuable, there may be minimal value to preventing copying.

- Make copying very difficult

  If the information sold is of very high value, then there is benefit to making it difficult to copy. Container technology or license keys for software can be appropriate mechanisms.

- Make tracing the thief easy

  This is analogous to dye packets in the teller's drawer. The dye doesn't make the bank hard to rob, but it makes it pretty easy to locate the thief. In information commerce, it is possible to watermark or fingerprint each distributed copy of content so that each copy is distinct and registered. If copies of a watermarked document come to light, they are easily traceable to the original customer.

- Make paying for copies easy

  If there is an easy-to-use, always available way to pay for copies, the majority of honest customers will use it. If no one knows who to pay or how to pay, then copying will flourish. This approach works especially well for information intended for professional customers. Such customers expect to pay for value received, and often pass along information charges to their customers anyway.

Summary

In this chapter we have discussed business models and business issues for three business segments which might benefit from Internet commerce: consumer retail, business-to-business cataloging, and information commerce. There are obviously many other business segments—government and health care are but two examples—that stand to benefit from applying Internet technology, but we hope our three choices cast a broad enough net to engage the reader into thinking carefully about the opportunities presented by the Internet and into analyzing carefully the complete customer value chain.

Within any business segment, related to the Internet or not, different participants have different goals. At a high level, for example, customers want the best products at the lowest prices, and vendors want to make as much money as possible. Understanding these differences and how to reconcile them in successful sales is a key part of any business strategy. Internet technology, and Internet commerce in particular, brings some thorny issues to the fore. In the next chapter, we look at some examples of these issues and discuss ways to analyze and address them in commerce systems.

CHAPTER 5

Conflicting Goals and Requirements

It is a very hard undertaking to seek to please everybody.
—Publilius Syrus[1]

The first rule in business is *know your customer*. If you know what your customer wants, and you deliver it better than anyone else, you can be successful. Often, however, problems arise because systems must serve more than one set of customers, who have conflicting requirements. Sometimes the customers don't know what they want, especially in an entirely new area. This chapter surveys some of the rough ground of Internet commerce: those areas in which the participants have different goals, or at least different priorities.

Goals of the Participants

Systems for Internet commerce have many masters. This section illustrates some of the resulting complexity by reviewing the goals and interests of some of the key constituencies.

---

1. Publilius Syrus, *Maxims.*

Buyers

In the context of this section, *buyer* means customer. It seems obvious that a commerce system must meet the needs of the customer, but different kinds of buyers want different things, and their interests are sometimes at cross-purposes with those of the sellers.

Retail Customers

By retail customers, we mean the buyers using systems for business-to-consumer commerce.

- Convenience

    The Internet is an alternative to driving and browsing, and an alternative to bulky and out-of-date paper catalogs. If using the network is not easier than the alternatives, few people will bother.

- Price

    Retail consumers are frequently very price sensitive, especially for products which are either commodities or for which there are several alternatives.

- Selection

    Consumers are interested in choosing from the broadest possible selection within their area of interest. Interestingly, this can be for two dissimilar reasons. A buyer may be looking for the best set of features and functionality among a broadly used product, or he may be looking for a rare or unusual product. In the former case, selection is for the purposes of comparison, whereas in the latter case, the consumer feels it more likely to find the niche product from a seller who has a broad selection. The Internet offers another alternative for the buyer of unusual items; because the network can reach a worldwide audience, even niche markets may be large enough to support a specialized retailer.

- Privacy

    Many consumers are very reluctant to part with personal information for fear of being the target of junk mail or advertising, or simply because they feel their private lives are no one else's business. These customers are likely to be offended to learn that their network browsing and buying habits are being carefully monitored.

- Service

    Some consumers are not price sensitive, but service sensitive. They patronize merchants who greet them by name, who keep them informed of new products, and who run establishments where the customer is always right.

- Security

    Consumers want to be assured that their credit card numbers and other sensitive information are adequately protected.

Business Customers

Business customers are buyers who are using Internet commerce systems in the course of their daily jobs (for example, an administrator reordering office supplies or an engineer specifying components for a new product design).

- Personalization

  Sellers would like their retail customers to be repeat buyers, but it is essential that business customers be repeat buyers. Much of the business world runs on purchasing contracts, special pricing, volume discounts, and the like. These aspects of commerce will also be reflected on the Internet. In a world with alternate suppliers and intense competition, sellers will work hard to personalize their services and to offer the best possible service, both to entice new customers and to raise disincentives for current customers to switch.

- Ease of use

  Since business customers are almost by definition repeat customers, ease of use becomes vital. For the office supplies customer, the seller will make it easy to call up and reuse previous orders. For the specifying engineer, the seller will make it easy to search and locate components. In both cases, speed is essential because browsing and purchasing are not the end goals of activity, but rather nuisances that take time away from the buyer's primary responsibilities.

- Security

  The security concerns of business customers are not so much about the security of credit cards as about keeping their competitors from finding out what they are doing and assuring the integrity of business records in company computer systems.

Sellers

In the context of this section, *sellers* include merchants engaged in business-to-business or business-to-consumer commerce or publishers and content providers engaged in information commerce.

- Reach new markets

  Sellers are interested in exploiting the potential of the Internet to reach new markets.

- Create and strengthen customer relationships

  It is the rare seller who has a unique product that is not available from an alternate supplier. Consequently, sellers are interested in moving up the value chain and offering products that are less commoditized or in other ways creating barriers to exit for their customers.

  Part of building customer relationships is learning about one's customers, which frequently includes gathering as much customer information as possible.

- Cost effectiveness

  Internet commerce systems can greatly reduce distribution costs and customer service costs.

- Security

  Sellers are extremely interested in the integrity of their marketing presence, their prices, their customer records, and their business records.

Conflicts can easily arise within a business planning an entry into Internet commerce.

- MIS or IT departments may feel they should own and operate any Internet commerce system because it necessarily involves computing.

- Conversely, MIS may be very reluctant to deploy an Internet commerce system because it is new and different.

- Sales departments may feel threatened by the ability of the Internet to collapse distribution channels.

Financial Processors

The financial processor operates the part of the credit card processing system that accepts transactions from merchants and forwards them to the merchant's bank. More broadly, we include financial authorization and settlement services independent of payment mechanism, credit card or otherwise.

- Security

  Transaction security is paramount for a financial processor. Security includes the privacy and accuracy of records, and the authenticity and integrity of requests.

- Transaction volume

  Processors make money either as a flat fee per transaction or as a percentage of the transaction amount. Consequently, they are keenly interested in raising transaction volume—either the number of transactions or their monetary total.

- Cost structure

  Processors are not paid on the basis of their costs, but on the work they do. The Internet as a communications infrastructure raises some intriguing possibilities of reducing telecommunications costs or even of transferring the costs to other parties.

- Added services

  Financial services are commodities. Like other suppliers of commodities, processors are interested in adding additional services to increase their ties to their customers.

- Risk management

Much of the complexity of the financial network connecting buyers, sellers, and financial institutions is concerned with allocating risk and responsibility for losses to the various involved parties. The processor is interested both in requiring the use of systems that minimize risk and to the extent possible in transferring risk to other parties.

Government

- Security

Government interest in security generally refers to national security. This area includes government controls on import, export, and use of cryptography.

- Legal controls

Governments are interested in assuring business and consumer compliance with laws and regulations. Access to certain kinds of information is illegal in many countries, and trade in certain kinds of products is illegal in different areas.

- Taxes

Governments get paid through taxes, and so have a strong interest in assuring collection of taxes and in closing loopholes.

Governments must be cognizant of the ubiquity of the Internet. An attempt by government to over-regulate the conduct of business may simply drive business elsewhere. Businesses may make a worldwide *choice of law* and conduct transactions in a legal venue most favorable to their needs.[2] Businesses incorporate in Delaware and register ships in Liberia for exactly these reasons.

Technologists

Technologists have a difficult task in creating systems for Internet commerce. In a new field, visionary customers buy products and adopt new technologies based on technical elegance and a common vision of the possibilities. Technology is almost never enough, however, to reach large markets, since visionaries rarely have the power to write large checks and there are not enough early adopters to build a volume market.[3]

In order to expand the market for Internet commerce, it will be necessary to build whole products around a technology core. This leads to the technologist's dilemma. The goal of a technologist is the simple and general system that solves most of the

---

2. As described by Dan Geer in testimony before the House Science and Technology Committee, February 11, 1997. The statement is available at http://www.house.gov/science/dan_geer.html.

3. Geoffrey A. Moore, *Crossing the Chasm: Marketing and Selling High-Tech Products to Mainstream Customers* (HarperBusiness, 1995).

problem. In fact, the market may demand increasingly complex and domain-specific applications that solve the complete problem in some market segments.

The Role of Standards

In information technology, a standard is a set of specifications that helps enable systems built by different parties to interoperate. In Internet commerce, standards serve two primary functions.

- Standards are a way of transferring power from vendors to customers.

  It is generally to the benefit of the vendor to have a proprietary technology base. Proprietary systems can lock in customers by raising extreme switching costs, and can reduce vendor costs by removing the necessity of testing against the products of other vendors to assure standards compliance.

- Standards are a way of assembling a complete system from multiple vendors.

  In an early-stage market, it may be that no single company can build the "whole product." To the extent that the complete system relies on components from others, standards help everyone. Individual vendors build components that comply with appropriate standards, and this permits system integrators to use components from multiple vendors to assemble a complete system.

The success of the Internet itself is a tribute to standards. In a way, the definition of the Internet is based on a standard. Systems that comply with the Internet standards such as TCP/IP *are* the Internet.

The main problem with standards is that it is difficult to make them simple enough to be widely adopted, yet complex enough to be useful.

Early versus Late Standardization

Standards efforts tend to follow one of two paths: early or late standardization.

Late Standardization

In late standardization, various parties work together cooperatively to build the market, or competing technologies arise and the market decides on a leader. Only after some market stability is reached do the parties get together and declare the result a standard. Most of the Internet-related communications standards have evolved this way, with experimentation and interoperability testing followed by mutual agreement on standards. The primary benefit of late standardization is that the resulting standards tend to be simpler and at least are known to match real requirements.

A second form of late standardization occurs when a proprietary system acquires such dominant market share that it becomes a standard, even though it may not happen in a cooperative manner. Standards arrived at this way tend to work effectively, but are more complex due to their origins.

Early Standardization

In early standardization, the parties involved get together and jointly agree on specifications. This can work out for the benefit of everyone, especially when the growth of the market would be greatly delayed by a period of fragmentation. On the other hand, early standardization tends to result in overly complex standards that attempt to answer customer needs that are not well understood. The parties involved sometimes add complexity merely so that all vendors will be equally inconvenienced. The standards efforts for music and data compact discs are an example of early standardization intended to grow the market, whereas the International Standards Organization (ISO) suite of internetwork protocols are an excellent example of a runaway standards process which ultimately failed in the market.

Standards for Internet Commerce

Are standards important for Internet commerce? As frequently happens, sometimes they are and sometimes they aren't. We don't sort the following list by good versus bad; these are merely ideas to think about.

- Standards aid interoperability.

  Unless one is able to obtain a complete system from one vendor, it is essential that the components interoperate. This problem is exacerbated when the system operator does not even control which components are used. For example, in a business-to-consumer Internet commerce system, the seller may rely on the customer to obtain an adequately functional Web browser, which must then interoperate successfully with the seller's Web server and content layout.

- The best is the enemy of the good.

  In the early stages of a market, system designers experiment with many different technologies and mechanisms. However, when each commerce site is completely different in style, design, function, and customer experience, the user base may be limited to those who thrive on newness and complexity. There is a strong benefit to consistency and standardization that leads to ease of use.

- The good is the enemy of the best.

  Standardization, and particularly premature standardization, restricts innovation. In addition, the more widely adopted a standard, the more resistant it is to change and evolution. In an early market, no one has any idea (or everyone has lots of ideas) about what technologies and design principles will ultimately succeed. At best, standardization will slow down the rate at which the market discovers and converges on successful principles.

Privacy versus Merchandising

Consumers would like to retain their privacy, releasing as little information as possible to sites on the Net; whereas commercial interests, beyond collecting information necessary to provide a service, frequently combine that information with other sources of data to build up a very detailed picture of their customer and sometimes resell that information to others. In addition, the very technologies that can be abused in profiling and exploiting consumers are necessary to build Web applications and make them easy to use.

The first problem is not the transfer of information alone, but how that information is used. A consumer will understand the necessity of entering a shipping address to order online, but that same consumer may be very unhappy if that address is sold to another organization for marketing purposes.

The second problem is that privacy does not seem amenable to purely technical solutions. As discussed later, the Web cookie facility has acquired a bad reputation, and many users now turn off cookies in their browsers. This prevents many Web sites (that use cookie technology for quite legitimate reasons) from providing any service at all.

Platform for Privacy Preferences

The Web community's reaction to the privacy issue combines technology and trust. The World Wide Web Consortium has launched a working group called the Platform for Privacy Preferences (http://www.w3.org/P3P/). The group's Web page states the following goal:

> The Privacy Preferences (P3) project will result in the specification and demonstration of an interoperable way of expressing privacy practices and preferences by Web sites and users respectively. Sites' practices that fall within the range of a user's preference will be accessed "seamlessly," otherwise users will be notified of a site's practices and have the opportunity to agree to those terms or other terms and continue browsing if they wish.

A number of organizations, including Netscape, Microsoft, Firefly, and Verisign are cooperating with the W3C's effort, using Firefly's Open Profiling Standard as a starting point. The idea is that whenever a site requests personal or profile information from a user, it can be provided automatically, so long as the site's stated intentions for using the information conform to the user's preferences.

Cookies

One technology caught up in the debate about privacy is the *cookie*.

Cookies are an interesting technical innovation added to World Wide Web browsers in 1995. In 1996, as knowledge and use of cookies spread, a controversy erupted about their privacy implications.

Cookies are a technology for turning stateless Web hits into *sessions*, for automatically recognizing a particular browser when it returns to a site after an extended interval, and for storing user profile information in the browser. These capabilities are enormously useful to both service operators and to users, but they also introduce privacy concerns.

What Are Cookies?

Cookies are a Web protocol and browser mechanism that permits a server to tell a browser to store a block of information on the user's hard disk, and to give it back on subsequent visits to the same server. No information in a cookie is sent to a server that wasn't first put there by the same server. When a browser connects to the server, the server says, "Take this envelope, and bring it back with you the next time you come in."

This capability can be used to accomplish three things:

- Tracking of a particular browser through a site—a session of related Web hits
- Automatically recognizing that a browser has returned to a site at a later
- Providing the ability to store user profile information at the browser

To the extent that the ability of cookies to store user profile information has caused a lot of concern, it should be noted that a profile can easily be stored at the server, and indexed by anything unique about the browser, such as a browser serial number or a cookie containing a unique ID. Some sites attempt to use the browser's IP address as a unique number, but this leads to problems because many users are shielded by proxy servers or use dynamically assigned addresses.

What Are the Benefits?

Cookies can provide the technical underpinnings for sessions, automatic user recognition, and user profile storage. Each of these capabilities provides valuable services for the user as well as the service.

- Sessions

  Without sessions, it is essentially impossible to provide a Web-based service that has more than one form. If a succession of forms is needed, there needs to be a place to store the state of the process between hits, and as a consequence a way to retrieve (index) that state on the next hit. In addition, if, during the succession of screens comprising a service, the user wishes to branch off into other Web content (help screens, for example), then there needs to be a way to pick up the service where the user left off. So one benefit to both service and user is that sessions permit an application to use a series of Web screens with embedded help. Another benefit is that the service can conduct log analyses to see what parts of the service are used, and how, so as to improve service.

Obviously sessions are extremely valuable information for advertisers and auditing bureaus, especially when coupled with demographic information, but whether that is a benefit to the user is more arguable.

- Automatic user recognition

Automatic identification of a particular user is the cornerstone of any secure service (which needs authentication) and also of any service which offers personalized views to individuals. Without hit-by-hit authentication, a service cannot offer secure content, because you don't know who is getting it. Without authentication, a service cannot offer any degree of personalized service.

There is also a place for recognizing a returning user—even anonymously. For example, if an online mall wishes to provide a shopping basket which is preserved across sessions, an anonymously issued user ID can accomplish it.

- Client-side user profiles

The final application of cookies is as a place to store things like user profiles or application state. One benefit of using a cookie for this is that the service does not suffer the performance impact of referencing a server-side database on each hit. Another privacy benefit is that there need be no central storage area where all sorts of information on all sorts of people is collected.

What Is the Downside?

- Unknown tracking

Cookies can be used by Web sites to store information on personal preferences and behavior without the permission of the person. Because the cookie uniquely tracks a particular browser, a Web site can obtain accurate information on repeat visits. But the information stored can also be inaccurate, particularly if a computer is shared by more than one person. This can lead to personal information of one user being revealed to another.

- Employer search

When company-owned computers are used by employees to surf the Web, cookie files may be stored on the company computer. The company may be able to search those files in order to obtain evidence of improper use of the machine. Indeed, one enterprising newspaper has sued a local government in Tennessee to obtain staff cookie files under the theory that they are official government records.

Secure Electronic Transactions

In late 1995, Visa and MasterCard joined together to develop the Secure Electronic Transaction (SET) protocol, a technical standard for safeguarding payment card purchases made over open networks. SET is a strong candidate to be the mechanism through which consumers make credit card purchases over the Internet.

Payment card purchasing is a complex process, and although we will review it in detail in Chapter 14, a preview is in order here. There are a number of entities involved in a payment card transaction, all playing different roles.

- Issuing bank—issues card to consumer, extends credit, and is responsible for billing, collecting, and consumer customer service
- Acquiring bank—forms relationship with merchant
- Consumer—makes purchases, pays the bill
- Merchant—sells products, receives payment
- Processor—service organization which operates the telecommunications infrastructure
- Card association—umbrella organization which sets standards

In the nonelectronic realm, a transaction works this way:

1. Cardholder presents card to make a purchase.
2. Merchant transmits transaction information to acquiring bank's processor.
3. Processor routes transaction through card association to issuing bank.
4. Issuing bank verifies credit standing of cardholder and approves transaction.
5. Transaction approval routed back to merchant.
6. Merchant later "settles" transaction, resulting in funds moving from issuing bank to acquiring bank for deposit to merchant's account.
7. Cardholder pays bill, moving funds from cardholder to issuing bank.

SET

SET is designed to mimic the traditional card transaction flow. In addition to the operational messages, SET includes the use of public key certificates to authenticate the parties to each other.

Consumer

In the United States, consumers assume little risk for fraud and misuse of credit cards. Under the Consumer Credit Protection Act, consumers are not liable for any misuse of a card once they report it lost or stolen, and are liable for at most $50 in any event. The idea behind the law is to transfer the risks inherent in the system onto those best able through technical means to minimize the potential losses.

Consumers also gain substantial customer service benefits through use of payment cards, including the ability to dispute charges and withhold payment in cases of merchant nonperformance or questionable quality of service. As card issuers have competed with one another, consumers have also benefited through extended warranty programs and frequent purchaser programs of various kinds.

In spite of these benefits of payment cards (and ignoring the issues of fees and interest charges), consumers are generally nervous about typing a credit card number into a computer. For consumers, SET has the goals and requirements shown in Table 5-1.

Goals	Provide confidentiality of information
	Authenticate merchant to cardholder
	Improve perception of safety of electronic commerce
Requirements	Obtain and install cardholder software (wallet)
	Obtain SET client certificate

TABLE 5-1. SET Goals and Requirements for Cardholder

Banks

In the traditional payment card system, banks manage risk. Issuing banks assume the risks of extending credit to cardholders, and acquiring banks assume the risks of providing card services to merchants. Several features of SET are aimed at reducing merchant risks: merchants are required to have SET certificates, which authenticate valid merchants, and SET permits merchants to accept transactions without learning the customer's card number. In the physical world, for example, unofficial merchants can clear card transactions indirectly by routing them through official merchants, in a process known as factoring. This cannot happen with SET, because the unofficial merchant would not have a certificate. Similarly, unless merchants are very careful with their storage of card numbers, a security breach at the merchant can reveal card numbers to unauthorized personnel. With SET, merchants do not need the actual card numbers, so this risk is reduced.

Merchants

In traditional payment card systems, when the customer is present at the point of sale and signs the payment card slip, and a variety of other procedures are followed such as the clerk checking the signature against the card, the transaction qualifies as a card-

Goals	Reduce merchant fraud
	Build electronic commerce volume
Requirements	Implement certificate hierarchy
	Implement certificate systems for cardholders

TABLE 5-2. SET Goals and Requirements for Banks

present transaction for a reduced discount rate, and the payment card system guarantees payment to the merchant. However, when the customer and card are not present at the point of purchase, as is usual in telephone sales, the merchant must pay a higher discount rate and the merchant must assume the risk that a stolen card number is being used.

Through the use of cardholder digital certificates, SET makes strong authentication of the cardholder possible. This means that after operational experience is acquired, a SET transaction over the Internet may qualify as a card-present transaction.

Goals	Easy integration
	Build electronic commerce volume
	Reduce transaction costs
Requirements	Implement SET merchant software

TABLE 5-3. SET Goals and Requirements for Merchants

SET Conflicts

The introduction of SET brings some conflicting goals and requirements. In this section we review the tension between banks and merchants, and between cardholders and the new complexities introduced by SET.

Banks versus Merchants

SET offers banks the potential for a reduction in merchant fraud losses by not revealing card numbers to merchants. On the other hand, merchants want easily to integrate SET-based systems into their existing operations. Usually, existing payment card systems will require access to the customer's card number, in opposition to SET.

SET does have options which reveal the card number to the merchant, which can be activated on a merchant-by-merchant basis, but this capability comes at a price of increased protocol complexity and a need for additional configuration mechanisms. Activation of this option also removes one of the greatest security advantages of SET, by permitting merchant personnel access to card numbers.

Cardholders versus Complexity

The purpose of requiring cardholders to obtain certificates for authentication is to greatly reduce problems of fraudulent use of card numbers obtained off-network. This benefit comes at the expense of increased complexity for the cardholder, in obtaining and managing the certificate, but the benefit does not directly go to the cardholder. If fraud is reduced, then eventually card discount rates will drop; then merchants will have the option of slightly reducing prices to consumers.

Summary

Whenever different participants in a system have different goals and requirements, there is a potential for conflict. This is particularly true in a new industry like Internet commerce, where there are few established standards. Our advice is to build a list of the participants in your system, and to be very clear about their goals, interests, and agendas.

Understanding the participants, their goals, and their interests is very important in framing both the business problem and the technical challenges to be overcome. Framing those problems and developing a core approach to solving them is the process of developing an *architecture* for the system, which we consider in the next chapter.

CHAPTER 6

Functional Architecture

Architecture...the adaptation of form to resist force.
—John Ruskin[1]

What Is Architecture?

The architecture of a system defines its basic components and important concepts, and it describes the relationships among them. There are many different ways to approach systems for Internet commerce, ranging from the simple to the complex. In part, the architecture depends on the nature of the business, and the system architecture developed for a consumer retail system might be very different from that for a publishing system. We believe that many design ideas span a wide range of commercial requirements, and that the similarities in systems for Internet commerce are much greater than the differences. This chapter describes a core architecture for Internet commerce systems, one that can be adapted for many applications.

Why should we have a general architecture? Why not simply build the systems focused on a single application? For us, a practical answer is that we have been building systems for Internet commerce for several years now, and reusing the architecture and design work where possible is best for our customers. More important, however, is that as businesses refine and evolve their goals for Internet commerce, their systems will need to evolve as well. That evolution may go well beyond the original requirements for the system, so the flexibility of the architecture is critically important in making that growth possible. For example, a software store may begin by taking

---

1. John Ruskin, *Val d'Arno,* 1874.

orders over the Internet and sending out boxes with manuals and disks. Later, it may wish to deliver software over the network as well. If the original system does not handle online delivery, the store may find itself facing significant development or upgrade costs to add this capability.

In this chapter, we describe the kinds of thinking that go into creating an architecture, explore some of those areas in more depth, and present some examples of practical architectures for Internet commerce.

Core Architectural Ideas

Architectures for commerce systems may look very different, but they all have to address the same issues and provide answers for a common set of questions. These issues must be understood no matter what approach is taken. In some cases, these common questions are considered explicitly during the design phase; in other cases, the questions and their answers are reflected in assumptions about various components in the architecture. In this section, we examine some of the primary elements that go into a commerce architecture.

One word of caution: it may sometimes seem that what we describe in the architecture is so obvious that it need not be written down, or that we are drawing unnecessary distinctions. In our experience, leaving the obvious as implicit can often lead to later confusion and misunderstanding, precisely because everyone thought it was obvious, but had a different idea of what was "obvious." If we are to be successful at designing and building computer systems, we must be very precise, not only in describing the computational steps but also in our understanding and description of what we are trying to do. The processes of doing business may seem natural because they are so familiar to us, and because people can handle many unusual situations easily and effectively. When we design computer systems to manage some of those processes, we must be especially careful because computers cannot figure out how to keep a customer happy when something unexpected goes wrong.

Understanding of Roles

Two of the most basic questions for any computer system are "Who uses it?" and "What do they do with it?" For some programs, there are a few kinds of users who share similar goals. For example, novices and experts both use word processors with the same goal—producing a document. Internet commerce systems are more complicated: their users include the buyers of goods and services, the sellers of goods and services, and the people who operate all of the machinery.

Understanding the various roles and kinds of users for a system helps us to focus our attention on making sure that each person can use the system effectively to accomplish their goal, whether that is making a purchase or creating the accounting reports.

Decomposition of Functions

A second important part of the system architecture is the way it decomposes the system into functional units. The specification of these functional units and the interfaces between them defines the architecture of the system. One of the differences between architectures is often the way that they group functions into units. Are all of the components integrated in a single system? Are the components distributed across multiple systems? What are the interfaces between functional units?

Linking Content to Transactions

The first two considerations for the system architecture, roles and decomposition, apply to the design of almost any computer system. A third part of the system architecture of an Internet commerce system is the way that content, such as a catalog, is linked to the transaction processing. In a paper-based system, the buyer transcribes item numbers and quantities onto an order form or requisition. Obviously we would like to do this electronically.

There are several key issues in this linkage.

- How the user makes the transition

  In many cases, the user sees a "click here to buy" button or can add items to a shopping cart for later purchase. The transition to the transaction takes place either at the "buy now" point or at "checkout" for the shopping cart.

- How the information is verified

  Depending on the underlying technology, it may be necessary for the transaction system to verify that the purchase information, such as price, item identification, and so on, was not modified when it was sent over the network. Because (as we shall discuss in more detail later), the Web uses a stateless protocol, commerce systems built on top of the Web must manage their own state. If that state is carried by the client in some way, the server must be able to ensure that it was not modified in transit.

- How the information matches up

  Some Internet commerce systems include a real-time inventory check to assure customers that items are in stock. If the system indicates that an item is in stock, however, how long is that indication good for? If the customer puts the item in a shopping cart for purchase some time later, does the system promise that the item will be available when the purchase occurs? If the system does make such a promise, how long is it good for? What if the customer never returns to the site to buy the items in the shopping cart?

The answers to these questions help make design decisions for the system. Because different answers can lead to very different designs, it is important to think through the issues early in the design process.

Trust Models

In any distributed system, different components trust each other to a greater or lesser extent. Some components may trust others completely for all kinds of access (for example, both reading and writing data elements), whereas other components may disallow any remote access to their data. The specification of these relationships is called the *trust model* for the system. Any system has at least an implicit trust model, but specifying one explicitly helps us to understand the details of the relationships between components when we need to analyze the security of the system.

Roles

Many different people interact with an Internet commerce system, and they need to do different things. Buyers require one set of operations; catalog designers, customer service representatives, and system operators each have their own sets as well. Even though these latter groups may all work for the merchant, they have different tasks to perform. For some businesses, especially smaller ones, the same person may perform all these tasks. Larger businesses have different people fulfilling different roles. Considering roles separately enables us to satisfy the requirements of businesses of all sizes, as well as making it possible to design a system that allows a smaller business to grow smoothly without having to reconsider what people do at each stage.

Speaking in terms of roles also helps to avoid confusion. For example, simply referring to the customer does not distinguish the cases when one person is selecting a product to be purchased and another arranges payment. By defining the operations required by a particular role, we can ensure that everything needed by the role is present in the system, rather than relying on the ability of one person to act in multiple roles.

It is important to keep in mind that there might be individuals playing many different roles in some organizations, and that there might be many individuals playing the same role in a larger organization. For example, larger organizations commonly have many people in the customer service role.

Next we describe some of the primary roles for both the buyer and the seller.

Customer Roles

In any commercial transaction, there is a buyer and a seller. We use many different words for the buyer: customer, consumer, purchasing agent, and so on. On the Internet, we sometimes use the words client or browser as well, referring more to the software than the person. But there are some subtle differences in these words, and the distinctions reflect different roles on the buyer side. In some cases, such as a consumer purchase, the same person plays all of the roles without even thinking about the differences. Businesses, however, often make purchases in different ways, so it is useful to consider the various roles.

- Specifier—this person selects what is to be purchased.
- Approver—this person approves a purchase recommended by the specifier.
- Buyer—this person negotiates the terms and conditions of a purchase and arranges for payment.
- Recipient—this person receives the delivered goods or services.

In addition, we can distinguish kinds of buyers based on their relationship with the seller: an *anonymous buyer* (sometimes referred to as a "walk-in customer") has no prior relationship with the seller and may not ever create one beyond making a simple purchase. *Member customers* are those who repeatedly buy from a seller and have established some kind of relationship, which we will call *membership* here. Members may sign up because an account is convenient, because it offers some special benefits, or because there is a business relationship that is reflected in the membership.

Membership accounts give rise to another role, the *member administrator.* A person acting in this role may modify or update any profile information stored about the member. If the membership encompasses several individual accounts, such as for different members of a family or multiple purchasing agents for a business, the member administrator may also be able to set limits on the use of the individual accounts. These limits might be on the kinds of items that can be purchased, the amounts that can be spent, the time of day for purchases, and so on.

In practice, of course, a single individual may fulfill more than one role. For example, a consumer buying a sweater selects one in a store, pays for it, and takes it home. In this case, the consumer plays all three roles, and we generally make no distinction among them. In contrast, consider the electrical components example described in Chapter 2. The specifying engineer determines what part will be purchased, a purchasing agent negotiates the payment terms, and the manufacturing group receives the components for inclusion in the final product.

What this breakdown tells us is that a general-purpose Internet commerce system needs a way for different people to handle different parts of a transaction, but it should also be very simple for a single person to handle all of them. Consumers do not expect to change roles explicitly at every stage, but they do expect to have a quick and easy process for buying. Companies, on the other hand, that do make distinctions in the various roles want to be able to hand off the transaction from one role to another smoothly and efficiently.

Business Roles

On the other side of a transaction is the seller. There are many roles in an Internet commerce system for sellers. Smaller businesses, and even larger ones beginning with small-scale efforts in Internet commerce, may have just a few people playing all the roles—so much so that the different roles enumerated here may seem overly complicated. Thinking about the roles early, however, makes it possible for an Internet business to grow more smoothly, as more people join the team and the roles become more distinct in reality. For the seller, there are two main groups of roles—the business and content creation team and the operations team. The following are the most important business roles.

- Business manager

  The business manager is responsible for the business approach on the Internet, creating and operating the Internet presence for the business, deciding what products and services are sold online, determining pricing, and establishing the key business relationships needed to make the venture successful. (We will discuss implementation strategies for these kinds of operations in Chapter 7.) This is primarily a business role, with particular attention paid to the success of the online business and the bottom line.

- Internet commerce architect

  The Internet commerce architect is generally a systems analyst who turns the business requirements into a system design that incorporates the creation and management of content (such as catalogs), the transaction processing, fulfillment, and technical aspects of customer service. In short, the architect fills in the next level of detail for the commerce value chain.

- Content designer

  The designer is responsible for the look and feel of an Internet commerce system, including the graphic design, page layout, user experience, and so on.

- Content author

  The author creates or adapts product information into a form that can be used for Internet commerce, working within the design laid out by the content designer.

- Implementor

  The implementor is responsible for creating any programs or software extensions needed to make the Internet commerce system work. For example, an implementor might write the software that takes product information from a database and dynamically renders it into a Web page.

- Database administrator

  If a database of product information is used, the database administrator (DBA) manages the creation and operation of the database to ensure its correctness, integrity, and performance.

- Sales and marketing

  The sales and marketing team is responsible for focused efforts in promoting Internet-based commerce for the business.

- Customer service representative

  Customer service representatives for the business answer questions about products, assist buyers with registration or the purchasing process, respond to inquiries about order status and problems after the sale, and handle product returns and payment disputes. Of course, a business may have different people specialized in different areas of this role.

Of course, a particular organization may have more than one person in one or more of these roles, or one person may act in many of them. Some of the decisions may be determined by software purchased from a particular vendor, in which case many people on the commerce team described previously must select which product to buy and how it fits in with their plans for Internet commerce. Some members of this team may be outside consultants, depending on the skills and availability of an organization's staff.

The operations team installs and operates the Internet commerce system, making sure that it is running and available for customers. Some specific approaches to system operation are discussed in Chapter 7. The roles include the following.

- Operations manager

  The operations manager is responsible for managing all service activities for the Internet commerce system.

- System supervisor

  The system supervisor manages the system staff.

- System administrator

  The system administrator is responsible for the technical operations of the computer systems and networks.

- Security officer

  The security officer ensures that appropriate security measures have been taken in the design and implementation of the Internet commerce system.

- Fulfillment agent

  The fulfillment agent is responsible for shipping and handling of physical goods or delivery of services. In the case of digital goods, the fulfillment agent is responsible for overseeing the operation (and staff, if any) of the fulfillment system.

- Accountant

  The accountant is responsible for ensuring that the proper accounting procedures have been followed for Internet-based transactions, managing the relevant business records, creating reports on the transactions handled by the system, and other accounting functions.

Roles and Reality

The roles we have described are probably not exactly the roles found at any particular business, and it is unlikely that there is any one-to-one correspondence between these roles and people doing real work. Thinking about roles instead of people, however, enables us to ensure that all of the work gets done, and that we are not missing an important function as we design a system and put together a team to operate it. Making these distinctions also helps if some of the work will be outsourced. As we shall see in Chapter 7, there are many approaches to implementing a system, and sometimes it makes sense to outsource all or part of the operation of an Internet commerce system. Some of the roles here—the operational ones, for example—can be outsourced relatively easily. Others, such as deciding what products go into the online catalog, are business decisions that cannot be handed off to others.

Components

Another important aspect of the system architecture is the set of components we have to work with. For Internet commerce, we frequently try to take advantage of general-purpose Internet applications, for three reasons.

1. If general-purpose applications can be used, we need not build them again.
2. General-purpose applications are widely distributed, so we need not create the distribution channels to put a specialized tool in the hands of the customers.
3. Customers are already familiar with the application, so they do not need to learn how to use a specialized tool.

In the next sections we introduce the basic components used for Internet commerce systems, with more detailed technical discussion of them in the second half of this book. Although our focus is on using general-purpose tools, such as the browsers and servers of the World Wide Web, there are, of course, times when it is appropriate to create and distribute a specialized tool for commerce. Even so, we think the components described here are a good starting point for designing such tools.

Customer Components and Clients

For customers, the primary tool for using the World Wide Web is a *browser,* sometimes called a Web *client.* We discuss browsers and other Web clients in Chapter 8. The system architecture is clearly influenced by the basic structure of the Web, and in particular by the capabilities of browsers. As we shall see, one of the important questions in deciding exactly how to structure a system is "What browsers do the customers have, and what are their capabilities?"

Some companies have also designed specialized client applications for commerce, particularly for payment. These applications, often called *wallets,* are designed to implement one or more payment methods that require additional processing, such as cryptographic operations, on the client computer. Wallets may also be used to keep track of what transactions have been made, check on order status, or manage other information related to transactions. The main problem with wallets is that if a system requires the customer to have a wallet, the customer must take some action to obtain and install the wallet software.[2] We look at different payment systems, including their requirements for client software, in Chapter 14.

Seller Components and Servers

On the other side of a transaction is the seller, whom we might also call the merchant or vendor. The seller provides all of the components of the commerce value chain, from content to customer service. In practice, a seller may provide some of the stages in the value chain directly and contract with others to provide the rest. Different sellers may make different decisions about which stages to provide directly and those decisions may even change over time. Again, therefore, we separate the stages of the value chain in the general architecture so that different components can be handled differently.

Some components of the value chain are more easily outsourced than others. Content, for example, is a presentation of the actual products or services offered by a business for sale. Although a company may look outside for creative presentation ideas or development of the actual content, what the products are and how they are sold are the foundation of the business. Payment services, on the other hand, are very important to the business, but the details of the processing can be hidden as long as the results are correct. Here are some of the components.

- Transaction processing system

  The seller's transaction processing system keeps track of all information related to transactions: what was ordered, who ordered it, how much it cost, the status of payment, the status of fulfillment, and so on.

---

2. When this book was written, wallets were not commonly distributed with browser software. If such distribution becomes common, and if wallets interoperate with merchant software from multiple vendors, then this problem disappears.

- Payment processors

  Payment processors manage the movement of money or other payment instruments in the system. For example, when a consumer pays using a credit card, the seller connects to a credit card payment processor to authorize the transaction (by checking for sufficient available credit) and, later, for settling the transaction.

- Fulfillment systems

  Companies operating mail-order businesses often contract with a fulfillment company to handle packing and shipping orders. A business taking orders over the Internet for tangible goods might do the same. Indeed, a business selling digital goods over the Internet might even work with a fulfillment company to operate the servers used to deliver the online products. Or, in both cases, a business may choose to manage the fulfillment process in-house.

One logical grouping of these functions results in what we will call the *front office* and the *back office*. The front office is concerned with marketing and selling goods and services. Content and presentation are very important, and the focus is on attracting the customer to buy the product or service. The back office is concerned with managing the details of the transaction, from placing the order to payment to fulfillment. Proper handling of the transaction is important, such as ensuring that the relevant information is delivered to the right places and that the payment is collected correctly.

Examples of System Architecture

As we have suggested previously, different answers to different issues can result in very different system architectures. In this section, we look at four different architectures and discuss how they are constructed. The four architectures are a Web server with an order form, a variation of the Web server with an order form that uses the Secure Electronic Transactions (SET) protocol, an approach to distributed transactions we have developed at Open Market, and an approach to business-to-business commerce developed by the Open Buying on the Internet consortium. There are, of course, many other approaches to Internet commerce; we chose these to illustrate many of the points discussed in this chapter.

For analysis of architecture, we have found it convenient to consider four primary components of Internet commerce systems:

- Client

  The client is a computer system, typically a PC, connected to the Internet directly via an Internet service provider (ISP), or indirectly via a corporate network. The buyer uses the client computer to browse and to purchase.

- Merchant

  The computer system or systems containing the merchant's electronic catalog and, in the case of online goods, which contain products for over-the-Net fulfillment.

- Transaction system

  The computer system or systems that process a particular order and which are responsible for payment, record keeping, and other business aspects of the transaction.

- Payment gateway

  The computer system that routes payment instructions into existing financial networks such as for credit card authorization and settlement.

Various architectures use these four components in different ways. In some systems, some of these components are combined into a single computer system, whereas in others these four system components are implemented by separate computer systems.

Once the designers of a commerce system have selected a gross division of function, there are still many decisions to be made at lower levels of functionality. For example, the order aggregation function, which permits the assembly of individual items into a complete order, can be implemented as part of the merchant, transaction, or client component.

Web Server with Order Form

A Web server with catalog pages and an order form is one of the simplest ways to construct an Internet commerce system. This approach is typically called a *merchant server*. A diagram of a representative system is shown in Figure 6-1 with a logical

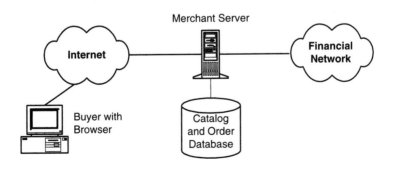

FIGURE 6-1. Merchant Server: Physical View

diagram of the structure of the merchant server shown in Figure 6-2. Many of the technical details will become clearer as we discuss the technology in later chapters, but we will sketch the basic ideas here.

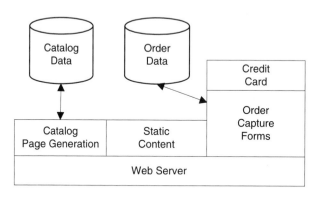

FIGURE 6-2. Merchant Server: Logical View

In this example, a single Web server provides both the catalog content and the order form. In other words, the merchant server and transaction server are combined into one system, and there is no explicit payment gateway. The catalog might consist of a set of Web pages describing items for sale, with embedded pictures, drawings, specifications, animations, video or audio clips, and so on. The Web pages may be created as static pages using an HTML editor, or they may be created dynamically from a database of items and descriptive information. Next to each item is a button that the customer can click on to buy it, or add it to a shopping cart for later checkout. When ready to buy the item (or items, if more than one is present in a shopping cart), the customer clicks on a *checkout* button that starts the payment part of the transaction.

Payment by credit card is the most common method used on the Internet today for consumer transactions (and we discuss it in detail in Chapter 14). A simple order form might consist of a listing of the items being purchased, and a set of fields for the customer to enter credit card payment information, including the card number, the expiration date, and the address for delivering the items, if they are physical goods. The form may also ask for the billing address, as some credit card systems use the billing address as part of verifying the holder of the credit card.

It is possible, of course, that the Web server might use a different payment mechanism. In the simplest version of this model, the Web client has no special capabilities for commerce, so the commerce application does not require additional software for payment mechanisms. Credit cards, purchase orders, and other kinds of account-based payment may be used with such systems, taking advantage of basic security capabilities common on the Web today.

This basic architecture may be appropriate and sufficient for some kinds of Internet commerce applications. Its primary virtue is its simplicity. On the other hand, it may be more difficult to expand it as the online business grows, or to incorporate new technologies and components as they become available.

Secure Electronic Transactions

SET, for Secure Electronic Transactions, is a standard for the way credit card payment transactions should be handled on the Internet. SET is discussed in more detail in Chapter 14. In this section, we provide an architectural introduction to SET. In a SET system, a payment gateway is added distinct from the transaction server.

The key differences between the Web server with order form and a system based on SET are in the way the order form is handled and in the way payment-related communications are handled. A physical, block diagram of a SET-enabled Internet commerce system is shown in Figure 6-3.

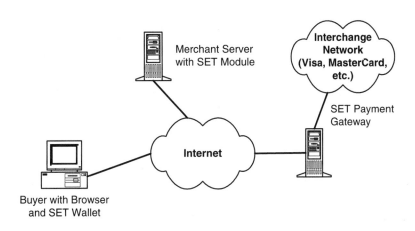

FIGURE 6-3. SET Architecture

In its simplest form, the SET architecture takes over from the merchant server order form at the point when payment by credit card is appropriate. The merchant server, rather than connecting directly to a credit card authorization network, instead incorporates a SET merchant module. When the SET module is called to handle payment, the following steps occur.

- The merchant module sends a message to the SET wallet located on the buyer's computer, containing a description of the order and the total price.
- The buyer uses the SET wallet to select a payment card and to approve the purchase.

- The SET wallet communicates via the merchant computer with the SET payment gateway at the merchant's acquiring bank.

- The payment gateway connects to a traditional financial network to authorize the transaction.

- The merchant computer stores the acknowledgment and sends a receipt to the buyer.

Open Market Commerce Architecture

The core architectural idea of this architecture is to separate the management of content from the management of transactions through a technology called *SecureLink*. This idea permits multiple catalog servers to share the capacity of a single transaction engine and allows the content-oriented parts of the system to scale independently from the transaction-oriented parts of the system. The approach also permits service organizations to become commerce service providers, who provide transaction management services on an outsourced basis to other companies. Figure 6-4 shows the physical architecture of this approach, and Figure 6-5 shows how functionality is distributed across different elements of the system. In this architecture, the transaction server is separated from the merchant server and there may or may not be a separate payment gateway depending on which payment methods are supported.

The authors participated in the design of the SecureLink system, which is described in more detail in Chapter 17 of this book.

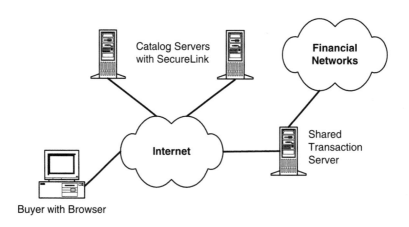

FIGURE 6-4. Open Market Commerce Architecture: Physical View

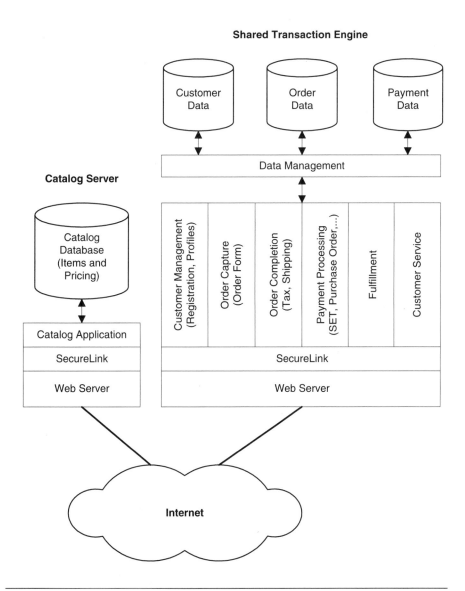

FIGURE 6-5. Open Market Commerce Architecture: Logical View

Open Buying on the Internet

Open Buying on the Internet, or OBI, is a standards proposal released by the OBI consortium. The consortium is a group of buy-side organizations, sell-side organizations, payment organizations, and technology companies that is addressing the problem of business-to-business commerce on the Internet. The core idea of OBI is to split the functionality of the commerce system between buy-side activities and sell-side activities so that each organization manages those functions logically connected to it.

The OBI design is based on a model of business commerce shown in Figure 6-6. In this model, the logical breakdown of activities is to place the customer database, requisitioner profiles, and approvals processes on the buy-side, and to place the catalog, order management, fulfillment, and payment on the sell-side. This structure results in the architecture shown in Figure 6-7. The key idea in OBI relevant to our functional components is the splitting of the transaction server into its sell-side and buy-side parts.

Browse   Request   Approve   Fill   Receive   Pay

FIGURE 6-6. OBI Business Purchasing Process

In order to make this architecture work, two elements of interoperability are needed between the buy-side and sell-side components: requisitioner authentication and order handling.

- Requisitioner authentication

  Because the buy-side organization assumes the responsibility in the OBI model for managing the pool of requisitioners, the sell-side must have a standardized means of authenticating prospective requisitioners as authorized by the buying organization. OBI uses public key certificates for this purpose. When the requisitioner browses the supplier catalog, he presents a certificate signed by the buying organization to validate himself. This approach implies that at the time the trading relationship between the companies is set up, the supplier catalog must be configured to accept the certificates.

- Order handling

  In OBI, the requisitioner builds up an order by interacting with the supplier catalog. That order is then sent in a standardized format called the OBI order request from the sell-side OBI server to the buy-side. Once there, any necessary approval processes proceed. After the order is finalized, it is returned to the sell-side as an OBI order to fulfillment.

The real benefits of the OBI choice of placing functionality can only be seen when there are multiple buy-side companies trading with multiple sell-side companies. When this happens, the buy-side is able to centrally manage its requisitioner database and approvals system and to use those systems seamlessly with multiple trading part-

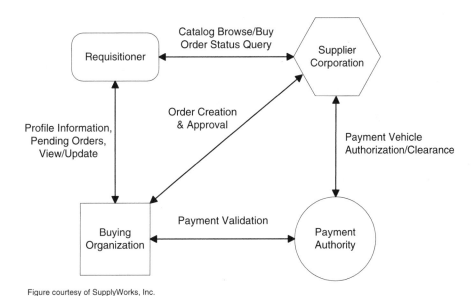

Figure courtesy of SupplyWorks, Inc.

FIGURE 6-7. OBI Architecture

ners. Similarly, the selling organization can leverage a master catalog and order management system against multiple purchasers. In this ideal situation, information is not duplicated on either side.

Transaction Flow in the OBI Model

In this section, we walk through an OBI transaction. The descriptions in this section correspond to the numbered arrows in Figure 6-8.

1. The requisitioner uses a Web browser to connect to the buying organization's purchasing server and selects a hyperlink to the selling organization's catalog server.

2. The selling organization's catalog server authenticates the requisitioner based on a digital certificate and then allows the requisitioner to browse, select items, and check out.

3. The content of the order is transferred from the catalog server to the selling organization's OBI server.

4. The sell-side OBI server maps the order into an OBI order request, encapsulated in an OBI object (with optional digital signature), and transmits the order request to the buying organization's OBI server over the Internet.

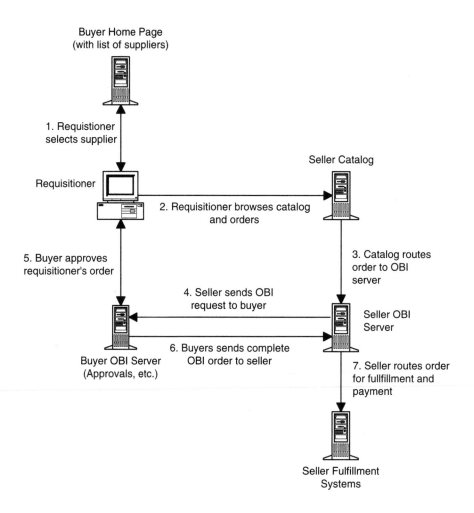

FIGURE 6-8. OBI Transaction Flow

5. The requisitioner specifies any necessary annotations to the order, and internal approvals processes take place.

6. The completed and approved order is mapped to an OBI order format, encapsulated as an OBI object, and transmitted back to the selling organization via the Internet.

7. The selling organization obtains payment authorization, if necessary, and begins order fulfillment.

For additional information on OBI, see http://www.supplyworks.com.

Summary

Ultimately, the architecture of an Internet commerce system (like the architecture of any complex computer system) has a tremendous effect on the long-term success of a project. It is almost always easier to slap something together quickly to solve a particular problem, but the resulting system won't be able to handle the challenges of tomorrow, and it will quickly be obsolete, even for its original purpose. By carefully creating an architecture, taking into account the business challenges to be addressed and possibilities for change over time, the system can evolve and adapt to growth, new challenges, and technology change. Over the long term, the up-front investment can have enormous return. Trading those advantages against "let's get it running now" is an important decision, and one that should be made very carefully.

Assuming now that there is an architecture—at least a simple one—in place, we can consider some strategies for implementing the commerce system, the subject of the next chapter.

CHAPTER 7

Implementation Strategies

Rome wasn't built in a day. If it were, we would've hired their contractor.

> —Boston Central Artery project billboard

Planning the Implementation

As anyone who has ever operated business computer systems knows, the hard part is not the design or even writing the code—it is operating the system reliably and effectively over the long haul. Conceptually, taking credit card numbers over the Internet is straightforward, but what happens when the connection to the financial processor isn't working in your West Coast office at 6 A.M. and your East Coast customers are trying to buy something? This chapter considers some approaches to implementing and operating an Internet commerce system. During different phases of design, development, and operation of a commerce project, choices must be made regarding the use of internal resources or outsourcing. Table 7-1 summarizes some of the options considered in this chapter.

In planning an Internet commerce system, there are five phases to consider:

1. Project design
2. Software development and integration
3. Content development
4. Deployment
5. Long-term operation

Within each phase, it may be appropriate to do the work in-house or to outsource it. In our discussion, outsourcing may include, for example, using off-the-shelf software from a vendor, as compared to doing in-house development.

	In-House	**Outsource**
Project Design	Marketing and IT staff	Business consulting
Software Development	Custom development	Off-the-shelf software
Content Development	Marketing staff	Web developer
Hosting and Operations	IT staff	Internet service provider
Transaction Services	IT staff	Commerce service provider

TABLE 7-1. Implementation Options

Outsourcing

With any ongoing service, it is useful to ask whether it is best performed in-house or outsourced to a specialized organization. Internet commerce is no different, and the rapid evolution of Internet technologies can often make it difficult to keep up without some assistance. Forrester Research developed one model of an outsourcing strategy, shown in Figure 7-1. It consists of four phases:

1. **Early outsourcing.** In the beginning stages, an IS organization can create a system more quickly and begin to develop the requisite skills by calling on the expertise of outside specialists. Such specialists typically develop expertise in new technologies more quickly than large corporate users.

2. **Internalization.** If the first phase is successful, appropriate IS groups who have already begun to develop the necessary skills can take over from the early outsourcing. The new skills, combined with detailed knowledge of the business, make it possible to expand deployment as well as customize the application to meet the specialized requirements of the business.

3. **Centralization.** As a technology spreads, it becomes possible to support the systems across the enterprise. This requirement, combined with the need to limit expenses, moves responsibility for the system to a central IS group.

4. **Late outsourcing.** As an application moves to legacy status, it may be important to continue operating it, but it may no longer be a core part of the business. In addition, it may also distract an IS team from new technologies and business opportunities. At this stage, outsourcing it to a specialized company may be especially attractive as the outsourcers can create economies of scale for operating similar applications for many customers.

This model is useful for many applications, but it is particularly appropriate to consider for Internet commerce applications. Outsourcing the implementation and opera-

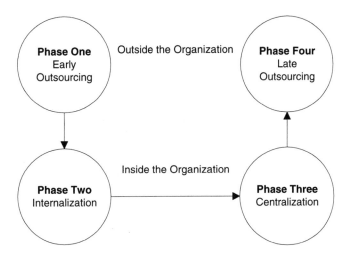

Figure courtesy of Forrester Research, Inc., Cambridge, MA, USA

FIGURE 7-1. **Life Cycle of Technology Outsourcing**

tion of an Internet commerce system allows an organization to establish its presence and direction more quickly. The early experience is invaluable in developing follow-on applications, which can be brought in-house as the internal teams learn the new technology skills and begin to integrate the commerce applications more closely with other parts of the business.

An alternate method of analyzing outsourcing versus internal development is to consider how closely the project is aligned with the business.

- Is the project a core competency?

  Are the development and operational skills required already available in-house? If not, would this project alone justify the hiring and training necessary for success? If the answer to these questions is no, then outsourcing may be appropriate.

- Is the technology a commodity?

  This is a difficult issue. If the technology involved is not a commodity, then the necessary development skills may only be available from a few specialized sources. Commodity technology may be less expensive to manage internally, especially if excess capacity is available. Operational considerations may be the reverse—if the operations of the project are a commodity, then outsourcing operations may have an economy of scale that makes them superior to in-house operations.

- What is the technology and project rate of change?

  Is the technology and project expected to change rapidly? If so, then internal development, closely coupled to the business, may be indicated. Slowly changing applications may be safely outsourced and (nearly) forgotten.

- To what extent does the project need to be integrated?

  If a project has few and well-defined interfaces with one's core business systems, then it may be a good candidate for outsourcing. On the other hand, if complex and custom integration work is required to interface the application with existing in-house systems, then internal development and operation may be more pragmatic.

Custom Development

One approach to developing an Internet commerce application is to create a custom application, either by doing the development in-house or by contracting it to an outside organization. The advantage, of course, is that the application—if developed successfully—will presumably meet the requirements for a specific business. In addition, a custom application may be better integrated with other systems at a particular business. These advantages are especially strong when the market for packaged application products for Internet commerce applications is still young, and the products are evolving quickly.

On the other hand, there are several potential problems with custom solutions, and they should be considered carefully in a "make or buy" decision.

First, rapid development is not always quality development. One of the attractions of custom development for Internet commerce applications is to "get something up fast." Indeed, it is not very hard to put together a simple catalog on a Web server, perhaps with a basic order form to collect credit card numbers. Sometimes it is important to get a system running quickly, to establish the presence on the Internet. But that short-term system may not be what is needed in the long term. How does it integrate with other systems? How is customer service handled? How does the system evolve with new technology? How are the security issues addressed? If Internet commerce is a strategic direction for the business, not just a tactical demonstration, it should be approached with an idea of the long-term directions.

Second, custom development may now take longer than using off-the-shelf products. The range of features, cost, and quality in products for Internet commerce applications is expanding rapidly, so there may be a product that meets, or almost meets, the requirements for a particular business.

Third, how will a custom application be maintained? Will an in-house staff continue to work on it, or will they have new projects to undertake? Or will the outside consultants or integrators maintain it? Are they committed to long-term maintenance?

Fourth, custom development often has hidden costs. There may be ideas or features that were missed in the original definition of the project, which require expensive changes later. Getting effective maintenance for a custom system—by definition the only one like it in the world—may cost more than expected. Finally, what are the costs of changing the system as the technology changes?

Fifth, the business requirements will undoubtedly change over time, and those changes will require changes in the software. The changes go well beyond maintenance, requiring modifications to the software, extensions to new applications, solutions to new problems, and so on. Although it is often difficult to predict how the requirements may change and what the implications for the software are, we can predict with great confidence that such changes will happen.

Finally, the technology will change, and likely will change quite rapidly. Will the custom application be flexible enough to evolve? Will the team working on it learn about the new technology quickly enough? Does a shift in technology require a rethinking of the way the entire application is structured?

These questions are important ones to understand in developing any important application for a business. In some cases, the requirements of the business are so specific that the custom development is justified. In others, the long-term costs suggest that building on off-the-shelf products, with some integration and modest customization, is a more effective approach, even if not all of the initial goals can be accomplished.

Packaged Applications

In the early days of Internet commerce, almost every system was unique, developed to particular specifications as a custom implementation. Over time, of course, many software products have come to the market for creating commerce applications. The applications available today vary considerably in price, capabilities, and how much work the application developer must do. Products for commerce fall into several broad categories:

- Content creation and management
- Order processing
- Fulfillment
- Integrated systems

Even within these categories, there is a wide range of products. Content tools, for example, range from simple HTML editors to sophisticated systems for creating, managing, and mapping entire Web sites.

The details of these kinds of products are discussed elsewhere in the book, but there are a few general issues to consider in choosing products.

- Does this product meet the requirements as a component of the application? (For example, does a content creation tool handle the desired kinds of content?)

- How does the product integrate with other products (if it needs to do so)? In particular, does it integrate with the best of the other categories?

- Can the product be integrated with necessary legacy systems (e.g., inventory management)?

- Does the product have a plan for its long-term evolution in Internet commerce applications?

- Can the product be customized to meet specific requirements?

- Is the product extensible?

- What kind of support is behind the product?

Whenever possible, it is important to look at the choices of products for commerce applications by how they fit in with the overall direction of the commerce project, rather than in isolation. The best tools are the ones that will be used to get the job done—which may be very different from the most sophisticated tool in each category. Finally, hybrid approaches may be appropriate, with packaged applications providing the core functions, and custom software integrating the applications to existing business systems.

The Role of Internet Service Providers

Internet service providers, called ISPs, supply many of the services required for Internet commerce. First and foremost, they connect individuals and organizations to the Internet so their customers can communicate with other Internet users. Second, they often provide *hosting services* for Web sites or other Internet applications, where the ISP installs and operates the server computers and software that make up the Web site. In such cases, the server systems are usually located on the ISP's premises, not the customer's. Third, ISPs may provide transaction services, such as payment systems, for the commerce operations of their customers. We refer to ISPs supplying such services as *commerce service providers*, which we discuss in more detail later.

Communications Services

The core of the ISP's service is providing communications. Typically that includes the fundamentals of Internet systems, including the routing of IP packets, the Domain Name Service (DNS), and electronic mail. The communications services may be available by dialup, ISDN, or a dedicated data circuit, such as T1, and they are available in many different bandwidths. The bandwidth effectively measures how much data can flow over the connection per unit time. How much bandwidth you need depends on your application, but experience suggests that a T1 connection (providing 1.54 Megabits per second), or at least a reasonable fraction of one, is required for adequate performance in Internet commerce systems.

The Domain Name Service is used to translate hostnames such as *www.my-domain.com* to an IP address such as 10.250.92.7. Most ISPs will also take care of registering a domain name, such as *my-domain.com,* so that others can find it.

When selecting an ISP, there are several important issues to address.

- Cost for the desired bandwidth

  The ISP can usually help size your application to select the most cost-effective bandwidth as well.

- Outbound connections

  The Internet is a collection of networks that interconnect with each other. That means that some ISPs are closer to the Internet backbone—the high-performance core of the Internet—than others. The effective bandwidth between your site and your customers depends not only on your ISP, but also on your customers' ISPs and all the other ISPs in between.

- Reliability

  How reliable is the ISP's service? How quickly do they respond to problems? As with any other service, it is frequently a good idea to talk with other customers of the ISP to learn about their experiences. Of course, higher reliability and better customer service may also cost more, so be prepared to take that into account as well. Some ISPs can provide redundant connections (at higher cost, of course) that may improve the overall reliability. If so, be sure to check how much redundancy there really is. For example, there may be two circuits between the same routers at your site and the ISP's site. Although that may guard against certain kinds of circuit failures, it certainly does not handle router failures. And because it is hard to tell where the circuits are physically routed, it may even be the case that they end up using the same fiber optic cable in the telephone system, which means there is hardly any redundancy at all.

- Extra services

  What additional services does the ISP provide? Do you need those services for your application? If not, will you be paying for services that you do not use?

The performance and reliability of your ISP are fundamental to the performance and reliability of your Internet commerce application, so it is very important to find an ISP that can provide the level of service you require at a price that fits your budget.

Hosting Services

Beyond the basic communications services, many ISPs offer additional services for hosting Web sites. That is, they operate the computers and software needed for a Web site on their own premises. For many businesses, this approach has several advantages.

- The ISP has a trained staff available for the operations.

- The ISP can (usually) provide round-the-clock operations and support, which may be difficult for smaller businesses to justify. (In other words, the ISP may have an economy of scale in hosting.)

- Because the Web site can be connected directly to the ISP's backbone, greater bandwidth to the users may be available compared to hosting at a corporate site.

- The cost of the operation may be amortized over a longer period of time or over many ISP customers, resulting in a lower cost of ownership for the business.

There are also some disadvantages, of course. The biggest one is lack of control: one is relying on another company to provide the critical operational services. The ISP may also constrain when and how one can update the content on the Web server. Even taking these limitations into account, however, it is often very effective to use an ISP's hosting services.

When selecting an ISP for hosting services, there are several issues that should be evaluated.

- What kind of hardware will be used for the Web server? Does it run the kind of software you will need?

- What kind of software is used for the Web server? Does it support your requirements? Can you provide your own programs for your application? Who controls the configuration of the software?

- What commitments for reliability will the ISP make? What has been the experience of other customers?

- What performance can be expected from the hardware, software, and network? Is it sufficient? What will happen if the performance turns out to be inadequate in practice? Will your application have its own system, or will it share a computer with other applications? Can the ISP handle peak loads for you as well as average loads?

- How do you update the content of your Web server? Can you use the tools you want to? If not, are the tools required by the ISP sufficient for your application?

- How is the security of the system managed? Are the operating systems reasonably well secured? Are they carefully managed? Is there a firewall in place? How does the ISP staff handle potential security incidents? Are the software components kept up to date with security-related patches from the software vendors?

- Is the ISP staff capable of providing the service you require? Are they too busy with other customers to give you the necessary attention?

- How much will it cost to get the level of service you require? Are there extra costs beyond the basic ones?

As with the basic communications services, it is important to select an ISP that can provide the services you require at a reasonable cost. Although it is possible to change ISPs, managing the transition can be difficult. It is therefore worthwhile to invest some time and effort in understanding what the ISP can do for you before setting up the site.

Commerce Service Providers

The next step beyond hosting services for Internet commerce applications are transaction services: providing the infrastructure for order capture, payment, and fulfillment. We call an entity providing such a service a *commerce service provider,* or CSP. Internet service providers are often CSPs, but other kinds of organizations may be CSPs as well. A bank, for example, may provide transaction services for Internet commerce as an extension of the services it provides to its merchant customers. Some *Internet malls* provide similar services as well.

It is common for CSPs to provide hosting services as well, although this is not always required. Some system architectures (as discussed in Chapter 6) require that content servers and transaction systems be located together, but others do not.

Here are some important questions for commerce service providers.

- What kinds of payment systems are supported now? What kinds may be added in the future?

- Does the CSP handle the kind of business model you require (e.g., information commerce, consumer retail, etc.)?

- What is the cost structure? Is the pricing based on a flat rate, transaction volume, transaction value, or something else?

- What kinds of reports are available to sellers?

- How and when are funds transferred to sellers?

- What customization of the ordering and payment processes can be performed for each seller? Does that meet your application requirements?

- Can the look and feel of the ordering and payment processes be customized to appropriately brand the site?

- Which tasks are managed by the seller, and which by the CSP?

Project Management

It may seem trite to say, but one of the keys to a successful Internet commerce application is getting the work done. A typical commerce project will involve software from several vendors, some custom development (or at least customization) by an in-house team or outside consultants, the operational services of several organizations, the integration of the new application into existing business models and practices, and many other activities. Without effective project management, it is unlikely that all the pieces will come together for a successful system.

This is not the glamorous part of Internet commerce, but it may well be the most important. Although projects will differ greatly in the details, there are some common issues for Internet commerce projects.

- Estimating costs

  What are the real costs of the project likely to be? This includes software products, time and effort to customize or extend the products, getting information about the actual products and services for sale up on the Internet, costs of Internet access, personnel requirements for developing and operating the application, and so on. A common mistake is to look primarily at the up-front cost of the software as being the dominant part, when in fact the costs of customizing or adding on to the base software may be much higher. The operating costs may also be much higher, depending on the details of the application. It is important, therefore, to look at the cost of ownership for the project, not just the initial software costs.

- Measuring benefits

  What are the expected benefits from developing the commerce application? Is this project a strategic investment or one for immediate return? Are the primary benefits expected to be lower costs (from having to print and mail fewer catalogs, for example) or increased revenues? Is this a pilot project to be replaced by a larger-scale (and possibly different) system, or is this the primary system? Having a good idea of the expected benefits—and making sure that the expectations are shared across the organization—makes it possible to measure them over time and to ensure that the organization can evaluate whether the project is successful or not.

- Sizing and performance

  It is especially hard to predict the required level of performance and sizes of the server systems for any Internet service, not just commerce systems. The usual problem is that an interesting site can attract a large number of people over a short period of time—word of mouth can spread very quickly on the Internet. When the site is overloaded, it can get a reputation for poor performance just as quickly. This phenomenon of intense periods of heavy use is sometimes called a *flash crowd*.[1] What this suggests is that we should plan systems for a high peak load with a desired service requirement, and a different set of expectations for load and service requirements on average. These plans should be separate from what would be considered a "successful" load or number of users on the system, since the goal of the planning is to handle the potential load. The potential load may be well in excess of what would be considered successful.

- Personnel

  Does the project have the necessary staff with the right skills to implement the application? Does it need consultants or contractors with specialized knowledge? Does the team need additional training on the software or technologies to be used?

- Maintenance, support, and upgrades

  What is the expected evolution of the commerce application? Are the software components on track with the expectations for the evolution? Who performs the maintenance and support on custom components or extensions? Will upgrades of software components have stable programming interfaces to enable reintegration with other systems? All too often, commerce applications are developed without a long-term plan, and the shifts in products and technology can leave them isolated over time. Although such shifts may happen even to the best-planned projects, careful planning in advance can avoid many such problems. Indeed, that is why we advocate paying attention to the architecture and long-term questions for Internet commerce in this book, rather than focusing on the details of what can be done today.

Staying Up to Date

One of the truisms of technology is that it changes. In the Internet world, especially, the technology is evolving quickly. We want to stay up with the latest and greatest technologies, whether they be the Web, real-time audio, Java, or exciting ideas yet to be invented. There is tension between the desire for stability and the drive for rapid evolution, the cost of change and the fear of being left behind. Therefore it is worth thinking through the benefits, costs, and implications of incorporating new technologies into an Internet commerce application.

---

1. The term "flash crowd" was coined by science-fiction author Larry Niven in a short story by that name (in *The Flight of the Horse,* Ballantine, 1971).

Issues for the Business

- How will the proposed change affect the existing system? In many cases, the change may have little or no direct effect on the application already running. Other possible changes may risk the stability of the running application; such changes must be evaluated and tested carefully.

- Will your team have the necessary skills? Changing technology requires continual development of new skills for the team implementing the application. Although the continuing education of the team is important, this must be balanced against a treadmill of technology change. One useful question here is whether or not the technology—or the skills—are strategic to the organization.

- What are the costs? What does it actually take to implement the new technology in the application? These costs might come from software, new or custom development, staff training, new hardware to run the new software, or added routine operations. No matter what the components of the cost, it is important to look at the overall cost of the new technology, which may be far greater than just acquiring a new software package.

- How much change can the customers and the organization handle every year? Even when all the other factors line up—the customers like (or at least don't mind) the change, the technology looks like a long-term winner, the costs aren't out of line, the team has (or can acquire) the needed skills—there may be a limit to how much change the customers (or an organization) can handle in a given period of time. Sometimes absorbing the change may be too much, in the context of all the other activity going on.

Issues for the Customers

- What software will your customers have? Some new technology features require that customers have additional software on their systems. For example, real-time audio applications may require special software for playing back audio files. To get the benefit of the new software, not only must the application be modified, but the customers must also install the extra components on their systems. In some cases, distributing the client software must be done as part of the application, which can result in added development and customer service costs. Do not forget that the required client software must also be available for the platforms (operating systems and other core software) that the customers are using.

  It is also important to keep in mind that the customers who use your system may not be the owners and managers of their computer systems. If the application requires particular client software, it may be necessary to negotiate with the IT department of each of your business customers to make sure the appropriate software is loaded and operable.

- What do your customers require? Do they care? Some customers may want very much to have a site with the latest technology—multimedia audio and video, Java applications, and so on—whereas others may have no interest in such technologies at all. Understanding the customers is therefore extremely important in making decisions about these technologies. A Web site aimed at teenagers, for example, will probably make much more extensive use of multimedia applications to attract customers than a Web site for electronics engineers to select parts.

- How will your customers react to change? Some groups of customers are uncomfortable with rapid technology evolution. Familiarity and stability are important to them, so changes in the application are likely to put them off.

- What are the expectations? Do your customers expect rapid deployment of new technology as a matter of course? Or do they expect a steady and deliberate evolution? Matching the technology development to the expectations can help customers have a sense of how your business operates, making it possible for them to plan more effectively.

- Is it a fad or a trend? Some technologies have a short life, whereas others become core parts of business computer systems. In the early stages, it is often difficult to tell them apart. Jumping into a fad can be a costly exercise in unusable technology, whereas missing a fundamental trend may lose valuable time to competitors. Though it is not always possible to tell which is which, thinking through this question may help make a decision about the investment. This is particularly important when dealing with exciting technologies that may or may not have a significant long-term effect on the business.

These questions are intended to help guide the process of adopting new technologies into commerce applications. In many ways, they represent a pragmatic view that is often opposed to the excitement and vision of new technology. On the other hand, it is easy to get caught up in such excitement, and asking these questions helps one arrive at a realistic understanding of the benefits as well as the costs.

The Role of Standards

Part of the core philosophy of the Internet is the use of standards to ensure interoperability among components from different vendors. TCP/IP, the core protocols of the Internet, is defined independently of any one vendor, and that definition is what makes it possible for two computers owned by different people, manufactured by different companies, running different software, to communicate with each other.

Just what is a standard, anyway? In the computer business, we often talk about two kinds of standards, *de jure* and *de facto.* The first, *de jure,* are the standards specified by designated organizations that are recognized to have some authority. These include organizations such as the International Telecommunications Union (ITU), the American National Standards Institute (ANSI), and the Internet Engineering Task Force

(IETF). These groups develop standards as a collaborative process among representatives from companies and other organizations which are involved in developing a particular technology area.

By contrast, a *de facto* standard is one that has become "standard" through widespread use. Sometimes such standards evolve from a particular company's technology becoming widely used by many vendors; the Network File System (NFS) developed by Sun Microsystems is one example. In other cases, the standard arises out of collaborative development, often including work from researchers and university labs. The TCP/IP family of protocols is an example of such development.

For our present discussion, standards serve two main purposes: they provide the basis for building interoperable applications and they provide a certain stability for longer-term development. In addition, some kinds of standards allow applications to be ported easily from one platform to another, which can simplify the evolution and deployment of an application. Building applications using a foundation of standard protocols can take advantage of years of work by others to develop a common approach to a problem, or to create other applications that work together. For example, using the standards of the Web as the base of a commerce application means that the user interface can be provided by commonly available Web browsers and the communications managed by a Web server.

Standards cannot always be a hard and fast requirement, however. When a technology area is developing rapidly, it often takes standards some time to catch up. In the early stages of such development, it may be difficult to predict which of several competing products may emerge as a standard (or at least as the basis for one). In such cases, it may be necessary to choose a technology solution in advance of standardization, based on the best available information and understanding of both the risks and the potential benefits.

In other words, standards are another tool for getting the job done. They can be very effective at times, but we must not be trapped into using only standards when new opportunities present themselves.

Round-the-Clock Operation

As we have said, the Internet is open for business around the world, 24 hours a day. Customers (and potential customers) from Australia are likely to be browsing sites in the United States at times when a normal storefront would be closed. Even within the same time zone, customers may be using the Internet for business late at night, whether for convenience or simply because they couldn't sleep. Many businesses, especially smaller ones, are not accustomed to operating under such conditions, so it is especially important for them to consider these aspects of the operation.

It might be observed that telephone-order businesses have many of these same characteristics: their catalogs are available to customers at any time, and the telephone may be used throughout the day or night. There are, however, some important differences, especially around what customers are coming to expect from Internet businesses. In most cases, telephone-order companies that are open during business hours have some geographic limitations for their base of customers. For example, almost all of their customers may be in the United States. The geography therefore limits the most common times of interest—during the day. On the other hand, many telephone-order companies are providing 24-hour service, because they recognize that customers will call around the clock.

Second, if the catalog is the Web site and the Web site isn't available, then the catalog isn't available. Part of the service—perhaps the main part—is providing the information to customers whenever they would like to get it.

Staffing is the most difficult part of providing service 24 hours a day, 7 days a week. If operations are not fully automated, then appropriate personnel need to be available at all times. It takes about five full-time-equivalent staff to keep one person on duty on a round-the-clock basis. Computer systems and network connections *will* operate around the clock unless something goes wrong, so there are two main questions for providing round-the-clock service.

1. Are there any routine operations that require a person to do them outside normal business hours? This question applies to any part of the Internet business that is not automated. For example, if a purchasing system requires a person to approve a purchase order, and this function must be available at any time, then someone must be present at all times to perform the task.

2. What should happen if the automated systems fail outside normal business hours? When something goes wrong with the computer systems or networks, it usually takes a knowledgeable person to diagnose the problem and repair it. How is the problem detected? How are the right people notified? Are there specific requirements for how long the failure can last? For example, a project plan might specify that certain kinds of failures must be repaired within an hour, other kinds within four hours, and so on.

Of course, different businesses will have different requirements for their availability and responsiveness, depending on the nature and expectations of the customers, the way that the Internet is being used for business, the availability of trained staff, and the amount the business is willing to invest in providing such a level of service. The important thing is to think through these requirements and make some decisions at the outset about what is desired for service, rather than to be caught by surprise when a computer or network connection fails.

Finally, as we discussed earlier, outsourcing the operation of the Internet commerce system is one way to provide a high-availability system. Most organizations that handle such outsourcing have plans and staff to make the systems available around the clock. It is important, of course, to ensure that they do and that both parties agree on the expected level of service and responsiveness to problems.

Security Design

Surveys often show that security is one of the primary areas of concern for those creating systems for Internet commerce. Indeed, the security of the system is of critical importance in a successful system over the long term. There are important security issues in the design, implementation, and operational phases of any Internet commerce project.

We discuss security issues, technologies, and solutions in detail in Chapter 13. In implementing and operating an Internet commerce system, however, we must emphasize the importance of continual monitoring and evaluation of the system from a security point of view. It does no good to set up a system correctly at the outset and then undermine the security with careless operation, in much the same way that it does no good to install a lock on a door if no one ever locks it.

Multiorganization Operation

Over time, developing a robust Internet commerce system will almost certainly involve coordinating the efforts of many organizations. In this chapter we have already looked at several possible participants:

- Internet service providers
- Commerce service providers
- Web and content developers
- Payment processors
- Software vendors
- Systems integrators
- Different organizations within a company

These participants are often involved not only with the creation of the Internet commerce system, but also with the day-to-day operation of it. So when problems arise, as they inevitably do, it is exceedingly important for the different groups to work together smoothly on solving them. Problems with networked computer systems are often difficult to diagnose, so the complete team must be able to cooperate to find it, instead of blaming each other for the problem. Once the problem is found, of course, it may be clear who is responsible for solving it, or it may require a team working together to do so.

Performance problems, in particular, are often extremely hard to find. Part of the problem is that it may be difficult to find the bottleneck in a complex system, with many components and a structure that may not be fully understood by anyone on the project team. Another part of the problem is that network systems are commonly designed to tolerate many kinds of faults, typically by sending data again if an expected result does not occur within a given period of time and by having redundant services. When these are combined, the failure of one service may go undetected, because the sender finds a different service after some time interval. Thus, a fault in the system (the failure of the service) appears to the users as a performance problem (the extra time taken to retransmit the data).

To maximize the chances for successful operation, then, there are several steps that can be taken in advance of problems.

1. Ensure that all participants understand both their role and the roles of the other participants in the operation of the system.

2. Bring all (or most) of the participants together to work on the routine operation as a team, so that when problems arise, the people and the organizations are used to working with each other.

3. Plan in advance how to handle particular problems, so at least the predictable problems have known paths to solving them.

4. Establish a set of problem-solving procedures—from detection to diagnosis to solution—that is familiar to all participants. The procedures then help the team work together in solving the problem, rather than trying to figure out who does what in an *ad hoc* fashion.

5. Prepare for problems by acquiring—by development or purchase— tools for monitoring the system and diagnosing faults. It is much easier to use well-understood tools to find a problem than to apply primitive tools and debugging techniques haphazardly. And the monitoring tools, if used correctly, can provide early warning of many faults before they become serious.

For the most part, these suggestions have little to do with technology; they are about working with people, teams, and organizations. In making an Internet commerce system a real success for the business, however, these are precisely some of the most important issues to be solved. The most wonderful technology in the world won't succeed if the team operating it doesn't succeed.

Summary

It is easy to be seduced by the lure of computing technology, whether for Internet commerce or any other application. The technology, though, is only one piece—albeit the flashiest—of the effective use of computer systems. In particular, an Internet commerce system must enable a business to deliver value to its customers. With the technology components in place, they must be operated in a way consistent with delivering that value, with the reliability, security, and performance expected by the customers. The operational task may not be glamorous, but it is absolutely fundamental to the success of the business, which is, of course, what the effort is all about.

The first half of this book has focused on the nontechnology parts of an Internet commerce system: understanding the business issues, focusing on the customer, developing an architecture, and executing a plan. With that view, we now turn to the technology components of Internet commerce systems.

Part Two

The Technology of Internet Commerce

CHAPTER 8

The Internet and the World Wide Web

Technology…the knack of so arranging the world that
we don't have to experience it.
—Max Frisch[1]

The Technology of the Internet

The first part of the book was primarily about the business issues for Internet commerce. Understanding the business is really the first part of planning a successful system for Internet commerce. In this part of the book, we delve into the technology used to make those business plans real. We will be discussing both the core principles underlying the technology (such as how to think about security for Internet commerce) and some current technology components (such as some of the communications protocols used on the Internet today). The core principles provide some guidance for making decisions in the face of rapid technological change, whereas the discussion of current technologies provides some understanding for putting them to work, as well as demonstrating how the core principles can be applied at one point in time.

In this chapter, we begin with a look at the technological underpinnings of the Internet, starting with the core protocols (TCP/IP) and moving to some of the key application areas, such as the World Wide Web. We also examine some of the fundamental design principles of the Internet. Understanding these principles not only helps with understanding the technology, but also helps us build on the accumulated experience of the Internet for designing new systems.

---

1. Max Frisch, *Homo Faber,* 1957.

The following chapters examine technology areas that are particularly important for Internet commerce. We look at the key building blocks for commerce systems, the creation and management of content for commerce systems, the uses of cryptography to provide security, issues of system security, payment systems, transaction management, and interfaces to auxiliary services for commerce systems. We then discuss how to tie these components together in an effective system design.

Development of the Internet

The Internet grew out of a research network originally funded by the U.S. Department of Defense. Development of this network, known as the ARPAnet after the Advanced Research Projects Agency (ARPA), began in 1969. Over time it grew slowly, as universities, defense agencies, and a few companies joined the network, mostly as participants in various research projects funded by ARPA. As the network grew, it was used for applications beyond research, such as electronic mail. With these other applications came increasing use by research groups working on other kinds of projects.

In the early 1980s, the current versions of the core Internet protocols, TCP and IP (which we discuss later), were introduced across the network. Shortly thereafter, as ARPA reduced its role in supporting the network, the term *Internet* came to be used as the name for the now global entity. The term "Internet" comes from the word "internetwork"—an interconnected set of networks. As we shall see, the Internet can grow with very little central control, as networks are connected to each other.

As shown in Figure 8-1, the growth of the Internet in terms of connected computers has been exponential since its inception in 1969. Since the Domain Name System (DNS) was widely introduced in the late 1980s, the growth in registered domains has tracked the growth of the network as a whole. In 1992, the Center for European Nuclear Research (CERN) released the first versions of World Wide Web software. Subsequently, the number of Web servers has grown even faster than the number of computers on the network.

One sometimes sees the term *internet* (with a small *i*) used to describe an internetwork distinct from the Internet (with a capital I). For a time this term was commonly used to describe networks belonging to a single organization, such as a large company, that used Internet technology. More recently, the term *intranet* has become the common term for such internal networks. We shall have more to say about intranets later in this chapter.

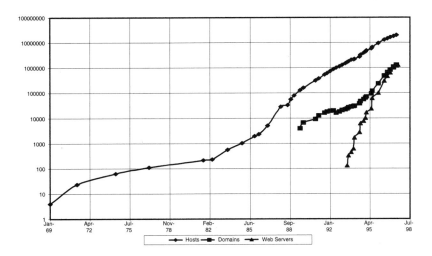

FIGURE 8-1. Growth of the Internet

Design Principles of the Internet

The Internet has been successful because of some fundamental decisions about its design made early in its history. These decisions are often invisible to the end user, and even to application developers, but understanding them gives insight into why the network is the way it is. In addition, we often find that such insight helps in making choices about building new applications. Even when such applications seem far removed from the core ideas of the Internet, those that match the spirit of the Internet design are more likely to succeed than those that do not.

The main design ideas in the Internet are as follows:

- Interoperability

  Independent implementations of Internet protocols actually work together. This may seem obvious today, but it took significant work in the early days of the Internet to make that happen. In fact, the Interop conference began as an event for vendors to test the interoperability of their products. Today, interoperability means that systems can be assembled using client and server computers and software from different vendors.

  In the context of Internet commerce, interoperability means that buyers and sellers do not have to buy and upgrade software simultaneously from the same vendor to conduct commerce. Of course, this is only true if the software from different vendors is based on open standards and does, in fact, interoperate.

- Layering

  Internet protocols are designed to work in layers, with each higher layer building on the facilities provided by lower layers. For example, TCP builds on IP to create reliable byte streams, and application protocols such as those for the Web or electronic mail build on the capabilities of TCP. This layered architecture is shown in Figure 8-2.[2]

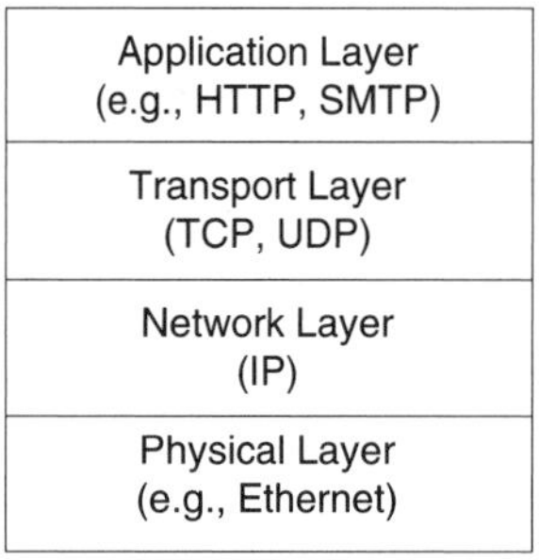

```
┌─────────────────────────────┐
│     Application Layer        │
│    (e.g., HTTP, SMTP)        │
├─────────────────────────────┤
│      Transport Layer         │
│       (TCP, UDP)             │
├─────────────────────────────┤
│      Network Layer           │
│         (IP)                 │
├─────────────────────────────┤
│      Physical Layer          │
│    (e.g., Ethernet)          │
└─────────────────────────────┘
```

FIGURE 8-2. **Layering of Internet Protocols**

- Simplicity

  One way to look at the layering of the Internet is that it grows both up and down from IP. IP itself is very simple, providing only addressing and formatting of packets. Below the level of IP, there is the complexity of many different kinds of network hardware, topologies, and routers, such as Ethernet, dial-up connections, and so on. IP hides that complexity from applications. Above IP, higher-level protocols such as TCP offer service abstractions that are easy for application programmers to understand and use. As a consequence, application developers and users are insulated from the complexities of different network devices as well as from the complexities of implementing low-level network protocols.

- Uniform naming and addressing

  The IP layer offers a uniform addressing structure that assigns a 32-bit address to each computer connected to the network. These addresses are commonly written in *dotted quad* form, such as 16.11.0.1. Addresses are hard for people to remember and work with, so the Domain Name System (DNS) offers a uniform way to translate human-readable names for computers, such as "www.openmarket.com" to the numeric address for that computer. These two systems, together with interoperability of implementations, let the Internet function.

---

2. Some readers may note that this model differs from the common OSI reference model for network layers. Internet applications typically do not fit the OSI model exactly, so we have used the simplified model here.

- End-to-end

    The Internet is designed around end-to-end protocols. That is, the interpretation of the data happens on the sending and receiving systems, but nothing in the network needs to look at anything but the destination address for delivering the packet. This is somewhat like mailing a letter: you put the recipient's address on the envelope and drop it in the mailbox. The postal service does not care what is inside (as long as it is not hazardous), and you do not care if it travels by truck, jeep, or airplane, as long as it arrives in a reasonable amount of time. By contrast, when you travel to a faraway city, you might take a taxi to the airport, an airplane to the other city, and a bus to the hotel. Each of these steps is booked and paid for separately. The analogous system in networking is hop-by-hop or link-by-link systems, in which intermediate systems are processing the data at the application layer.

    End-to-end protocols have several advantages. They hide the internal structure of the network, including the wide range of physical hardware used on the Internet, from users and applications. In addition, they can provide simple abstractions to programmers, shielding them from such things as the messy details of recovering from low-level errors.

From these simple ideas comes a powerful, robust, and reliable network that has scaled to a global level. The standards and specifications for the Internet protocols are developed by the Internet Engineering Task Force (IETF), which is open to participation by anyone who would like to contribute. Over time, the IETF has brought together vendors, users, researchers, governments, and others to develop and improve the technology of the Internet.

Core Network Protocols

The Web depends on a number of lower-level protocols, particularly IP, TCP, and DNS. Several comprehensive works on the networking and protocol technology of the Internet are listed in Resources and Further Reading.

Physical Layer

The Internet, as the name suggests, is a network of networks. At the physical layer, no single technology is used. Various parts of the Net run over local area networks using Ethernet, token ring, Fiber Distributed Data Interconnect (FDDI), Asynchronous Transfer Mode (ATM), and other technologies. Wide area networks have been built with point-to-point data circuits, dialup, frame relay, ATM, and other services. All of these network technologies are used to transport and route Internet traffic. Within one of these lower-level networks, routing is handled by whatever means are built into that network. In most cases, even the addressing is distinct from Internet addressing. For example, Ethernet uses 48-bit universal identifiers for addressing and routing.

When an IP network is built using an Ethernet, the end systems use a special protocol, the Address Resolution Protocol (ARP), to translate IP addresses into Ethernet addresses.

Internet routers are used to connect these constituent networks. These routers forward packets from network to network until they reach the network connected to the destination system, whereupon the router can deliver the packet directly. Each router has a local map of the network that tells it where to forward a packet next, based on the destination address in the IP header. The information about where to forward a packet next, which can be quite complex in a large network, is distributed using various *routing protocols*. More information about routing can be found in several of the references in Resources and Further Reading.

Security at the physical layer depends on the network technology used. Some network systems, for example, include encryption of all data on the physical network. This encryption does not, however, extend to data when it travels off that particular physical network. The security of router configurations depends for the most part on simple passwords, on the obscurity of these devices, and on the detection of the side effects of tampering (which are usually obvious).

Routers are often used as the first line of defense against network attack. Router configurations are part of network firewalls, and in particular they are set up to carefully segregate "suspect" traffic that originates from outside an organization from presumably authorized traffic which originates on the inside. We shall have more to say about firewalls in Chapter 13.

Internet Protocol (IP)

The term *TCP/IP* is commonly used as the name of the fundamental networking protocol of the Internet. In fact, TCP and IP are two separate protocols, though most applications on the Internet use both. IP is the Internet protocol, the one that most defines the Internet. IP deals only with packets of data, which are labeled with the network addresses of the source and destination computers. The network is responsible for trying to deliver the packets to the destination, but it does not guarantee that it will do so. Within the network, packets may be lost or duplicated, and they may arrive out of order. This "best efforts" approach may not seem useful at first, but in fact it is a very powerful substrate for building networked applications. Other protocols can build on the foundation of IP to meet the needs of different kinds of applications. Such protocols are identified in an IP packet by a protocol identifier, which enables a destination system to select the correct protocol for processing at the next layer up.

IP itself does not offer any security services. Attackers with physical access to the network can listen to packets going by, introduce forged packets, and potentially intercept and alter legitimate packets. Addresses can be forged easily, so many applications must be careful about believing the addresses on a packet. Ultimately, it is the responsibility of higher-level protocols to manage these problems, but network layer techniques such as firewalls are often used to create protected network environments in which applications simply do not worry about these sorts of attack.

IP has been used in its current form for many years. Over the past few years, the IETF has been defining the next generation of IP, now known as IP version 6 (or IPv6). IPv6 includes many improvements to IP, including a larger address space, better scaling for the routing system, and security services. It has been carefully designed to allow a gradual transition, since the Internet is already so large. There will likely be a lengthy cutover period to IPv6 as vendors upgrade their software and network users install it at their sites. During the transition, some of the improvements, particularly the security services, will likely be deployed with the current version of IP. We discuss these security services, known as IPSec, in more detail in Chapter 13.

Unreliable Datagram Protocol (UDP)

The two most common transport protocols on top of IP are the Unreliable Datagram Protocol (UDP) and the Transmission Control Protocol (TCP). UDP provides a very simple datagram (or packet) service to applications. It gives them access to the basic facilities of IP, while adding a few additional features. These features include a checksum for basic data integrity and a *port number,* which is used to identify which application is the real destination for the packet (recall that the IP address only identifies the system, not the application running on the system). UDP does not provide any services for reliable delivery or ordered delivery, so packets may arrive out of order, or they may never arrive at all. Applications that use UDP must provide reliability to the level they need, but they also have great flexibility in how to do that. Two notable Internet applications that use UDP are the Domain Name System (DNS), which we discuss in more detail below, and Sun's Network File System (NFS).

Transmission Control Protocol (TCP)

The Transmission Control Protocol (TCP) is the most common transport protocol on the Internet. Building on the packet-oriented foundation of IP, it provides the abstraction of a reliable byte stream. That is, an application sends data, and the receiver gets it in the order it was sent (unless, of course, an error occurs that is too serious for TCP to recover from). It also provides a flow control mechanism to ensure that a receiver is not overwhelmed by a sender transmitting data too fast. TCP works by having the receiver send back an acknowledgment for the packets it received. If the sender does not get the acknowledgment within a certain period of time, it transmits the packet again. Each packet also contains a sequence number, so the receiver can put them into the right order. An application using TCP thus has the illusion of a continuous ordered stream of data, without having to worry about the details of how the data gets through the network. Most familiar applications on the Internet use TCP, including the Web and electronic mail.

TCP itself does not have any native security mechanisms. Although an eavesdropper can pick up individual packets and easily reconstruct the conversation, it is much harder for an attacker to change the data in a TCP stream. More unfortunately, it is easy to attack an end system by sending many "new connection requests" without following through on the rest of the protocol. This ties up operating system resources and can block legitimate connections. Because several such attacks have occurred, vendors are currently deploying countermeasures to this and related attacks. To a certain extent, network firewalls can also help limit the problem.

Domain Name System (DNS)

The Internet uses 32-bit numeric addresses to route packets to a particular network adapter on a particular machine somewhere on the Net. Humans, however, like to use names for networked machines or services, rather than numbers. Aside from relieving the user from the necessity of remembering and transcribing numeric addresses, names serve some valuable purposes.

1. A service can move from machine to machine (and, hence, from address to address) while keeping the same name. That way, people (and other systems) need only remember the name of the service.

2. A service can be supported by multiple machines, with independent addresses, but which share the same name.

The problem of translating human-sensible names into numeric addresses is handled by the Domain Name System, or DNS. The DNS is a very fast, very scalable method of translating names to addresses. A DNS name such as *www.openmarket.com* consists of a machine name, in this case *www*, and a hierarchy of domains, *openmarket* and *com*, separated by periods. Generally speaking, a *domain* is the name of an organization that assigns names to computers and services, whether that be a company, university, or other kind of entity. As shown in Figure 8-3, DNS names are structured in a hierarchy. The name is processed from right to left, with the root of the hierarchy represented as a dot at the end. When a program needs the network address for a machine, it queries local DNS servers, which may, in turn, query remote servers as well. Root DNS servers are responsible for top-level domains such as *com, edu, gov,* and *mil,* as well as geographic domains such as *us, ca,* and *jp* (which designate the U.S., Canada, and Japan, respectively). These root servers know only which other lower-level servers know about the *com* domain. DNS servers for the *com* domain then know which lower-level servers are responsible for the *openmarket* domain, but they do not know anything about names within the *openmarket* domain. Finally, the *openmarket* DNS servers are responsible for knowing the IP address of the machine *www.*

In addition to these authoritative servers, DNS information may be temporarily cached by other systems, and most clients are configured to accept such nonauthoritative information (nonauthoritative because it is not necessarily up to date).

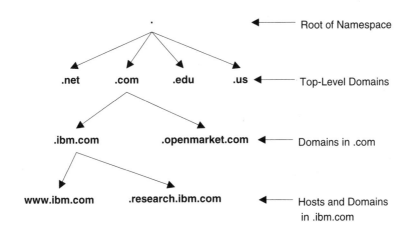

FIGURE 8-3. Structure of the DNS Naming Hierarchy

The DNS is also used to translate IP addresses to names. If we want to find the name associated with the address *199.170.183.2,* for example, we reverse the order of the numbers and use the *in-addr.arpa* domain for the lookup, resulting in *2.183.170.199.in-addr.arpa.* That looks almost like a regular domain name, and we get back the answer *relay.openmarket.com.* This process, often called a *reverse lookup,* works because the hierarchy of network addresses (which read from left to right) is very similar to the hierarchy of DNS names.

This ability to translate addresses to names is often used for both access control and logging. An incoming connection has no name associated with it—only the IP address of the sender. Because logs and access control rules are often read and written by people, it is much easier for them to read and write names, so applications commonly translate addresses to names.

Using DNS information for access control can be risky, however. DNS is very widely used on the Internet, but the security of Web systems that use it will depend both on the source information fed into DNS and on the security of intermediate DNS servers between the client and server. As an example, consider a Web server configured to provide access only to hosts in *openmarket.com.* A connection arrives from IP address *199.170.183.2,* and the server uses a DNS inverse name lookup to find out if indeed this address is assigned to Open Market. One problem is that this works well if in fact the address *is* one of Open Market's, but if it isn't, then the DNS inverse lookup will retrieve the answer to this question from the attacker's DNS server! One way to guard against this is to look up the name again in the DNS to see if the address entries match. For most applications, the usual course is to use DNS to translate names to addresses, but not to depend on the DNS results for authenticating the source of the messages.

The World Wide Web

In 1992, Tim Berners-Lee at CERN released the first implementation of the World Wide Web. Because of its power and accessibility, the Web has grown in popularity to the point that many people do not distinguish between the Web and the Internet itself.

World Wide Web—Summary

The WWW project merges the techniques of networked information and hypertext to make an easy but powerful global information system.

The project represents any information accessible over the network as part of a seamless hypertext information space.

W3 was originally developed to allow information sharing within internationally dispersed teams, and the dissemination of information by support groups. Originally aimed at the high energy physics community, it has spread to other areas and attracted much interest in user support, resource discovery, and collaborative work areas. It is currently the most advanced information system deployed on the Internet, and embraces within its data model most information in previous networked information systems.

In fact, the Web is an architecture which will also embrace any future advances in technology, including new networks, protocols, object types, and data formats.

Tim Berners-Lee on the World Wide Web, circa 1992
From *http://www.w3.org/Summary.html*

Web Fundamentals

The World Wide Web is a global hypertext network of over a million Web servers and untold millions of Web browsers[3] connected by the Hypertext Transfer Protocol (HTTP) and its variants. Like the Internet, the Web is growing rapidly, so it is hard to say exactly how big it is at any given time. Web servers supply, and browsers display, pages of multimedia information. Pages are frequently defined by the Hypertext Markup Language (HTML) and can contain text, graphics, audio, video, and even pieces of software called *applets* that are automatically downloaded from the server and run on the desktop. The most important elements of Web pages are hypertext

---

3. As of the summer of 1997, there were approximately 25,000,000 computers connected to the Internet. No one knows how many users of the Web there are.

links to other pages on the same or different servers. These links appear as highlighted text invoked with the mouse, but portions of images may contain hypertext links as well. By simply clicking on the links, a user can easily move from page to page, without having to worry about the location of the information or about the underlying details of communications.

Each hypertext link contains a visible part, called the *anchor*, which the user sees on the screen. The anchor usually describes the link or gives a title for the referenced page. Hyperlinks can also be represented by images, so Web pages can be created with icons representing links. The target of the link is described by a *Uniform Resource Locator* (URL) such as

> http://servername.domain/path/name/of/object.html

which can refer to a page on the same server or to one anywhere on the Web.

The World Wide Web is a nearly pure client-server system. Content is held by Web servers and requested by clients. With a few exceptions, servers do not initiate activities, and clients merely display the content they have retrieved from a server. Exceptions include *server push*, in which a client holds open a network connection and the server continually updates the client, and *applets*, in which code is automatically downloaded for the client to execute, usually to provide more complex interactive behavior.

Uniform Resource Locators

The structure and flexibility of the URL is central to the use of the Web for electronic commerce.

As shown in Figure 8-4, a URL such as http://www.w3.org/example/path/index.html is composed of several parts.

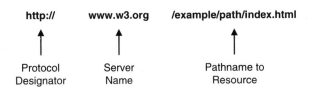

FIGURE 8-4. Components of a URL

- Protocol designator (*http:*)

  This tells the browser what protocol to use in connecting to the server, in this case HTTP. Most Web browsers can use other protocols as well, such as FTP (ftp:) and SMTP (mailto:) for file transfer and electronic mail, respectively.

- Server name (*servername.domain*)

  This is a Domain Name System (DNS) name. The browser will use the DNS to translate the name to an IP network address.

- Pathname (*/path/name/of/object.html*)

  This is frequently the full name of a file on the Web server, but it may be interpreted by the server to mean that a program or database query should be executed to generate the results for the client. By convention, the extension (in this case, .html) means that this is an HTML document, but this convention is not required.

This particular URL refers to a static HTML page of information somewhere in the filesystem of a server. Much of the power of the Web comes from two additional capabilities: pages can be constructed dynamically by applications software, and information can flow in both directions. When a page is constructed dynamically, the Web server passes the path portion of the URL to an application program, which can return an HTML page or other content constructed on the fly by the application itself. In addition, HTML pages can contain forms to be filled out by the user, and the input data for the forms sent back to the server.

Web Protocols

The Web actually employs several network protocols. Some of them, such as the File Transfer Protocol (FTP) originated elsewhere but have been assimilated into the Web. Others, such as the ones described here, have been created for the Web itself.

Hypertext Transfer Protocol (HTTP)

HTTP is the original Web communications protocol. With HTTP, the client opens a TCP connection to the Web server, and transmits an HTTP header. The header contains an HTTP command, such as GET, PUT, or POST, and the path portion of the URL. The HTTP header may also include information for authenticating the user, as well as information about acceptable document formats. This information allows the client and server to negotiate about what formats will be returned by the server, so (for example) a client that can handle images only in the GIF format will not receive images that use the JPEG format.

Clients use the GET command in HTTP to retrieve documents, and PUT to upload files to the server. The POST command is used by the client to send the results of a form filled out by the user. With the PUT and POST commands, the client simply transmits the information immediately after the HTTP header.

When the server has completed processing the request, it transmits a reply header back to the client followed by the page to be displayed. One of the header fields sent by the server specifies the format of the data being returned, which permits the client to locate the proper module or application for it. This capability enables Web browsers to display many different kinds of data (e.g., text, HTML, images, etc.). Moreover, a browser may be *extensible*, which allows it to invoke other applications to handle data formats it does not understand itself.

Secure Sockets Layer (SSL)

SSL, developed by Netscape Communications Corporation, is the most widely used security protocol on the Internet. In our simplified model for protocol layers, SSL fits in between TCP and the application, where it can provide security services for any stream of data. In addition to encrypting the communications, SSL provides for the use of digital certificates to authenticate the server to the client. With SSL Version 3, certificates can be used to authenticate clients to servers as well. The Internet Engineering Task Force (IETF) has a working group on Transport Layer Security (TLS) that is standardizing a protocol based on SSL. SSL and TLS are described in more detail in Chapter 13.

Secure HTTP (S-HTTP)

S-HTTP is a security protocol for the Web originally developed by Enterprise Integration Technologies (EIT).[4] It never became widely used, but it is interesting because it provides various security services at the application layer rather than the transport layer. S-HTTP allows Web clients and servers to specify authentication and privacy capabilities independently of one another, and it enables them to negotiate the cryptographic algorithms to be used. Furthermore, S-HTTP builds on Web protocols because each link in a hypertext document can carry information about the security properties of the target document. This capability increases the complexity of authoring secure content, but makes the management of security much more automatic.

Over time, the Web has grown to embrace more and more protocols, making it possible for a Web browser to become the primary interface to the Internet for many users.

Other Web Tools

The foundations of the Web—HTTP, HTML, URLs, and so on—have become the basis for many applications. Search engines, for example, are one of the most popular applications. A search engine is a tool for finding information on a web, whether that is the World Wide Web or a web used internally by a company or other organization. The index created by a search engine may be created in different ways. Some are

---

4. EIT created a spin-off company called Terisa Systems to pursue the S-HTTP work. Terisa has since been acquired by Spyrus.

created and maintained by people, giving the engine the organized feel of a library. Others use *Web robots* to download information from all over the Web, indexing the text in some fashion. Web robots typically work by keeping a list of Web pages to index, and downloading them one by one. Each one is indexed from the text, and any hyperlinks on the page are added to the list of pages to index, if they have not already been indexed recently. On a well-connected web, then, a robot can index nearly all of the static pages that it can read. If you do not wish your site to be indexed by robots, there are some ways to prevent it (see the references at the end of the chapter).

Other Web tools make it possible to use the Web when you are not connected to it. For example, mobile computers (such as laptops and notebooks) are typically connected to the network only part of the time. For many users, then, an *offline browser* enables a user to download Web content in advance and in bulk, rather than downloading each page as it is clicked on. Later, while the system is disconnected, the user can browse the pages just as if the network were present. (Of course, this does not work well for interactive applications or dynamic pages with changing content.)

The Web has become so powerful and ubiquitous that many applications have embraced it in one way or another. For example, some programs offer help by linking back to the vendor's Web site for information, rather than providing it with the program. Or they may augment the help files with updates and frequently asked questions on a Web site. Word processors, spreadsheets, and other applications may allow the user to embed other documents into their own by providing a URL, so the data is fetched over the Web as appropriate.

From the point of view of Internet commerce, these are all components that we think about when designing a system. For example, does the commerce system need to work with offline browsers? What about with the Web embedded in other applications? Does the commerce-enabled Web site work well with search engine robots that may try to index it? The answers to these and other related questions should be part of the requirements definition for commerce services.

Agents

The term *agent* has been used to mean many different things, ranging from spell checkers that work as you type to artificial intelligence programs that find the information you need before you ask for it. To be practical today, agents are typically more limited in capability, though many research projects are exploring what agents might be able to do.

In the realm of Internet commerce, the most common idea of an agent is something like a personal shopper, which finds various items you might be looking for and presents them with comparison information. Taken a step further, such an agent may even be authorized to make purchases under certain conditions.

Personal shoppers may sound interesting to buyers, but they are worrisome to sellers. Agents that discriminate mainly on price, for example, drive a market toward low-price sellers. Since the agents are automated, it is difficult (if not impossible) to build a relationship with the actual customer. Already, the Net has seen sellers react against prototype agents of this type. In most cases, the sellers developed countermeasures to keep agents from using their systems. Agents are still too new to the Internet, and especially to Internet commerce, to make predictions about how they will ultimately be used in commerce applications. It is very likely that they will be put to such use, and the developers of any evolving commerce system should keep an eye on where this technology is going.

Intranets

The term *intranet* has come to be used for applications of Internet technologies on internal networks of companies and other organizations. Intranets most commonly include Web technology in one way or another. For Internet commerce, intranets have two interesting properties. The first is that the intranet can be used to create a unified experience for customers by drawing on the resources of many different parts of the company, pulling together functions such as product information, technical details, customer service, ordering for products and services, as well as any other specialized organizations within the company. Second, Internet commerce applications can be deployed for internal use as well, making it possible to use the same applications for internal ordering, transaction processing, and service for internal "customers."

Extranets

Similar to the word *intranet,* the term *extranet* has come to be used to describe a network connecting an organization with its partners, suppliers, and close customers. Sometimes the term simply means using the Internet for communicating with them, but frequently it refers to networks that connect them together more closely than a typical Internet connection. The network may use the Internet, or it may use Internet technology on a private physical network. Typical applications include sharing information for joint projects, direct connections into a supplier's ordering system, or direct access for customer service and support.

Such activities include many that we have discussed for business-to-business Internet commerce. Indeed, an Internet commerce system may be the basis for an extranet, bringing closer relationships for both buyers and sellers. In a sense, the extranet is providing an exterior security boundary that protects the organizations from the open network, while providing lower security boundaries for greater sharing of information between the partners.

Consumer Devices and Network Computers

As the Web has grown, so has the range of devices that can connect to it. Many of these devices do not have all the capabilities we associate with desktop computers; they may be limited in computing power, storage, network bandwidth, display capabilities, and so on. Some of these devices, such as WebTV, are aimed at a broad consumer market. Others, such as various kinds of network computers, intend to take full advantage of the Web and related technologies. They are based on the premise that the useful resources for users are all on the network somewhere, and the primary goal of the desktop device is to connect the user to those resources. These so-called *thin clients* are really built around the Web as the basic interface to computing.

Thin clients of various kinds have some important implications for commerce applications. In particular, application designers must understand what range of devices they expect to be used with the application. For example, an application built using Java for execution in a browser rules out the use of any browsers that cannot run Java. Such a limitation may be an acceptable trade-off for some applications, but others may want to reach the broadest possible group of customers. As the various types of devices develop further and gain broader use in the marketplace, application designers should consider how to evolve their applications to keep up with what their customers are using.

The Future of the Internet: Protocol Evolution

Like other technologies, the Internet is evolving quickly, and changes are inevitable. Although many of the core principles remain the same, the details will be different. All of the technologies mentioned in this chapter are changing to some degree.

TCP/IP is evolving with the development of IPv6, the next generation of the Internet Protocol. IPv6 builds on the long experience with IP (which is officially version 4), and it brings improvements in scalability, security, and support for real-time media. Because it changes the fundamental protocols of the Internet, it will be quite some time before the entire Internet is running IPv6, though many IPv6 products are on the market today. In fact, some of the security technology developed for IPv6 is also being developed for use with the current version of IP.

Fortunately, IPv6 has little direct effect on Internet commerce. Because of the layered architecture of the Internet, applications for commerce are largely insulated from the changes in the lower layers. Thus, as IPv6 is deployed, commerce applications will continue to work, while the overall network benefits from the new capabilities. Over time, as the IPv6 security infrastructure comes into widespread use, commerce applications can use the IPv6 security features to enhance their security as well.

The Web is changing, too—both HTTP and HTML are active areas of work. New versions of HTTP promise better performance and more flexible interactions between clients and servers. The changes to HTTP may affect applications more than IPv6 does, simply because it provides capabilities closer to the application's logic. Because the changes are designed to be compatible with earlier versions, applications need not change right away, and they can be modified when it is appropriate to take advantage of what is new in the protocol.

As for HTML, the follow-on development gaining rapid acceptance is the Extensible Markup Language (XML). In effect, XML allows applications to define their own markup extensions, which (among other things) enables them to define documents that include application-specific tags for data items as well as rules for displaying them on a screen. For example, a commerce application might use XML to define an order form, where the prices, descriptions, quantities, and so on are tagged appropriately. This enables a display application, such as a browser, to show a nicely formatted form on the screen, while the application can parse the order form to extract the information needed to process the order.

Although changes in the technology of the Internet are inevitable, it is not necessary to adopt each one immediately as it becomes available. Each evolutionary step (and the occasional revolutionary one) must be evaluated for how it affects the value delivered to customers by the commerce application, along with the costs of implementing the change. There is also some risk that such changes will not become common in the marketplace, leaving an application at a dead end. For Internet commerce applications, we recommend aggressive caution and prudent revolution.

Summary

Though the Internet has become widely used only in the last few years, its roots go back more than two decades to work in academia and research. Some key architectural principles of the Internet, such as interoperability, layering, and common addressing and naming, have created a network that could grow to a worldwide scale, supporting a tremendous variety of applications. The core protocols of the Internet make it possible for computers around the world to communicate with each other.

Building on this foundation, the World Wide Web brought a new generation of information management and usability to the Internet. The Web is itself another layer in the foundation for many kinds of applications, such as the Internet commerce systems we describe in this book.

In the next chapter, we look at some of the primary building blocks for Internet commerce systems.

CHAPTER 9

Building Blocks for Internet Commerce

I found Rome a city of bricks and left it a city of marble.
—Augustus Caesar[1]

Components in an Internet Commerce System

The building blocks of Internet commerce are the technologies of the World Wide Web: its protocols, browsers, and servers, along with application development structures such as Java, ActiveX, and CGI. This chapter begins with a look at the basic content machinery of the Web, then surveys the protocols and mechanisms for getting content to the user. We then turn to current technologies for building content pages at the server and the evolving technologies for adding programmability to the browser. We conclude with a look at the changes to basic Web technology which are important for adding commerce facilities to the Web.

Content Transport

There are two ways for content to get from a server on the Internet to the screen of the end user. Either the user's client program (browser) goes to the server and retrieves the content, or the server initiates the connection and delivers content to the desktop. These two mechanisms are called *pull* and *push* content delivery, respectively. In addition, a variant of push content is *broadcast*, where the same content is delivered to many clients simultaneously.

---

1. From Suetonius, *Augustus.*

Pull Content

Pull content has been the traditional mode for the World Wide Web: the client opens a connection to a server whenever the user clicks on a hypertext link. Most Web browsers can use a variety of network protocols to retrieve content, but the Hypertext Transfer Protocol (HTTP) is the most common. The fundamentals of HTTP were described in Chapter 8. Here are some of its more subtle points.

Protocol Variations

In the original design for the Web, a browser used a separate HTTP connection for each component on a page. For example, each included image (the most common kind of component after the Web page itself) required a separate connection.[2] Each connection requires a certain amount of overhead and time to set up. Of course, when the page components come from different server systems, separate connections are necessary; but when the components all come from the same server, a single connection could suffice. Some HTTP client and server implementations support a protocol option called *HTTP Keepalive*, which permits the same connection to be used for multiple requests. The proposed HTTP 1.1 protocol similarly permits multiple requests on a single connection, while also reducing the overhead of the protocol in many other ways.

Caching

Fetching a document, especially a large one, from a remote server can take some time, especially with a slow Internet connection. To improve the performance as seen by the user, many browsers save temporary copies of Web pages and their components. The repository of copies is called a *cache*. There are several obvious cases where browser caching is effective.

- Images such as a logo or toolbar are used on multiple pages in the same site.
- The user clicks the Back button on the browser, causing a recently seen page to be redisplayed.
- A site is visited repeatedly over time.

In addition to the browser cache, Web contents are often cached in proxy servers. A proxy server typically sits between a group of users on an organizational network and the Internet at large. They are also sometimes used as part of an Internet service provider's network. Used as part of a firewall, proxy servers provide some security advantages. By providing caching, proxy servers can also reduce the network traffic between internal users and the Internet, as well as providing better performance for the users.

---

2. This is the reason why some sites have a single image with an *image map* for a toolbar—it is more efficient than using separate small images for the different buttons.

There are two big problems with caching.

- The cache is missing something you wish it had.

  When the browser makes a request, and the requested page or image is located in the cache (called a *cache hit*), the user gets fast and predictable performance. When the requested item is not in the cache (called a *cache miss*), the user has to wait for the main content server to respond. The net result is unpredictable performance. Statistically speaking, caches tend to improve the average performance of the Web, but increase the variance. This effect can irritate users.

- The cache has something you wish it did not.

  When the browser makes a request, and the item is in the cache, the user gets a response right away, but the real page back on the content server may have changed. The HTTP protocol has some ways to deal with this problem, but they are not always successful.[3] As the network grows, caching is likely to become more common in the quest for good performance. On the other hand, the software must also evolve to do a better job of caching correctly. Web browsers typically have a Reload button that forces a page to be fetched from the primary server, but users have to guess when they need to select it.

Effects of Caching on Commerce Applications

Caching can have bad effects on commerce applications. An outdated page can confuse users, disrupting their use of the commerce application. Here are some examples.

- A catalog page is cached and does not display current prices.

- A catalog application displays different prices to different corporate customers, but due to proxy caching, a user from one company sees prices relevant to another.

- An order form page does not display the correct total, because the user receives a cached copy reflecting an earlier stage of the order.

- The application uses *hidden fields*[4] to store part of the application state. The user resubmits a cached copy of a form containing information inconsistent with the rest of the application.

The solutions to these problems are different. For example, one way to solve the last one is to avoid using hidden fields that store part, but not all, of the state of the application. In other cases, it is important to make sure that the Web server is sending the appropriate HTTP cache directives so that Web pages are cached properly.

---

3. The HEAD command in HTTP can be used to ask a server if a page has changed since a specific time, and various header fields such as PRAGMA NOCACHE can inform proxy servers and other caches when and how long it is safe to cache.

4. HTML forms provide hidden fields as a way to carry information in the form that is posted back to the server, but this information is not displayed to the user. For example, a form might be asking for a customer's payment information, with the order number carried in a hidden field so the application can match up the payment data with the right order when the user submits the form.

Offline Browsers

Like many Web users, we are often frustrated by slow or unpredictable performance of the Web. We often know ahead of time what we want, and it would be easy to say simply, "Computer, turn on overnight and make a copy of Web site such-and-such on my local hard disk." In the morning, we can browse through it quickly, and we can even read the Web pages without being connected to the network. This magic is what *offline browsers* do. An offline browser is a desktop application that can preload content onto the local hard drive in a way that is transparent to normal operations of the Web. They are especially useful for laptop users and for those who visit the same sites over and over again. However, offline browsers do not work well for dynamic or interactive sites. Increasingly, offline capabilities are being integrated with browsers as a basic function.

Some offline browsers require the end user to specify what content they want to automatically retrieve, whereas others allow creators of content to create *packages* to which the user subscribes. Packages turn a *pull model* offline browser into something more like a *push model,* because the content creator defines exactly what is distributed to the users. The user decides when to download the package, however.

A similar set of tools can be used for a different application: replicating a Web site. In order to provide higher effective performance or to enhance reliability, a Web site may actually consist of multiple Web servers with identical content. Replication can be difficult when the site is dynamic, since the underlying applications and databases must be replicated, not just a collection of HTML Web pages. It is also difficult for users to find the "best" replica, since there is no good way to find the least-loaded server or the one that is "nearest" on the network. However, users benefit even from simple replication schemes, since they generally perceive improved performance and reliability.

Push Content

The Web began with users requesting documents from servers. As an alternative, a server might deliver content to the end user proactively, without a direct request. From a technology perspective, a user signs up for a *channel* of content and the relevant information is automatically delivered to the desktop. Like a television or radio channel, a push content channel can contain material meant for real-time viewing, but unlike television or radio, a channel can contain arbitrary information bundles. By way of analogy, imagine that the television station could control your VCR, automatically recording for you the programs you signed up to see. More dramatically, push systems, if implemented for the physical world, could automatically update all the books, magazines, videotapes, and music recordings in your entire house. Push technology can be applied to any kind of content, including multimedia intended for end users and software intended for computers.

If a push system is used to deliver applications and databases to the desktop, or in conjunction with real-time server connections, it can be effective for dynamic and interactive content as well as static information.

Extension Mechanisms

Web browsers typically include built-in support for HTML and many other data types such as images, text, and audio. Most browsers also include various extension mechanisms, so that additional capabilities can be added in the field, either with user intervention or automatically. Some of these mechanisms include the following.

MIME Types

MIME is an acronym for Multimedia Internet Mail Extensions, an Internet standard for multimedia electronic mail. With MIME, each document is tagged with a type to identify what kind of data it is, such as HTML, text, images, and so on. Some common MIME types for the Web are shown in Table 9-1. HTTP has borrowed much of the MIME type mechanism from its original application, although the details are occasionally different. The browser interprets the MIME type to decide how to display the downloaded data. If the MIME type is not handled directly by the browser, most browsers can be configured to launch an independent viewing application. For example, a user may install a video application that can display video clips downloaded from the Web. The installation process configures the browser to start the application when the clip is downloaded. When it is launched, the helper application operates independently of the browser.

MIME Type	Description
text/html	HTML document
image/gif	GIF image
image/jpeg	JPEG image
text/plain	Plain text
application/pdf	Adobe Portable Document Format (PDF)
audio/x-pn-realaudio	RealAudio
video/mpeg	MPEG video
video/quicktime	Apple QuickTime video

TABLE 9-1. **Example MIME Types**

HTTP also allows the browser to inform the server of its capabilities, by listing the MIME types it can handle. This makes it possible for a server to deliver data in different formats, depending on what the browser can handle.

Unfortunately, the extra installation and configuration, as well as the separate operation, mean that this mechanism can be awkward for users. For many applications, it may be more useful to use one of the other extension mechanisms. However, the MIME-type mechanism allows extension applications to be independent of the underlying browser, which can be advantageous as well.

Plug-ins

Some browsers, such as those from Netscape Communications Corporation, have a *plug-in* mechanism, which permits software developers to add new capabilities to the browser using a defined programming interface. One such capability is the ability to display a new type of data using the browser itself rather than starting a separate application. The software containing such add-on capabilities is itself called a plug-in, and must be manually installed by the user before the new data type can be used. Another similar approach is the use of Microsoft's Object Linking and Embedding (OLE) technology, which is used in Microsoft's browser.

Browser plug-ins can modify the behavior of the browser in very complex ways, such as adding new toolbar commands and menu items. They must be implemented to work with a specific version of a specific browser (though a browser vendor may provide good upward compatibility). Consequently, the plug-in mechanism is powerful but inconvenient for many commerce applications, unless they gain widespread use among buyers who can use them for many different sellers.

Scripting

Browsers such as Navigator, Internet Explorer, and others permit executable scripts to be embedded in Web pages. Scripts are written in languages such as JavaScript or VBScript, and they are executed by an interpreter in the browser when the page is displayed. For security reasons, these scripts have limited power, but they can modify the display and increase the interactivity of the Web. A common application, for example, uses a script to check the validity of form entries supplied by a user. This allows errors to be corrected more quickly, without a visit to the server to verify the input.

Applets

Netscape's Navigator, Microsoft's Internet Explorer, and other browsers are able to execute applets written in Java. Java applets are downloaded on demand from a server when a Web page requires them. The applet then executes in the Java virtual machine supplied by the browser, which limits the ways in which the applet can affect the system. We discuss Java and Java applets in more detail later.

Controls

Microsoft's Internet Explorer introduced the notion of ActiveX controls. ActiveX controls are software modules that are automatically downloaded and installed when a Web page containing them is encountered. Unlike Java applets, however, an ActiveX control has free run of the user's computer. ActiveX controls are discussed in more detail later.

These extension mechanisms can all be used to make the Web a more dynamic and interactive environment. Using them, however, may require a fair investment in development and maintenance as browsers evolve over time. In addition, it is still difficult to write extensions that are at once easy for users to obtain and install, while still being portable across different browsers. Understanding your customers, their software, and their willingness to be flexible is important in making decisions about how to take advantage of browser extensions.

Client Software Requirements

This discussion of browser software leads us to one of the trickiest problems in Internet commerce: should the commerce experience be designed to use only the capabilities common to nearly all browsers, or should it take advantage of more advanced features? If advanced features are required, then one can restrict the set of users to those who have the right software, or one can make it possible for users to obtain the necessary software easily. In either case, there is an additional problem when the user population is split among different platforms, such as Windows, Macintosh, and Unix. There are a number of possible approaches.

- The commerce site adapts to the capabilities of a particular user. For example, it may dynamically select between presentation that makes heavy use of images or one that is limited to text. This selection may be automatic if the site can identify the capabilities of the browser, or it may ask the user to choose the style of interaction by clicking an appropriate link.

- The commerce site requires the user to have particular software installed, such as an animation plug-in, commerce module, or particular version of a browser. This solution may be appropriate in a closed user community, where a single organization has substantial influence over the users.

- The commerce site "looks best" when viewed with particular software, such as a particular browser version. It may or may not look good, or even work, with other software. If one or two types of client software have a dominant market share among the targeted user base, this may be an acceptable system.

Note that it is possible to shift among these approaches, both as you gain experience with customers and as the software evolves. At one time, for example, few users had browsers capable of rendering tables in HTML, but now most browsers can do so.

Therefore, a choice that was appropriate at one time may not be appropriate as the available software changes.

Server Components

The original concept of the World Wide Web was very simple. Web servers stored pages coded in HTML in their filesystems. These pages could be retrieved by browsers using HTTP. The URL of a page was simply the hostname of the server plus the filename of the document.[5] Later, it was realized that HTML Web pages could be produced by programs as well as stored as files. In this mode, the URL specifies the hostname of the server, the name of the program to run, and possibly some arguments for that program. In the most general case, a Web server is free to attach any interpretation at all to a URL and to use any mechanism to create and return the page contents to the browser.

The Common Gateway Interface (CGI)

The Common Gateway Interface (CGI) defines a standard interface between a Web server and an independent application program which is responsible for some portion of the URL name space. These applications are sometimes called gateways because one of the first uses of CGI was to create gateways between the Web and a variety of existing applications. CGI has also served as the interface for entirely new applications designed for the Web, but not integrated directly into a Web server.

CGI was originally designed and implemented for Unix platforms, but it has been carried across to most other Web server platforms as well. In CGI, the path portion of the URL identifies the application, which is launched by the Web server as a separate program. The standard input and output streams of the application are wired to the network connection from the browser. The input from the browser (such as a posted form) thus goes to the application, and the output of the application is sent to the browser. The server mediates this connection and ensures that the HTTP protocol is followed. In addition, the server provides some details about the request to the application using environment variables. Examples of some common CGI environment variables are shown in Table 9-2.

Beyond CGI

CGI is very general, because the application is completely decoupled from the Web server. Unfortunately, that generality comes at the cost of performance, since the application must be launched independently for each request. In addition, because the

---

5. Actually, Tim Berners-Lee's original concept of the Web included the ability to create, update, and annotate content from the desktop—capabilities which have only recently become common.

application exits after a request, there is no convenient place to store state between Web requests. These limitations of CGI have led to the development of several other interfaces between Web servers and applications.

All server APIs, CGI included, must solve a number of problems:

- Starting and stopping application
- Passing data from the client to the application
- Passing data from the application to the client
- Status and error reporting
- Passing configuration information to the application
- Passing client and environment information to the application

CGI Variable Name	Meaning	Sample Value
GATEWAY_INTERFACE	Version of CGI in use	CGI/1.1
SCRIPT_NAME	Name of the CGI program being executed	/payment.cgi
PATH	Search path for finding other programs	/sbin:/bin:/usr/sbin:/usr/bin
HTTP_USER_AGENT	Version identifier of browser	Mozilla/4.0
REMOTE_HOST	Name of client machine	mypc.somewhere.org
REQUEST_METHOD	HTTP command	GET
REMOTE_ADDR	IP address of client machine	10.0.25.10
HTTPS	Indicates SSL in use	OFF

TABLE 9-2. **Example CGI Variables and Values**

Server APIs

Netscape, with NSAPI, and Microsoft, with ISAPI, have each defined application programming interfaces which permit application software to be integrated directly with a Web server. Although they differ in detail, both permit application code to be loaded and executed in the same process context as the server itself. This structure yields high performance, but it removes the security of isolating the application process from the server, as well as isolating multiple applications from each other. Server APIs also generally limit the application programmer's choice of programming language and may limit other aspects of the application design.

FastCGI

FastCGI, originally developed by Open Market and now supported by a number of servers (including the popular Apache server), is an attempt to deliver the performance of an integrated server API while preserving the isolation and safety properties of CGI. In addition, FastCGI permits applications to run on separate systems, remote from the Web server. FastCGI works by communicating between the application and the Web server using a lightweight protocol carried over TCP or other stream protocol, such as local interprocess communication. The use of a communications link between the FastCGI application and the Web server permits the application process to be persistent, yet provides a high degree of isolation for reliability and security. A persistent application provides both a convenient way to keep track of the state of a multirequest process and the performance advantage of starting the application process only once.

Server-side Scripting

There is a middle ground between pages of static content kept in the filesystem and pages of dynamic content created by a complete application: server-side scripting. In these schemes, base pages (also called templates) are kept in the filesystem, but these pages contain a mix of HTML and instructions in a scripting language which are executed by an interpreter embedded in the Web server itself.

- Server-side includes

  Server-side includes represent a very simple form of scripting, in which certain tags in a page are replaced by the results of running a program or by certain information, such as a timestamp, already known to the server. Such scripting languages are limited to specifying these program names and their arguments.

- Server-side scripting

  It is possible to embed a language interpreter in the Web server. Web pages stored in the filesystem can contain scripts or programs which are interpreted on the fly. The nonscript portions of the Web pages are combined with the output of the script portions to produce the final page sent to the browser. The embedded languages most commonly used are Java, JavaScript, and VBScript.

  Embedded languages must run in some environment to be useful. Microsoft's version, Active Server Pages (ASP), is an execution environment for server scripts and control. ASP permits the page designer to combine JavaScript and VBScript scripting with ActiveX controls written in any programming language. Netscape's version is LiveWire, which permits server-side JavaScript.

Database-driven Templates

Mechanisms for connecting the Web to database systems are structurally similar to server scripting. The usual approach is to define a template language for the pages, which are stored in the Web server filesystem. Special tags in the templates permit embedded SQL statements to create database queries. Results from the queries are then substituted in the pages delivered to the browser. There are many systems on the market for linking databases to the Web, and they can be an effective part of an Internet commerce system.

Programming Clients

Before the Web, systems intended for geographically distributed users were built either as a mainframe with a terminal network or as a client-server system. In terminal network applications, the application logic lives on the host computer, and the terminals have little capability beyond perhaps local editing and printing. By contrast, client-server systems take advantage of the processing capabilities of the client computers—typically PCs; the application data remains on the host, while much of the application logic moves to the client.

Early Web browsers were much like very fancy terminals with some multimedia capabilities. They had excellent displays, local editing, and complex forms, but no programmability. Web browsers were termed the *universal client,* but at the cost of moving application logic back to the server. Web applications tend to be three tiered, with Web browser clients fronting a tier of application servers, which in turn front database servers.

The current generation of Web browsers goes very much further, offering essentially full programmability to the application designer. As we have seen, clients can be programmed in different ways, including scripting, Java applets, and ActiveX controls.[6]

Scripting

Scripting refers to the practice of embedding small programs in the source form of an interpreted language directly in a Web page. Scripts run when encountered on a page or when specified events happen, such as the user clicking on a button or editing a field of a form. They can be very useful for performing interactive functions such as checking form contents for consistency and validity.

Netscape and Microsoft browsers support scripting in the JavaScript language, which is an object-oriented scripting language developed by Netscape. It resembles Java in some ways, but does not have Java's strong type system.

Scripting languages are very powerful for rapid development of simple applications, but their lack of compile-time checking makes it difficult to adequately test even a moderately sized script. Beyond a relatively modest complexity, it is better to use Java applets or ActiveX controls.

---

6. We limit our discussion here to programming mechanisms that automatically deliver and integrate new functionality to the browser. Browser plug-ins certainly add functionality, but the user must explicitly install them.

Java

Java is an object-oriented programming language developed by Sun Microsystems. It is now being widely adopted for general programming tasks as well as for creating browser applets for the Web. Java includes not only a specification of the language, but also a specification of the *virtual machine* which forms the execution environment for Java programs. Rather than being compiled to the native instruction set for a particular processor (such as a Pentium or SPARC), Java applications are compiled to an instruction set that executes on a well-defined abstract machine. The language and virtual machine together permit a Java program to be completely portable. A Java program compiled to Java byte codes will run the same way on any platform that implements the standard Java virtual machine.

Browsers from Netscape, Microsoft, and others include a Java virtual machine and extensions to HTML which permit Web pages to contain references to Java applets and their parameters. When an applet is encountered, it is automatically downloaded into the browser virtual machine and executed. The virtual machine includes Java class libraries which let the applet draw on the screen, interact with the user, and communicate with the server from which it came. The virtual machine implements a so-called *sandbox,* which prevents the applet from reading the user's hard drive or from taking over control of the user's computer.

The portability of Java applets and the standardization of the virtual machine mean that applet creators do not need to worry about supporting many different versions of the applet for different client computers in use by the users. A single applet will run exactly the same way on all platforms. Java and the Java virtual machine are still evolving rapidly, so the applet author does need to worry about different versions of the Java environment.

Security for Java applets is based on a sandbox model, in which the applet is prevented from doing anything that might be dangerous. Unfortunately, this also prevents the applet from doing many things that are useful. Extensions to Java, such as signed applets in Java 1.1, and the new mechanisms in the Java Electronic Commerce Framework, make Java applets very useful for many commerce applications.

ActiveX

In 1996, Microsoft introduced ActiveX. ActiveX is an evolution of Object Linking and Embedding (OLE), which Microsoft developed earlier to enable diverse applications to work closely together. ActiveX controls are software objects referenced by a Web page, which can be automatically downloaded and installed on a user's PC at the time of first reference. On future references, the control is automatically activated, without having to be downloaded again. Unlike Java applets, ActiveX controls have full access to the resources of the client system.

The security model for ActiveX is based on code signing, rather than on a sandbox. ActiveX controls have full access to the user's computer. In order for users to be willing to install such potentially dangerous pieces of software, each control is digitally signed by its authoring organization (digital signatures are described in Chapter 12). The user then makes a decision to trust the organization that created the control before running it.

ActiveX controls are very powerful, but they contain binary computer code, making them dependent on particular platforms. At this time, ActiveX is restricted to various versions of Microsoft Windows. In addition, the flow of a user's experience at a Web site may be disrupted when an ActiveX control is installed if the user must interrupt the process to answer a question about trusting the creator of the ActiveX control. ActiveX currently has no provision for removing controls once they are installed, so frivolous or seldom-used controls will accumulate and consume the user's system resources.

Sessions and Cookies

The HTTP protocol is designed to be stateless. Each request is intended to be independent of every other request. As the Web has come to be used as the foundation for complex applications (for commerce and other areas), cookies and other technologies have been developed to maintain persistent application state on top of the stateless protocol.

Why Sessions Are Important

As originally conceived, the Web was a very large collection of documents. Browsers would request a document, the user would work with it for a while, and then request another document. In this environment, a stateless protocol makes a lot of sense. With large numbers of browsers and smaller numbers of servers, it makes sense to make the server stateless so that it uses few resources per request.

With the growth of the Web, this design idea has begun to break down.

Complex Pages Require Many Connections

In HTTP, each graphic element on the page requires a separate network connection. This leads to poor performance for the user, since several packet round trips across the network are necessary even for the smallest page elements.

High Overhead

In an intranet environment of static pages, the server does not have to do much work to return a particular page. However, on the open Internet, privacy and authentication requirements lead to a great deal of server work for each connection. Consequently, the connectionless protocol may be counterproductive.

Web Applications

Almost any interesting Web-based application, particularly Internet commerce applications, requires a whole series of actions by the user and the server, working through a number of different Web pages.

State and Sessions

What is really going on in an application that has a series of interactions with the user? At the most basic level, the application has to remember state, and to make changes to the stored state as a result of interactions with the user. The situation is also complicated by the fact that there may be many users, whose interactions with the Web application are interleaved with one another. Sessions are a way to remember which state information is associated with which user.

The way to approach this problem is to consider the possible places to keep application state. The general context is shown in Figure 9-1. A Web browser communicates with an application running on a Web server, and the application has access to a database. State can be kept in the database, in the application, or in the client.

State Kept in Database

In this model, the application itself is stateless, perhaps a CGI application which is restarted on every client request. If the application requires a series of interactions with the user, intermediate application state is stored in the database. On each client request, it is necessary to locate and read the state from the database. This can be done by using Web basic authentication, which supplies a username and password on each request, or it can be done with a cookie or other session mechanism (discussed later).

State Kept in Application

If the application intermediate state is substantial, and the intermediate state does not require transaction safety, it may be kept in allocated storage inside the application. In this case, the application must be persistent (not restarted between client requests), as is possible with FastCGI, ISAPI, and NSAPI. Again, a session mechanism must be used to associate the particular user with a particular block of stored state information.

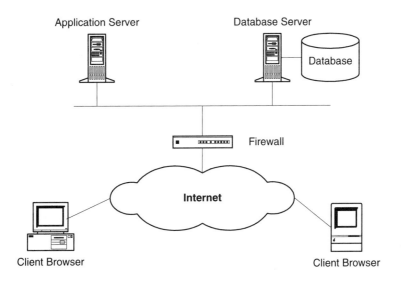

FIGURE 9-1. A Generic Web Application

State Kept in Client

For simple applications, it may be appropriate to keep application state in the client between requests. In this model, when the application server responds to a client request with some intermediate results, it also sends to the client any intermediate application state that will be necessary to resume the application on the user's next request. This requires a mechanism for handing state information back and forth between client and server.

Session and Client State Mechanisms

There are a number of techniques available for identifying sets of user requests as belonging to the same session and for passing state information back and forth between client and server. In addition, it is important to note that the difference between a session mechanism and a state mechanism is subtle. State is the application information itself, whereas a session identifier is a reference to state stored somewhere else.

Authentication Mechanisms

Any authentication mechanism, such as basic authentication or client certificates, can serve as a session mechanism. Because these authentication systems identify the user to the server on each request, state information can be stored at the application or application database and looked up on each request by using the user identification.

Dynamic URLs

By embedding a user ID or other information in every URL used for a sequence of pages, the URLs in use by a particular user will be different from the URLs used by any other user. This creates a session mechanism. The difficulty is that these dynamic URLs can be easily lost if the user clicks out to some other Web site for a while and then reenters the application later. In addition, dynamic URLs can present a security challenge unless they are cryptographically protected from forgery or tampering. Open Market's *Digital Tickets* are one way to create protected dynamic URLs.

Cookies

Most of the current generation of browsers support cookies, an idea originally introduced by Netscape. A cookie is a block of information transmitted from server to browser, and stored there. On subsequent requests to the server, the browser sends back the cookie along with the Web request. Cookies can be used to store session identifiers or to store application state. In addition, cookies can be set to be persistent across browser sessions. The privacy implications of cookies are discussed further in "Privacy versus Merchandising" on page 76. Because cookies are accessible to the savvy browser user, they must be protected from tampering.

Forms

If the Web application consists of a series of HTML forms, application state or session identification can travel along with the form as hidden fields. Hidden fields are a special type of HTML form field that is not displayed to the user, but merely returned as is to the server. Like dynamic URLs and cookies, hidden fields are subject to tampering if not protected.

Applets

As Web applications move from HTML and forms to more client-server style, applets, controls, and client scripting can be used either to store session identifiers or application state.

Object Technology

Object technology has become the subject of intense marketing, as competing companies apply the label to whatever they were doing anyway. Consequently, it is necessary to dig fairly deep to understand exactly what is going on. The essential idea of a software object is a package containing both some *data* and the *methods* which operate on that data. This packaging has several good results.

- Encapsulation—Objects hide the details of their implementation.

  Objects are a step beyond subroutine libraries, or APIs, as they are now called. The programmer who develops software using APIs must understand how data is represented and stored. With object technology, the object is responsible for the data, not the programmer making use of the object to accomplish some higher goal. Encapsulation not only makes it unnecessary for the programmer to learn about the internal details of the object, it makes it impossible. This sounds heavy-handed, but it greatly reduces both immediate problems and latent bugs.

- Polymorphism—There can be multiple implementations of an object.

  Once a particular concept, such as a bank account, has been represented as an object, variations of the concept, such as a checking account or a savings account, can be represented as different implementations of an object, each with the same interface. When this is done, applications which operate on the account, such as the application which computes interest due each month, do not even need to know that there are different kinds of accounts.

- Language Binding—Objects can be implemented in different languages.

  The internal communications between one part of a program and another part are usually orchestrated by the language and its compiler. However, because the object technology carefully defines the ways in which one object can call another, there is no need for all the objects in a system to be coded in the same language. Instead, each language system provides a translation to the standard communications machinery defined by the object system.

At one level, object technology is about better and more efficient ways to construct large software applications; disciplined use of abstraction and encapsulation make software more reliable, whether or not development is done using an object-oriented programming language (OOP) like C++ or Java. At quite another level, object technology provides the possibility that complex systems can be built using software piece parts designed and implemented by different groups or different companies. This idea is called *component software*.

An object model is not sufficient to achieve component software. The object model supplies a base set of assumptions and necessary conditions for interoperability—similar to a standard gauge for railroad tracks. Having the rails the same distance apart is obviously necessary for cars to run on different railroads, but not sufficient. Component software systems also impose additional sets of standard interfaces that compliant objects must obey in order to assure interoperability. Returning to our train example, standard interfaces for car coupling and brakes are also necessary for interoperability.

Beyond component software is the notion of distributed object computing, where the application is composed of software objects located on multiple computers connected by a network. Distributed object computing requires not only an object model and language bindings, but wire protocols, naming, and a security model as well.

- Wire protocols

  When objects communicate over a network, they must agree on the format and order of transmission of information. Network communication is related to the problem of object persistence, in which an object can record its data on disk. In achieving object persistence, the object serializes itself on disk—essentially writing out a copy of its data in a linear format. In object network communications, the source object creates a serialized message in a standardized format so that the recipient object, potentially running on a computer of a completely different architecture, can successfully receive and interpret the message.

- Naming

  In any distributed system, the software components of an application must establish communications with each other. Since on the network any pair of computers can potentially communicate, objects use a naming and addressing system to look up each other's network addresses and establish the proper communications channels. This problem also arises in the nondistributed world of component software; but in traditional applications, the binding of all the objects together is done by the programming environment at build time, rather than dynamically at runtime.

- Security

  In a distributed system that must operate over open networks like the Internet, security is a major issue. Software components must assure they are communicating with the correct objects (authentication) and that their communications are private (via encryption) and trustworthy (via integrity checking). In Internet commerce, a third aspect of security becomes essential, that of trust. In many situations, not all the software objects making up an application are running on computers controlled and operated by a single organization. The system designer must determine precisely what degree of trust to place in computations done by computers run by customers or by different organizations.

CORBA

The Object Management Group's Common Object Request Broker Architecture, or CORBA, is the result of a 15-year effort by a consortium of companies to define a reference model for objects, as well as encouraging companies to produce interoperable implementations for multiple languages and platforms.

CORBA is based on the idea of an Object Request Broker (ORB), which is the basic mechanism through which objects make requests to and receive responses from other objects. The ORB provides naming and communications services. CORBA objects are described by an Interface Definition Language (IDL) that formally defines their interfaces. IDL is a language for defining objects. It solves the language binding problem through language-specific translators which take an IDL description of an object and translate it into a specific set of language bindings.

CORBA also supplies object services, common facilities, and a number of domain interfaces that define common objects for particular application domains such as finance and health care.

CORBA works over the Internet through the Internet Inter-ORB Protocol (IIOP), which defines the way CORBA objects communicate over a TCP/IP network.

COM

Microsoft's Component Object Model, or COM, is the most widely used object system, as it is an essential part of Microsoft's desktop operating systems and applications. Beyond the basic object model which defines communications standards, Microsoft provides a number of other levels of functionality under the blanket name OLE.

- OLE automation

  OLE automation defines a set of standard interfaces which, if implemented, make a COM object scriptable, so that it can be used from a scripting language like Visual Basic. The ability to link potentially complex objects by using veneers of script can enable rapid application development. Scripting languages may have high overhead, but because the bulk of runtime is spent in compiled objects, an application built this way may not suffer from poor performance.

- ActiveX

  Also known as OLE controls, ActiveX objects are COM objects which implement additional sets of standard interfaces which make them usable as component software. One of the most interesting aspects of ActiveX is a definition of both design time and runtime behavior. ActiveX controls can be configured at design time through one set of interfaces in an integrated programming environment such as Visual C++, and then operate at runtime through another set of interfaces. This distinction between design time and runtime helps to make well-designed ActiveX controls useful as component software.

- Distributed COM, or DCOM

  DCOM uses a version of DCE RPC (Distributed Computing Environment Remote Procedure Call) for its wire protocol, permitting COM objects located on different computers to communicate.

Java Beans/RMI

Java is the newest member of the object community. Java is an object-oriented programming language, and Remote Method Invocation, or RMI, is the standard way for a Java object to communicate with another across a network. As an object-oriented language, Java has an object model built in. The other key feature of Java is *write once, run anywhere*. Java applications are built to run under the control of the Java virtual machine, a kind of abstract computer. Platforms which support Java (almost all platforms, these days) implement the virtual machine, and then any Java program can run.

Java Beans are the Java version of component software. Beans implement a set of standard interfaces and behaviors which, similar to ActiveX, permit bean behavior to be customized at design time. Java Beans can also use a set of bridges, which permit beans to interoperate with RMI-based objects, ActiveX controls, or CORBA objects.

Implications of Object Technology for Internet Commerce

Object technology has a number of implications for the design of systems for Internet commerce.

- Rapid application development

  Object technology generally permits more rapid application development than earlier methods of programming. Obviously, this advantage is not at all unique to Internet commerce.

- Distributed applications

  Object technology permits applications to be distributed across multiple computers without the development staff necessarily having to be experts in all aspects of network communications and security.

- Flexibility of deployment

  Object technology, particularly the availability in the Web context of download-able applets and controls, gives great flexibility to the designers of the Internet commerce application in designing multitier applications, placing functionality at the servers, or migrating functionality all the way to the client desktop. Automatically moving part of the application to the desktop can provide great advantages of interactivity and interoperability, but also introduces some complex security and trust problems, since the desktop computer may not be a trustworthy computing platform.

In practice, object technology will likely have a role in almost all Internet commerce projects.

Commerce Client Technology

The machinery of browser programmability has been applied in various ways to Internet commerce. As discussed in the previous section on object technology, commerce functionality can be distributed to the desktop, with advantages in privacy, convenience, and interactivity, but also potential disadvantages in security, universality, and reliability.

Advantages of Clients for Commerce

- Privacy

  Information such as the user's profile, preferences, and purchase history can potentially be stored on the desktop, rather than becoming part of a central database. If the proper care to protect these sorts of information is taken, client storage can enhance personal privacy.

- Convenience

  Commonly used information such as billing and shipping addresses can be stored by desktop software and automatically supplied to merchant servers. This can relieve the user from the burden of repetitively entering the same information at site after site, and can also help ensure the information is accurate when used. Of course for these benefits to be realized, the information storage and supply mechanisms must be standardized.

- Interactivity

  Perhaps the key benefit of moving functionality to the desktop is interactivity. Because the software is running directly on the user's computer, a very high-bandwidth, low-latency channel is available between the user and the application. This permits highly interactive metaphors such as drag-and-drop to be used which would be impossible for a purely server-based implementation.

Disadvantages of Clients for Commerce

- Security

  The security technology for Java and ActiveX applets is designed primarily to protect the desktop computer and its user from hostile software. Neither Java nor ActiveX does much to protect a distributed application from a hostile user or untrustworthy client computer. Any use of client software for Internet commerce must be carefully evaluated to make sure that errors, accidental or malicious, in the operation of the client software cannot damage the integrity of the application.

- Universality

  Until client technologies such as Java are universally available, requiring client capabilities can merely reduce the audience for a commerce application. If the user does not have the equipment or environment for the client software, that user cannot use the application. More subtly, if the user must take special action such as installing a plug-in or control, the barrier is set higher for use of the server application.

- Reliability

  Many of the potential benefits for client software require that persistent state must be maintained on the client computer. This can cause problems in usability and reliability. If the user habitually uses several computers—an office desktop and a laptop, for example—the stored state on the two computers may be incomplete and incompatible. If the user's computer crashes, which is not unusual, stored state may be lost. It may not be adequate to depend on the user for backup of application-critical information.

Client Functionality

In designing a commerce system, it is appropriate to consider each element of functionality for potential deployment to the desktop. We discuss some possibilities here.

- Receipt and coupon storage

  The desktop is a natural place to store Internet commerce purchase receipts and coupons. If these items are not stored and indexed on the desktop, then the user has the problem of remembering all the various commerce locations he has visited.

- Payment credentials and applications

  Some Internet payment protocols, such as SET, require client software to function. Others, such as entering a credit card number into a secure HTML form, can benefit from desktop software that could, for example, automatically enter one's information into the form.

- Shopping cart

  Shopping cart functionality may be placed at the transaction engine, for cross-store purchasing; at the catalog server, for complex pricing; and at the user desktop, for maximum interactivity. With client software, drag-and-drop item selection can be implemented, as well as highly interactive pricing calculations and order modification.

- User profile

  User profile information, from the prosaic, such as shipping address, to the sublime, such as preferences in colors and styles, is a natural candidate for client storage. By keeping such information at the client, it can be used across multiple Internet sites and potentially kept more private.

Commerce Client Examples

There are a number of current examples of the use of client software for Internet commerce.

- Wallets

  CyberCash, IBM, JavaSoft, Verifone, and others have built *electronic wallets*. These applications store user payment credentials for SET and similar protocols, and may also play a role in receipt storage.

- Shopping application

  Peapod, among others, has built specialized commerce applications for the desktop. Peapod software is specialized for the needs of grocery shopping. As such, it is highly interactive and has excellent support for repeat and recurring orders.

- Applets

  A number of sites use Java or ActiveX applets to display the contents of the user's shopping basket. These display applications typically also make use of browser frames to provide a separate windowpane for the shopping cart, distinct from the frame used for catalog information.

Technology for Fulfillment of Digital Goods

As discussed in Chapter 4, fulfillment for digital goods is accomplished online. In information commerce, the content itself is the product.

Securing Delivery

When the content is the product, the commerce system must provide the link between the sale and fulfillment. Once payment is made, fulfillment must be automatic. There are several mechanisms available.

- License key

  In the case of software purchased and fulfilled over the network, the software package may be freely downloadable, but not operable without a specific license key. Rather than purchase the download, the customer in effect purchases a license key. The key is usually tied both to the software and to a particular computer, so that the same key will not work for more than one copy of the software. This technique is also applied to purchasing specific rights for information databases located on a CD-ROM or on a network server as well as for secure containers (discussed later).

- Access control database

  Once payment is taken for a particular content package, the commerce system can make an entry in the access control database for the content server. Thereafter, the end user logs in to the content server using traditional Web access control mechanisms, such as name and password, via basic authentication. This scheme has a number of problems, notably that the user's credentials are kept in lots of different places, so that it is difficult for him to remember which password is used where or to update all the servers when a new password is chosen. It may also be awkward for the system operators to maintain all the access control databases when multiple content servers are involved.

- Digital receipt

  Once the payment transaction for digital goods is complete, the commerce system can create and sign a *digital receipt*, stating that payment has been received and that delivery is authorized. This approach is taken by Open Market's products. An Open Market *digital receipt* is a URL which points to the electronic fulfillment area, and which contains a *ticket*. The ticket is analogous to a movie theatre ticket. If you have one you get in; otherwise you don't. The digital ticket contains information on the access rights given, the term of those rights, and a reference to the transaction which created it, for audit purposes. In this system, a central transaction engine can provide commerce services for distributed digital goods fulfillment servers. Because the receipt is a URL, it is automatically managed by Web browsers, and can be bookmarked and saved by the user.

- Public key attribute certificate

  Many Web browsers offer the ability to use X.509 version 3 public key certificates for security purposes. These certificates primarily offer authentication, but can also be used for access control. Version 3 of the X.509 specification allows for an extensible set of attributes to be attached to the certificate, which can be used to specify access rights for digital goods fulfillment. In this model, when digital goods are purchased, the commerce system can prompt the user to create a new public key, and then turn that key into a certificate by signing it (acting as a certificate authority) and attaching attributes describing the necessary access rights for digital fulfillment. This approach can work, but it is awkward because of the complexity of creating, installing, and using a certificate. This topic is discussed more fully in Chapter 12.

Failure Recovery

Customers tend to object when they pay for things and then don't get delivery. From the buyer's perspective, this is a usability issue: delivery should be reliable or at least easy to retry. If it isn't, the customer will go elsewhere. From the seller's perspective, the reliability of fulfillment is a cost and customer satisfaction issue. If delivery is unreliable, he may lose customers. If the mechanism for retry or failure recovery is too expensive, then it becomes a cost of customer service problem.

These are the approaches to failure recovery.

- Too cheap to complain

  If payment for digital goods is on a per-page basis, using microtransactions, then it may be acceptable to simply charge for all pages, successfully viewed or not.

- Time-based charging

  If payment for digital goods is based on the time spent connected to the service, and if unsuccessful downloads are infrequent or resolved quickly, then it may be acceptable to charge for all time used, productive or not.

- Separate bulk transfer from the transaction

  By permitting free download of bulk data in encrypted or inactive form, and then charging for an unlocking key or license key, the reliability of fulfillment can be improved. Because the downloading of the bulk data is not protected, the consumer can retry as needed. The download of the particular license key needs to be reliable, but at least it is small and fast.

- Permit retry based on transaction records

  If the transaction records are persistent, the commerce software can automatically redeliver after a failed download attempt. The buyer will have to authenticate himself to the satisfaction of the commerce system as in fact being the original purchaser. Open Market's software, for example, provides persistent proof of purchase in the form of online statements and digital receipts.

- Grant access, not a download attempt

  Upon payment, the commerce system can make an access control entry stating "This customer has access to the download area for the next hour," on the basis that an hour is enough time for several download attempts, even if the first is unsuccessful. Subscriptions work this way, as does Open Market's concept of digital receipts.

Auditability

Related to the concept of failure recovery is the concept of auditability. Generally, a commerce system is auditable if the system stores enough records that a reasonable person would agree that a particular transaction happened as claimed. These sorts of records are valuable for multiple purposes.

- Dispute resolution

  When a customer dispute arises, it is frequently in the form that a particular service or product was not delivered, or that the price charged was incorrect. If the commerce system provides adequate records, there will be a complete audit trail of all essential features of the transaction: date and time, means of authenticating the customer, price, description, and evidence that indeed the product was delivered or service rendered. This information can refresh the customer's memory or assist a customer service representative in resolving the dispute.

- Failure recovery

  One interesting case arises when the audit trail provides an indication that service was not rendered to the buyer. In this case, for digital goods, the goods or services can be redelivered. The system may err in this direction since the marginal cost of delivery is near zero.

- Audit

  Audit has precise technical meaning, but in this context, we refer to a more general sense of checks and balances that help assure that all customers have paid, that all payments are matched by buyers, and that goods and services have been successfully delivered.

Rights Management

Rights management refers to the problems associated with intellectual property rights, and in particular to the problem of assuring that, in a commerce setting, payment is made for a particular use of content, and that the use made does not exceed the use authorized. For example, the content owner may wish to charge one price for searching a database and viewing the results on a screen, and a higher price for printing the search results.

In discussing rights management, it is very useful to draw a distinction between facilitating compliance and rights enforcement. In a business-to-business context, the buyer may have no particular incentive to steal content, particularly if the charges would be passed on to the buyer's client. Instead, what is needed is an easy way to pay. Facilitating compliance has many design issues, but on the whole the problem is much easier than operating in a potentially very hostile business-to-consumer environment where software designed to let users steal commercial content may be widely available.

Generically, rights management requires some means for specifying what rights are desired and what rights are granted, plus a means for paying for those rights (in the case of facilitating compliance) and a means for securing the content against unauthorized use (in the case of rights enforcement).

Secure Container Technology

The generic name for rights enforcement technology is *secure container technology.* The general idea is that the content is carried around the network in encrypted form, and unlocked only at the point of use. In addition to the concept of unlocking information only at point of use, secure container technologies can also control some aspects of the computing environment, so that the Print button, for example, might be disabled if the document does not convey the right to print. It is always possible for the end user to manually transcribe information received off the screen and to rekey it, but secure containers can make it difficult or uneconomic to misuse protected content.

Examples of secure container technology are IBM's Cryptolopes and InterTrust's DigiBoxes. These technologies can also offer *superdistribution* which can implement an entire distribution chain from author to publisher to distributor to end user, with economic and security models maintained at every point.

Copyrights

One important aspect of digital goods is the management of intellectual property rights. Information is fundamentally different from physical artifacts in that exact copies can be made. If Susan gives a copy of an electronic document to Mary, they both have it. This fact has always been true of information, but the advent of first the copy machine and then electronic documents has greatly lowered the cost of copying. Improper use and redistribution of copyrighted materials is a sufficient problem that content owners are reluctant to make their information available on networks unless adequate controls to prevent or discourage misuse are in place.

Fingerprinting and Watermarks

As discussed previously, it is useful to distinguish between facilitating compliance and rights enforcement. At some level, these are opposing terms: facilitating compliance is about making it easy to pay; rights enforcement is about making it difficult to copy. There is also a middle ground—making improper use traceable. For example, suppose a protected document is improperly copied and republished on the Internet. If it were possible to identify the original purchaser of that copy, it would serve to discourage improper use. It turns out that this kind of tracing is possible, through digital techniques called fingerprinting or watermarking. In these schemes, each copy of a document is made subtly different, in a way that is not obvious, and which encodes a serial number or other tracing information.

Here are some fingerprinting methods.

- For images, a trivial amount of *noise* can be added to the encoding of the image. This noise can have no effect on the appearance of the image, but a decoding computer that knows what to look for can recover the added noise and decode it to a serial number.

- For text, slight variations in the spacing of the words or the line breaks can encode a serial number.

The technical name for hiding a message in another message in a way that the existence of the hidden message is also hidden is *steganography*. Watermarks do not have to be hidden, but if they are not, a technically astute attacker might be able to remove the watermark. It is usually a good idea also to place an explicit copyright notice in a protected document. The notice, together with the real prospect of improper use being discovered and traced, helps to set the social context of copyrighted information in electronic form.

Summary

Unlike many systems based on information technology, systems for Internet commerce depend on client software and server software which may be supplied by different vendors, operated by different organizations, and yet which must interoperate across an open network. This chapter has focused on basic client and server technologies, digital goods fulfillment, and a brief survey of object technologies. These components provide the basic wiring and Internet infrastructure for commerce systems. The next several chapters discuss the architecture of Internet commerce systems and the various supporting technologies such as cryptography, security, and transaction processing.

CHAPTER 10

System Design

The contact with manners then is education…history is philosophy
learned from examples.
—Dionysius of Halicarnassus[1]

The Problem of Design

The following chapters will examine many of the key technology areas for developing systems for Internet commerce. A logical question, of course, is "How do they go together?" In this chapter, we consider the problem of design: given a set of components, how do we put them together to create the most effective solution? Although we are saving details of the components for later, the discussion in this chapter is intended to frame an understanding of the role each component plays in the overall system.

From a software engineering point of view, many design methodologies have been put forward. Such techniques as object-oriented design, rapid prototyping, formal methods, and so on can all be used in the design of Internet commerce systems. We do not advocate here any particular method or set of such methods. The methods appropriate for your team depend on your own views and experience, the views and experience of the team, the tools available to you, and many other factors.

In this chapter, we look at some of the main design issues that have arisen in our own experience with Internet commerce systems. For the most part, these issues are not

---

1. Dionysius of Halicarnassus, *Ars Rhetorica*, XI.

unique to Internet commerce, but they do tend to be very important in such systems. We begin first with some principles of design—those ideas that are mostly independent of particular choices of technology and that apply to a wide range of systems.

Our Philosophy of Design

The design of a computer system, like any engineering design, is really part art and part science. The science is very important: for computer systems, it tells us what kinds of problems can be handled successfully by computers, how to evaluate, measure, and select algorithms for a particular problem, and provides some guidance in proper development of computer programs. Designing a complex system, however, requires a certain degree of insight, experience, and even good taste combined with the science.

Understand the Customer's Requirements

There is no substitute for a good understanding of the target customers and what they want. In many cases, they cannot say explicitly what they want, so it is necessary to ferret it out in other ways. Is convenience important? What about access to good information? What inconveniences might they tolerate in exchange for certain services? How much are they willing to pay? The result of such understanding may be a product or service that never occurred to the customer, but once they see it, they know that it is what they want. A particular challenge in Internet commerce is that there are many new and unforeseen opportunities. It's impossible to predict with certainty what buyers will prefer, so flexibility becomes very important as well.

Plan for Evolution

If a computer system of any kind is going to be around for a long time, we should plan for it to incorporate technology changes and evolve over time. The performance of computer hardware, such as processor speed or memory density, tends to double approximately every two years, for approximately the same cost. Network performance, measured in bandwidth, is also increasing. By planning for this evolution, we can take advantage of these changes to provide superior service and performance over a long period of time. In addition, software is changing rapidly. Only a few years ago, for example, almost no one had heard of the World Wide Web. Although we may not foresee every technology change that may arrive, we can imagine that some kinds of changes are at least possible, and plan appropriately so that the system can evolve in many different directions.

Start Small

It is often tempting to build a large, comprehensive system to solve all the known problems. Such attempts frequently take a long time to design and build, and they often end up being canceled before they can deliver anything at all. Getting started with a small system provides an opportunity to learn from those first explorations and adapt the evolution of the system appropriately. This approach is particularly important in the rapidly changing world of the Internet, because a large and complex system is likely to be obsolete by the time it is deployed. Incremental development, by contrast, allows a system to take advantage of technology changes as well as improved understanding of the customers and the business.

Keep Options Open

The design process is largely about making choices. We often find, however, that some choices limit our future options more than others. For example, we might design our system around a particular payment method, such as credit cards. Although credit cards may be quite sufficient today, they may not be sufficient in the future. We may not be able to predict what else we may need, but we could also design the system to handle payment methods in a generic fashion, with a particular module that implements credit card payment. In that way, we have the option to add other payment systems later. If done early enough in the life of the system, the added flexibility frequently has little additional cost. In making design choices, then, when all other things are (nearly) equal, it may be wise to choose the path that allows the most flexibility in the future.

Develop an Architecture

As we saw in Chapter 6, the architecture of a system contributes a great deal to its long-term development and evolution. Early attention to creating the architecture, with particular focus on design issues such as the ones we discuss here, paves the way for a system that can grow and develop over a longer period of time. A system architecture is a framework for solving individual design problems. There is obvious benefit from such a framework at the time of initial design, but an architecture is even more powerful later, as a framework for solving problems that were not envisioned at the time the original system was built.

An Architectural Approach

In the following sections, we discuss some of the most important issues in system design. These issues cut across many phases of developing an Internet commerce system (and, of course, they are relevant to many other kinds of computer systems as well). By this we mean that each issue must be considered as part of the overall architecture, the detailed system design, the implementation, and the operation of the system. For example, an architectural decision to build on a distributed system has implications for how the system scales compared to a centralized system. But a perfect architecture for scaling may not mean much in practice if the detailed system design does not provide for the necessary facilities, or if the implementation omits them.

The fundamental design issues we consider here are:

- Performance and scaling
- Reliability
- Transactions
- Managing state
- Security

Each of these, we believe, is fundamental in the sense that it is both important in an Internet commerce system and cuts across the different phases of development, as we have discussed.

Performance and Scaling

Simply put, scaling is the question of how big a system can grow in various dimensions to provide more service.[2] There are many different ways we can measure the scale of a system, such as the total number of users, the number of simultaneous users, the transaction volume, and so on. These dimensions are not independent, and scaling up the size of the system in one dimension typically affects other dimensions as well. The side effects may help other areas or hurt them, depending on the changes made. For example, increasing the CPU performance on a system often helps several areas. In contrast, increasing the size of a database to handle more users may sometimes decrease the performance.

Therefore it is important to evaluate possible changes to the system to improve the scaling or performance in the context of the entire system, not just for one component. Having a clear set of priorities for the system (such as "the most important thing is to serve millions of users") makes it easier to make trade-offs when needed, as well as to justify investment in new hardware or software changes to make the desired improvements.

---

2. Anecdotal evidence (and our experience) suggests that something unexpected becomes a serious problem every time a system increases its size (in some dimension) by a factor of 10. This tells us that system designers, in general, have some difficulty looking beyond order-of-magnitude changes. We can compensate for this either by trying harder (since we know about this problem) or by planning to deal with something unexpected at the points where the system has grown that much. This also means that a particular design problem can only be addressed when the order of magnitude of the problem is known and planned for.

It is often the case that the system architecture enables or limits certain kinds of changes for scaling. For example, a system designed to operate all of its components (catalog server, payment system, user account management, and so on) on a single computer means that the primary means of scaling up the system is to buy a larger computer. Such a system is therefore ultimately limited by the size of the available computers. In some cases, the natural technology evolution of computers (faster CPUs, bigger memory systems, bigger disks) will allow the system to scale with the required level of service, but often it will not (especially since the basic software—operating system, database, and application—often consumes a considerable part of the additional resources). Distributed applications, in contrast, may often be less efficient for small-scale systems, but they may scale up much better as demand grows.

One additional (and often overlooked) point about scaling up Internet services is how fast the scaling can be done. Internet services often become popular very quickly (the *flash crowd* effect mentioned in Chapter 7), so it may be important to add capacity to the system rapidly in order to keep up with the demand. If, for example, a system can be scaled up by adding additional servers as needed, the increased capacity may often be added without disrupting operation of the existing service.

For many systems, poor performance is often an inconvenience, a source of complaints, perhaps, but the users keep using the system. In Internet commerce systems, performance problems are often much more than an inconvenience—they can be a disaster for a business, putting off customers and giving competitors an advantage.

The performance of a system can be measured in many ways, so it is important to decide what measurements are important and relevant. Two common kinds of metrics examine *latency* and *throughput*. Latency is a measure of how long it takes to complete a given operation. For example, how long does it take to download a Web page? Throughput is a measure of how many operations can be completed in a given time: how many Web pages can the server deliver in an hour? These two measures may seem almost the same, but they actually tell you very different things. Latency tells you about the experience of a particular individual user (on average), whereas throughput tells you how many users the system can handle. Also, the two measures may interact with each other: as throughput increases, for example, the latency as seen by any given user may increase. This is like driving on a highway in heavy traffic: the number of cars moving down the highway is greater (throughput), but the average speed is lower (yielding higher latency).

To get a good characterization of a system's performance, you should decide what you want to measure in advance, then measure it and work to improve it. Although your ideas of what is important to measure may change over time, this is the only way to really improve the system. All too often, the performance metrics for a system are chosen to make it look good, without regard to getting an accurate idea of how the system performs for its users.

Reliability

Many business computer systems require a high degree of reliability, and this is particularly true of Internet commerce systems. The special challenge of Internet commerce is the risk of being embarrassed in public. When the system is not working, neither is the business. In other situations, people can work around the computer's failures. The front-line operators for a mail-order business, for example, can write orders on paper if needed, but at least the phones are being answered. On the Internet, if the server is down, one may not even be able to tell easily if the company is still in business!

Reliable systems are often built by using redundant components, so that when one fails, another is available to take over. In many network protocols, such as TCP, the sender of a message on the network expects an acknowledgment and will retransmit the message until it receives one (or until it gives up after trying too many times). Such attempts to recover from difficulties may also mask failures. But if those failures are not reported to the operators, the system may not be repaired—until the last redundant component fails. At that point, all the redundant design is for naught. Keep an eye on the system to make sure that broken components are fixed soon after they break.

Transactions

The term *atomicity* comes from the world of transaction processing. In many applications, it is important that a transaction be atomic. That is, it must not happen that one part of a transaction completed and another part did not. For example, when money is transferred from one bank account to another, we can think of this transaction as consisting of two parts: debiting the amount from one account and crediting it to the other. It seems clear that we either want both parts to happen (in which case the transaction has succeeded) or both parts not to happen (in which case the transaction fails). If only part of the transaction completes, such as the debit operation, the result is both incorrect and confusing. This kind of failure can also result directly in unhappy customers (and errors that may be hard to correct), so it is well worth the effort to avoid it. Here we introduce a few key concepts about transactions, before diving into more details about transaction processing in Chapter 16.

Transactions for Internet commerce often have this requirement: they must be atomic. In addition, they must satisfy three other requirements: consistency, isolation, and durability. Consistency means that all parties have the same view of the outcome of the transaction. Isolation means that independent activities don't interfere with one another, and durability means that the outcome of a transaction cannot be undone by a hardware failure.

In a distributed system, such as a client-server system for Internet commerce, there may be several messages exchanged between the two parties to complete an operation. If so, the system should be resilient against failures in the network that may lose, duplicate, or even reorder the messages. We can think of a transaction as beginning with the first message and ending with the last one, so that the complete transaction should be atomic. If the network fails in the middle of the transaction, the state of the system should be consistent. Ideally, it is also clear to both sides whether or not the transaction succeeded, but when it is not, it is usually straightforward for the two sides to sort it out.

It is easy to see how this property of atomicity should apply to a payment transaction—the transfer of money should clearly be atomic, as in the previous example of bank accounts. Atomicity is also important in other parts of a complete purchase transaction. For example, payment is just one part of the purchase transaction; we must also include recording the purchase as being complete as part of the transaction. If the money has moved but the merchant loses track of what was purchased, the goods may never be delivered.

The general problem of recovering from various kinds of failure is related to atomicity. Indeed, we can look at implementing certain transactions as atomic to be a way of avoiding or recovering from certain kinds of failure. The most common kind of failures for an Internet commerce system are network failures and system crashes. Let's look at the problems caused by each of these.

In a network failure, there is some problem in communication between two systems, though both of them are functioning correctly otherwise. If some care is not taken in designing the application, the consequences of a network failure may be rather confusing. For example, a client may not get service that it has requested, or a server may have delivered a response that never reached the client. More specifically, suppose that a customer has purchased a software package for download. If the downloading is interrupted by a network failure, how can the client complete the download?

Different systems may have different ways to deal with this problem, but it is an important one to address. One way, for example, for a system to recover is that the server has an account for each customer that contains a listing of all completed transactions. After customers experience a network failure, they can identify themselves to the server, examine the listing of transactions, and resume a failed delivery. Another approach might be to issue the equivalent of a store receipt, which can be used to resume downloading the software after a failure.

System crashes, on the other hand, must be handled somewhat differently. The crucial issue in preparing for a crash is ensuring that important information is *durable,* and recorded on stable storage at the proper times.[3] By *stable storage,* we mean a storage medium, such as a disk, that will hold the information across crashes and power

---

3. Of course, another approach is to ensure that systems never crash. This approach usually requires special hardware and software, as well as careful attention to seemingly mundane issues like redundant sources of power.

failures. For example, the system should record that a purchase has been completed before informing the client of this fact. This ensures that if the server crashes before completing delivery, at least the server is certain about what happened, and the client does not think that the operation completed when, in fact, it did not.

How a system recovers from failures is not just an abstruse technical issue. It can have real consequences for the way that customers perceive the system and on the kinds of problems that must be solved with customer service. When evaluating a product for use in a commerce system, understanding how a system deals with these problems can often provide useful insight into how carefully the system designers worked through the difficult issues in creating an application.

Managing State

In any distributed system, a key question is where different pieces of information—the *state* of the system—are stored. One way to think about this is that the underlying information is stored in a database, whether it be a "real" database system or a collection of files that represent the information stored by an application. When we talk about managing the state of the system, we are really talking about the variables in the process of being modified. For example, there may be several steps in making a particular transaction, and the system must keep track of the progress of each step and its results. Eventually, those changes are committed to the database as updated information, or they are discarded.

With a client-server system such as the Web, the choice is essentially about which of these two stores particular information. In a three-tier Web application, there are three possible places: the client, the application logic, and the third-tier database. Some of the choices are clear: information private to the client or that may be relevant for several different services may be stored at the client. The server is a good place to keep information that is not specific to a particular client or user. In between, there is a range of information about the state of completed transactions, user account information, and transactions in progress that must be stored somewhere. Such information is often kept at the application server in a three-tier system, but it may be split between client and server if only the two systems are involved.

Because early Web browsers provided few, if any, methods for keeping track of user-specific state, commerce systems have typically managed all of the state information themselves. Some applications, notably payment systems, have attempted to manage more of the state on the client side. Each of these approaches has its advantages. Here are some of the advantages for the server.

- No special client software is required.

- Customers can use the system from wherever they happen to be, whether it be home, office, a kiosk, or someone else's computer. They are not tied to the computer with the right software and configuration.

- The server can control the security of the information, based on business and application security requirements.

- The set of information recorded can be extended without requiring updated software to be distributed to clients.

- Customers are not faced with a multiplicity of additional applications that they need to do business online.

- The server may have an aggregation of information that can be used for applications such as special marketing programs.

Storing information on the client side has some strong advantages for customers. The primary one is that important information about payment credentials, transactions in progress, and perhaps a transaction history are kept private on the customer's system. A client application may also store such items as receipts for on-line purchases. Of course, some of that information will be tracked by merchants for accounting and marketing purposes no matter where the official copy used by the customer may be.

For many applications, the costs of developing a client component have been prohibitive. As we discuss in Chapter 9, this may be changing as the tools for developing client applications using technologies such as Java and ActiveX become more common. The real value of a client-side application comes where that application provides some unique functions not possible with a pure server implementation, or when the client application (with some real utility) can be used across many different servers. How best to use client components is still a matter for the system designer to weigh carefully.

Security

Security is often cited as the biggest concern about the technology of Internet commerce. A common question is "Is the Internet safe for commerce?" In a sense, this is the wrong question; a better one might be "Can the Internet be safe enough for my business?" Just as we use different locks for houses than for bank vaults, there are many different technical components used for security in Internet commerce, and they depend on such questions as the risks, costs, and the value of the information involved.

We can break down the issues of security into four main areas.

- System security

  How secure is the operating system of a computer? Can unauthorized users log in to it? Can information be protected from different users on the system, or can any user on the system read (and modify) any information on the system? Is the system physically secure? Who can get into the room? These are basic questions about the system underneath an application, and they are extremely important, because it is impossible to build a secure application on an insecure foundation.

- Communications security

  It is often important to protect the contents of a message from eavesdroppers or others who might otherwise see the message. A common example for commerce applications is protecting a customer's payment credentials, such as a credit card number, when the customer sends it to a merchant's server. In such cases, we typically use some kind of encryption mechanism to keep the messages private.

- Data security

  After data has been communicated securely, we must worry about how it is protected on the end systems. In some cases, it is processed immediately and discarded, so no additional protection is needed. In other cases, we rely on the protection mechanisms of the operating system to safeguard the data. For particularly sensitive data, such as a customer's credit card number, we may choose to encrypt that data when it is stored on a disk.

- Authentication and authorization

  Authentication is the means of answering the question "Who are you?" in a reliable manner. Passwords are a common method for authenticating users to computer systems (and you probably have several), although there are others. Authorization is the means of answering the question "What are you allowed to do?" For example, a system may contain a list of people allowed to perform a particular task. In a commerce system, authorization often consists of having proof that you paid for something.

These aspects of security are important for any Internet commerce system, and they should be included as part of any system design or product evaluation.

Building on these core ideas, there are three main principles of security to keep in mind when designing or evaluating a system.

1. **The security requirements are determined by an understanding of the business requirements and the associated risks.** We would create different security systems for applications that handle million-dollar transactions and those that handle ten-dollar transactions. We would never assert that a system is absolutely secure. Rather, we look at whether or not it has an appropriate set of security technologies in place for the perceived risks and threats.

2. **Securing a system means securing the whole system, not just individual components.** It is easy to put together a number of components that have their own security properties, but the resulting system is not necessarily secure. Different components may interact badly with each other, or there may be gaps between different components that can be exploited by an attacker. Designing a secure system requires attention to the complete system.

3. **The operation of a secure system is the most important element in keeping it secure.** If we don't lock the front door of the house, it doesn't matter whether the door has a lock or not. Similarly, the continuing operation of a secure system must include detailed attention to whether or not the users and operators of the system are using it as intended. In particular, users may sometimes subvert the security of the system (intentionally or not) in order to make it more convenient or easier for them to use. It is therefore especially important for the system operators to be vigilant about how the system is used, so they can detect misuse as well as attempts to break the system.

Understanding these principles goes a long way to helping ensure that a secure commerce system can be designed, implemented, and operated. In Chapter 12, we discuss in some depth the subject of cryptography, used to create many components of a secure system. Building on the use of cryptography, we examine detailed issues of security technology for Internet commerce in Chapter 13.

Design Principles versus "Technology of the Day"

One of the hardest parts of buying a PC today is knowing that it is obsolete the moment it is unpacked. The rate of change in computer hardware is breathtaking, and that of computer software is dramatic as well. In only a few years, the Web has become the basis for most Internet commerce systems as well as many other applications. The technology of the day changes very quickly, so it is impossible to say in this book what technologies, or what products, are best suited for a particular commerce application.

Therefore, instead of focusing on specific technologies, we have examined the fundamental issues in designing a system for commerce. These principles can be applied with many different technologies, and used to evaluate many different products, in order to develop a specific application that satisfies specific business requirements. More important, by stepping back to look at these principles, it becomes possible to see what is really important about the system, and how it will evolve over time. Rather than choosing components and building an application around them today, only to be faced with potential obsolescence in a very short time, we think it is important to develop an approach to strategy and design that enables a business to design the system it needs, and then bring in the products or custom development required to realize that vision.

As we discussed earlier, this is why the system architecture is so important. The architecture provides a framework for evolution and for making decisions about what technologies to adopt, and when. It helps keep evaluations focused on the business problems being solved, rather than the hype that often surrounds new technologies.

Summary

This chapter has discussed the important aspects of designing a system for Internet commerce. Although these issues are common to the design of many kinds of computer applications, they are especially important for Internet commerce applications. Of course, different applications will ultimately have different designs that are appropriate for the requirements and architectural approaches chosen for those projects. Even though the answers may be different in each case, any successful design must confront these problems at one point or another.

With these basic principles in mind, we now turn to more detailed descriptions of some of the main technology areas for Internet commerce. Throughout these next chapters, the principles and design issues discussed in this chapter form the backdrop for how the technologies fit into an overall system for Internet commerce.

CHAPTER 11

Creating and Managing Content

To him who in the love of Nature holds
Communion with her visible forms, she speaks
A various language.
—William Cullen Bryant[1]

What the Customers See

The first point of contact for customers doing business on the Net is *content:* the information, catalog, brochures, and so on available on a Web site. For most Web sites, compelling content that draws in customers and encourages repeat visits is essential, and commerce sites are no exception. The precise look and feel of Web content is a creative and marketing design issue, but the design of Internet commerce systems requires a general understanding of the mechanisms of Web content and the tools available to create and manage it. This chapter provides an overview of Web content technology and how it works with Internet commerce.

This chapter includes brief overviews of several Web-related software packages. By no means do we have a complete list of the available tools. Over time, of course, the details of these packages will change, so you should make appropriate evaluations of the packages when you are building your application.

---

1. William Cullen Bryant, *Thanatopsis*, 1817.

Basic Content

Content in the World Wide Web is made up of multimedia hypertext pages typically described in HyperText Markup Language (HTML). Web pages are *multimedia* because they can include text, images, audio, video, and other kinds of data. In fact, the Web protocols are extensible to deal with any kind of media. Web pages are *hypertext* because instead of following a linear sequence like the pages of a book, any Web page can link to any number of other Web pages, in arbitrarily complex ways.

HTML is a description language for structured documents similar to SGML (Structured General Markup Language), which has been the standard for professional publishing for many years. A fragment of an HTML document is shown in Figure 11-1. *Tags* in the document source[2] describe the semantics of the document, and the details of the visual representation are left to the client software. This is a distinctly different model of description than a system like Postscript, which describes the appearance of a document but not its structure.

In the most common mode of operation, a Web browser retrieves pages coded in HTML from one or more Web servers. Web pages are identified by Uniform Resource Locators (URLs). Part of the URL tells the browser how to locate the proper server and what protocol to use to retrieve the page. The rest of the URL is sent to the server to locate the particular page on that server.

If a page is merely linked to the next page, there would still be a linear ordering of pages. In HTML, however, any location on a page can contain a link to another page on the same server or on another server anywhere in the world. The location of a link is called an *anchor*. Anchors can occur in a list of pages, such as a table of contents or index, in running text, or as portions of clickable images. This ability of pages to each link to many other pages turns the collection of pages on servers around the world into a web.

Basic Formatting

Using HTML, Web browsers have built-in abilities to handle several standard types of content.

Text

Text encompasses a variety of facilities for structuring documents such as headings, typefaces in different sizes and styles, and layout directives such as centering.

---

2. With HTML, a tag is marked by <tagname> in the document. If a tag is used to mark a region of text, the region will start with <tag> and end with </tag>.

Lists

HTML provides support for lists of items with arbitrary nesting levels. Standard HTML provides for three kinds of lists: unnumbered (with bullets) lists, numbered lists, and definition lists, which are used for text such as glossaries.

Images

Web browsers handle images in several ways. A document may just be an image, in which case the MIME type of the document specifies the format of the image. As an alternative, an HTML page may embed images inside it using special tags, and the browser retrieves separate files that actually contain the images. In addition to displaying pictures or diagrams, Web pages often use images and small graphics for visual appeal, icons, and toolbars. This technique gives the Web page designer a great deal of flexibility in creating the appearance of Web pages.

Forms

Much of the Web's power comes from its ability to create interactive applications. The simplest form of interactivity is the *form*. An HTML form can contain such elements as checkboxes, menu selections, and text entry fields. The user can fill out such a form and submit it to the Web server, which can then return information based on the contents of the form. Forms are discussed in more detail later.

Advanced Formatting

In addition to these basic capabilities, most browsers today can handle more advanced features of HTML.

Tables

Tables are a mechanism for achieving more control over the representation of arrays of content. In early versions of HTML, for example, the only way to line up a column of figures was to switch to a fixed-pitch font for that region of the document. The table formatting capabilities of HTML use a very general description of rows and columns of content, giving the designer many choices for layout.

Frames

Frames are a structuring mechanism that permits several independent Web pages to share display space in the same browser. One application of this is to maintain different views on a set of pages. For example, a site might keep a navigation view in one pane while displaying detailed content in other panes.

Image Maps

Web browsers usually display hyperlinks as highlighted text, indicating that a click on the text will call up the linked Web page. Often it is possible to click on an image as well, making small images useful as icons to represent hyperlinks. Image maps are an alternate means of representing and activating links. Using an image map, parts of a graphic image can be active, so that a hypertext link can be activated by clicking on a portion of an image. Image maps can be handled at the server, in which case the browser sends the click coordinates to the server, or at the client, in which case the server sends along a description of the *hot* regions of the image to the browser.

Controlling Appearance

Unlike many document description languages, HTML describes the semantics of a document rather than its appearance. Instead, browsers control how the various tagged elements of an HTML page should be displayed. This means that HTML documents can be displayed on a wide variety of devices, because the browser can render them differently depending on the capabilities of the device. It even makes it possible to render HTML for the visually impaired, while still providing information about the structure of the document. This does mean, however, that the designer of a page does not control its ultimate appearance.

Historically, obtaining close control over the appearance of a Web page on the user's display has been a big problem for Web authors. Frequently, page creation teams must test their HTML pages using the most popular browsers, adjusting the HTML coding as needed. Sometimes they even use peculiar techniques to control appearance, such as inserting transparent or invisible images on the page to obtain precise control over spacing.

For some applications, this lack of control can be a frustrating limitation. In order to give authors greater control over the display of HTML, the Web community has developed *Cascading Style Sheets (CSS)*. This proposal permits a Web page to reference a set of style sheets, which describe how the various elements should be displayed. Even more advantageous, an HTML page can link to several sets of style sheets, which can define the preferred representation of the page on different devices. For example, a high-resolution PC display could use one, a low-resolution television set could use another set, and an Internet browser for the visually impaired could use a third.

Other solutions to this problem are in development as well, such as Dynamic HTML and XML. Application designers should watch the development of content markup languages, since they are a core part of making the commerce experience compelling for users.

Web Pages and Forms

Fill-out forms are a powerful method of interactivity on the Web. Forms consist of HTML tags that create on the browser screen an editable set of fields intermixed with standard HTML markup. Each field has a name, which is not displayed for the user, but is used by the server to keep track of the various fields. The form is created by the Web server, either as a static page or as the dynamic output of a program. Dynamic forms might be used to vary the set of fields to be completed, as appropriate to the application. The initial values of the fields may be filled in by the server, or they may be left blank. After completing the form, the user clicks on a "submit" button (which may have a different display). At this point, the field *names* and contents are sent to the Web server as a series of name-value pairs. An application running on the Web server receives and interprets the form contents. Figure 11-1 shows the HTML source for a form, and Figure 11-2 shows the corresponding Web page as displayed by one browser.

HTML forms can contain the following kinds of fields.

- Checkbox—Used to select options.
- Radio button—A set of pushbuttons, only one of which can be activated (like the station selector on a car radio).
- Text line—An editable line of text.
- Scrollable text line—An editable line of text than can be larger than the box.
- Text area—An editable text box with multiple lines.
- Pushbutton—A button used to submit the form or reset its contents to their original state.
- Image—A pushbutton may be rendered as an image instead of as a button with a textual label.
- Drop-down menu—A drop-down menu contains a list of alternatives.

These elements can be combined in different ways to create many interactive Web applications.

Images

HTML documents can contain embedded images in formats such as GIF or JPEG. Embedded images are not stored by encoding the image itself within the HTML file, but are stored as separate image files on a Web server. The author of the HTML file merely inserts an *image source* tag within the HTML source:

```
<img src="Rocks80E3.gif" width="528" height="30">
```

When the Web browser encounters a tag like this, it retrieves the image using HTTP and then renders it in place. The *width* and *height* attributes are hints to the browser

```
<!DOCTYPE HTML PUBLIC "-//IETF//DTD HTML//EN">
<html>
<head>
<meta http-equiv="Content-Type"
content="text/html; charset=iso-8859-1">
<meta name="GENERATOR" content="Microsoft FrontPage 2.0">
<title>HTML Example</title>
</head>
<body bgcolor="#FFFFFF">
<h1>HTML Example</h1>
<p>This page contains HTML examples for <u>Designing Systems for
Internet Commerce</u>.</p>
<p>An HTML page can contain headings, text, lists, graphics, and
so forth. This page was prepared using Microsoft FrontPage.</p>
<p>Here is an HTML Unnumbered List:</p>
<menu>
    <li>This is the first item</li>
    <li>This is the second item</li>
</menu>
<p>Here is an HTML table with two rows and two columns:</p>
<table border="0" cellpadding="3" cellspacing="4">
    <tr>
        <td>Row 1</td>
        <td>Column 2</td>
        <td>Column 3</td>
    </tr>
    <tr>
        <td>Row 2</td>
        <td>Cell 2,2</td>
        <td>Cell 2,3</td>
    </tr>
    <tr>
        <td>Row 3</td>
        <td>Cell 3,2</td>
        <td>Cell 3,3</td>
    </tr>
</table>
<p>Right below this line is a graphic image of a line of rocks.</p>
<p><img src="Rocks80E3.gif" width="528" height="30"></p>
<p>Here is a simple &quot;request for assistance&quot; form:</p>
<form action="sendmessage.cgi" method="POST"
name="sendmessage.cgi">
    <p>Priority: <input type="radio" checked name="R1"
value="V1">Normal
    <input type="radio" name="R1" value="V2">High <input
    type="radio" name="R1" value="V3">Emergency</p>
    <p>Message: <input type="text" size="44" name="T1"></p>
    <p><input type="submit" name="B1" value="Submit"></p>
</form>
<hr>
<p>The end.</p>
</body>
</html>
```

FIGURE 11-1. An Example of HTML Source

about the size of the image, so that the browser can leave the right amount of space for the image and proceed with rendering the rest of the page. The image can be filled in later, since it may take some time to download. This technique lets the text part of pages display faster on slow Internet connections without the need to reformat the display when the actual image is finally available.

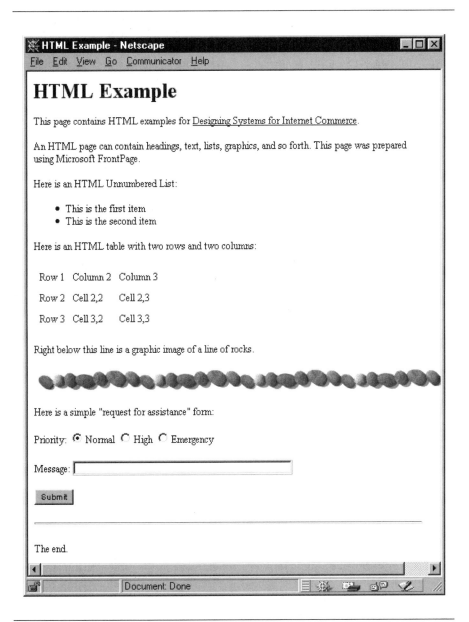

FIGURE 11-2. **Screen Shot of the Rendered HTML from Figure 11-1**

Image Maps

In HTML content, the anchor for a hypertext link can occur in text, as an image, or as part of an image. A common Web paradigm is to use an image containing multiple links to other pages. The geometric definitions of the regions (or *hot zones*) of the image can be kept at the server or sent to the client. Image maps were originally interpreted only by the server, but most browsers today can use the client-side version as well. Client-side image maps have a number of advantages: they take load off the server, different parts of the image can link to different servers, they can be more interactive for the user, and they can be used more effectively by text-only browsers.

Multimedia

Web content is not limited to text, graphics, and images. Audio, video, and animation are also available. Animated images can be built using features of the GIF image encoding format, client scripting, Dynamic HTML, or even with extension languages such as Java. Audio, video, and other media types may be handled by external applications or by adding a plug-in to the browser to render the data in place.

Other Types of Content

HTML, along with its programmable extensions such as Java, JavaScript, and ActiveX, is the most widely used data type on the Web. Some others are becoming increasingly popular.

VRML

The Virtual Reality Markup Language (VRML) is used to define a three-dimensional virtual world. Once a VRML model is downloaded to a suitably equipped browser, the user can navigate the world interactively on the desktop.

PDF

Adobe System's Portable Document Format (PDF) is a further development of the popular Postscript language, which describes documents for printing. The objective of PDF is to make Postscript a useful environment for browsing documents online. PDF adds searching, interactive use, hyperlinks, and annotation to Postscript. The key difference between HTML and PDF is that HTML describes the structure of a document without controlling its rendering, whereas PDF tries very hard to give the author full control over the appearance of the document on the screen. The objective is that a document viewed online should look exactly the same as the same document on paper. PDF has become popular as a means to distribute paper forms, journal articles, and other carefully formatted items online. Today, many businesses use PDF for documents where precise appearance is important, and governments use PDF for distribution of official documents and materials such as tax forms.

Tools for Creating Content

There is a wide range of tools available for creating content. Each of the following is described in more detail later.

- Many desktop publishing tools have been extended to create Web content. They are intended for use by end users, and they are generally most useful for static content that does not change frequently.

- Database connectors can be used to publish content dynamically from a database by using templates for page layout that are combined with the results of database queries. They are mainly intended for use by Web developers.

- Authoring environments have been developed specifically for creating and managing more complex Web sites. They are mainly intended for use by Web developers, but they may be appropriate for some end users as well.

- Complete applications have been created for specific purposes such as banking or Internet commerce catalogs. These tend to be used by specialists in the specific area, but they can be very useful in simplifying some of the work.

In addition, the basic technology of the Web, described in Chapter 8, permits Web pages to be created dynamically by an arbitrary application.

Desktop Publishing Tools

Although HTML can be created by manually entering the tags with a text editor, there are many desktop publishing tools that provide *what you see is what you get* (WYSIWYG) editing. These tools allow the creation of HTML pages while displaying them as they will be rendered by a Web browser. There are many such tools on the market, including ones from Netscape and Microsoft.

Netscape Composer is a part of Netscape Communicator that can create or modify HTML and publish the results directly to a Web server, using either the HTTP protocol or the File Transfer Protocol (FTP). Composer works at the level of individual Web pages.

Microsoft FrontPage has two main components: an editor in the style of desktop publishing tools, and the FrontPage Explorer, which shows different views of an entire linked set (a *web*) of pages and images. The Explorer can show a hierarchical view of the files and directories that make up a web, as well as a *link view,* which is a graph showing how the pages are linked together.

FrontPage also has the notion of a *bot,* which is an active component one can add to a Web page. Bots are similar to ActiveX and other sorts of controls in that they have a design-time aspect, for configuration, and a runtime aspect, which operates when the page is viewed. FrontPage uses bots to implement limited forms of dynamic Web pages. Bots are also a FrontPage extension mechanism, so third parties can implement bots which add to the native functionality of FrontPage.[3]

FrontPage works on an entire web of pages as a group, and it includes extensions to some Web servers that enable FrontPage to upload pages to the server.

In addition, many traditional desktop publishing applications, such as Microsoft Word, Corel WordPerfect, and Adobe FrameMaker, can save documents in HTML form (although this sometimes loses formatting information compared to the native form).

Database Connectors

When a Web site must publish hundreds or thousands of very similar pages, such as stock quotes or catalog items, it makes sense to store the basic page layout as a template, while the actual information is stored in a database. Database connectors manage this process.

Database connectors typically define a language for writing page templates, and the templates are stored in the Web server's filesystem. Special tags are used to embed database queries in the templates. Results from the queries are then substituted in the pages delivered to the browser. This technique has a number of advantages.

• By changing the template in one place, the look and feel of thousands of Web pages can be changed at once.

• The generated pages automatically track changes in the information stored in the database.

• Complete pages are never stored, thus saving storage space on the server.

• The same data can be provided in different forms to different users, or shared by many applications.

As with HTML publishing tools, there are many database connector products available. Two examples include Microsoft's Active Server Pages and Universal Web Connect from Informix.

Microsoft Active Server Pages

Active Server Pages (ASP) were introduced by Microsoft as a standard component of Internet Information Server 3.0. With ASP, a Web developer can use server-side scripting, built-in ActiveX components, and new components created specifically for a particular application. Active Server Pages are based on template pages that contain

---

3. For example, Open Market, Inc., has a series of *CommerceBots*, which add commerce functionality to pages produced with FrontPage. They allow *buy buttons* and *digital coupons* to be added with a simple dialog.

both HTML and fragments of a scripting language. ASP scripts can be written in VB-Script and JavaScript, as well as other ActiveX scripting languages. The scripts can in turn call ASP built-in components or any other ActiveX control on the system.

ASP has a number of built-in components.

- The Data Objects component connects the application to any ODBC-compliant database.
- The Filesystem component provides read-write access to the server's filesystem.
- The Content Linking component manages links between pages.
- The Advertising Rotator component selects different content based on a statistical model. This control is intended for displaying different banner advertisements according to a set of weights.

In addition, ASP includes some *intrinsic components* that provide access to the HTTP request and response messages, information about browser capabilities, and a method for managing sessions. These intrinsic components give access to the basic Web system, rather than to other system resources.

Informix Universal Web Connect

Like other database connectors, the Informix Universal Web Connect (IUWC) system uses special server-side tags in HTML content pages to select and merge information from an Informix database. The environment includes the following.

- Persistent application state

    IUWC enables long-lived applications by separating the application code from the CGI Web driver, and it provides services for managing connections and sessions. In operation, the Web server launches a small driver application using CGI. The Web driver in turn opens a connection to the application module. This lets the application stay running between invocations, which reduces startup overhead and allows the application to maintain state for lengthy transactions.

- Application management

    IUWC stores the entire application content, both templates and data, in the database. This makes it easy to provide for application testing and staging, and makes it straightforward to roll an application back to an earlier version if necessary.

Authoring Environments

One step beyond tools for creating pages from the contents of databases are tools for the design, construction, and maintenance of complete Web sites. Microsoft FrontPage can be viewed this way, since it works on multiple pages at once and has some support for dynamic content via FrontPage bots, but it is primarily a desktop publishing application.

Bluestone Sapphire/Web

Sapphire/Web is an environment for developing, deploying, and managing Java and Web-to-database applications. The basic idea is to bind user interface components, such as buttons or Java applets, to data objects, such as database data, stored procedures, or user-written code. The application can then be deployed on a variety of Web servers, using different middleware and transaction support environments. Once the application is deployed, Sapphire/Web provides management capabilities that support application operations.

*   Development

    Sapphire/Web includes an integrated development environment, which provides project and code management, visual development, wizards, and extensive collections of Java classes and middleware components.

*   Deployment

    Sapphire/Web applications can run using a wide variety of Web servers and databases. The developer can choose from multiple middleware packages to interconnect different application components, including Java and CORBA packages.

*   Management

    Sapphire/Web applications can span multiple servers for load balancing, partitioning, and fault tolerance. The management console provides a visual interface to the entire collection of servers, with facilities to start, stop, and test components dynamically.

Other Authoring Environments

Some other examples of Web authoring environments are Allaire's Cold Fusion (http://www.allaire.com/) and Vignette's StoryServer (http://www.vignette.com/).

Complete Applications

In addition to the general-purpose tools for creating Web content, there are many packages becoming available for more specialized Web applications. These provide in-depth capabilities for particular needs, such as catalogs or publishing. For Internet commerce, some examples of packaged applications include Open Market's LiveCommerce, Folio's siteDirector, and iCat's Electronic Commerce Suite.

Open Market LiveCommerce

LiveCommerce is an application for the creation and deployment of industrial parts catalogs on the Web. It provides tools for importing or creating catalog data, stores the information in an object-oriented database, provides easy-to-use tools for searching and sorting the catalog, and integrates with Transact, Open Market's order management application. Here are some of the capabilities of LiveCommerce.

- Catalog creation

  LiveCommerce provides flexible methods for importing catalog data into its internal object-oriented database. Information can be loaded from other databases, from files, or created anew. In addition, LiveCommerce can manage product configuration, making it unnecessary to enter information for all possible variations of a product. For example, a family of computer products with different combinations of processor, memory, and disk capacity can be described as a set of choices, rather than enumerating all possible combinations.

- Navigation

  A key issue in large catalogs is finding what you want. LiveCommerce provides hierarchical navigation, with the ability to *orient*, *view*, and *sort* the catalog. For example, a software catalog might permit the user to orient the catalog toward low-price products, view only PC-compatible products, and sort by manufacturer. A separate navigation window provides constant feedback to help keep the user from getting lost in the data.

- Parametric search

  LiveCommerce also provides *parametric search* capability. In this technique, catalog items may have arbitrary sets of attributes and their associated values. Parametric search permits the use of any set of attributes in any order to narrow the search space. If the number of search results is small, LiveCommerce simply displays them. Otherwise, the system lists the number of matching items and displays other attributes that may be used for selection, enabling the user to continue the search.

- Personalization

  LiveCommerce provides the ability for users to register with the system. Information from the user can then be used to modify the display of the catalog. As an example, users from different companies might see the part numbers and prices appropriate to their respective companies.

Folio siteDirector

Folio siteDirector is an application for publishing information databases (called *infobases*) as HTML over the Web. A typical use of the system is for disseminating legal, tax, or accounting information. siteDirector can automatically generate a table of contents as well as provide fast searches on the information. A related product, Secure-Publish, provides authenticated subscription access to infobases.

- Media independence

  Folio infobases can be published on the Web (using siteDirector), on LANs, or via CD-ROM for isolated or disconnected use. Incremental annotations and updates are fully integrated into the infobase, and they can be searched as well.

- Unstructured information

    Unlike a parts catalog, which is usually very structured, infobases frequently contain highly unstructured text information. Consequently, siteDirector provides efficient full-text searches and queries that permit the user to zoom in on candidate documents that may be appropriate. The system uses relevance ranking to present candidate documents to the user in order from most likely to least likely.

- Commerce capability

    siteDirector includes a programming interface that allows developers to add access control, pay-per-view, and usage-based billing capabilities to the system. The SecurePublish version of siteDirector uses the distributed, on line subscription capability of Open Market's Transact to control access to infobases on a subscription basis.

iCat Electronic Commerce Suite

iCat's Electronic Commerce Suite is intended for small to medium-size retail or business-to-business catalog sites. The product includes the tools necessary to create, manage, and host online product catalogs, including a secure transaction capability. Rich graphical information about items is included, along with a set of catalog templates. The system uses templates to create displayed pages, with product information pulled from any database usable with ODBC. The transaction capability is provided through a CyberCash, Open Market Transact, or First Virtual system.

Choosing Applications

Off-the-shelf application software is almost always less expensive to deploy and operate than a solution developed and maintained internally, provided that the application meets the needs of the organization. Some of the reasons for this include the following.

- Development costs are amortized over many customers.

- Maintenance and support are handled by the vendor.

- Regular releases provide periodic infusions of new functionality. This is particularly important for Internet applications of all kinds, because the general rate of technology change is so fast.

As an example of packaged applications, consider accounting software. In the early days of information technology, companies frequently wrote their own accounting systems. Now, almost all companies use packaged accounting software. Available products range from simple applications like Intuit's QuickBooks to large and complex systems like Oracle Financials.

Managing Content

Creating content has an essential creative aspect, but it also has a procedural aspect, in which the path from the creative keyboard to a production Web site is carefully defined and scrupulously followed. This procedural work is sometimes called the editorial process flow or the publishing phase of Web content. This section follows content through its life cycle: creation, editing, staging, testing, production, and archiving.

Creation

Content comes from somewhere. It may be written from scratch, collated from other sources, or delivered by a live feed from other sources. Beyond the creative part of creating content, the procedural part consists of a series of conversion and formatting steps that different items go through before they are ready to become part of the live Web site.

Format conversions move documents from various desktop publishing or source formats into HTML or whatever standard format the site may use. These steps may be manual, using desktop conversion tools, or they may be automated. In either case, there is some danger that the output document may not look at all correct. Desktop publishing documents are formatted to achieve a certain appearance when printed, and there are usually several ways to achieve this appearance. For example, a section heading may be coded as a section heading paragraph with a standard type style, or it may be coded as a body paragraph with a nonstandard type style. HTML, in contrast, expects section heads to be coded only as section heads. Automated conversion tools can sometimes give unexpected results, especially if the input format lacks the semantic information used for HTML. Issues like this must be solved with a combination of experience, standards, training, and testing.

Formatting applies standard templates to documents that will become part of a site. These templates may be applied in the creation of each individual document if desktop publishing tools are used to prepare content, or they may be used in the generation of content by automatic tools driven from a database. In both cases, the value of the templates comes from the consistent presentation to the user, as well as in simplifying the use of repeated elements such as logos, toolbars, and navigation aids.

Editing

After an item has been created and converted to the correct format, it will go through a number of editing steps.

- Does the item conform to corporate standards of look and feel?
- Are the spelling, grammar, and other aspects of the presentation correct?
- Are all the facts correct?

- Are the correct links for hypertext in place?

Except for the hypertext links, these steps are similar for both print and the Internet. The challenge of these processes in the Internet case is first, to achieve a fully electronic process, and second, to meet the real-time demands—the deadline for new content may not be weekly, but every 10 minutes!

Transactional Aspects of Content

The Internet is not like a magazine or newspaper. In print, each new issue is assembled completely while still hidden from public view. Only the full issue is delivered, all at once, to the subscriber. In contrast, Web content can be visible to subscribers at all times. If a site attempts to exploit the ability of the Internet to always deliver up-to-date content, the site can literally be changing under the eyes of the reader. Careful design is required to be able to update the content of a production site while at the same time assuring that the content is internally consistent, that all the links actually work, and that all required testing has been done. Not only must the system be designed to accommodate such updates, but the processes that go along with doing the work must be designed and followed carefully.

Here are two particular dangers.

1. Multiple authors

   Any time that multiple authors are at work, there is a danger that more than one will attempt to change the same document at the same time. Depending on the details of how this is done, one of them may "win" with the other changes lost. In the worst case, the resulting document may become scrambled. The usual solutions to this problem include the application of *source control* tools that lock documents before update or the use of a document repository that can maintain multiple versions and identify conflicts.

2. Changing multiple pages

   Often a change to a Web site means that many pages must be updated. Unless this is done carefully, an active user may see the pages in an inconsistent state, viewing old versions of some pages and new versions of others. This problem is sometimes exacerbated by caching in browsers and proxy servers, which may show old versions for some time after the new ones are available. A common approach to solve this problem is to change all affected pages in one atomic action, such as by renaming a directory or committing the changes in a database. In addition, it is important to make sure that the appropriate hints for caches are provided.

Staging and Testing

Of course, not all sites need to be updated continuously. If changes are made less frequently, it may be useful to make all changes on a "staging" system before any modifications are made to the production system. The content on the staging system can be extensively tested before it is made available on the production site.

Content Testing

If the site's content is HTML, it is a good idea to check the HTML for syntactic correctness. For example, every tag must have a matching closing tag, with appropriate nesting, and only sanctioned tags should be used (since some organizations may have policies on HTML style). Such checks are especially important for HTML written by hand. In some cases, it may be possible (and appropriate) to use automatic tools for preparing versions of the content for display by different browsers as well as a text-only view for those users with slower-speed network access.

Link Testing

Few things irritate Web users more than stale or disconnected hypertext links. Links that are internal to a site are straightforward to manage, although it is useful to test them for consistency. Links to other sites should be tested periodically to ensure that you catch problems before your customers do. Some Web publishing environments, such as Microsoft's Active Server Pages, provide mechanisms for making links correct by construction, by only creating and inserting the link when the page is viewed.

Commerce Testing

If the site is commerce-enabled, then staging is the right moment to check that all items are enabled correctly, with accurate prices, sales tax classifications, and so forth. In addition, test transactions can be run to verify that fulfillment of both physical goods and digital goods works properly and that all reports are correctly generated.

Indexing

If the site uses a full-text search engine to help user navigation, withdrawn pages must be dropped from the index, and new or changed pages added. Ideally, the production index always exactly matches the production pages.[4]

---

4. A related issue is that content on one's own site may be searched and indexed by a central search engine such as AltaVista, Lycos, or Excite. These massive search engines only poll individual sites occasionally, and may be woefully out of date.

Editorial Review

Because the staging system represents a fully functional but private version of a Web site, it is an appropriate place to run any final human editorial checks on content.

Archiving

It is an excellent idea to save at least one old version of a site, with a procedure to rapidly put the archived version into production.

*   The archives form an audit trail of changes.

*   Archived copies of individual documents (or even the entire site) may be part of the site, with some value to users.

*   An archived version is useful if the production content version is damaged or vandalized. The archived version can be put back in production, providing a means of rapid recovery from such problems.

Multimedia Presentation

By far the largest amount of Web content is HTML, but other data types are also in widespread use. A hypertext link in HTML can link to an arbitrary data type. When the Web server returns a page, a hypertext transfer protocol header carries data type information to the browser. Browsers have built-in support for many data types, can accept plug-in extensions to handle other data types, and can launch a completely different application for still others.

*   Built-in

    Popular browsers implement native support for HTML and image formats such as GIF and JPEG.

*   Plug-in

    Adobe Systems provides a freely distributed reader for Acrobat format files. When installed, the reader plugs into the browser to add support for the Acrobat data type. When the user clicks on an Acrobat document, the reader plug-in takes over the browser window and displays the document in place.

*   Separate application

    A Web document catalog might contain a Microsoft Powerpoint presentation. When the user clicks on the associated link, the user's copy of Powerpoint would be launched to handle the file.

There are some widely used data types.

- Animated images

  Some image formats, such as GIF, have the ability to sequence through a series of images packaged together. These are widely used for creating small animations.

- Applets and scripting

  Applets and client scripting can create animation effects and other interactive behavior in the browser. Dynamic HTML has similar capabilities.

- Video data

  Video clips can be integrated with other Web content, using standard encoding types such as MPEG, QuickTime, and AVI. To date, most video works as downloaded clips which are played locally, but as network bandwidth improves, streaming video[5] will become increasingly common.

- Audio data

  Audio clips can be put on the Web using WAV files, SND files, and the aforementioned AVI files. In addition, protocols such as RealAudio permit streaming audio to be used. (There is also an active area of interactive two-way audio over the Internet, which can be used to replace or augment telephone service.)

- Shockwave

  Shockwave files are complete multimedia animations, produced by the popular Macromedia Director animation creation tool.

- VRML

  Finally, VRML, the virtual reality modeling language, deserves special mention. VRML is a format for describing three-dimensional virtual worlds. A VRML page, really a 3-D model, is downloaded to a VRML-capable application and then the VRML world can be explored locally.

Different Faces for Different Users

One of the most interesting things about the Internet is that an information creator can interact directly with an information consumer, instead of having intermediaries such as publishers, distributors, and so on. To some, this aspect of the Internet spells doom for middlemen, but it also represents an opportunity to strengthen customer relationships. In business-to-consumer commerce, for example, businesses compete for customers on the basis of price, convenience, and service. Since the network gives more

---

5. Streaming audio or video is a tricky concept. A traditional audio or video clip works by first downloading the entire audio or video file to the client machine, then launching an application to play it. Streaming media works by starting to download the media file, then starting to play it before the download is complete. As long as the download stays ahead of the playback, this will work well, and result in lower playback latency.

or less equal access by the consumer to all businesses, price and convenience may quickly reach parity across providers. At that point, the primary basis for competition will be service and relationships, and the network provides excellent tools for improving both.

Unlike a broadcast channel such as print, television, or radio, where most consumers receive the same content, each Internet user has an individual channel to the on line presence of a business. Instead of providing the same content to everyone, a site can provide individually personalized content to each user.

Personalizing a site may be done for business functions, or for unabashed merchandising purposes. Users of a business-to-business catalog, for example, may see the different prices negotiated for their respective companies. A retail site may send personalized electronic coupons to frequent shoppers.

There are three key elements to personalizing a site: authenticating the user, creating a user profile, and generating custom content.

Authentication and Identity

The first step in personalizing a site is authenticating the user. In this context, it may not be necessary to know an individual's true identity. Instead, it is sufficient to assure that a series of visits by a user represents the *same* person, even if the precise identity is unknown. In other cases, it is important to have formal authentication, as in the preceding business example. In this kind of application, some techniques for authentication include the following.

Browser Cookie

Once a user has registered, the site may record a persistent cookie in the user's browser. This technique provides automatic sign-on at future visits, but it breaks down if the user disables cookies or tries to use the service from a different computer. Cookies do have the advantage that they can track users through a site, and even identify users on subsequent visits, though there may be no explicit registration or identification at all. (There are other techniques for maintaining session state that do not use cookies, but they have similar properties.)

Name and Password for a Single Site

One common technique is to register users of a site with a name and password on the first visit. On future visits, the user is prompted for the name and password before being permitted to enter the site. Unfortunately, this can be a burden for the user, who ends up with individual accounts at many different sites. The result has several problems. If the user chooses the same name and password for many sites, it may be easy to remember, but a compromised password exposes all of those sites. In addition, all of those sites know the password, so an unscrupulous operator can abuse that knowledge. On the other hand, users who choose different names and passwords for each site are more likely to lose track of them. Users with lost passwords can be a significant source of customer service problems.

Central Authentication Database with Delegation

Many sites may share a central authentication database. The customer has one set of credentials, so they are easier to remember and protect. The affiliated sites get greater security, can share the costs of the authentication database, and may gain access to a larger group of users. For Internet commerce, organizations that offer commerce services to a number of businesses may also offer a registration database, such as that in Open Market's Transact engine. Another place where a single authentication database occurs is in a large online service like America Online, where affiliated businesses can rely on the central registration service. However, since there is no standardized Internet authentication and registration system, a business cannot count on obtaining user authentication from an arbitrary Internet service provider.

Personal Digital Certificates

Public key digital certificates are digital objects in which a trusted third party attests to the binding between a user name and a security key. Whenever the security key is used to set up a secure connection, the server at the other end can find out the associated name and which organization stands behind it. Certificates were just beginning to get widespread acceptance in 1997, and they are still awkward to use. The use of certificates for authentication is discussed further in Chapter 13.

Profiles

After the system identifies a user, it can retrieve a stored profile about the user. Sometimes, if the profile is small, a site may use a browser cookie to store the profile on the client, rather than storing it in a database. User profiles can contain a wide variety of information. We discuss some common categories.

Registration Information

Many Web sites have registration forms. Users may fill out these forms in order to gain access to the site or as part of making a purchase. There is a wide range of information that is collected, ranging from name and address to payment credentials (such as credit card numbers) and demographic information.

Optional User-supplied Information

Profiles help to personalize sites. Sites frequently request information about the preferences of users in order to provide better service. For example, one can register favorite authors at Amazon.com in order to receive notification of new books by those authors. These types of profiles are optional and generally linked to a specific benefit for the user.

Linked Information

Once authentication is available, profile information can be automatically generated. For example, if an authenticated user completes a commerce transaction, the user and transaction become linked. Appropriate reporting software can record actual or contemplated purchases in the associated user profile for merchandising purposes. Profile and transaction information obtained online can also be linked to personal information obtained from sources off the network.

Browsing Information

At the finest level of detail, individual browsing patterns in a site can be collected into the user profile along with such information as search keywords entered. The Web is the first medium in which such finely detailed tracking of individual activities is possible, and it is not yet clear how best to use the information for personalization. At a minimum, areas that are frequently visited by a user might be given links on a personalized home page for the user.

Storing Profiles

There are several ways to keep and maintain profiles.

- Browser cookie

  As mentioned previously, cookies can be used to store user identification information, often for tracking sessions. Cookies can also be used to store profile information directly. The advantages are that the site need not allocate storage for profiles, and that the profile data is directly available to Web applications at the site without querying a database. The disadvantage is that if a user switches computers (or simply deletes the cookie), the profile information is lost. The site also will not have all users' profile information available at once for reporting or marketing analysis.

- Site local storage

  User authentication information can be used to retrieve profile information from a local database. This works well until the Web site grows to more than one location.

- Shared storage

  A shared system can store user profile information. For example, a transaction engine or authentication system that serves multiple sites can also provide a common user database with shared profile information. The advantage is that the information need only be kept up to date in one place.

- Browser wallet

  One additional storage site for profile information is a browser-based "wallet." This method is not widely used, but it may become more common. Originally invented as a way to store payment credentials for commerce, browser wallets can also store profile information such as name, address, and personal preferences. These can be released to requesting Web sites automatically, on approval of the end user, or under the control of privacy software such as the Open Profiling Standard.

Custom Content

Given user authentication and profile information, the final problem to be solved is how to generate personalized content. The details will necessarily vary with different applications, but here are a few examples.

Personal Newspaper

The objective of our example personal newspaper site is to attract users by offering a custom-tailored newspaper. The concept is to save users time by putting the information they want on a personalized front page. The site could be funded either by paid subscriptions or by advertising.

Users are asked to register an interest profile, which includes the following elements on a registration form.

- Name and password, for signing on to the site on future occasions.

- E-mail address. This will be used as a location to send an e-mail version of the personal newspaper, if desired.

- Postal code. This will be used to create a custom weather report for the user's home city.

- Favorite sports teams. This will be used to select news items about the teams, including up-to-date scores.

- Stock market ticker symbols for companies of interest. This will be used to generate a custom portfolio report and news items about the companies.

The user profile and authentication information is stored in a database at the Web site. When a user clicks into the site, a sign-on screen asks the user to sign on or register as a new user.

After the user signs on, the Web application uses the user name to retrieve the user's profile from the database. The standard front page is a template with placeholders for weather, sports, and business, but no content in those areas. The Web application uses fields from the user's profile to select an appropriate weather report, team scores, and company news, and populates the template, which is then returned to the user. A periodic batch job searches the database for users who have selected the e-mail option and queues personalized e-mail messages for transmission.

If the site is supported by advertising, advertisers can learn a great deal from the profile, such as the postal code. The profile can be used to place advertisements that are more likely to be of interest to the user.

Custom Catalog

The objective of our example catalog site is to deliver office supplies to medium-sized corporate customers. The purpose of the Web ordering system is to reduce ordering costs by having the end user requisitioners order supplies directly. This service is provided to a number of customers, and the supply catalog must be customized for each buying organization. The customizations include an order form reflecting the look and feel desired by the respective buying organizations, a set of supplies offered which is limited by contract, and a set of prices and discounts which reflect the volume of orders. Personalization for individuals also reflects individual purchasing limits.

In this example, which follows the design of the Open Buying on the Internet (OBI) standard, the selling organization operates the catalog and provides organization-level customization. The buying organization is responsible for authenticating requisitioners and authorizing purchases according to individual purchasing limits. For convenience, Figure 11-3 reproduces the OBI architecture diagram from Chapter 6.

To create a purchasing relationship, the buying and selling organizations agree on services, items covered, and contract pricing. This information is placed in a buying organization profile stored at the seller's catalog system.

The buying organization creates digital certificates for requisitioners, which record their user names, as assigned by the purchasing department.

When a requisitioner enters the seller catalog, the site uses the information in the digital certificate to select the proper discounts, price tables, available items, and the proper order form for the buyer. When the order is complete, the catalog routes the order to the buyer's approval system, along with the user name from the certificate.

The buyer approval system uses the user name from the certificate to select the proper purchasing limit. If the order is approved, it routes the order back to the seller along with the proper shipping address.

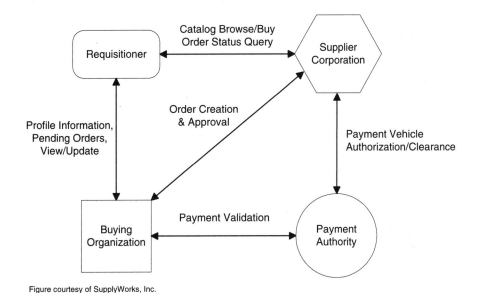

Figure courtesy of SupplyWorks, Inc.

FIGURE 11-3. OBI Architecture

In this example, the storage of the profile is split between buyer and seller systems. This division makes sense for this application, because the same requisitioners may purchase from multiple suppliers, and there is no need to store the same profile in multiple places.

Merchandising

The objective of our example merchandising site is to attract traffic by offering coupons and special offers to create repeat customers. In order to be as unobtrusive as possible, there will be no registration or sign-on requirements.

For this system, authentication will be done by using a browser cookie to store a unique ID number. If a browser comes to the site for the first time, no cookie will be present, so a new ID number will be allocated and stored as a cookie. The purpose of the ID number is to recognize repeat visitors and to adapt site behavior over time.

At first, the user profile will be empty, and the site home page will display generic special offers. Should the visitor make a purchase, however, the ID number will become linked to the user's profile (particularly the postal code) and transaction records.

The postal code will be used to select special offers appropriate for the user's apparent demographics, which is already common practice. After the first transaction, when the user visits the site, the home page will display offers more likely to be of interest to the user.

The order form for the site will also permit the user to enter an optional e-mail address, in case the user wishes to be informed of a delay in shipping or of any special offers. A notice indicates that the site will not resell address or e-mail information, in order to assure the user of privacy.

A weekly batch job uses the available profile and transaction information to occasionally send electronic coupons to the users who have registered e-mail addresses. The electronic coupons are URLs which bring the user back to the site.

Summary

Personalized content depends on identifying or authenticating the user, storage of appropriate profile information, and a site architecture which permits dynamic construction of content according to that profile. Custom content is an important mechanism for sites to build stronger relationships with customers, which can help the competitive position of the site in an environment which tends to flatten other competitive factors such as price and convenience.

Integration with Other Media

As the Internet becomes more and more integrated into everyday life, there are increasing opportunities to link other media into the Web for commercial purposes. Four essential characteristics of the Internet make this exciting.

- Capacity. Except for modest storage expense, the marginal cost of Web content is essentially zero. Product information can be voluminous and detailed.

- Currency. Content on the Internet can be kept up to date. Catalogs, pricing, inventory, and financial and regulatory information all change frequently.

- Transactions. In other media, an advertisement exhorts one to telephone for a transaction. On the Internet, the transaction is right there.

- Bandwidth. Internet bandwidth is large and increasing, but not unlimited. Individual access to the network is frequently over dial-up telephone lines using modems running at 28.8 Kbps or below. In addition, more laptop users work in a disconnected mode while traveling, with no immediate access to the Net. Many users, however, are able to access the Net using high-speed corporate LANs, 56 Kbps modems, ISDN, cable modems, or satellite links.

With these factors in mind, several types of cross-media integration seem particularly important.

URLs in Advertising

In traditional print and broadcast media, space is at a premium: every square inch of print advertising and every minute of broadcast advertising comes with a substantial price tag. With ubiquitous Internet access, print and broadcast advertising can concentrate on brand recognition, and link to online sources for detailed product information. Already a substantial percentage of magazine and television advertisements include URLs, linking these media to the Web.

CD-ROM and DVD

CD-ROMs are already in wide use for distributing applications, catalogs, and reference information. CD-ROMs have the advantages of large capacity and bandwidth, and they work even when disconnected from the network. CD-ROMs lack currency and transaction capability, but by integrating network access when available with local CD-ROMs, an application can have the capacity and bandwidth of the CD-ROM and the currency and transaction capability of the Internet. Updates to CD-ROM content can be pulled from the network or pushed by the network to client systems, and applications delivered on CD-ROM can easily link out to transaction and information systems on the Internet. Digital Video Disks, or DVDs, are similar to CD-ROMs except they have much greater capacity.

E-mail and the Web

E-mail is a familiar medium to Internet users, but it has only recently been integrated with the World Wide Web. The current generation of e-mail clients can display most messages formatted in HTML, and they can activate a Web browser from a URL in an e-mail message. These capabilities make it easy to use e-mail to communicate with customers and to distribute special offers and coupons. The recipient can easily store and forward these messages, as well as jump immediately to interactive or transactional Web sites.

Summary

Creating and managing content that is compelling and easy to use is as important on the Internet as in other communications media. With any new medium, however, we find new capabilities, new tools, and new constraints. The Web offers powerful mechanisms for integrating many kinds of media, and for providing an experience that is rich in detail for users. Moreover, the presentation can be tailored to the personal interests and characteristics of an individual customer, an ability unmatched by any other medium.

Discussions about the Internet and the Web often focus on technology, but ultimately it is compelling content that brings customers back to a site. Take advantage of the technology, but focus on the content.

CHAPTER 12

Cryptography

> The King hath note of all they intend,
> By interception, which they dream not of.
> —Shakespeare, *Henry V*

Keeping Secrets

Cryptography—from the Greek word for "secret writing"—is the science of communication over untrusted communications channels. Historically, cryptography has been associated with spies, governments, and the military. It has been used in warfare for thousands of years, with some of the most famous cases, including the German Enigma machine, coming from World War II. Over the last 50 years, however, cryptography has acquired a sound mathematical and practical foundation, and has moved from being an almost exclusive tool of military and diplomatic application to embrace commercial applications as well.

Used properly, cryptography can keep a message secret, positively identify its sender, and assure the recipient that it was not modified in transit. In some cases, cryptographic techniques can help prove that a message was sent in the first place, and by whom.

As a short example, let us apply these attributes of cryptography to a problem of electronic commerce over a network: Alice, a purchasing agent, wishes to order some widgets from her supplier Bob. What are the requirements for this transaction?

- Alice wants to be sure that she is really dealing with Bob and not an impostor (authentication).

- Bob wants to be sure that Alice is really Alice and not an impostor (authentication), because Alice gets special prices as part of a contract already negotiated.

- Alice wants to keep the order secret from her competition, and Bob does not want other customers to see Alice's special prices (privacy).

- Alice and Bob both want to ensure that crackers cannot change the price or quantity (integrity).

- Bob wants to make sure that Alice cannot later deny having placed the order (nonrepudiation).

These are some of the properties that Alice and Bob may want to have for their communication, and cryptographic techniques can be used to provide them. We will return to Alice and Bob's communication as we delve into the details of each part. Table 12-1 provides some more details about these properties.

Privacy	The message is secret: only the sender and intended recipient know the contents of the message.
Authentication	The recipient knows that the message is not a forgery, but was in fact sent by a particular sender. The sender knows that the message is going to the proper recipient.
Integrity	The recipient knows that the message was not modified (intentionally or accidentally) while in transit.
Nonrepudiation	The author of the message cannot later deny having sent the message.

TABLE 12-1. **Functions Provided by Cryptography**

In this chapter, we discuss some basic principles of public and private key cryptography, then discuss how these technologies are used to create secure communications channels, digital signatures, and other solutions. We close with a discussion of key management, the little appreciated linchpin of cryptography.

Types of Cryptography

In cryptography, an ordinary message (the *plaintext*) is processed by an encryption algorithm to produce a scrambled message (the *ciphertext*). The receiver uses a matching decryption algorithm to recover the plaintext from the ciphertext. If these algorithms were known to everyone, there would be no security, because anyone could decrypt the ciphertext. Therefore, in addition to the algorithm, there is an additional piece of input data called a *key*. The key is secret, even though many people may know the algorithm. The principle is the same as that of a combination lock. Many people may use locks with the same design, but each one chooses a different combination. The combination of the lock is equivalent to the key of the encryption algorithm.

There are two basic types of cryptographic algorithms: secret key systems (sometimes called *symmetric*) and public key systems (sometimes called *asymmetric*). In secret key cryptography, both encryption and decryption operations use the same key (that is, the key is used symmetrically). In public key cryptography, the encryption and decryption operations use related but different keys (in other words, the keys are asymmetric). As we shall see, having two keys means that one can be published—that is, made "public"—which gives public key cryptography its name. The other key is kept secret, and is sometimes called a *private key*. Secret key systems have been around for many hundreds of years; public key systems are a recent invention, dating from the mid-1970s. Both types of systems allow for secret communications, but public key systems can more easily grow to worldwide scale and more easily permit unaffiliated persons to communicate securely. Public key systems can also be used to provide *digital signatures,* which are analogous to handwritten signatures on letters, contracts, or other documents. We shall have more to say about digital signatures later in this chapter.

In practice, cryptographic systems often use secret key and public key cryptography together. Secret key algorithms are usually much faster than public key algorithms, so it is more efficient to use a secret key algorithm to encrypt the actual data. The system generates a random key for the symmetric algorithm, and then encrypts that key using the public key algorithm. The receiver first decrypts the symmetric key using the public key algorithm, and then decrypts the data using that key.

Algorithms, Protocols, and Key Management

There are three main components in the use of cryptography for real systems: cryptosystems, protocols, and key management. The term *cryptosystems* refers to the cryptographic algorithms and their characteristics. *Protocols* refers to the ways in which cryptographic algorithms are composed and applied to real problems, such as the securing of a communications channel or information in a database. Finally, *key management* refers to the essential problems of creating, distributing, and storing keys.

The design and analysis of cryptosystems is extremely specialized, so we limit ourselves to a brief survey of those systems that are commercially relevant today. Protocols are very important for electronic commerce, as they are used for protecting content and information as well as for payment systems. Finally, key management, perhaps the least-appreciated component, is actually the most important to the attainment of real security in an adverse environment.

We begin with a discussion of how to think about the security of systems using cryptography, and then continue with a discussion of algorithms, protocols, and key management.

How to Evaluate Cryptography

The operational security of a system that uses cryptography is determined by the security of the cryptographic algorithms in use, the correct design of the cryptographic protocols, and, above all, proper key management.

- Algorithms

  The design of cryptographic algorithms is very specialized. Don't try this at home. Instead, choose an established and well-understood algorithm that offers the features you need, and that is sufficiently strong for your purposes. Because cryptography is still a rapidly developing field, it is prudent to be prepared for unpleasant surprises. When possible, design systems so that the cryptographic algorithms can be replaced with new ones. If you choose an algorithm that can use different lengths for keys, be prepared to change the size, typically by using longer keys. Someone may try to sell you a new cryptographic algorithm with better security, better performance, or some other advantages. Using such an algorithm can be dangerous, because you can't really tell how good it is. Staying with the well-known algorithms may seem boring, but it is certainly safer.

- Protocols

  The design of cryptographic protocols is perhaps more accessible than that of algorithms, but even the simplest-appearing protocols are fraught with an amazing number of subtle bugs. Don't try this at home either. Whenever possible, use established protocols (and where it's not possible, try harder to find one that works). As with algorithms, the use of modular components allows you to introduce new protocols from time to time. This is especially useful if weaknesses are discovered in an older protocol, as is sometimes the case.

- Key management

  Key management is the most difficult part of cryptography, though it is also the least discussed. Really, don't try this at home (except that you may have to if the systems and components you want to buy don't do it). Key management includes the generation, distribution, storage, and update of keys. Since modern cryptographic algorithms and protocols are very strong, key management systems are a tempting target for attackers. When evaluating a secure communications system, it is important to ask hard questions about how the built-in key generation, storage, and distribution work. Sometimes, however, these are left to the user of the system, and there is no choice but to design and implement them yourself.

Cryptographic Strength

The right way to think about the security of a cryptosystem is that the key encapsulates the entire security of the system, as long as it employs a sufficiently strong algorithm. In particular, we would be suspicious about any system that depends on the secrecy of an algorithm. A public algorithm that has withstood the efforts of cryptanalysts for years is a much better bet.

How then does one measure the strength of a system? First, suppose that the algorithm itself is available to all. Second, suppose that the attacker has access to the system and is therefore able to submit plaintext and receive the corresponding ciphertext, encrypted using the current key. (This is called a *chosen plaintext attack*.) This would seem to give the attacker every advantage, other than knowing the key ahead of time. If the attacker still cannot decrypt your messages by any means other than by trying each possible key, then you are in good shape.

One way to attack a cryptosystem is to try all possible keys to decrypt a message. This process is known as *exhaustive search*, or a *brute force attack*. It is impossible to prevent a brute force attack, but mounting one can be prohibitively expensive if the number of possible keys is extremely large.

If attacking the system requires trying each possible key, then there need to be enough possible keys to make this task computationally infeasible. Key length is measured in bits. For example, the Data Encryption Standard (DES), specified by the U.S. government, has a 56-bit key. For a key with n bits, there are 2^n possible keys. Every bit added to the key length doubles the work of the attacker. For example, DES with a 56-bit key has 2^{56} possible keys, or about 72,100,000,000,000,000 different keys. This may seem like a large number, but this turns out not to be the case! A research group at Digital Equipment Corporation built a chip capable of 16,000,000 DES operations per second. If one were to build a machine with one thousand such chips, a DES-encrypted message could be broken in less than eight weeks. On June 17, 1997, a team led by Rocke Verser broke a DES-encrypted message by marshaling the efforts of some 78,000 computers on the Internet, over a period of several months.

Such an effort may be beyond the reach of a casual cracker, but may be possible for a criminal syndicate and very likely exists within the code-breaking organizations of national governments.

A related piece of bad news is that the performance of computers at constant cost is doubling about every 18 months. This technology trend, known as Moore's Law, has held for nearly 30 years and shows no sign of letting up. In round numbers, by 2010, machines and their components will be at least 1,000 times faster per dollar than they were in 1996. More speculatively, nanotechnology or biotechnology may make massively parallel code-breaking efforts possible at some future time.

Luckily, the computational cost of attacking a cipher increases exponentially faster than the cost of improving its strength.

In January 1997, RSA Laboratories announced the RSA Secret-Key Challenge, a series of symmetric key cryptographic contests. The first challenge to fall was a 40-bit key version of the RC5 algorithm—in 3 1/2 hours! A stronger 48-bit version of RC5 took 313 hours and DES took 140 days, as mentioned previously. RC5 has a variable key length, and some stronger challenges remain unsolved.

Operational Choices

Leaving aside for the moment questions of protocol and algorithm, the first choices to be made are the cryptographic strength of the system—embodied by choices of algorithm and key length—and some of the key management questions. The most important elements are to choose truly random keys that are long enough, keep those keys secret, and change keys "often enough."

Again, this all supposes that you have selected a good cryptosystem—all the security of the system lies in the keys, and none in the algorithm itself.

We will consider key randomness and key secrecy shortly. For now, let us consider the selection of key length and the frequency of key updates.

Key Length

Given a reasonably strong algorithm, how well the data is protected depends largely on the length of the encryption key. Fundamentally, an encrypted message must remain secret for the useful life of the information. To a large extent, the value of the information in the encrypted message will govern the resources used to attack it. For example, an attacker would be foolish to spend one million dollars to obtain information worth one thousand dollars, but he might spend one million dollars to obtain a secret worth two million dollars. Here are some examples.

- Financial credentials must remain secret beyond their validity period.
- Contract bids must remain secret beyond the contract award.
- Editorial material must remain secret until published.
- Confidential personal information must remain secret beyond the lifetime of the individual.

Today, a common recommendation is a minimum of 75-bit keys for present-day security and 90-bit keys for information to be kept secure for 20 years. These figures are for symmetric cryptosystems such as DES, IDEA, and RC4. Current public key systems have shortcut attacks such as factoring, which make it possible to avoid trying all possible keys. For these systems, keys must be much longer—768 or 1024 bits for an RSA key, for example.

Key Lifetime

Keys do not last forever; they need to be updated from time to time. The proper lifetime of a key is a function of the value of items encrypted, the number of items encrypted, and the lifetime of the items encrypted. We have already discussed lifetime. If a key can be broken by a properly equipped adversary in two years, and the lifetime of information encrypted under the key is six months, then the key must be changed at least every 18 months, so that an attack mounted on the first item encrypted will not succeed until after the last item encrypted loses its value.

The number of items encrypted is an issue for two reasons. First, if individual encrypted items have a market value, then the sum of the values of all encrypted items is the proper measure against which to balance the resources an attacker may bring to bear. Second, some cryptosystems can be attacked more easily when a large body of ciphertext is available. This effect is more difficult to quantify, but again, it is a good idea not to use a key for too long.

Another factor which leads one to short lifetimes for keys is paranoia. The longer a key is in use, the greater the chance that someone has compromised the key storage system and obtained the key by subterfuge rather than brute force attack.

It is important to note that changing keys does not change how long it takes an attacker to find it using brute force (or any other cryptographic attack). Changing keys does limit the amount of information revealed if any particular key is found. For example, if the encryption keys are changed every month, then only one month's worth of information is disclosed if a key is discovered.

One-Time Pad

Is there a perfect cryptosystem? Surprisingly, the answer is yes. It is called the one-time pad. In the original scheme, you fill the sheets of a pad of paper with completely random characters. You make exactly two copies of the pad, and by hand deliver one copy to your correspondent. To send a message, you write it on the pad, one letter per letter on the pad, and simply add the letters pair-wise, where A=1, B=2, and so forth, and Z wraps back to A. The resulting letter sequence is the ciphertext. Your correspondent reverses the process, subtracting from each letter of the message the corresponding letter on the pad, revealing the plaintext. Once a sheet of the pad is used, it is destroyed. If the pad contains truly random letters, this scheme is absolutely secure. The attacker does not know what is on the pad, and must guess—but there is no way to know when he is right! By changing the guess, the attacker can decode the ciphertext into *any* message, be it "attack at dawn" or "negotiate surrender."

The one-time pad offers perfect security, and is indeed used when perfect security is needed, but the system has many disadvantages.

- The pad must be truly random. Any structure at all can be used to break the system. Creating truly random characters is difficult, and creating a vast quantity of them is more difficult.

- The pad must never be reused. If a sheet is used twice, then the two sections of ciphertext encrypted using the same page can be compared, possibly revealing both.[1] Since the pad is consumed as messages are sent, the pad has to be very long or frequently replaced.

- The pads must be distributed and stored with absolute security. Since the ciphertext cannot be successfully attacked, the obvious point of attack is to copy or substitute a pad.

- Every pair of correspondents must have a unique pad, leading to immense practical difficulties of distribution.

These practical difficulties effectively restrict the use of one-time pad systems to situations in which cost is no object. For most other situations, cryptosystems are used in which the key is a fixed size and can be attacked by exhaustive search.

Secret Key (Symmetric) Cryptography

In a symmetric cryptosystem, shown in Figure 12-1, the message, or plaintext, is encrypted using a key. The resulting ciphertext is sent to the recipient, who decrypts the message using the same key. Note that the same key must be known to both parties. Perhaps the best-known secret key system is DES, the Data Encryption Standard. Table 12-2 shows how symmetric cryptography achieves privacy, authentication, integrity, and nonrepudiation.

Suppose that Bob and Alice wish to communicate using secret key cryptography. To get started, they must agree on a key, which only they will know and which they will keep secret from all others. Once Bob and Alice have a key in common, each can encrypt messages to the other. Authentication is assured, because each knows that only the other knows the key. When a message arrives, there is only one person it could be from. Message integrity can also be assured, provided that a message digest or message integrity code is included with the message.

---

1. This has actually happened. In an effort to save money during World War II, the Soviet Union issued duplicate pads to multiple offices. By intercepting both ciphertexts, the United States was eventually able to decode many of these "Venona" messages.

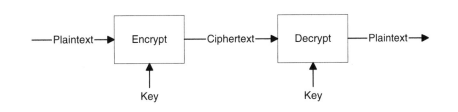

FIGURE 12-1. Symmetric Cryptosystem

Block and Stream Ciphers

A block cipher algorithm is designed to take a fixed-length block of plaintext, perhaps 64 bits, and encrypt it with the key to produce a fixed-length ciphertext. A stream cipher uses the key to produce a pseudorandom key stream, which is then typically exclusive ORed[2] with the plaintext to produce the ciphertext. Both methods have some practical disadvantages. Because each block of a block cipher is independent, an eavesdropper may notice that certain ciphertext blocks are repeated, and he will know that corresponding plaintext blocks also repeat. With the simple application of a stream cipher, the key stream repeats with each new message, making analysis easy. To combat these problems, an Initialization Vector (IV) is used. For block ciphers, the IV is prepended to the message and encrypted. Then the first block of ciphertext is exclusive ORed with the second block of plaintext, and so on. This technique is called *cipher block chaining*. The IV is different for each message. With a stream cipher, the

Privacy	Only those who know the key can encrypt or decrypt messages.
Authentication	If separate keys are used for each pair of communicating parties, then the receiver of a message can be assured that the sender was authentic. The sender knows that only the intended recipient can decrypt the message.
Integrity	Symmetric encryption does not provide message integrity without some effort. However, a message integrity code (MIC) can be added to the message. A MIC is a message digest of the message combined with the secret key.
Nonrepudiation	Symmetric cryptography does not provide nonrepudiation, since either the sender or the intended recipient could have created the message.

TABLE 12-2. Functions Provided by Secret Key Cryptography

---

2. The exclusive OR operation produces a '1' if either input bit is a '1' but not if both inputs are '1' or both are '0.'

IV is used somewhat differently. In this case, the IV and the key are used to initialize the key stream generator, so that it produces a different sequence for each message. The IV itself is sent in the clear before the ciphertext is started.

Secret Key Cryptosystems

This is by no means an exhaustive list of current symmetric cryptosystems, but is rather a quick list of interesting and commercially important systems.

- DES

  DES, for Data Encryption Standard, is a block cipher which uses a 56-bit key to encrypt a 64-bit plaintext block into a 64-bit ciphertext. DES is defined by FIPS 46, published in November 1976. The most common mode of operation of DES is called cipher block chaining (CBC). In this mode of operation each output block of ciphertext is exclusive ORed with the next input block to form the next input to the DES algorithm. The process is kicked off by a 64-bit Initialization Vector. Without CBC, individual blocks of ciphertext can be replaced by an attacker to disrupt communications, and because 8-character blocks of 8-bit data like ASCII fall naturally on 64-bit boundaries, a cryptanalyst can identify when blocks are repeated and can gain substantial insight into the plaintext.

  DES has been in use for over 20 years, and although it has withstood intense scrutiny from cryptanalysts, its 56-bit key size is becoming suspiciously small. (It turns out that inverting both the key and the plaintext inverts the ciphertext, which reduces the effective key length to 55.)

- Triple DES

  A recent variation of DES, called Triple DES or 3DES, uses three 56-bit DES keys to encrypt each block. In a Triple DES encryption operation, the data block is encrypted with the first key, decrypted[3] with the second key, and encrypted again using the third key. The middle operation is a decryption, so that if the three keys are chosen to be the same, then Triple DES reduces to ordinary DES. In its three-key mode, Triple DES requires a 168-bit key.

- IDEA

  IDEA (International Data Encryption Algorithm) is a block cipher developed by Lai and Massey, originally in 1990. IDEA uses 128-bit keys to encrypt 64-bit blocks. IDEA is widely used as the bulk encryption cipher in older versions of the Pretty Good Privacy (PGP) system.

---

3. When we say "decrypted with the second key," we mean that the DES algorithm is run in decryption mode with that key. Clearly, the decryption operation does not yield the plaintext, since a different key was used.

- RC4

  RC4 is a variable key length stream cipher designed by Ron Rivest for RSA Data Security Inc. RC4 is widely used on the Internet as the bulk encryption cipher in the Secure Sockets Layer protocol, with key lengths in the range of 40 to 128 bits. Although RC4 is a proprietary cipher of RSA DSI, and therefore violates our principle that publicly analyzed ciphers are best, in 1995, someone published on the Internet the source of a program which appears to duplicate the RC4 algorithm, so it is now receiving more study.

- Blowfish

  Blowfish is a variable key length block cipher designed by Bruce Schneier of Counterpane Systems. Blowfish is freely available, and is very fast, nearly three times faster than a DES implementation on an Intel Pentium processor. Blowfish is widely used in PC file encryption applications, secure tunneling applications, and others. The key length is variable from 32 to 448 bits, which makes it interesting for variable security applications. (See http://www.counterpane.com/blowfish.html.)

- CAST

  CAST is a variable key length block cipher designed by Carlisle Adams and Stafford Tavares for Entrust Technologies. The key length is variable from 40 to 128 bits. CAST is the standard bulk encryption cipher in the Pretty Good Privacy system. In January 1997, Entrust released a version of CAST for free use in both commercial and noncommercial applications.

Public Key (Asymmetric) Cryptography

In an asymmetric cryptosystem, shown in Figure 12-2, the encryption key is different from the decryption key. Typically, each participant in a public key system creates his own key pair. Then one member of the pair, called the private key, is kept secret and never revealed to anyone, whereas the other member of the key pair, called the public key, is distributed freely. Either key may be used for encryption or for decryption, but the most important point is that the private key never be revealed. The best-known public key cryptosystem is RSA—Rivest, Shamir, Adleman—which is named after its inventors. Continuing our analogy of a safe, a public key system is somewhat like a safe with a slot in the top. Anyone can put items into the safe, but only the person who knows the combination can get items out.

Table 12-3 shows how public key cryptography achieves privacy, authentication, integrity, and nonrepudiation.

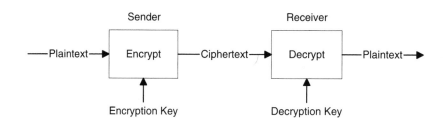

FIGURE 12-2. Asymmetric Cryptosystem

A Public Key Cryptography Example

Suppose that Bob and Alice wish to communicate using public key cryptography. To get started, Bob and Alice each create a key pair, and each pair has a public and a private key. Next Bob and Alice publish their respective public keys in the town directory.

Suppose now that Bob wishes to send Alice a message M. He encrypts the message in Alice's public key. The ciphertext can only be read by Alice because only she knows her own private key. Alice decrypts the message using her private key, revealing the original message.

Privacy	A message is encrypted by the recipient's public key. Only the recipient has the proper private key to decrypt the message.
Authentication	The recipient can authenticate the sender of a message by verifying a digital signature—a message digest of the message encrypted using the sender's private key.
Integrity	A digital signature of the message provides message integrity. A message digest of the message is encrypted using the sender's private key.
Nonrepudiation	Nonrepudiation can be provided using digital signatures. However, long after the fact, a dispute can arise about whether the signature was created at the same time as the message. For this problem, a digital timestamping service may be useful.

TABLE 12-3. Functions Provided by Public Key Cryptography

The first problem with this scheme is that anyone could have sent the message! Because Alice's public key is published in an open directory, anyone can send a message to her. If the message says, "Meet me at the trellis at midnight—Bob," how can Alice tell if the message is really from Bob or perhaps from her father who is testing her? An answer to this problem, and an application of authentication, is for Bob to apply a digital signature to the message. Suppose that Bob takes the message M and encrypts it using his private key, creating a signed message S. Anyone can decrypt this message by using Bob's public key, so it isn't secret; but only Bob could have sent it, since only Bob knows his private key.

The solution to Bob and Alice's problem—sending a secret, authenticated message—lies in the combination of these techniques. Bob first signs his message using his own private key, and then he encrypts the signed message using Alice's public key. Only Alice can decrypt this message, and once she has, she can verify that Bob sent it.

The next problem with public key cryptography is the authenticity of public keys. When Bob sends a message to Alice, he looks up Alice's public key in the directory. Suppose Alice's father has substituted his own public key in the directory. Now when Bob sends a message, he unwittingly encrypts it using not Alice's public key, but her father's key. If Alice's father is clever, he will decrypt the message, then reencrypt it using Alice's real public key. The substitution may not be discovered until Alice thinks to check the directory to see if the key listed under her name is the right one.

One solution to the problem of the security of key directories is the use of public key certificates. A public key certificate is a document containing a name and the corresponding public key, signed by a trusted certificate authority. Suppose the town clerk is operating as a certificate authority. Alice, when she first creates her public key, appears in person before the clerk with a document attesting that the public key is really hers. The clerk signs the document using her private key. The resulting signed document is a public key certificate. Anyone can verify its authenticity by checking the signature using the clerk's public key. Of course, the clerk's public key must be beyond reproach. Once Alice has a certificate, she can place it in the directory and Bob can be assured the key he uses to send messages is really Alice's key.

Certificate authorities are often organized in a hierarchy (like the DNS), which enables administrators to distribute the process of issuing the certificates. To create the hierarchy, higher-level certificate authorities sign certificates for lower-level authorities. The certificate authority at the top of the hierarchy is called the *root,* and its public key is called a *root key.*

Public Key Cryptosystems

This section reviews the RSA and elliptic curve public key cryptosystems.

RSA

The preeminent public key cryptosystem is Rivest, Shamir, Adleman (RSA). The security of RSA is based on the difficulty of factoring large numbers. An RSA public key is a modulus n and a random encryption key e. The corresponding decryption key d is kept secret. The keys e and d are chosen randomly, but these numbers are related such that $ed = 1 \mod (p - 1)(q - 1)$, where p and q are prime and $n = pq$.

RSA encryption is the mathematical operation

$$c = m^e \bmod n$$

where m is the message, c is the ciphertext, e is the encryption key, and n is the RSA modulus. Decryption is

$$m = c^d \bmod n$$

There are a number of important things to know about the RSA algorithm.

- The numbers p and q must be primes and certain "weak" forms must be avoided.

- A particular choice of p and q must never be used with multiple keys e and d—if this is done, the cipher is easily cracked.

- RSA is a block cipher where the size of the block is the size of the modulus n. Information to be encrypted must be shorter than a block, or the message must be broken up into multiple blocks.

- The message cannot be too short. If m^e is smaller than n, or only wraps a few times, then the message is easily decoded.

- There are several formatting rules for one-block messages, which make life difficult for cryptanalysts.

The best source for recommended use of RSA cryptography is the *Public-Key Cryptography Standards* (PKCS) series published by RSA Data Security Inc.

As was mentioned previously, other than the "be careful about this" items above, the security of RSA is equivalent to the problem of factoring. If the (public) modulus n can be decomposed into its factors p and q, then the private key d can be recovered. In recent years, very substantial progress in factoring has been made, with the best current algorithms being the General Number Field Sieve (GNFS) and the Special Number Field Sieve (SNFS)—which is applicable only to numbers of a special form. Table 12-4 shows some estimates for the amount of computing power necessary to factor numbers of certain sizes popular in the use of RSA. Generally speaking, the RSA modulus must be about a factor of 10 longer than a symmetric cryptosystem key of equivalent security. The constant "10" is only illustrative and changes (downwards!) as improvements are made in factoring algorithms.

Elliptic Curve

Cryptosystems based on Elliptic Curve algorithms are now being introduced. EC cryptosystems are based on the difficulty of the discrete logarithm problem, rather than on the difficulty of factoring. Barring unusual progress in solving the discrete logarithm problem, Elliptic Curve systems can achieve a particular level of security

Number Size (in Bits)	Arbitrary Integers (Using GNFS)	Special Integers (Using SNFS)
512	3×10^4	1×10^5
768	2×10^8	3×10^7
1024	3×10^{11}	3×10^7
1280	1×10^{14}	3×10^9
1536	3×10^{16}	2×10^{11}
2048	3×10^{20}	4×10^{14}

TABLE 12-4. **Computing Power Required to Factor (in MIPS-Years)**[a]

a. Andrew Odlyzko, AT&T, RSA Cryptographer's Conference, September 1996.

with shorter keys than systems based on the difficulty of factoring. Several standardization efforts are under way for EC systems in groups such as ANSI X9, ISO/IEC, and IEEE

The major difficulty with Elliptic Curve systems is that they are new. They have not survived years of intense scrutiny as have DES and RSA. However, what passes for popular opinion in the cryptographic community is that elliptic curve systems are coming up fast.

Protocols

A protocol is a series of steps taken to accomplish a task. In fact that is also the definition of an algorithm, but we use *algorithm* to refer to the attainment of internal, mathematical results like encrypting a block, and *protocol* to refer to the attainment of user-visible results such as secret communication and digital signatures.

Communications

Obviously, most of the previous discussion of secret and public key cryptosystems has been about their use in communications, but complete application of cryptography to communications also addresses some issues beyond simple encryption and decryption of blocks.

- Session keys

  A session key is a cryptographic key adopted for use for a particular message or during a particular session of communications. The use of session keys arises for two purposes: to achieve a gain in performance, and to limit the amount of information encrypted with a master key. Frequently a communications system will use a relatively low-performance public key cryptosystem only to communicate a session key, which is then used for high-performance symmetric key encryption of the bulk message data. The second reason for using session keys is to limit the amount of information available for cryptanalysis of the master key. Because only the random session keys are ever encrypted by the master key, the attacker cannot exploit any statistical properties of the actual messages to assist in the attack on the master key.

- Message integrity

  It may be possible for an attacker to alter or substitute different ciphertext somewhere along the communications channel between sender and intended recipient. It is therefore necessary to assure that the message received is the same as the message sent. Sometimes an alteration would be obvious because the received message would decrypt to gibberish, but computers are much worse than people at detecting gibberish. To solve this problem, either a message digest can be added to the plaintext before encryption, or a message integrity check or digital signature can be included as part of the ciphertext.

- Protection against replay

  It may be possible for an attacker to record an entire message, then replay it later. If duplicate messages are not detected and discarded, the attacker can cause considerable mischief. For example, if an encrypted order for widgets with instructions to charge a credit card can be replayed, then the attacker could run down the seller's widget supply or cause the buyer an overdraft.

  Duplicate messages can also arise accidentally. For example, if the communications channel goes offline during a transmission, the sender may retransmit the most recent message. But was the message lost or just the acknowledgment for it?

- Data compression

  Data compression and encryption do not mix. Or rather, they mix only when combined the right way! Data compression refers to the problem of encoding a message in the minimum amount of space. In order to do this, data compression algorithms such as the familiar ZIP and COMPRESS algorithms exploit statistical properties of the source file to encode the same information in fewer numbers of bits. Encryption destroys the very statistical properties that compression algorithms exploit, so in general it is not possible to compress an encrypted message. It is, however, possible to encrypt a compressed message! This odd property has a couple of readily apparent effects. First, a modem which depends on data compression for achieving a high bit rate will get a much lower bit rate on encrypted materials. Second, a compressing file system like the popular Stacker or Doublespace systems for PCs will not achieve any space savings when used on encrypted files.

Arguably, compressing a file before encrypting it may slightly improve security, because compression reduces redundancy, and redundancy of the plaintext can be exploited during cryptanalysis. The main point here is that encrypted files are essentially incompressible.

Chapter 13 describes some of the secure communications protocols in use on the Internet.

Message Digests and Hash Functions

Hash functions, also known as one-way functions, take a variable length message and collapse it to a fixed length, such as 128 bits or 160 bits. The result is often called a *message digest* or *hash* of the message. Hash functions are an essential element of digital signatures and of message authentication codes. Rather than create a digital signature by, say, encrypting the entire message with one's private key, one encrypts the hash of the message instead. This creates a signature whose length is a small fixed size, independent of the length of the message. Good hash functions have the property that given a particular hash (output value of a hash function), it is infeasible to guess a message that would have that hash. In addition, it should be infeasible to find any two messages which have the same hash.

Here are some widely used hash functions.

- MD5

    MD5 (the MD stands for Message Digest) is a public domain algorithm designed by Ron Rivest. It accepts as input a message which is a multiple of 512 bits long, and reduces it to a 128-bit output. Some recent results have found some weaknesses in a variant of MD5, which makes it prudent to choose alternative functions when possible. To date, such attacks do not apply to the use of MD5 for message authentication codes, so MD5 MAC algorithms continue to be acceptable. Other recent work is beginning to question nearly any 128-bit hash algorithm, so it is appropriate to choose algorithms with outputs of at least 160 bits for new system designs.

- SHA-1

    SHA-1, the Secure Hash Algorithm, was developed by the U.S. National Institute of Standards and Technology (NIST), with assistance from the National Security Agency. It accepts messages which are a multiple of 512 bits long, and produces a 160-bit output.

- RIPEMD-160

  RIPEMD, for RACE Integrity Primitives Evaluation Message Digest, is a 160-bit hash algorithm developed by the European Community's Research and Development in Advanced Computation Technologies in Europe effort.

- MDC-2 and MDC-4

  MDC-2 and MDC-4 are hash algorithms which use DES block encryption. MDC-2 was designed by IBM and is specified in ANSI X9.31 for use in financial security applications. MDC-4 uses four DES encryptions per 64-bit block of input data to produce a 128-bit output.

SHA-1 and RIPEMD-160 are on track to become ISO standards.

Message Authentication Codes

In communications, messages are often protected against accidental damage by attaching a checksum, cyclic redundancy check, or error-correcting code. The sender uses the message to compute the checksum, then sends both to the recipient. The recipient uses the message as received to recompute the checksum. If the received checksum is different from that locally computed, then a transmission error has occurred. Checksum algorithms are designed to guarantee that all errors involving fewer than so many bits are detected, and to detect all other errors with very high probability.

A message authentication code (MAC), does a very similar job, but protects the integrity of the message against both deliberate and accidental tampering. MAC algorithms use the message and a secret key (which is not transmitted with the message) as input, and produce a fixed-length output. MACs are constructed using hash functions. An attacker knows the message, but not the key, so the attacker cannot reproduce the computation. Message authentication codes are sometimes referred to as message integrity codes (MIC), because the secret key can be used to ensure both the authenticity and the integrity of the message.

Early MAC algorithms simply concatenated the key with the data and hashed the combination. Such simple approaches turn out to have cryptographic weaknesses, so recent work has focused on making stronger algorithms. An example MAC algorithm is HMAC, which can work with nearly any hashing algorithm. It is commonly used with MD5 or SHA-1.

HMAC is defined as follows:

$$HMAC = H(k \parallel opad, H(k \parallel ipad, message))[4]$$

---

4. In this formula, ‖ refers to concatenation.

In this formula, *k* is the key, and *ipad* and *opad* are padding strings of 0s necessary to pad the key up to the natural block length of the underlying hash algorithm.

Digital Signatures

A digital signature is an information block attached to a message which could only have been created by a particular individual. Using public key technology, this can be done by creating a message digest of the message, and encrypting the message digest with one's private key. Anyone can validate a signature using the corresponding public key. A digital timestamp can be used to assure the signature was created at a particular time. This is important, since if the private key is ever lost, arbitrary signatures can be created and backdated.

Timestamps

An unforgeable method of digitally timestamping a document is important when non-repudiation is important. For example, if Alice digitally signs a contract, but later wishes she hadn't, she can declare that her private key has been lost or stolen, and claim that some unknown miscreant has used her (now public) private key to sign and backdate the contract. A timestamp can prove that the document was signed and delivered before Alice claims her key was stolen. There are various ways of constructing digital timestamps; one way is for the timestamping service to digitally sign a document consisting of the document being stamped and a clock value. Obviously, one could argue that the private key of the timestamping service itself is suspect, but a solution is to place all the timestamped documents into a sequence, and to create a running message digest of them. Periodically (weekly perhaps), the current digest value is widely published, so even the timestamping service itself cannot cheat. *Surety, Inc.* operates such a service (see http://www.surety.com/).

Certificates

A public key certificate is a digital document containing a public key, the name of the key's owner (called a *distinguished name*), dates of validity, and other information, all digitally signed using the private key of a certification authority. This is a sufficiently important subject to devote a whole section to: Certificates, Certificate Authorities, and Trust Models (see page 232).

Key Exchange

Because public key technology is fairly slow, it is frequently used only for authentication and for exchange of a session key, which is then used for symmetric cryptography. However, if there is some other mechanism available for authentication, then key exchange can be used to exchange a session key. The best known key-exchange algorithm is Diffie-Hellman.

Key exchange is relevant because the combination of key exchange, symmetric cryptography, and digital signatures offers a suite of functionality essentially identical to that of full public key cryptography. This is interesting in turn because the patent protection for Diffie-Hellman expired in 1997, and there are public domain signature and symmetric cryptography algorithms.

Secret Sharing

Keeping only a single copy of a secret is safest from a security point of view—put all your eggs in one basket, then watch that basket—but it raises the prospect of a catastrophic event or natural disaster destroying the only copy. Keeping multiple copies of the secret is risky because then if any copy is lost, the secret is out. Now suppose the secret is broken up into three parts, such that any two can be used to reconstruct the secret. This is secret sharing and can be made quite general. A secret can be divided into, say, n parts, any m of which are necessary to recover the secret (m less than or equal to n). If fewer than m parts are available, no information about the secret is revealed. This technique provides safety for the secret, since any $(n - m)$ parts can be lost before the secret itself is lost, and provides substantial security, since m independent attacks must be made. (And the first attack may give warning that evildoers are afoot.)

A related idea is secret splitting, equivalent to secret sharing with $n = m$. Secret splitting is sometimes used for key distribution, with the parts of the key being sent through different communications channels.

Key Management

Key management is the hardest part of cryptography.

Key management has to do with the creation, distribution, storage, and destruction of cryptographic keys. A key is at least as valuable as all of the information legitimately encrypted with it. We say "at least" because if an attacker has a key, he can also create unauthorized messages and introduce them into the system.

Key Generation

Sometimes a cryptosystem will have some keys, or some patterns of keys, which are known to be weaker in some way than the average randomly chosen keys. The key generation procedures must avoid these weak keys, but a much more stringent requirement is that keys be random. True randomness is very difficult to achieve. An early version of a popular secure Web browser, for example, created cryptographic keys which were based in part on the time of day, as given by the machine's clock.

Since the attacker knows the time of day fairly accurately, the amount of randomness in the keys was greatly reduced, leading to a successful attack in only a few minutes of computer time.

There are true random number key generators available, which are based on such natural physical phenomena as radioactivity or shot noise. These devices are not broadly deployed and are expensive. For keys generated by computer software, two solutions are popular.

- User input

  For long-term keys, key generators rely on input from outside the computer. Typically, the user is asked to type randomly for a while. The letters typed are ignored, and instead slight random variations in the interarrival time of keystrokes are used.

- Pseudorandom

  For moment-to-moment creation of short-term keys, key generation is pseudorandom, combining unpredictable pieces of information such as the process identifier, the computer's real-time clock, the number of hardware interrupts received, and so forth. None of these items are random enough alone, but the idea is that by combining all of them, a *randomness pool* is created, from which one can draw keys which are sufficiently random for most purposes.

In addition to these methods, there may be real random numbers available to software. There is some recent work suggesting that air turbulence within computer disk drives may be a source of natural randomness that can be exploited for key generation.

Passwords intended for human use are also keys. When people choose their own passwords, they tend to choose poor ones. The trouble with machine-generated passwords is that they are difficult to remember, and they get written down, which is also not good. (Actually, in an era of network threats to security, writing down a really good password and sticking it in your purse may be the best choice. To protect against insiders, write down only part of the key and remember the rest.) The usual advice is to use a long, memorable password, such as a multiword *pass phrase* or a password composed of multiple words separated by weird punctuation.

Key Storage

Proper short- and long-term storage of cryptographic keys is essential to good security.

- In memory

  When a key is used by a computer, it must necessarily be in memory. This is a problem on most computers, because the contents of memory may be available to other software running on the same system. On a PC, there is no real defense against this issue. On multiuser systems, memory is protected from other users, but usually a privileged user or a debugger necessarily has access to the memory of other processes. For these reasons, an online key is only as secure as access to the machine and the system administrator password.

To reduce somewhat the effects of online storage, good practice includes zeroing out all storage used for keys before the memory involved is released back to the operating system.

- On disk

  Cryptographic keys are frequently stored in disk files. This is done because they are too long and too random to require they be entered by hand. Key files on disk are frequently stored in encrypted form. The good news is that stealing the encrypted file may not benefit the attacker. The bad news is that the security of all the keys in the file is only as good as that of the master key, which is frequently a human-sensible password, not a true random key. In addition, one should understand where the file password itself is kept! If the system needs to be able to automatically start after a power failure, then the key file password needs to be online somewhere. If automatic restart is not required, then an operator may be prompted to enter the key file password. In this case the operator might wonder if he or she is really talking to the real key unlocking software or to a clever imitation seeking only to steal the key file password.

  Because of these limitations, security for encrypted key files generally also reduces to the physical security of the computer combined with the security of the administrator password. And do not forget that the key file will be present on backup tapes. How are they handled and stored?

- In protected hardware

  Commercial systems frequently use protected hardware devices such as cryptographic accelerators or smart cards both to store keys and to do cryptographic operations. The idea is that since the key never leaves the device, and the device is designed to be tamperproof, the key can be given physical security.

  One problem is that although it may be impossible to steal a key so stored (at least the theft would be detected!), it still may be possible for rogue software to command the use of the keys to decrypt or encrypt messages on behalf of unauthorized parties.

- Offline storage

  Truly valuable keys may not be kept online at all, but used only on isolated computer systems and when not in use kept in a vault. If the safety of a single copy is worrisome, *secret sharing* may be used to split the key into a number of separate parts, some subset of which are needed to recreate the key.

  When keys, or the keys to unlock encrypted key files, are kept offline, there needs to be documented procedures for who has access to the keys, how they are to be handled, and how they are to be stored and destroyed.

Key Destruction

Cryptographic keys remain valuable long after they leave service. An attacker can record all the ciphertext encrypted under a key and hold it for long periods. If the key becomes available later, all the saved ciphertext can be decrypted easily.

- Keys stored in RAM—Zero immediately after use.

- Keys stored on disk—Overwrite multiple times with 0s, 1s, alternating patterns, and random patterns. It turns out that it is possible to analyze "erased" magnetic media several layers deep.

- Keys stored on paper—Burn or shred with a confetti shredder, not a strip shredder.

- Keys stored on backup tapes—If you must keep backup tapes of keys, keep them on segregated tapes which contain no other vital information. Then they can be destroyed.

Key Distribution

Sometimes keys do not need to be distributed. For example, when cryptography is used to encrypt files on the disk of a personal computer, there is no need to distribute the key to anyone. In most situations, however, cryptography is used in situations where two or more persons, located at some distance from one another, must exchange keys. When two people are involved, the situation is fraught with peril. When a whole network of keys must be distributed, the situation gets complicated.

There are several methods for sharing a key between two people.

- Meet in person

  This procedure is the simplest to understand, but it doesn't scale well to thousands of people, and it is expensive. A whole batch of keys can be exchanged in advance this way, but then they must all be stored securely.

- Send the key by courier

  The essential problem is whether to trust the courier! One can split the key and send the parts by different routes, but this adds to the expense.

- Use a master, or key exchange, key to encrypt session keys

  This is a time-tested method, especially if the key exchange keys are stored in protected hardware.

- Use public key cryptography or a key exchange protocol

  These schemes permit the secure exchange of keys with someone, but who? The problem is translated from privacy to authentication. The public key solution is a certificate, and the key exchange protocol solution is either a digital signature or an out-of-band confirmation such as a telephone call to confirm delivery. It is particularly important to guard against man-in-the-middle attacks, in which an attacker pretends to be each party to the other.

When more than two parties must communicate, pairwise key exchange quickly becomes unmanageable.

When keys must be exchanged among multiple parties, either a key distribution center (KDC) is used, or public key certificates are used.

- Key distribution center

  In these schemes, each member of the network has a key exchange key in common with a central, trusted server. Either the KDC distributes the necessary pairwise keys in batch, or the KDC can operate in real time to create keys as the need arises.

- Public key certificates

  As mentioned earlier, a certificate connects a public key to a name, by having a trusted third party (the certificate authority) sign the certificate. These certificates can be freely published, or exchanged over open communications channels. Parties wishing to communicate use the public key from the certificate of their chosen correspondent to encrypt a session key.

Each scheme requires a central authority of some sort. Either an online key distribution center creates keys as needed, or an offline key distribution center distributes keys, or an offline authority certifies public keys. The trade-offs are in the details. Is a reliable online service required? How are keys revoked? Does the KDC have the ability to read all messages? The public key systems seem to be the most powerful when communicants with no prior relationship wish to communicate, provided that each is willing to trust a third party to authenticate the other.

Certificates, Certificate Authorities, and Trust Models

A public key certificate is a message containing a public key, a name, and some dates of validity, all signed by the private key of a trusted certificate authority (CA).

The primary purpose of a certificate is to attest to the connection between the public key and the name of its owner. One should read a certificate as, "I, the certification authority, attest that the attached public key belongs to the entity named herein." Certificates are very useful, because they permit a solution to the problem of authentication without requiring an online key distribution center. Parties who wish to communicate go independently to the CA and have their public keys signed. Then when Alice wishes to communicate with Bob, she sends Bob her public key certificate along with her signed message. Bob is able to validate the certificate because the public key of the certification authority is (must be) known to everyone. The other situation in which a public key certificate is very useful is when Alice wishes to send an encrypted message to Bob. Alice must either already have Bob's public key, or must obtain it from Bob or from a directory service. In either case, Alice needs to know that the key is really Bob's, or that the directory has not been tampered with. A certificate is freestanding—built into it is the statement from the certification authority that the public key is Bob's. (The next step is to wonder if the person using Bob's certificate is really Bob! This step is accomplished because only Bob has the private key that matches the public key in Bob's certificate.)

The standard format for certificates is the ISO standard X.509. Two versions are in common use. X.509 Version 1 certificates contain a public key, the distinguished name (an X.500 name) of the owner, dates of validity, the distinguished name of the certificate authority, and the signature of the CA. X.509 Version 3 certificates also contain a flexible set of attribute/value pairs.

The best-known commercial certificate authority is Verisign (see http://www.verisign.com), but other organizations are setting up to issue commercial certificates as well, including the U.S. Postal Service and other PTTs. A number of companies sell public key systems, including certificate-issuing systems, which can be used to set up a complete public key infrastructure.

Summary

Cryptography provides the essential tools to provide privacy, authentication, message integrity, and sometimes nonrepudiation on an open network. Cryptography provides the machinery which makes possible such technologies as Secure Sockets Layer for Web communications and Secure Electronic Transactions for credit card transactions on the Internet. In effect, cryptography makes it possible to accomplish at a distance, over an open and untrustworthy network, what would otherwise require face-to-face meetings.

Security

You can wear a flak jacket, but still be hit by a bus.
—Shikhar Ghosh

Concerns about Security

Security is often cited as one of the greatest barriers to Internet commerce. Of course, security is important to Internet commerce systems in many ways, but it is really part of the way that business is enabled by the technology. Indeed, the security of systems for electronic commerce is a business problem, not merely a technology problem. Technologies such as public key encryption provide critical components of an overall solution, but they are not enough. In this chapter we suggest some ways to think about the security of the whole system; we review the technologies of security; and we discuss a number of related areas, such as export control. Although many of the topics here are relevant for Internet security in general, not just for commerce, our focus is on what is necessary to build Internet commerce applications.

Although there are good reasons for caution around security issues, it is possible to do business on the Internet today with a secure system, using the principles described in this chapter. These principles apply both to systems designed from scratch as well as to systems built around off-the-shelf products for Internet commerce.

Readers less interested in the technical details should read the first few sections to understand the basics, then skim the remainder of the chapter. Those interested in more depth than we provide here should refer to the references at the end of the book.

Why We Worry about Security for Internet Commerce

Many people have heard vague stories and statements about the security of Internet commerce, and their first reaction is caution (sometimes, paralyzing caution). Others wonder what all the fuss is about, since we do not spend much time worrying about the security of transactions in the physical world. Why is the Internet different? Why does it inspire such worries?

There are actually many reasons why the Internet is different, and why we should be cautious.

The Physical World Does Worry about Security

Many of the issues we call "security problems" for Internet commerce are the online analogues of real-world business issues. We want certain kinds of business communications to be private; we expect to be paid with real money; we require personal signatures on contracts, etc. These expectations, and the means by which we accomplish them, have been developed over thousands of years—through the entire history of commerce. On the Internet, we are faced with these issues in a different context, so we are forced to make them explicit and to develop new solutions, all over a comparatively short period of time.

Our Computers Are Connected

Through most of the history of computers, one had to be in the same room to use one, or at least on a directly connected terminal. As long as only trusted users had access to the rooms and the terminals, the security of the system itself was not so important. On the Internet, we are allowing anyone in the world to use our computers, if only (we hope) in a small way, such as to fetch a Web page. But now we have created a hole in the dike, and we must be careful with how we design, implement, and operate our systems to ensure that the entire dike is not swept away.

The Network Is Public

An "internetwork" is an interconnected collection of networks, and the Internet (with a capital "I") is the biggest interconnected data network in the world. The individual networks are owned by thousands of different individuals and organizations, and there is no central control of the network at all. What holds the Internet together is an agreement on common protocols to use and the fact that networks carry traffic for each other. For example, in the early days of the Internet, it was common for network packets to traverse university networks where any sufficiently motivated and clever undergraduate could read them. By contrast, in most countries, the telephone system evolved under the control of a single entity. But even in the early days of the telephone, privacy was a problem. Party lines were common, with multiple people sharing the same line. Telephone operators, especially in small towns, could—and did—listen to conversations. As the system evolved over many years, the technology and the organizations changed so that we now expect our telephone calls to be private. Indeed, so strong is this expectation that many people are surprised when cellular phone conversations are recorded, despite the fact that cell phones are radios.

The Network Is Digital

Given access to the telephone system, it is still difficult —or at least time-consuming—to get useful information by listening to telephone calls. If one can target a particular person directly, of course, it is much easier. But if one simply listens to random telephone calls, it may be quite a while before one gets so much as a credit card number. A computer network, on the other hand, makes it possible to listen to many "conversations" simultaneously. Moreover, a computer can sift through the conversations looking for particular patterns, such as the numeric pattern of a credit card number, without the attacker having to do any work personally.

Computers Collect Data

Suppose that we keep a (paper) file on each customer in our file cabinet, and that one item in each file is a credit card number. An attacker with access to the file cabinet can go through each file to collect a list of credit card numbers—a feasible though tedious attack. If, on the other hand, we have a single sheet of paper listing all the customers and their credit card numbers, then the attacker's job is much easier. Computer systems are frequently like that: the desired (and sensitive) data are easily accessible, or programs can be used to perform searches. The use of the computer by itself may make certain kinds of attacks possible, so we must address problems that are not "realistic attacks" in the noncomputer (or precomputer) world.

Computers Can Be Programmed

As we have just seen, one of the problems is that an attacker can use a computer to sift through data looking for important information. Computers can also be programmed for other nefarious activities: submitting hundreds (or thousands) of fraudulent orders, or probing for ways to gain access to a computer system. In particular, sophisticated attackers can write and distribute programs that are used by unskilled attackers, which makes the unskilled attackers dangerous. It is as if one could easily get a simple-to-use machine for picking locks, rather than having to learn and practice in order to be an effective lock picker.

Without Good Security, Computer Fraud Is Untraceable

On an insecure computer system, an attack may leave no trace. Crimes in the physical world always leave some physical evidence—a witness, footprints, fingerprints, pictures on a security camera, and so on. Security and cryptographic subsystems both protect the system and provide some traces of what actions have been performed, and by whom. Because we create the entire environment on the computer, we must also create these subsystems—there are no properties of nature to help us.

Computers Are Not Perfect Replacements for Humans

In many respects, computerized order taking is cheaper and more efficient than having a person answering a telephone call to write down an order. On the other hand, a person can be more flexible in working with a customer, or can observe something unusual about an order or pattern of orders. Machines do not have that flexibility. It may even be the case that some people are more willing to lie to a computerized system than they are to a person on the phone, so the potential class of attackers is suddenly much larger.

The Internet Seems Anonymous and Distant

In many ways, communication over the Internet seems more abstract, more impersonal, or less real, than communication in person, or even over the telephone. This "virtualness" means that some people may try to defraud, confuse, or play a prank on a distant, faceless Web site, when they would never think of doing something like that to a neighborhood store. Conversely, this distance means that it is all the more important that consumers be assured that they are dealing with the business they intend to. It is hard in the physical world to fool someone into thinking they are at a well-known department store, but such deception can be much easier online. Even in the physical world, problems like this can arise: there have been instances where fake ATMs were set up to collect account numbers and PINs.

Information Commerce Is Different

Many of our security concerns are especially true for information commerce. Online information is easy to copy, distribute, and modify. If we are selling information, we want it delivered only to the buyer, not to anyone who happens to be eavesdropping. In the physical world, the mail carrier could copy a magazine, but doing so requires a fair bit of effort, whereas copying the electronic version requires just a few keystrokes. As buyers of information, we want to be sure that the information sent is what we receive. Again, it requires substantial effort to intercept and modify a piece of physical mail, but it is much easier electronically. As sellers of information, we usually want to deliver it immediately, so we have no opportunity for later checks as we do in mail-order retail, or we have no existing business relationship. We do not even have a delivery address in the physical world, so it is exceedingly difficult to track down a fraudulent transaction.

The Legal System Must Catch Up

Many of the issues that we have described here are handled by the legal system. But the legal system relies on many physical pieces of evidence—contracts on paper, signatures, delivery addresses, and so on—in establishing a case. We take it for granted that a person's signature is so difficult to forge that it is very hard to prove that one did not sign something if the signature appears to be legitimate. What substitutes for the signature in Internet commerce? In most cases (if at all), we use digital signatures. But this is not only a relatively new technology, it takes some effort to understand the subtleties of digital signatures. Similarly, other areas of the law—many of them so familiar that we hardly think about them—are challenged by the changes in technology.

There Are Proven Paths of Attack

Computer systems have proven vulnerable in the past to attackers, so we must be careful and vigilant with new systems for Internet commerce. There is a perception that there is a problem. Internet security has become front page news for the *New York Times* and the *Wall Street Journal,* so many people—both buyers and sellers—are concerned about the security issues. Even where the risks may seem lower than some in the physical world, today the perception is that the risks are much higher, so it is important that they be addressed in the design and implementation of systems for Internet commerce.

Because We Can

One of the remarkable things about cryptography is the kind of protection it gives us for many applications. Internet commerce applications are among the easiest to secure with cryptography, but it will increasingly find its way into other applications in the physical world, as we understand better how to combat many kinds of crime by judicious use of strong security systems originally developed for the online world.

Risk of the Unknown

Finally, we always worry about diving into uncharted waters. Our current business and legal systems are so familiar that we tend not to think about how we got to where we are today. It is often useful to recall the evolution of money, bank vaults, the law of contracts, and the telephone system as we recapitulate much of that evolution over a very short period of time.

Thinking about Security

Most experienced practitioners find it appropriate to think of security as a problem of managing risk. This is true for three reasons. First, the security you need depends on what you are trying to protect. Banks use different security systems than retail stores, for example. Second, additional security almost always comes with additional cost, inconvenience, or delay. At some point, the costs of adding security outweigh the advantages. Third, there is no point in making the security of one area of a system very much stronger than at another point, for a chain is only as strong as its weakest link.

In reality, security is a property of the whole system. The security of a bank, for example, depends on its vault, guards, video cameras, motion sensors, the vigilance of employees, and the procedures for operating all of the equipment and handling problems. Similarly, the security of an Internet commerce system requires appropriate technology, but it also requires a clear understanding of what is being protected, along with careful operation and monitoring by the people running it.

Technology

In effect, technology components are the tools in the security toolbox, to be used in constructing a secure system. These components include cryptographic mechanisms, secure communications protocols, ways to store sensitive information, and so on. Most discussions about security, especially for Internet commerce, focus on these components, and we describe them in more detail later in this chapter.

Policies and Procedures

A security policy defines what is being protected, and why. It outlines the threats against the system that we want to defend against. By doing so, it allows us to design a security subsystem to protect the application as well as to evaluate the resulting implementation to see if the security goals are being satisfied. Over time, the policy can also be used to guide an evaluation of whether or not the system is operating correctly. Of course, the policy itself may evolve over time, with corresponding changes in the implementation of the security subsystems. It is especially important for the policy to evolve along with changes in the business, since such changes may change the nature of the risks involved. For example, a larger business may simply attract more of the wrong kind of attention than a smaller one.

Procedures record how the system should be operated to comply with the policy. Writing them down allows the right things to be done again and again, instead of being done when (or if) someone remembers to do them.

People

It is often said that people are the weakest link in any computer security system, since they can be tricked, persuaded, or coerced into assisting attackers. Much of the time, they might not even be aware of what they are doing. This is why proper training about security issues is essential, and not just for the operators. Everyone involved with the system should be aware of the security policy, the mechanisms used to implement the policy, and their own responsibilities for safeguarding information. We outline some specific ideas later in this chapter.

Security Design

With these issues in mind, we turn to the high-level design of secure systems. The security design should be part of a project from its very beginning, for it is much more expensive to add security after the fact than to design security into the system from the start. We recommend following a five-step process for the security design of a system for electronic commerce.

1. Create the security policy.
2. Add appropriate security mechanisms to the application.
3. Design the security of the physical, network, and computer system environment.
4. Develop feedback, monitoring, and auditing mechanisms to observe the system in operation.
5. Use the results of monitoring and auditing to refine the design, implementation, and operation of the system.

This cycle is depicted graphically in Figure 13-1.

Create the Security Policy

The first step in a security design is the creation of the security policy. A policy should cover the whole system, including information systems (computers and networks), data (development, production, and backup information), and people (operators, maintenance personnel, customers). The policy should include a discussion of what is being protected, what kinds of protection are needed, who is responsible for different parts of the system, any necessary training, and what kinds of monitoring and auditing are required.

Design the Environment

The second step is to design the environment for the application. The environment design includes all of the components outside the application itself, such as the computers, operating systems, networks, and physical location. Often the environment may provide some capabilities or protection for the application, so the application need not duplicate them. (Note, however, that such capabilities should be documented, so that the application can be recreated elsewhere should the need arise.) In other cases, the environment may constrain the application in certain ways, or require that special security measures be taken by the application because they are not part of the environment.

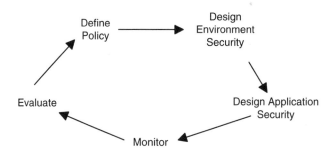

FIGURE 13-1. Security Design Cycle

For example, suppose an application operates on systems protected by strong physical security. Furthermore, the operators perform all of their work on local consoles. In this case, the application may place less emphasis on authentication and access control for management operations, because it can assume that the operators must have been authenticated to gain access in the first place. An application designed to be managed remotely, however, would have a very different set of concerns. Note, however, we did not say the application would have *no* emphasis on authentication and access control. It is still good practice for the application to have its own means of authentication and access control, because it is possible for the physical security mechanisms to fail.

In practice, the design of the environment and the design of the application security mechanisms may interact a good deal. Some security problems may be easier to solve in the application than the environment, and vice versa. In some cases, especially in product design, the application may impose some requirements on the environment it will be used in. The important thing is to consider the design of the whole system—application and environment—in developing the security design.

Design the Application Security Mechanisms

The third step in security design is providing security mechanisms for the application itself. The general design of the application, along with the security policy, should already provide the requirements for what is being protected and give some guidance on the kind of protection needed. The security design, then, can apply technology components, such as cryptography, authentication, and authorization systems. In addition to these generic mechanisms for controlling access to information, there may be some specific requirements of the application itself. For example, if the application is for the sale of software over the network, the security system might include product keys that permit the software to run only on the particular customer's computer. As in this example, the security required for an application often goes well beyond simply encrypting communications on an open network or protecting against attackers breaking into a computer system.

Monitoring and Auditing

Beyond even the special requirements of a particular application, security requires feedback mechanisms to insure that the security mechanisms are working correctly, containment mechanisms to limit the extent of damage, and recovery mechanisms in the event of a problem. In the physical world, there is still a role for the watchman, who makes sure that the locks on the doors are actually locked. In the electronic realm, these checks and balances take on the form of audit trails, velocity checks, and customer service. The information provided by such mechanisms can be used in many ways: recreating what happened if a problem occurs, checking to ensure that attacks are unsuccessful, verifying that the operation complies with the security policy, and evaluating whether or not the security policy, design, and mechanisms are effective for the application.

Computer security experts often point out that security is a property of the whole system. The designers and operators of a service must think carefully about the application, the risks, and the value at stake before deciding on the level of security to be provided, and within each level, they must think about the relative strength of the security mechanisms deployed.

Analyzing Risk

Part of designing an appropriate security policy is to determine what level of protection is warranted against what kinds of threats. A bank, for example, faces different risks than a homeowner, and the bank is therefore willing to pay more to protect itself against those risks. Many choices in computer security are determined by how much the security measures cost (which may be in money, performance, or inconvenience). Without a good understanding of the benefits of particular security measures, it is impossible to evaluate the choices from a business point of view. In this section, we look at how to analyze computer security risks and evaluate means of reducing those risks.

Adversaries

The first step is to "know thy enemy." People often begin by focusing on types of attacks and the ensuing damage, but means of attack are merely the tools. A determined attacker, for example, may be willing to work very hard to penetrate a system, whereas a casual attacker may give up easily. Both may try the same kind of attacks, but the persistence can make a big difference. Hence, it is important to ask the following questions.

1. Who are your adversaries?

2. What are their intentions?

3. What are their resources?

Here are some potential groups to think about.

- Crackers

  Crackers are the *cyberpunks* who like to break into computer systems for fun, vandalism, or to show off. Crackers may use off-the-shelf attack software from the Net or from magazines, perhaps without really understanding it. Crackers typically do not have powerful computing resources, and their intentions are frequently not inimical. They often cause substantial damage, whether from vandalizing systems, disrupting operations, or just taking up the time of systems staff trying to figure out the damage and repair it.

- Researcher

  A researcher may work very hard to expose weaknesses in secure protocols, and publish those weaknesses on the Net. Their revelations cause publicity and embarrassment, but lead indirectly to more secure systems. Researchers typically do have access to very substantial computing resources, from networks of idle networked computers to special-purpose hardware or supercomputers.

- Criminals

  Even without the Internet, there is an immense amount of white-collar crime, much of it exploiting weaknesses in computer systems. Because the Internet is both ubiquitous and anonymous, it has become an attractive venue for crime. Internet crimes range from simple fraud with stolen credit card numbers to sophisticated attacks for access to money or information. Criminals may not have the resources to break encryption schemes, but they can easily afford to bribe employees or other individuals with access to electronic commerce systems. The intentions of the criminal are financial gain.

- Competitors

  A competitor might not break into your computer systems to steal money or destroy records, but access to your customer lists or business plans may be very valuable to them. In addition, a competitor who learns of weaknesses in the security of your systems might use that information against you in competitive sales situations or to generate bad publicity for you. Although corporations may have large resources, they are not likely to spend a large amount in an illegal or unethical way.

- Governments

  In an intensely competitive world economy, more and more government intelligence agencies are working to the economic advantage of domestic industry at the expense of foreign industry. Such organizations typically are not after direct financial rewards, instead they focus on proprietary design information, pricing information, and accurate intelligence about competitive sales situations. Government intelligence agencies will have immense resources at their disposal.

- Insiders

  Disaffected, disgruntled, or greedy employees may be the most serious threat to the security of electronic commerce systems. Insiders, by definition, have access to sensitive systems and information. There are technical ways to safeguard systems, such as protected hardware devices, but audit trails, cross-checks and good employee relations are essential. One of the most important decisions in designing an application is how much security is oriented toward external threats and how much toward internal threats.

- Anyone with physical access

  Anyone with physical access to facilities is a potential security threat. Cleaning crews, delivery personnel, contractors, visitors, and temporary workers all have access but may not be subject to the same training, scrutiny, and supervision as full-time staff.

Different organizations will assess the risks posed by each of these groups differently, but it is important to think through all of them (and any others you might think of).

Threats

With some idea about who the possible attackers are, we can consider what the possible attacks might be. For example, communications over open networks are exposed to many threats, such as eavesdropping, masquerading, and others. Furthermore, the client and server computers may be attacked, and an application itself may be subject to attack entirely outside the client-server realm. Here are some attacks against these systems.

- Service interruption or degradation

  This type of problem can be caused by equipment failures, such as disk, computer, or network failures. More ominously, a *denial of service* attack from the outside may disrupt operations. For example, an attacker could exploit a bug in the operating system of a server—perhaps one unrelated to the commerce application—to crash the system. In such an attack, no private information is disclosed, but the attack does interfere with the effective operation of the business.

- Theft and fraud

  An unauthorized user may be able to fraudulently obtain goods or services. This could happen due to a failure of authentication, in which the unauthorized user successfully impersonates an authorized user. For example, an attacker, by guessing passwords, may be able to gain access to another user's account. In a more complex situation, a user may be able to manufacture unauthorized discount coupons.

- Misappropriation

  Payments from legitimate users may be directed to an unauthorized party. Although this may be difficult when credit cards are used, other payment systems may be more susceptible. For example, one seller, appearing to be legitimate, might sell access to another seller's content. The payment would go to the wrong party, with the buyer unaware of the diversion.

- Data contamination

  Records kept by the system may be destroyed or become untrustworthy. This may be caused by a software bug or an equipment failure, or it may be an active attack. Such an attack can take several forms: the attacker might alter legitimate records or inject false information into the system. A problem with contaminated data may go well beyond any actual modifications. For example, if business records are lost, anyone who is aware of the problem can challenge transactions, knowing that the records cannot be used to defend against the dispute.

- Theft of records

  An attacker may gain access to your business records, confidential information about your system, or private information about your customers. For example, an intruder may steal customer files, perhaps including credit card numbers.

- Content alteration

  Attackers may break into a system and modify its content. For instance, crackers may break into a Web site and paint graffiti over its image files.

- Masquerade

  Attackers create a "look-alike" Web site, which draws unsuspecting users. For example, attackers might spoof the Domain Name System (DNS) to lure customers to a false site.

The methods used to implement these sorts of attacks are complex and varied. Here are some of the attack mechanisms, which can be combined in interesting ways.

- Eavesdropping

  An intruder listens to the messages going by on the network. The messages may or may not be encrypted, but even if they are, they can still be recorded for later analysis.

- Traffic analysis

  An intruder learns that certain clients are talking to certain servers. Historically, traffic analysis has been very valuable in military and diplomatic situations. For example, a sudden increase in message traffic between the command center and units in the field may indicate an attack is imminent, even if the messages cannot be decoded. In commercial situations, it may be useful to know that two supposed competitors are talking. Most electronic commerce systems, or Internet systems in general, make no attempt to avoid traffic analysis.

- Cryptanalysis

  An intruder tries to decode encrypted messages. There are many different techniques in this category, including brute force attempts to guess decryption keys, attacks on algorithm and protocol weaknesses, and attacks on the systems for generating and distributing keys.

- Authentication attack

  An intruder masquerades as the server you think you are talking to, or masquerades as a legitimate customer. This is also a broad category, including guessing passwords, stealing a legitimate user's credentials, and so on.

- Substitution attack

  An intruder substitutes all or part of a message with something different.

- Skimming

  An intruder may attack the system a little at a time, spread out to such a degree that the overall impact remains undetected. For example, if an attacker has a large supply of stolen credit card numbers, each may be used only once.

Basic Computer Security

Computer security is a subject worthy of several books, and some good ones are listed at the end of this book. In addition, it is always changing. New hardware and new software arrives constantly, and the pace of change for Internet technologies only compounds the problem. New systems, and even changes to existing systems, require new security analyses. Beyond the technology evolution, changing business requirements demand system changes as well.

Key Security Issues

Computer security has many enemies, including complexity, flexibility, and people. Complex software has bugs, which can be exploited by an adversary. Very flexible software is difficult to configure correctly, which leads to errors. Too many users leads to diffusion of the responsibility for security.

- Complexity

  Software has bugs, and more complex software has more bugs. Sometimes bugs are fairly harmless. When they are not, they may open a path of attack. This kind of bug often occurs when software is given unexpected inputs. Although it may work when the input is within bounds, it may fail in dangerous ways when an adversary drives the software outside its intended regime.

For example, a network application may fail to check the length of character strings submitted over the network. An adversary sends a very long string, which overwrites the application's stack, causing it to execute code sent by the attacker. The adversary now has all the privileges of that application—which may be access to the entire system.

- Flexibility

Complex systems are often difficult to configure correctly. Configuration entries may appear innocuous but have great consequences for security. Systems that are changed frequently are particularly vulnerable to such problems, and frequent change is common for Internet systems responding to changing business requirements.

For example, suppose that a user asks that a file be made readable to everyone temporarily. When the immediate need is over, no one remembers to change it back, leaving a part of the system unprotected.

- People

Generally speaking, the more people who have access to a computer, the less secure it will be. Although most multiuser computers go to some trouble to isolate users from one another, that isolation is effective only if carefully administered.

Security Principles

When constructing electronic commerce applications or other applications of networked computers, the following principles are useful.

- Keep the security system very simple.

Complex applications may be unavoidable, along with their attendant bugs. One way to help protect such a system is to isolate it from some kinds of network access with a *firewall*. A firewall limits the kinds of network traffic allowed through to the end system. In practice, a firewall system should be simple to evaluate the correctness of the firewall implementation and configuration. *If you have some complex software, keep it from the bad guys with some simple software.*

- Limit changes to system configuration.

Every change to the configuration of the system is a potential source of security problems. Obviously, a mistake in configuration may open a hole, but sometimes even a seemingly correct change may cause a problem in combination with other configuration options. In any event, careful records of changes are essential. *If you do not understand the configuration of the system, you do not understand its security.*

- Consider new versions carefully.

  New versions of software may offer attractive new features, but they may also have unknown security problems. You may need some time to learn how to operate it securely. Of course, it is important to track and install patches for security problems as quickly as possible, but other changes should receive cautious deliberation. *New software is seductive, but it may be dangerous.*

Basic Internet Security

The Internet is a worldwide collection of interconnected computer networks. Generally speaking, a computer is connected to the Internet if it has an Internet Protocol (IP) address and can exchange packets with other similarly connected computers. This is possibly too strict a definition, because many machines, located on corporate, government, or university networks, are partly isolated from the general network by firewalls. These partly isolated machines may not have the ability to exchange low-level network packets with the main Internet, but if they have the ability to send and receive electronic mail and the ability to connect to World Wide Web sites, then we will consider them to be connected.

For convenience, we divide the computer population into clients and servers. Generally speaking, clients are desktop machines whose function is accomplishing a wide variety of computing tasks for an individual. Server computers, on the other hand, are set up to deliver a more constrained set of services to a wide variety of users. This difference leads to Internet clients and servers generally operating in widely different environments, running different application and communications software, holding different kinds of data, and being subject to different sorts of security problems.

Client Security Issues

The typical Internet client computer is an Intel PC, Macintosh, or desktop workstation, with a TCP/IP stack and a number of Internet client applications. (If the PC is running server applications, then we will consider it to be a server.) There are two key issues to client security to be considered: how does the attacker get at the client and what does he do once there?

Methods of Attack on Client Computers

The following are potential methods of attack on client computers.

Physical Access to the Computer

Take a few minutes to wander around your company offices. Count the unattended computers. If machines are left logged in but unattended at night, then they are accessible to the cleaning staff and whoever else has physical access at night. Even if unattended machines are only a problem during business hours, what are the site policies about escort of visitors? If visitors are not a problem, insiders who might not want to use their own computer accounts for mischief might feel free to use others'.

Opportunistic Introduction of Software (Viruses)

Because personal computers, both IBM PC clones and Macintoshes, were not designed to be multiuser machines, they are quite vulnerable to computer viruses. The problem is that any program running on a PC has essentially complete access to all hardware and software on the system. A virus can flash messages on your screen, alter other programs to propagate itself, or erase your hard disk. Anti-virus software attempts to combat these problems by matching new software against a library of known viruses and by intercepting suspicious system calls.

Classically, viruses get into PCs by riding along with new software as it is loaded. Whenever a floppy disk is written by an infected machine, the virus adds itself to the disk. When the disk is run on another system, the virus has a new home.

Software in the original packaging is not immune; viruses can be introduced into software during manufacturing if the master disk becomes infected before duplication. When this happens, it is a source of huge embarrassment to the vendor, but that doesn't help the victims.

Network Security Problems

Personal computers are capable of using network file servers and are usually capable of exporting or publishing the content of the local hard disk to the network. If the security settings of such network file systems are set improperly or not set at all, the computer or the information on it may be compromised.

In addition, since client computers sometimes run network servers, such as personal Web servers, many of the security aspects of operating server computers apply also to clients.

Directed Attack over the Network

After more than a decade of computer viruses, personal computer users are beginning to appreciate the dangers of loading new software on their machines. A computer connected to a network, however, is subject to additional forms of attack, based on content and automatically installed software, rather than user-installed software.

PC mail software has the ability to transmit attachments in addition to straight text. Attachments are arbitrary documents intended for manipulation and display by particular applications. If the application has security holes, such as unguarded scripting languages, a virus can be sent along with the document. When the unwary user clicks on the document in order to see what is in it, the associated application is launched and the virus is in.

World Wide Web applets have similar problems. An applet is an executable program attached to a page of Web content. Applets are typically written in the Java programming language or as ActiveX controls. The designers of applet systems appreciate the security risks of running arbitrary programs on an unguarded computer, and the Java and ActiveX communities have taken different approaches to the problem. Java applets run in what is called a sandbox. The idea is that the applets' activities are confined to the sandbox, so it cannot do anything harmful. The problem with sandboxes is the tension between a sandbox that is sufficiently restrictive to be safe, yet sufficiently open that the applet can accomplish something useful. ActiveX controls take a different approach; they have full access to the machine, but are digitally signed by the vendor, so that the question is not "Is this applet safe?" but rather "Do I trust that XYZ Corporation has made sure it is safe?" The Java community is also developing code-signing technology, so this may be the wave of the future—at least until personal computer software is no longer subject to virus attacks.

Protocol Attacks

An attacker may occasionally be able to exploit knowledge of the client computer to mount an attack against a network security protocol, without actually breaking into the client at all. In 1995, students at the University of California at Berkeley, for example, used knowledge about client computers to mount an attack against the key generation software in a secure Web protocol. This permitted messages to and from that particular computer to be read.

Purposes of Attacks on Client Computers

Once a malevolent piece of code gains access to the desktop computer, what are its intentions?

Annoyance

Some attacks do nothing overtly harmful, but do display messages on the screen or cause a slowdown. Although not destructive to information, these attacks are a source of great irritation, and the user must react as though the attack were dangerous because it is disruptive and *might* be destructive.

Use of Resources

An attacker may have no particular evil intent against the owner of the compromised machine. Instead, the purpose of the attack may be to accomplish some computation too difficult for the perpetrator's own resources. For example, if the attacker wishes to break a cryptosystem by brute force attack, a virus may distribute the computations among hundreds or thousands of unsuspecting machines.

Destruction of Information

The viruses that people fear are those that alter or erase information. Having one's hard drive erased is certainly inconvenient and frequently irrecoverable, since many people do not back up their machines.[1] If information is subtly altered, the changes may not even be detected.

Theft of Information

As personal computers are used more frequently for electronic commerce, information of real commercial value, such as account numbers or credit card numbers, may be stored there. This information is a potential target. A virus that steals credentials, sends them out via e-mail, and quietly erases itself may be an effective way to anonymously and remotely gather large quantities of card numbers. Even if the credentials are kept in encrypted files, the virus need only wait around until the next time the file is unlocked.

Use of Credentials

One approach to the problem of a virus stealing credentials is to put the important information onto a smart card. A private key, for example, may never leave the protected hardware of the card, so it is not subject to theft by a virus. However, a virus might still install itself between the keyboard and screen of the computer and the card, so when the user wishes to digitally sign one document, the virus is really arranging for the smart card to sign something else entirely. This sort of problem may only be really solved when at least part of the user interface is inaccessible to viruses—such as a smart card with a built-in display.

---

1. There is also a school of thought that erasing everything on a PC and starting over every six months or so is a good way to combat the general accretion of software and files. Still, one would like to make the choice for oneself.

Server Security Issues

Server computers generally run applications software or provide a set of services to a large number of different users. Sometimes the users will have the ability to log in to the server, whereas in other situations only the administrators can log in. Server computers generally run multiuser operating systems such as Unix or Windows NT.

Methods of Attack on Server Computers

Computer attacks are many and subtle. Sometimes an attack may have limited objectives, such as access to a particular file or application, but more frequently the objective is the ability to install new software or run applications with *root* or administrator privileges.

Logging in as an Ordinary User

Often the first step in an attack on a server computer is to obtain a login or shell session as an ordinary authorized user of the computer. There are many ways to do this, such as obtaining or guessing a password, locating an unattended terminal, or taking over an existing communications session.

- Guess a password.

  Use a dictionary of common words and names to guess probable passwords. Telephone the help desk posing as a legitimate user and have the password reset. Spy on network traffic to catch passwords going by. Use a keyboard sniffer virus to grab passwords.

- Take over an existing session.

  Locate an unattended terminal. Use TCP sequence number attack to hijack a connection.

- Inject commands into an existing session.

  Use improper permissions in the X Window System or on terminal answer-backs to inject commands into an existing session.

- Exploit poorly set security controls.

  Break into a trusted host, or masquerade as one, and use a protocol such as *rsh* which permits login without supplying a password at all.

Once user privileges are obtained, the attacker can explore the system, looking for security weaknesses permitting greater privileges or looking for incorrectly set security controls. In some cases, user privileges are sufficient. For example, if the log files for a business application are configured with world-read protections, then any ordinary user account will have access to them.

Exploiting Bugs in Applications

Because server computers typically use commodity operating systems, many people have access to the software. Attackers can search for possible weaknesses at their leisure.

*   Out-of-range input

    Many applications are not written defensively, and do not check their input for content or size. For example, if an application uses fixed-size buffers, but does not check the length of input, an attacker can feed a very large message to the application, causing the application memory to be overwritten. If the buffer is allocated on the stack, the attacker can actually overwrite the program return addresses and seize control of the application. If the application has privileges, so does the successful attacker. Even if the attacker cannot get control, the application may crash.

*   Failure to check input syntax

    Applications which use interpreted languages such as TCL or PERL, or applications which pass commands for evaluation to other applications, are at risk if they fail to carefully check their input. If the attacker can persuade the application to execute an input message as a program or to perform variable substitution on a reply message, then security is at risk.

Exploiting Incorrectly Set Security Controls

Even if the server applications are bug free, they can be operated in an insecure manner.

*   Incorrectly set file protections

    Server operating systems have elaborate file protection mechanisms which are relatively easy to get wrong. If application files are read-accessible to an attacker, valuable information may leak out. If application files or queue directories are writable, it may be possible to trick an application into executing an attacker's instructions with elevated privileges.

*   Debugging code left accessible

    If networked applications are installed with debugging code accessible, it may be possible for an attacker to use privileged debugging commands remotely. In some well-publicized incidents, debugging access to mailer software has led to penetration of computers on the Internet.

Purposes of Attacks on Server Computers

In general, all of the purposes of attacks on client computers also apply to attacks on servers, but these purposes have special significance when applied to servers because a break-in may affect services delivered to many individuals and because the concentration of information in a server may have great economic value.

Access to Information

A break-in of a client computer may reveal a single transaction to an attacker, but a successful break-in of the server may reveal all transactions. For example, if credit card numbers are logged on the server, an attacker may obtain thousands of numbers as the result of a single successful attack. (Preventing this result is one of the design goals of the Secure Electronic Transaction protocol.)

Alteration of Information.

Electronic commerce servers may store business records. Destruction or alteration of these may make it impossible for a business to function, report on taxes, or defend against customer disputes. Alteration of the security configuration can leave a trap-door for later access by the attacker.

Access to Security Credentials

Servers may store security credentials for many users or for communications with other computer systems. For example, in a network protected by cryptography, the cryptographic keys may be kept on disk. Theft of these keys may compromise the entire network.

Denial of Service

An attack on a server computer may be aimed at denial of service to the entire community. If the server can be made to crash repeatedly, or to become bogged down dealing with unauthorized requests, the system can become unusable.

Achieving Application Security

Achieving computer security is difficult, but some general principles apply.

- Limit access to the system.

  The fewer people with login access to a server, the better. Try not to use an application server for general logins. Make sure that system administrators use good passwords and do not leave logged-in terminals unattended. Consider disallowing network access for system administration.

- Use available security tools.

  There are a variety of system configuration checkers and monitors. These tools can probe a system from the outside for known security weaknesses and can also survey file system protections for suspect usage.

- Protect complex systems with simple ones.

  Most server computer operating systems are too complex to be trusted. Firewalls (discussed later) are systems which carefully limit access to the server and which are simple enough to trust. Firewalls may also perform audit and logging functions.

- Make sure the system is *inside the envelope.*

  Many applications work well in the common case. If the behavior of the server is not understood when disks fill up or when the CPU is overloaded or when too many users are connected, put limits in place that trigger alarms when unusual operating conditions are encountered.

- Record configuration changes.

  Put procedures in place to maintain records of system configuration and an audit trail of changes.

- Create backups.

  Elementary as it sounds, make sure that server software and application data is backed up regularly. Make sure that the security controls for access to backup tapes are appropriate for the information on the backups.

- Assure that software is properly installed.

  New installations of software are a leading cause of improperly set security controls.

Firewalls

A firewall consists of hardware, software, or both that isolates a private system or network from a public network. The term may be somewhat inappropriate, because the firewall is intended to prevent problems from occurring as well as to prevent a problem from spreading.

Firewall functions include the following.

- Packet-level filtering

  Firewalls typically include packet-level (network-level) filters which control basic connectivity. Internet protocol packets, for example, can be accepted or rejected based on source and destination IP addresses, source and destination port numbers, and packet type. These capabilities are used to allow connections from outside the firewall only to particular services on the inside. Another important capability is to reject any packet arriving from the outside which has a source address purporting to come from the inside.

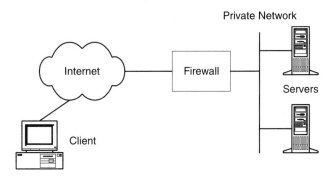

FIGURE 13-2. Example Internet Firewall

- Application relay

  Firewalls typically implement application protocol relay functions. For example, a relay for the Telnet virtual terminal protocol might permit an outside client to establish a terminal session with an inside host only if the outside user were equipped with a one-time password system like S/Key or a hardware login token like SecurID.

- Audit and logging

  Firewalls create log files of communications activity which are completely independent of the internal server machines. These independent audit trails aid containment, because even if an internal system is penetrated, the attacker has no way to erase his traces.

- Concentration of security administration

  If there are multiple server systems inside the firewall, there may be a diffusion of the responsibility for security. The firewall serves as a choke point through which all external communications must pass. As such, it is much easier to manage and operate than multiple independent systems.

Authentication

Authentication is the process of establishing identity as an individual, a function, or a member of a class of individuals. Authentication procedures generally use one or more *factors:* something you know, something you have, or something you are. A high-security application generally requires a two-factor authentication process.

- Something you know

  A password or secret that is known by an individual but not by anyone else. Generally, passwords should not be written down, but arguably this restriction should be relaxed for use on networks. The problem is that people tend to choose poor passwords, so they do not offer much security. Good passwords may be too difficult to remember. Another approach is the use of a pass-phrase consisting of several words.

- Something you have

  A physical key, access card, or passport that is in the physical possession of an individual. In the electronic realm, this may be a hardware token or smart card. Arguably, a complex password or code that is written down is in this category, rather than something you know.

- Something you are

  A fingerprint, retinal pattern, or other so-called *biometric* that is a physical property of an individual.

Authentication is frequently confused with authorization—an example is an ordinary house key. Possession of the key *authenticates* one as a member of the class of people *authorized* to enter the house. Computer systems generally separate the concepts of authentication and authorization—a known user name and password let you log in, but after that your rights are determined by separate *access control lists*.

Passwords

Passwords are used so broadly that we devote a section to them.

Passwords are frequently used to log in to a computer system or network. The user name and password as entered are checked against the password file. If they match, the login is permitted.

Passwords can be very secure, but as with most things in security, the devil is in the details.

Password Choice

People tend to choose bad (insecure) passwords, such as words from dictionaries or their spouse's name, but if you do not let people choose their own passwords, they tend to be written down, rather than remembered. In the worst case, passwords wind up on notes stuck to monitor bezels. The usual solution to this problem is to require passwords at least so long, with a mix of letters and numbers.

Password Change

In order to preserve security over a long interval, passwords must be changed regularly. Left to themselves, people tend not to do this, or tend to cycle through a small set of different passwords. Some sophistication in the password software is needed in order to enforce regular changes.

Passwords Used at Multiple Sites

When an individual has accounts on multiple computers, or at multiple sites on the Internet, there is a strong tension between using the same password at multiple sites or using different passwords at each site. Using the same password everywhere raises the stakes if the single password is guessed, but using different passwords everywhere makes it very likely that the user will forget one or more of them and be forced to write them down. In either case, having passwords at many different sites compounds the problem of enforcing periodic changes of password.

Password Storage

The password storage system at a password-required site is an obvious security target. The passwords of many individuals are stored in one place, making it a tempting target for attack. The usual way of lessening this problem is to not store passwords in cleartext, or even encrypted, but rather to store a hash of each password. It is very difficult to invert the hash function, so the password cannot be recovered from storage, but it is easy to check for a match. In addition to the hash, so-called *salt* is used as well. Salt is a random number stored with the password file entry that is different for each entry, and which is part of the hash computation. If an attacker succeeds in obtaining a copy of the entire password file, she must attack each entry individually, rather than using a dictionary attack against all entries at once.

Other Authentication Technologies

Here are some other authentication technologies.

One-Time Passwords

One problem with passwords is that if the password is ever transmitted over an insecure communications channel, the security of the password is suspect. This issue arises, for example, when one logs in to the office computer over a public network or from a customer site. One solution to this problem is to issue each user a whole set of passwords, each of which can be used only once. Typically this is done by printing a card, and then crossing out each password as it is used. One such system is S/Key, in which a one-way function is used to create a chain of passwords—each successive password is run through the function to produce the next password. The trick is to use the passwords in reverse order, so that an eavesdropper cannot reproduce the sequence. The central site must store the first password in the sequence and the last one used.

Hardware Tokens and Smart Cards

Because the weaknesses of passwords are well known, higher-security applications support the use of hardware devices for authentication. Devices which are restricted to authentication are usually called *tokens*, whereas smart cards can be used for authentication as well as for more general security purposes. Two common types of tokens are made by Security Dynamics and by Axent. The Security Dynamics SecurID card has a window on the front which displays a cryptographically generated random number which changes once a minute. The matching authentication server can duplicate the computation to check the number. The user simply copies the number from the card along with a PIN code into the system. The Axent Defender card is a small calculator-like device with a key pad and display. In operation, the system sends the user a challenge code, which is entered into the card along with the user's PIN. The user copies the response code from the card into the system. The server executes the same computation and compares the result.

Smart cards are small cards containing a processor and some memory. These cards may be credit card sized (sometimes called chip cards) or larger, such as PCMCIA size. Generally, the card memory contains some secret keys for either symmetric or asymmetric cryptography.

Web Authentication

The World Wide Web uses a stateless protocol, in which each browser request to a server stands alone and does not depend on any context for what has gone before. In addition, the authentication problem is symmetric—the user wants to know he is talking to the right server, and the server wants to know it is talking to the right user.

Client Authentication

Client authentication is the process of establishing the user's identity to the satisfaction of the server.

- Basic authentication

  The only authentication mechanism built into HTTP 1.0 is basic authentication. Normally a Web browser making a request to a Web server provides no authentication information. When this is unacceptable to the server, the server responds to the request with an "unauthorized" code and a realm. The realm is a text string whose purpose is to let the user know which name and password are being requested. Typically the browser will display an authentication pop-up box, with the realm displayed at the top and entry fields for user name and password. When the user clicks on OK, the browser retries the original request, this time supplying the name and password in the HTTP header of the request. The name and password are encoded in uuencode format, which makes them unreadable by eye, but trivial to decode with a program. Because the Web is stateless, these credentials must be supplied on every request. Browsers remember which sites require passwords, and supply them automatically on subsequent requests. Some browsers even remember name and password credentials between sessions, so the user need not even remember them (however, they may be available to anyone who uses the same computer).

The main issue about basic authentication is that the credentials of the user are sent in the clear across the network. This problem can be overcome by using SSL or another encryption protocol, but these protocols introduce a substantial performance penalty when used all the time.

- Digest authentication

Digest authentication is a proposed mechanism for use with HTTP 1.1. It is a challenge-response protocol, in which the server sends the browser a challenge, and the browser uses the locally stored password to compute a response. Since the user's password is not sent across the network, digest authentication is much more secure than basic authentication, while introducing only a very small performance impact. The digest authentication proposal also includes an optional opaque data field, which the server gives to the browser and the browser hands back to the server. The server can use this field to send an encrypted message to itself, and this message can be used to avoid any database lookups during response validation.

- Client certificates

The capability to use public key certificates for client authentication over the Web first appeared in the S-HTTP protocol in 1994, but this protocol was never widely used. The Secure Sockets Layer (SSL) protocol introduced by Netscape Communications Corporation introduced the capability for client certificates in SSL version 2, but the capability was not widely deployed until SSL version 3, supported by Netscape Navigator 3.0 and Microsoft Internet Explorer 3.0. The use of client certificates proceeds in two phases. A client certificate is first created during a conversation with a certificate-issuing server, and thereafter it is available for use with other servers.

During certificate creation, the user fills out forms with identification information and creates a public key pair. The public half of the key, together with the identification, is submitted to the certificate-issuing server, which uses its certificate authority root key to sign the user's public key, creating a certificate. The certificate is returned to the user's browser for storage together with the corresponding private key.

Once a client certificate is available, a server wishing to use it for client authentication uses SSL protocol headers to send a request for a certificate to the browser. The browser typically displays a pop-up box allowing the user to select an appropriate certificate from those available, and to unlock it with a password. The password protects the private key from other software running on the user's computer.

The certificate is transmitted to the server, along with a message signed with the corresponding private key. The certificate creates a connection between the user's identification information and the private key, and the message signed by the private key indicates that the key is indeed in the possession of the user. Together, the server knows that the user is the individual named in the certificate.

Server Authentication

The weakest method for server authentication is to depend on the integrity of the Domain Name System. When the user types "www.xyzcorp.com" into the browser, there is a good chance the connection is made to the right server. However, this depends on correct management of many computers, together with constant vigilance by their operators, so stronger methods are useful.

The most effective means of server authentication available today is the public key certificate. Secure Web protocols such as SSL permit the server to deliver to the client a public key certificate signed by a third party—the certification authority. The user must have the root key for the CA embedded in his browser, and communications must be conducted using SSL; but if so, the user knows that the certification authority has verified the identity of the server. In a commercial context this may or may not be adequate, however.

Suppose that the user wishes to do business with XYZ corporation, which has an online store. The Web pages for this store may be hosted on a shared computer together with pages from other companies. Consequently, the server certificate may read "Joe's hosting service" rather than "XYZ Corporation," which has a good chance of confusing the user.

This problem was handled in the little-used S-HTTP Web protocol, because every hyperlink in the Web could contain information about the expected security properties of the destination page. Once the user was satisfied with the initial page, the security properties of subsequent pages would be handled automatically.

Web Sessions

As mentioned earlier, the basic Web protocols are stateless, such that each request (or *hit*) stands on its own. Consequently, each request must be independently authenticated. This is exactly what happens in basic authentication, where the user's name and password are passed to the server on each request. The user experience is not bad, because after the first request for name and password from a site, the browser remembers to supply the credentials on subsequent requests. However, the server must independently validate the name and password on every hit. In addition, although the use of a secure protocol like SSL can overcome the problem of transmitting passwords in the clear, these protocols may not be warranted for all communications, because the content being viewed may not be intrinsically valuable. Digest authentication can solve these problems by making the authentication fairly secure and fairly lightweight, but it is not widely deployed.

The technique most often used to enable authentication but not to require that all content be encrypted is to create a session on top of the basic stateless Web protocols. When the session is entered, the user is asked to authenticate, and thereafter the authentication information is not required on every hit, but rather the information that a hit is part of session XYZ is passed along from request to request. There are two ways to create a Web session today: custom URLs and cookies.

In the custom URL method, the identification of the session is carried in the URL, either as part of the URL query string,

  http://www.xyz.com/url/path/name/script.cgi?query&string&with&session_ID

or buried in the URL,

  http://www.xyz.com/<sessionId>/url/path/name

The former approach requires that all user interaction be handled by a particular server application (CGI script) which manages the session, and the latter approach requires that the session validation be built into the Web server itself.

In the cookie approach, the session identification information is stored in the browser cookie, so that the browser automatically presents it to the server on every request. This works very well, but there are several problems: not every browser supports cookies, Web proxy servers do not always handle them correctly, and users may configure their browsers to reject cookies. Even when the mechanism works, if the client communications are not encrypted, the cookie may be stolen by an eavesdropper.

For encrypted communications, SSL version 3 offers an interesting alternative—the client certificate may be requested on the first request to a site. Thereafter, SSL session key caching can be used to reduce the average cost of the authentication by applying it across multiple requests. SSL version 3 offers the additional capability of authentication-only connections, which do not encrypt the content or incur the associated performance penalty.

Summary

We have argued that security needs to be a property of the whole system. The essential problem of the security officer is that security has to be strong everywhere, because the attacker needs to find only one weak spot or lapse of operational attention. The solution to this issue is best found in containment—build in strong security, but make sure there are feedback mechanisms and recovery mechanisms.

CHAPTER 14

Payment Systems

Money alone sets all the world in motion.
—Publilius Syrus[1]

The Role of Payment

In many respects, online payment is the foundation of systems for electronic commerce. The ability to take payment distinguishes an electronic commerce system from one that provides only advertising or other communications capabilities. Incorporating payment abilities, however, adds considerable complexity to a system. First, the security of both the payment mechanism and the overall system must be sufficient to protect the system. Second, the system must provide a high degree of integrity for transactions—the system must not lose or inadvertently change a payment transaction.

This chapter considers what happens once the buyer and the seller have agreed on what is being sold and its price. We examine payment systems from several points of view. First, we look at real-world payment systems to understand how we might construct analogous online systems. Second, we describe some of the systems already developed for online payment. Next, we consider how payment for so-called microtransactions might be accomplished. We conclude with a brief discussion of the abstract issue of payment and its role.

---

1. Publilius Syrus, *Maxims*.

A Word about Money

Before talking about payment, it is prudent to talk about money. It is convenient to think about two kinds of money: *token* and *notational.* Tokens are like coins or paper money: they have value in and of themselves. In the earliest days of token-based money, the tokens were valued for what they were made of. Today, it is usually the case that token money has value by fiat, because a government has issued the tokens and declared their value.

In contrast, notational money refers to something that represents value stored some-where else. For example, a check has no intrinsic value, but it represents a commit-ment to transfer money. The check cannot be freely transferred around, either. It is useful only to the party named on it. Payment instruments that extend credit are a variation of notational money. When one uses a credit card, for example, one agrees to pay the designated amount at some point in the future, and the transaction is guar-anteed by the financial institution that issued the credit card.[2]

On the Internet, and the electronic world in general, most systems today use nota-tional money: credit cards, purchase orders (which really represent a promise to pay at some time in the future), and electronic funds transfer. Some newer systems, such as various forms of electronic cash, have not yet gained widespread use, but they are actually uses of token money in electronic form.

Real-World Payment Systems

In many respects, payment online is not very different from payment in the real world. Because we want payment transactions online to have value off the network as well, online payment systems are usually based on existing payment mechanisms. In this section, we review several common payment methods. In particular, we look at the properties that make them attractive for use online, or that must be captured in an online analog.

Cash

Cash is perhaps the most familiar and most widely accepted form of payment outside of the network. For the consumer, it has many important properties.

1. Wide acceptance. Cash is accepted for nearly any transaction (although it is not very common for large ones).
2. Convenience. Cash is easy to use and easy to carry in small quantities.

---

2. Under some circumstances, the bank that issued a credit card may not guarantee the transaction. This is often true for mail-order transactions, where the customer and the card are not physically present.

3. Anonymity. One need not identify oneself to pay in cash.[3]

4. Untraceability. Once cash has been spent, there is no way to trace it back through the chain of those who have possessed it.

5. No buyer transaction costs. The buyer sees no additional cost for using cash. This makes cash especially useful for small transactions, where the overhead of a check or credit card is large compared to the value exchanged. The buyer does have an opportunity cost for holding cash rather than investing the money.

    Note that a merchant does have some costs for handling cash—transporting it safely to the bank, having it counted by the bank, and so on. Anecdotal reports place these costs at up to 10 percent.

These properties make *online cash* mechanisms attractive for many transactions online, but they also pose some technical challenges in creating such mechanisms. We will discuss some technologies and proposed systems for *electronic cash* systems later.

Credit Cards, Charge Cards, and Debit Cards

Credit cards are very familiar to many consumers, as are various other kinds of charge cards. A credit card, such as those from Visa or MasterCard, operates by extending a buyer credit at the time of purchase, with the actual payment occurring later through a monthly bill. The usual distinction between a *credit* card and a *charge* card is that the balance on a charge card must be paid in full each month, whereas a credit card may carry a balance from month to month, albeit with interest accrued. Cards from Visa and MasterCard are usually credit cards, whereas cards from American Express are usually charge cards. From a merchant's point of view, these cards operate in essentially the same way, and the only difference is whether or not the merchant accepts a particular card brand. Individual merchants may also have their own store-brand charge or credit cards, for which they handle all of the credit and payment processing.

A related form of payment is a certain class of debit cards which are linked to demand-deposit accounts, such as checking accounts, in banks. These cards usually carry a Visa or MasterCard logo, and they are accepted anywhere that Visa or MasterCard is accepted. Instead of a transaction extending credit, however, the payment is drawn immediately from the linked account. From a merchant's point of view, they operate exactly as credit cards do. This type of card is called an *offline debit card* because the transaction need not be authorized in real time.

By contrast, an *online debit card* requires a real-time authorization using a Personal Identification Number (PIN). Such cards are often ATM cards, and merchants often

---

3. Except for very large transactions, which (in the United States, at least) must be reported to the Internal Revenue Service.

accept them from local banks for some kinds of transactions. Like offline debit cards, payment is transferred immediately from the corresponding demand-deposit account.

Merchants pay for the ability to handle credit card transactions. The fees charged vary by acquiring bank, size of the merchant, size of transaction, volume of credit card transactions, and type of the merchant's business. For example, a mail-order merchant usually pays more for credit card transactions than a comparable store, because the customer is not present to sign a charge slip. This kind of transaction, known as a "card not present" transaction, carries a higher risk that it will not be paid, because the buyer may have stolen the credit card. A typical fee for a retail merchant is twenty-five cents plus 1.5 to 3.0 percent of the total transaction. Mail-order fees can be much higher, in the range of 2.5 to 5 percent of the transaction.

Credit cards are very popular for online payment for consumer retail transactions, especially for transactions similar to those performed with credit cards in retail or mail-order businesses off the Net, including ordering subscriptions to magazines, newsletters, or online information services. Because of the costs associated with credit card transactions, they are inappropriate for individual small transactions. For example, using the rates just given, more than half of the revenue in a fifty-cent transaction would go to pay for the credit card transaction. Some approaches to handling small transactions are described in the Micropayments section.

Packaging a Payment System

Most consumers think of a credit card as a fairly simple device. We use them for buying things, and later our bank sends a bill. The reality is quite a bit more complex. A credit card is a complex bundle of services.

- Consumer credit

    Most credit cards extend credit to the cardholder. If the cardholder carries a balance from month to month, interest charges accrue. Generally, if the cardholder pays his bill in full each month, no extra charges are made.

- Immediate payment

    Like cash, but unlike checks, credit card transactions result in immediate (overnight) payment to the merchant. This rapid payment can reduce the merchant's requirements for financing inventory.

- Insurance

    Unlike cash, there is no substantial risk of loss to the cardholder. Merely by notifying the card issuer, the card can be disabled, and even without notification, the cardholder's risk is limited.

- Financial clearinghouse

  Credit cards work even when the cardholder's bank is different from the merchant's bank. This simple and perhaps obvious fact makes commerce much easier and is in contrast to, for example, checks. A check drawn on a faraway bank is less likely to be accepted than a local check.

- Global service

  Credit cards handle multiple currencies automatically. The merchant deals in his own local currency, and when the credit card bill arrives, the transactions have all been converted to the cardholder's local currency.

- Record keeping

  Credit cards send periodic statements, which are very useful for reconciling expenses.

- Customer service and dispute resolution

  When a dispute about the quality of product or nondelivery arises, the cardholder can complain to his card issuer. The merchant's acquiring bank can withhold or reverse payment to the merchant, and this gives the consumer considerable bargaining power to obtain satisfaction.

- Enable merchant trust

  To a great degree, consumers can trust merchants who have credit card association logos in their window. The logo not only means that credit card payment is accepted, it also means that if there is any trouble down the line, the consumer can complain—not to the merchant encountered once in a faraway city, but to his own card-issuing bank.

- Enable consumer trust

  To a great degree, merchants can trust consumers who have credit cards. Provided the card is valid and the customer signature matches, the merchant is guaranteed payment. This greatly facilitates commerce.

Credit cards may be an expensive means of payment, costing 2 to 5 percent of transaction value, but they provide a complex set of services. It is a very interesting thought experiment to disaggregate the credit card and to consider the value of each of the services separately. In addition, when evaluating other payment mechanisms, it is a useful exercise to compare them, feature for feature, against the breadth of services offered by the ubiquitous credit card.

How Credit Card Transactions Work

The steps in a typical credit card transaction are shown in Figure 14-1. After a cardholder gives a credit card to a merchant, the merchant sends an authorization request to the merchant's bank (called an *acquiring bank* or *acquirer*), requesting that the amount of the purchase be reserved against the buyer's credit. The acquirer forwards the request through an interchange network (such as the ones operated by Visa or

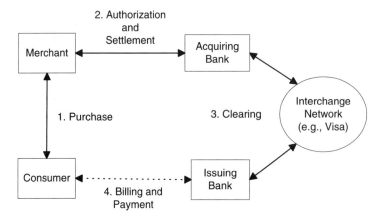

FIGURE 14-1. Credit Card Transaction Flow

MasterCard) to the bank that issued the buyer's card (called the *issuing bank*). If the credit is available, the issuing bank authorizes the transaction, sending the response back through the network. If not, the issuing bank denies the authorization. The authorization is valid for a specified period of time (three days is common), and it expires at the end of that time unless the transaction has been settled or the authorization renewed.

In most cases, transactions are settled some time after they are authorized. Authorization responses include codes used for later settlement. Retail store transactions, for example, are typically settled in batches at the end of the day. Mail-order transactions are not settled until the goods are shipped, a requirement usually imposed by the card association rules.

In some cases, it is appropriate to authorize and settle the transaction at the same time. For online systems, this is common for delivery of information products, where the delivery occurs immediately on receipt of payment. Some electronic payment systems combine the final step of payment with the delivery of the information product. Such systems give the buyer greater assurance that the product will be delivered, and they are discussed further later.

In addition to this routine processing of credit card transactions, there are several exceptional cases that must be handled by an online credit card payment system. These include reversing an authorization that is no longer needed, giving a credit for a returned item, and applying the appropriate charges when only part of an order can be shipped. In addition, it is very important for vendors of information products to have clear policies for handling customer disputes, since it is difficult to return the goods as with traditional mail-order merchants.

Computer systems used for processing credit card payments typically connect to computers at acquiring banks for authorization and settlement services. In many cases, the acquirers delegate operation of those computer systems to other organizations, known generically as *card processors.* These companies handle all aspects of the transaction processing, and sometimes can act as acquirers themselves. A merchant's banking relationship determines which systems are used for the transaction processing.

As the credit card business evolved, many different communications protocols were created to manage credit card transactions (over 1,400 of them, by some counts). In addition to standard protocols created by the card associations, many banks created their own to provide enhanced services. Several years ago, the ISO adopted a standard protocol, ISO 8583, for such transactions. ISO 8583 is commonly used for managing card transactions outside the United States, but it is not widely used in the U.S. now. One consequence of a standard emerging from so many different protocols is that the ISO standard has quite a number of optional fields. This variety usually requires specific changes for operation with a given acquirer. To ensure proper operation, acquirers normally require implementations to be certified with a test system before it is put into production use.

Credit card payment is appropriate for a wide range of consumer retail applications. These are the primary issues.

1. Privacy of the credit card number and associated information. We describe several methods to provide such security later.

2. Whether or not the transaction values are appropriate for credit card transaction costs. Credit cards are relatively expensive to process, and they may result in chargebacks (with resulting costs to the merchant) if buyers are dissatisfied with their purchases.

3. Whether or not the merchant can create the banking relationship necessary to accept credit cards. Because banks may be reluctant to extend such privileges to new or unfamiliar merchants, it may be difficult for a new business to begin taking credit cards immediately.

Risk Management

There are many aspects to risk management in credit cards; we mention a few here.

- Consumer risk

  In the United States, the Consumer Credit Protection Act limits the liability of the cardholder to $50 in the event his card or card number is used fraudulently. After the cardholder notifies his bank that the card has been stolen, there is no further liability. Frequently, issuing banks do not charge consumers even the $50 on the grounds that it is simply bad public relations. The effect of this law is to place the responsibility for the security of the credit card system on the shoulders of the system designers and operators.

Consumers also have substantial recourse in the event of nonperformance by a merchant following a transaction paid for by credit card. The consumer can dispute the charge and the merchant's bank will retract payment to the merchant until the dispute is settled.

- Merchant risk

  When the cardholder appears in person at the merchant, and his card is swiped in an electronic terminal, and the merchant checks the cardholder signature (generally, if the merchant follows an official protocol for these "card present" transactions), then the merchant's acquiring bank accepts the risk that the card is stolen or fraudulent, and guarantees payment to the merchant. On the other hand, when the card is used by mail or telephone, in a so-called card-not-present transaction (also called MOTO for Mail or Telephone Order), then the merchant is liable in the event of a fraudulent transaction. So far, all Internet transactions are classified as MOTO, although SET may change this.

  The credit card authorization networks do offer some assistance to the merchant to assess their risk. One service is the Address Verification Service. The merchant requests the cardholder's billing address from the cardholder, and sends it along with the card authorization request. The purported address is checked against the issuing bank's records and the response indicates whether there is a match. The merchant can then choose to accept the transaction or not. MOTO merchants also build up their own fraud control systems, based on customer history and whatever other information is available.

International Issues

The model of credit card use may be international, but there are regional differences that can affect the design of Internet commerce systems. Two examples illustrate the sort of issues that arise.

- From and to valid dates

  In the United States, credit cards are usually issued with only an expiration date marked. The expiration date must be entered as part of the authorization request to the card network, so commerce software typically has an order form with fields for card number, card type, and expiration date. In Europe, however, cards are usually issued with both the beginning and the end of the period of validity, and both pieces of information are necessary to authorize a purchase. This means that Internet commerce software for this market must request additional information from the user and route it to the authorization network.

- Bonus payments

  In Japan, it is very common for a substantial portion of annual compensation to be paid to workers in the form of semiannual bonuses. In reaction to this, the retail use of credit cards in Japan has evolved so that the consumer can designate, at the point of sale, that the purchase will be paid for with bonus money. As a consequence, the merchant point-of-sale system has a way to designate a purchase as a bonus payment, and the credit card authorization network passes that information back to the issuing bank. As electronic commerce in Japan grows, Internet commerce software must support this capability as well.

These two examples are both relatively minor items whose effects ripple throughout software for Internet commerce. The user interface for the order form needs new fields with new validation routines; the transaction database needs new storage fields for the new capabilities; and the payment processing interfaces need to route additional information to the financial authorization networks. This complexity is difficult to manage, but successful commerce requires getting such details correct.

Checks

Checks are another familiar form of real-world payment. Both consumers and businesses use checks for payment. Consumers use checks for point-of-sale payment as well as payment of bills. After taking checks as payment during the day, a merchant deposits them in the bank, where they are *cleared* (in the United States) through the Federal Reserve network for the actual funds transfer. Clearing can take several business days, during which the merchant assumes the risk that the customer will not have sufficient funds to cover the check. Because merchants take the risk of nonpayment, they often require substantial identification, such as a driver's license and a credit card, to authenticate the customer. In addition, merchants impose significant penalties for checks that fail to clear. These penalties cover both the merchant's cost in handling the bounced check as well as the fee charged by the bank to the merchant for it.

Because they involve moving paper, checks are relatively expensive to handle, both for merchants and the banking system. Electronic analogs for checks have been devised, and we discuss them briefly later. In practice, the use of credit cards or debit cards is likely to be far more common in online transactions than electronic checks. Debit cards provide nearly identical behavior from the consumer's point of view, in that the funds are deducted immediately from a demand-deposit account. (Note, however, that the funds are deducted from the account immediately, without the "float" that checks provide.)

Electronic Funds Transfer (EFT) and Automated Clearinghouse (ACH)

Electronic funds transfers (EFT) move money directly between bank accounts, providing same-day or overnight payments. EFT is commonly used, for example, for large interbank transfers. EFT systems were some of the earliest electronic payment systems, although they have always been on private networks, not on an open network such as the Internet.

EFT transactions move over a variety of networks, such as SWIFT, FEDWIRE, CHIPS, and ACH. The first three of these are primarily used for large transfers, whereas automated clearinghouse (ACH) transfers are used for many smaller-valued electronic payments, including payroll direct deposit and preauthorized withdrawals for bill payment, as well as online payments by businesses. For many business-to-business commerce applications, ACH provides a familiar payment method that can be integrated with purchasing over the Internet.

ACH transfers are also used by home banking and bill payment applications in cases where the bank account information for the recipient is known.

Purchase Orders

Strictly speaking, purchase orders are not a payment mechanism, but we use the term to refer to a particular kind of transaction between businesses. Transactions between two businesses are typically handled differently than purchases by a consumer. In most cases, the seller extends credit to the buyer, and the seller bills the buyer for the transaction, with an agreement on when the buyer must pay (such as within 30 or 60 days). A specific purchase is usually tied to a purchase order, which is used by the buyer to track transactions. From the seller's point of view, the purchase order is merely a convenient means to track transactions. Final payment is usually done by a check or wire transfer.

How does this translate to the online world? First of all, there must be some means of establishing the business relationship upon which credit is extended. The seller typically has a process for verifying the creditworthiness of the buyer, and this process would normally extend to online transactions as well. The initial verification is not usually performed in real time, so it may be handled through preexisting channels, or there may be an online registration system used to initiate the relationship. Such an online credit application process must capture the information required by the seller's traditional credit application process, which typically includes the name and address of the business, purchasing contact, and credit reference information. In addition, the online system should gather information, such as a password, used to authenticate authorized buyers from the customer's organization. Of course, the online system should be able to import information about existing relationships so that current customers can purchase online as well, and then augment the existing information with authentication data used to identify customers for online purchases.

Once the relationship is established, online purchasing works almost like other on-line transactions. As part of the order capture process, however, instead of collecting payment information such as a credit card number, the system must collect a purchase order number (or other buyer reference information) as well as authenticate the buyer to ensure that only authorized buyers are making purchases for a particular organization. In addition, the system should be able to check in real time to ensure that the purchase request falls within the available credit extended to the buyer's organization, in case that organization has taken on too much credit or has failed to pay its bills on time. This verification is very similar to the credit check done as part of authorizing a credit card transaction, but it is performed internal to the selling organization. As part of providing good service to customers, the system may also include the ability to handle an emergency request to increase the available credit, with a quick response by the seller that allows the transaction to proceed if appropriate.

Finally, of course, the online purchasing system must be integrated with existing billing and accounts receivable systems, so that the appropriate bills and invoices can be generated and tracked. Those systems may also be extended to the Internet system to provide up-to-date information for customers about such things as account balances and overdue amounts, as well as the ability to settle outstanding balances using online means of payment, such as credit cards or electronic checks.

Affinity Programs

Affinity programs are those that provide some kind of benefit or reward for buying from a particular business or using a particular payment mechanism. Frequent flier miles are one common example, in which buying the product (an airline ticket) provides some points toward a future reward (usually another airline ticket). Many issuers of credit cards provide affinity programs as well, ranging from cash rebates to points good for purchase from a particular catalog, to points good for purchase at a particular store. The goal of these programs, of course, is to increase usage of the payment system or sales at a particular business.

All of these programs can be made part of an Internet commerce strategy as well. There are three primary parts to affinity programs in Internet commerce: collecting and tracking the accumulated *points*, enabling buyers to redeem those points online, and enabling buyers to see their affinity account balances online.

Collecting and tracking the points is usually straightforward. The main issue is integrating the tracking system with the existing system for managing the affinity program. In the case of co-branded credit cards, this is often transparent, because any credit card purchase using that particular card will trigger the addition of affinity points. When points are tied to specific items or specific stores, the accounting must be added to the online transaction system, and then integrated with the existing affinity tracking system.

Second, buyers would like to redeem points online. This can be easy or hard, depending upon the software selected for the Internet commerce system. In one sense, redeeming points is just another kind of payment, so a system that accommodates multiple payment mechanisms can often be extended easily to handle redemption. Of course, this almost certainly includes the ability to authenticate the buyer to ensure that the legitimate account owner is the one making a purchase. At that point, the main question becomes whether or not items should be priced in a conventional currency, such as dollars, as well as affinity points. Some merchants prefer to avoid pricing items both ways, so that there is no implicit conversion rate between points and currency. Others are content to provide both prices, in effect giving two price tags for an item. Some Internet commerce systems tie the payment mechanism so closely to the catalog, however, that they do not provide the kind of flexibility needed to add redemption systems.

Finally, buyers may wish to check their affinity account balances online. Here the Internet system must be tied into the affinity accounting system, along with some kind of authentication to ensure the buyer's identity. As a convenience (or a marketing tool), the online account statement may include links to catalog pages useful for redeeming points, in order to encourage buyers to use them.

The ability to support affinity programs may not seem important at the beginning of an Internet commerce strategy. But, as we have observed, business models and requirements may change significantly over time, and the flexibility to add affinity programs later may be very important in choosing a software system for Internet commerce.

Private-Label Cards

Many businesses, especially retailers such as Sears Roebuck, J.C. Penney, and Macy's, issue their own credit cards for purchases from that business. In the abstract, such cards behave much like Visa, MasterCard, or other payment cards. In practice, providing such cards as payment instruments for Internet commerce means integrating the Internet system with the card payment system of whatever card is being used. The main technical steps, such as authorization, settlement, credits, and so on, will be processed much like other credit cards. The flexibility of the Internet commerce system is the key point here, because integrating such payment cards into the system will typically be handled for particular sellers, rather than being part of a general solution.

More recently, many retailers have begun issuing co-branded Visa or MasterCard credit cards, usually with some affinity benefits tied to the card. These cards, of course, behave just as normal credit cards for purposes of payment processing. They may have some special affinity features for online purchasing, such as special catalogs or online account statements, as we discussed for affinity programs.

Over time, we may also see private-label cards adopting credit card payment protocols such as SET for their transactions. Such adoption would leverage the infrastructure investment made for those protocols, while providing a greater degree of security than would ordinarily be obtained without specialized development.

Money Orders

Money orders are similar to checks, except that payment is guaranteed by a trusted third party, such as the U.S. Postal Service. The primary use of money orders has been to enable mail-order transactions in a way that protected the merchant from the risks of bad checks from remote customers. The customer pays the postal service (including a small fee) to issue the money order, which can then be sent to the merchant for redemption with the postal service. Money orders are safer than sending cash in the mail, because they can be redeemed only by the entity named on the money order. In the physical world, then, money orders provide three basic capabilities.

1. Insurance against certain kinds of loss (compared to, say, sending cash in the mail).

2. A certain level of privacy and anonymity (less than cash, more than using a credit card directly). Of course, most physical money orders are for mail-order goods, so there is a physical shipping address associated with the order.

3. Matching between buyers and sellers with different payment instruments. If a mail-order merchant does not accept credit cards, for example, a customer can use a credit card to purchase a money order used to buy goods from that merchant.

In an online money-order system, the first capability is not so important, because a properly designed online payment system does not risk losing cash. However, the anonymity properties can be stronger, especially for delivering digital goods. Because there is no physical name and address associated with the delivery, the seller cannot tie the transaction to anything more than an IP address on the network. The issuer of the money order has, at most, knowledge of the seller and possibly of the buyer, depending on the actual payment instrument used. Such an issuer may choose to adopt various policies regarding the disclosure of such information. When the issuer can be trusted to follow such policies, both buyers and sellers may have confidence in an appropriate level of privacy for their transactions.

Corporate Purchasing Cards

Many purchases made by businesses are relatively small, such as for office supplies, off-the-shelf software for personal computers, and so on. These purchases often need to be completed quickly and easily, and they commonly require little in the way of approval by others in the organization. In such cases, the corporate overhead of completing a requisition form, creating a purchase order, selecting a vendor, establishing a credit relationship if one does not already exist, receiving an invoice, and paying the bill can be very costly compared to the value of the items being purchased.

One solution to this problem is the *corporate purchasing card.* A corporate purchasing card is essentially like a credit card issued to an individual on behalf of an organization. For the most part, it behaves like a credit card as well, except that most transactions require some additional information about the item being purchased. This information allows the authorization system to make decisions based on the type of item as well as the availability of credit for the buying organization. For example, one individual may be allowed to buy basic office supplies, whereas another may buy personal computer software as well. As long as everything is in order, the buyer presents the credit card, the transaction is authorized, and the sale is completed.

Effective use of purchasing cards in the online world depends on the ability to capture this extra information about the item being purchased. Without that information, the authorization system cannot make a determination about whether or not the cardholder is permitted to make the transaction. As we have noted before, the flexibility of the payment system (and, in this case, its connection to the catalog system, which has the specific item information) are very important in making it possible to use purchasing cards effectively.

Coupons

In general, a coupon is an offer to discount a purchase made under specific conditions. Manufacturer's coupons are perhaps the most familiar, offering "fifty cents off" or "buy one, get one free." Individual stores may issue their own coupons, and sometimes they accept coupons issued by their competitors. Coupons take many forms, but all are intended to encourage consumers to purchase a particular product. In most cases, coupons are distributed separately from the point of sale of the product, so they help entice customers to visit a store to make a purchase.

Strictly speaking, of course, coupons are not a payment mechanism, but they do share some characteristics with payment. In most cases, we can view coupons as simply altering the final price of a set of goods or services, rather than as paying for the set. At that point, any payment mechanism may be used for the purchase.

Before we examine some of the technical ways that coupons can be implemented, let us look at some different kinds of coupons in the physical world. Coupons are typically issued by two kinds of entities: manufacturers and retailers. A coupon from a manufacturer is usually accepted by any retailer selling the product, and the value is reimbursed by the manufacturer. Retailers also issue their own coupons, which are intended for use only at the retailer's stores. In some cases, competitors may also accept the coupons, though the value is (of course) not reimbursed by the issuer. The kinds of discounts that are offered by coupons can vary widely, but here are some of the most common.

- Get a fixed discount.

  The price of an item is discounted by a fixed amount. For example, "fifty cents off when you buy product X."

- Get a percentage discount.

  The price of an item is discounted by a percentage. For example, "20 percent off when you buy product Y."

- Buy one, get one free.

  The price of a second item is reduced to zero if another item of the same kind is purchased. This kind of offer has many variations, such as "buy one, get one for 50 percent less" or "buy two, get one free."

- Buy X, get a discount on Y.

  This offer ties two products together, discounting the price of a second kind of product if another kind is purchased.

- After *N* purchases, the next one is free.

  In this case, the discount is applied after a history of repeated purchases has been established. A common way of doing this is for a consumer to keep a card that is punched for each purchase. When the card is fully punched, the discount can be taken.

Of course, coupons can be constructed in many other ways; the ones just listed are perhaps the most common. The question, then, is how can we translate such coupons into the online world? One way to look at coupons is that they provide a discount rule of the basic form, "If certain conditions have been satisfied, then the total cost of a set of items is changed in a particular way." The fixed-discount case, for example, has the form, "If one item of type X is being purchased, its price is reduced by a fixed amount." A more complicated coupon, offering "buy two, get one free" has the form, "If three items of type X are being purchased, the total price is two times the per-item price."

Although it may seem cumbersome, looking at the discount rules of coupons in this way allows us to write rules for online coupons that can be processed automatically by computer systems. The coupon mechanism can also be very general, which permits the use of different promotional approaches to determine the most effective means of attracting sales.

Smart Cards

A *smart card* is an object about the size of a plastic credit card that contains a processor, memory, and an interface to the outside world. The term is sometimes used to include PCMCIA devices with similar properties, and the cards that are exactly the size of plastic credit cards are sometimes called *chip cards*. Smart cards are being used for an increasingly large set of applications, including payment. We make a distinction between smart cards and the kind of handheld authentication tokens described in Chapter 14: smart cards provide at least data storage and often some computation based on that data, rather than the (relatively simple) authentication computations used by such tokens.

In practice, there is a wide range of smarts on cards. The differences come in the performance and capabilities of the processor, the amounts of RAM and ROM, the speed of the interface to the world, availability of specialized components for cryptographic operations, and whether or not they can be programmed for different applications. Different applications require different kinds of operations, so it is often important to speak precisely about the application and the kind of card used.

In order to be useful, smart cards require a *reader* of some sort to connect the card with a computer system. There are several different kinds of readers, depending on the technology being used. Chip cards typically have exposed contacts that match up with those in a reader when they are inserted into a slot. This approach is common for smart cards used at retail point-of-sale terminals. Other cards are "contactless" and use infrared communication to exchange data with the reader. A PCMCIA smart card, of course, uses a standard PCMCIA slot on a laptop or desktop computer. No matter what the mechanism is, however, the site where the card will be used requires a reader. For traditional retail applications, the reader would be attached to a cash register. For a building access system, readers would be mounted next to doors. For Internet commerce, the computer used by the holder of the smart card must have a reader for the card to be of any use. Over time, it may become common for PCs to be equipped with smart card readers to enable many kinds of authenticated applications, including payment transactions, but at the moment this is a significant barrier to the use of smart cards for Internet commerce.

In the abstract, smart cards provide several capabilities.

- Portable storage

  Because the device is carried around by its owner, it can be used anywhere the owner goes. In particular, it means that the information stored on the card is available wherever the owner takes it, which means that the owner is not chained to a desktop computer in order to use an advanced payment system.

- Secure storage

  A smart card has the potential to provide secure, tamperproof storage for all or part of the information stored on it. This is especially valuable for such things as cryptographic keys or data representing money, as well as for other especially private information.

- Trusted execution environment

  Smart cards are not vulnerable to the viruses and intrusion risks that plague desktop computers. Because the application runs in this protected environment, it can be given a greater degree of trust.

Some common applications today include the following.

- Prepaid telephone cards

  This use does not require very sophisticated cards, as the main technology used is a set of electrical fuses on a chip that are progressively burned up by the reader. When no more fuses remain, the prepaid value has been consumed and the card is no longer useful.

- Credit and debit cards

  This use is not very common inside the United States, but it is widespread in many other parts of the world. The chip on the card is used to authenticate the card at the retail point of sale, and the cardholder gives a PIN for authentication as well. The use of the smart card provides a greater degree of security than an easily forged piece of plastic with a magnetic stripe.

- Electronic purses

  Several electronic payment systems, such as Mondex and Visa Cash, rely on smart cards as the carriers of value in the system. The goal is to replace cash for small transactions by storing value on a card that can be replenished. Some technologies require that value can only be transferred from a card to an authorized vendor, whereas others (such as Mondex) allow card-to-card transfers as well. This latter capability means that users can pay each other for goods or services, just as they can use cash today.

Many other smart card applications are under development, ranging from simple stored-value or authentication systems to sophisticated uses of public key systems for signing and encrypting documents and payment instructions.

Historically, one of the problems with creating applications for smart cards has been the lack of standard interfaces for communicating with the devices. RSA Laboratories has been leading the development of a standard called PKCS-11, which specifies an API for cryptographic devices such as smart cards. The API, also known as *Cryptoki*, is intended to present a technology-independent view over a wide range of devices.

In a similar vein, the Java Card API is an initiative by Sun Microsystems to use the Java programming language to develop applications for smart cards. The use of a standard programming interface would make it possible for card-based applications to run on many different cards, rather than programming them individually. Many people are also looking for "multiapplication" cards that may be used in many different contexts (e.g., different payment systems, medical records, authentication, etc.), rather than requiring people to carry separate cards for different purposes. A common programming interface (Java, in this case) makes it easier to create such multiapplication devices.[4]

Smart cards come to Internet commerce applications in two ways. The first is that the smart card is used on an Internet client to support a standard protocol (such as SSL or SET). In this case, there is no difference from the server's point of view, because the protocol is standard. The client could employ the smart card in many different ways, depending on the security requirements of the application. One use is for the card to authenticate access to encrypted credentials stored on a desktop computer. A second use includes the card in the processing of protocol messages, either by executing the protocol on the card itself or by using the card for cryptographic operations (such as digital signatures) and storing the keys and certificates used for the protocol.

A second way to use smart cards in Internet commerce applications is to develop new protocols that take advantage of the special capabilities of smart cards, in particular for cryptographic operations and key storage. In some cases, the application requirements for the use of cryptographic hardware will also include such hardware at the server as well as the use of smart cards. This approach can be very effective for creating high-security applications, but it does increase the overall development costs substantially.

As we have noted, the biggest obstacle to the use of smart cards for Internet commerce is the availability of card readers on computers used for commerce, whether they are in homes or in offices. When card readers become a mass-market device, it will become common to include the use of smart cards in Internet commerce systems. Until then, the use of smart cards in Internet systems is likely to be confined to specialized applications where the security requirements demand the extra capabilities of smart cards.

Internet Payment Systems

The commercial development of the Internet has led to the creation of several payment systems specifically designed for Internet commerce.

---

4. Carrying one smart card instead of many clearly has some advantages for the person carrying the card. There are two possible problems: One is that having multiple applications on a card may tie together different applications that a person wants to keep separate (for example, there is no real need to link a credit card with medical records), so privacy is a concern. The second problem is that plastic cards bearing logos are a form of promotion, and card issuers may be reluctant to give up that promotion in order to join a multiapplication card with another organization's logo on it.

First Virtual

First Virtual has developed a system called VirtualPIN that uses electronic mail for confirming purchases. When consumers make purchases, they provide a First Virtual account number to the vendor. Vendors submit the transactions to First Virtual, which requests confirmation by electronic mail from the buyer. The buyer can confirm the purchase or flag it as a possible attempt at fraud. This model is commonly used for digital goods, although some First Virtual merchants are selling tangible goods as well. For further information, see http://www.fv.com.

CyberCash

CyberCash was founded in 1994 by Dan Lynch and Bill Melton. The company is focused on payment technology for Internet commerce. CyberCash has introduced three payment systems so far. CyberCash operates payment servers and gateways that connect the Internet to external financial networks. The company business model is as a payment service provider, with fees based on transactions, rather than as a software vendor.

Credit Card

CyberCash introduced its credit card service in 1995. The model for the credit card service is essentially identical to that of SET, discussed in "Secure Electronic Transactions (SET)" on page 285. The buyer downloads and installs a wallet application, which interacts with a merchant "cash register" module. Payment instructions are sent to the CyberCash gateway, which relays them into standard credit card authorization networks. For the credit card portion of its service, CyberCash is transitioning to support of SET.

CyberCoin

In early 1997, CyberCash introduced its coin service, intended for small-value payments. Subscribers buy coins using a traditional financial instrument, and the value is then held in escrow by CyberCash. An Internet payment using the coin service works by debiting the customer account and crediting the merchant account. Later, the merchant can transfer accumulated funds into a regular bank account.

CyberCash Check

In early 1997, CyberCash introduced the PayNow electronic check system, which permits payments to be made directly from demand-deposit accounts, without previous transfer of funds into an escrow account. In effect, the instructions for payment of a check are transmitted across the network. The system differs from the check-writing parts of home banking applications in that the payment happens at the point of sale. This system is useful for product purchases, but it is especially valuable for online bill payment.

In online bill payment, which CyberCash calls *interactive billing and payment*, companies which normally send bills to consumers by mail and accept check payments by mail in return, instead use the Internet for both activities. In the first *bill presentment* phase, the vendor uses an interactive Web site to display detailed statements of account to its consumers. In the payment phase, the consumers can use the PayNow check service to pay the bill. The vendor avoids the costs of mailing statements and the consumer avoids the effort of writing and mailing checks.

Online Credit Card Payment

Credit cards have become the most common means for consumers to pay for goods and services on the Internet. This is not surprising, because many Internet transactions are very similar to mail-order transactions. For consumers, credit cards are a familiar way to pay, and the credit card system lowers the risk to the consumer if something goes wrong. From a technical point of view, it is much easier to create a system for processing credit card purchases than to invent a new payment technology. Finally, from a business point of view, many merchants who wish to do business online already accept credit cards, so taking advantage of online opportunities does not require establishing a new banking relationship.

Secure Communication

The first credit card transactions on the Internet were not protected against eavesdropping. Early transactions consisted of credit card numbers (and related information) sent by electronic mail, Telnet, or the World Wide Web without encryption for privacy. As electronic commerce systems began to be deployed more widely (primarily on the World Wide Web), system designers took two other approaches: obtaining credit card numbers for a customer account over telephone, rather than over the Internet, or developing encryption systems and security protocols for transmitting the information. Two of the first encryption protocols for the World Wide Web, Secure HTTP and the Secure Sockets Layer (SSL), were developed in part to enable commerce applications.

For many credit card applications, strong cryptography using a protocol such as SSL provides a high degree of communications security.[5] Developing an application is often simplified because the application need not provide additional security or manage a complex protocol.

---

5. As discussed in Chapter 12, the security afforded by export-grade cryptography in general-purpose communications software may not be sufficient for financial applications.

Secure Electronic Transactions (SET)

The Secure Electronic Transactions (SET) protocol was developed jointly by Visa and MasterCard, along with some technology partners, to provide secure credit card transactions over open networks such as the Internet. The protocol includes strong encryption and authentication of all of the parties in a credit card transaction: the buyer (or cardholder), the merchant, and the merchant's bank. Although it is still in the early stages of deployment, SET is the emerging standard for handling credit card transactions on the Internet.

As described in the Business Description portion of the SET specification, SET was designed with several goals in mind:

1. Provide confidentiality of payment information and enable confidentiality of order information that is transmitted along with the payment information
2. Ensure integrity for all transmitted data
3. Provide authentication that a cardholder is a legitimate user of a branded payment card account
4. Provide authentication that a merchant can accept branded payment card transactions through its relationship with an acquiring financial institution
5. Ensure the use of the best security practices and system design techniques to protect all legitimate parties of an electronic commerce transaction
6. Ensure the creation of a protocol that is neither dependent on transport security mechanisms nor prevents their use
7. Facilitate and encourage interoperability across software and network providers.

In accomplishing these goals, SET also enables the use of the Internet for authorization and settlement of credit card transactions as well as enabling secure communication of payment information from the cardholder to the merchant. As discussed earlier, without SET, a merchant typically connects to an acquiring bank (or other financial processor) using a leased telephone line or dial-up connection. SET makes it possible for merchants to use their Internet connection for such connections, thereby avoiding the extra cost. (Note, however, that there are some disadvantages to this approach as well, which are discussed later.)

In addition, because SET focuses on encrypting financial credentials, it is intended to allow implementations to be exported from the United States using strong cryptography, while meeting the export regulations of the U.S. government. (We discuss the export of cryptographic software in more detail in Chapter 12.)

A diagram of a SET transaction is shown in Figure 14-2. Before the transaction occurs, the merchant and the consumer must set up for SET transactions by obtaining software and certificates. The merchant interacts with the acquiring bank to obtain a SET merchant certificate. This public key certificate is signed using the acquiring bank's key, which in turn is signed using the card brand key (Visa or MasterCard, for

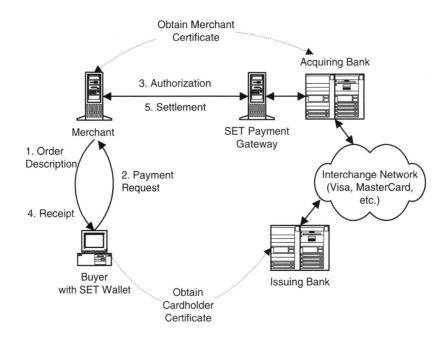

FIGURE 14-2. Flow of a SET Transaction

example). This certificate is used to authenticate the merchant to both the cardholder and to the payment gateway during the transaction phase. Similarly, the consumer interacts with his issuing bank to obtain a certificate signed by the issuing bank. The cardholder certificate is optional in the protocol, but if present is used to authenticate the cardholder to the merchant during the actual transaction.

During the transaction, the following steps occur.

- The customer interacts with the merchant Web site to select goods for purchase.
- The merchant sends an order description that wakes up the customer SET wallet.
- The customer checks the order and transmits a payment request back to the merchant's SET module.
- The merchant sends the payment request to the payment gateway.
- The payment gateway validates the merchant and the customer, and obtains an authorization from the customer's issuing bank via an interchange network.
- The payment gateway sends an order capture token back to the merchant.
- The merchant sends a receipt to the customer wallet.
- Later, the merchant uses the order capture token to settle the transaction.

The protocol definition for SET specifies the message formats, encodings, and cryptographic operations to be used. It does not require a particular method of transport, so SET messages may be carried in HTTP for World Wide Web applications, electronic mail, or any other method. The messages do not need to be exchanged in real time, which permits, for example, effective SET implementation based on electronic mail or other asynchronous systems.

Electronic Cash

Generally speaking, *electronic cash* is a class of technologies that provides an analog of cash represented in electronic form. Electronic cash systems attempt to replicate many of the properties of cash for online transactions: convenience, low (or nonexistent) transaction costs, anonymity, and so on. Although not all electronic cash systems try to satisfy all of these properties, most do try to enable quick and easy online transactions for small amounts of money.

Some electronic cash systems require smart cards (plastic cards with processors and memory) for operation; others can be performed entirely in software (although use of smart card hardware may bring an extra degree of security). When smart cards are used, losing the card means losing the money, just as losing a twenty-dollar bill means the money is lost. The card is just like cash, so the story goes, and it should be treated as such. Software systems may provide for backup of the value represented in storage, but losing all copies still means that the value is lost.

Visa Cash

As noted earlier, one of the limitations of traditional credit cards is that they have relatively high transaction costs, and therefore they are not suitable for small transactions. To address this problem, Visa has developed *cash cards* that can be used for low-priced items, in stores, vending machines, and other venues. The cards contain a processor and a few kilobytes of memory. The processor is capable of performing the cryptographic operations needed to debit the card and prevent counterfeiting. Some of these cards can only be used until their original value is consumed; others can be reloaded.

The communications between the card and a reader is presumed to be a secure channel, so the technology is not suited for transactions on open networks at this time.

Mondex

Mondex began as a joint venture between the National Westminster Bank and Midland Bank in Great Britain. In the Mondex system, smart cards are used to carry value. Value can be transferred between a customer's card and a merchant's terminal, from a bank to a customer's card over a properly equipped telephone, or even between two Mondex cards owned by individuals.

The Mondex system was deployed in a pilot phase in Swindon, England, in 1995.

As with the Visa Cash cards, the Mondex system was not originally designed for operation over open communications networks such as the Internet, but it is readily adaptable for that purpose. In 1997, AT&T Universal Card Services, in cooperation with Hewlett-Packard, Mondex, and Open Market, began a trial of Mondex use for Internet commerce. For further information on Mondex, see http://www.mondex.com. For information on the AT&T Universal Card Services trial see http://www.att.com/mondex.

Digicash

Digicash is an electronic cash system based on technology developed by David Chaum. Chaum's goals in developing Digicash were to match the properties of cash as closely as possible, particularly the properties of anonymity and untraceability. Unlike Mondex, Digicash does not require a smart card. The result is that Digicash developed a method for detecting so-called double spending. If the electronic cash is spent only once, all parties remain anonymous. However, if the same electronic coins are deposited at the bank twice, then the identity of the person who copied the money becomes traceable.

In October 1995, Mark Twain Bank in St. Louis became the first bank to issue Digicash electronic money. In October 1997, Deutsche Bank launched a trial of Digicash use on the Internet. For more information, see http://www.digicash.com.

Micropayments

The term *micropayments* is used to mean many different things. How big a micropayment is usually depends on how big an average or common payment is for the person using the term. Thus, for corporate transactions, a micropayment may be anything under $100, whereas for a credit card system it may be anything under $10. In general, we use the word *micropayment* to describe small-valued transactions—say, a few dollars or less. In most cases, micropayments are intended for use with online delivery as well: for example, fifty cents for a magazine article.

The term *nanopayment* is sometimes used to describe payments much smaller than micropayments, such as for transactions valued at less than a penny.

Business Models for Micropayments

From a business point of view, the most obvious thing about micropayments is that you really do have to make it up in volume. The arithmetic is simple: if the average transaction size is fifty cents, then it takes two million transactions to gross one million dollars. Out of that gross comes the costs of the computers for handling the transactions and fulfilling the orders, the software for processing microtransactions, the salaries of the operators to keep them running, power and air conditioning, and so on. At this stage in the evolution of Internet commerce, micropayment systems do not yet seem to pay for themselves on a large scale.

On a small scale, micropayments may indeed be successful. Consider an individual—not a professional writer—who publishes essays of political commentary on the Web. If ten thousand readers are willing to pay ten cents per essay, that comes to $1,000 our essayist might not otherwise receive. Even with fairly high costs for operating the micropayment system, the writer may come out ahead financially, as well as gaining from the exposure and visibility generated by the essays. This is a far cry from the financial returns needed to sustain a publishing business, however.

The technology side of micropayments is technically exciting and challenging, as is the vision of the future painted by micropayment proponents. One day it may be that micropayments are a common form of Internet business, but it appears for the moment that successful micropayment business models have yet to be developed and deployed.

Technical Micropayments Systems

There are a variety of technical micropayment systems either under active development or published. As this is a rapidly evolving area of technology, the best approach to further research is probably to type "micropayment" into an Internet search engine. Here is a quick survey of some systems.

Millicent

Millicent is a system designed by Mark S. Manasse of Digital Equipment Corporation's Systems Research Center in Palo Alto, California. A view of the entities and relationships in Millicent are shown in Figure 14-3. Millicent creates merchant-specific scrip, which is only exchangeable for goods at a particular merchant. Brokers provide a degree of vendor independence by selling scrip on behalf of multiple merchants. Millicent uses cryptography to protect the system against abuse by the end user, such as forgery or double spending of scrip. The other entities in the system have some protections as well. The protections offered by Millicent are not ironclad, since the system is intended for low-value transactions. The system does not provide transaction audit trails or receipts. The design center for Millicent is the exchange of scrip coins for individual Web pages. There is no protection for occasional download failures. The model is similar to that of a vending machine. If an occasional coin is lost, most people will just put in another coin. For further information, see http://www.millicent.digital.com/.

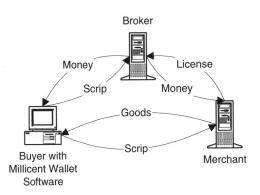

FIGURE 14-3. Millicent System Design

NetBill

NetBill is a system developed by Marvin Sirbu and Doug Tygar at Carnegie Mellon University. NetBill provides both for payment and transactional delivery of digital goods. By *transactional* we mean that either payment and delivery of the goods takes place or neither takes place. The system design, shown in Figure 14-4, prevents delivery without payment or payment without delivery.

Before any purchases are made, the NetBill customer downloads and installs the MoneyTool wallet application, which works with a Web browser. The customer also uses a traditional payment system like a credit card to purchase NetBill currency. The customer balance is stored on the NetBill server.

To make a purchase, the following steps occur.

- The customer browses the merchant's site and selects a digital good for purchase.
- The merchant system downloads an encrypted copy of the goods to the customer, along with the price and a timestamp.

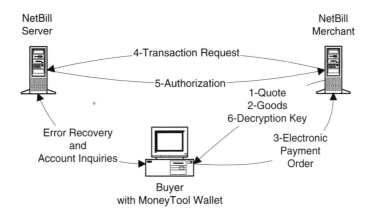

FIGURE 14-4. NetBill System Design

- The customer's MoneyTool wallet wakes up, and composes an electronic payment order (EPO), containing the price, checksum, ID of the product, and the timestamp, all signed by the customer's cryptographic key. The EPO is sent to the merchant server.

- The merchant server sends the electronic payment order, along with the decryption key for the goods, to the NetBill server.

- The NetBill server validates the EPO, debits the customer account, credits the merchant account, and records the decryption key, all in a transaction. This step assures the eventual success of the purchase.

- The NetBill server returns a success message to the merchant, who sends the decryption key to the customer.

- The customer can now decrypt and view the goods.

Should the customer fail to get the decryption key, or in case of other failures, the customer can communicate directly with the NetBill server to obtain the key or perhaps learn that the transaction was never recorded (and money not spent).

For further information on NetBill, see http://www.netbill.com/.

Aggregation

The business problem to which technical micropayment systems appear to be a solution is that of handling small-value transactions which cannot justify, for example, a credit card authorization. In some cases, this business problem can also be solved by transaction aggregation. In these schemes, small transactions are grouped together until the total is of a size suitable for handling by a traditional payment system. There are two modes of aggregation: *taxi meter* and *parking meter.*

In a taxi, charges accumulate as the taxi moves or waits. The passenger settles the bill at the end of the trip. Taxi mode, or *charge-up* transaction aggregation, works the same way: charges accumulate on the account of a customer until a threshold is reached, or until the end of a session or billing period. At that time, the total accumulated amount is settled using a traditional payment system. In this system, the seller is extending credit to the buyer, but the sums are small so not much is at risk. The seller can also simply refuse to do further business with the buyer until the bill is paid. In a variation of the taxi meter scheme, an authorization, or credit reservation, may be made at the beginning of a session, with settlement at the end when the true charges are known.

In a parking meter, a driver parking a vehicle deposits coins in the meter upon parking. The meter then decrements the amount of credit remaining as time is spent. Parking meter mode, or *draw-down* transaction aggregation, works the same way: the buyer prefunds an account with a traditional payment system, and then microtransaction debits are made to the account. In this system, the buyer rather than the seller assumes the risk. Variations include whether or not refunds of partially used credit can be made.

One very interesting difference between these two modes of operation is the allocation of risk and the consequences of it. Because the buyer takes the risk in parking meter systems, the system can be made available to anonymous customers. In contrast, because the seller takes the risk in taxi meter systems, these systems are typically available only to registered, authenticated buyers.

Transaction aggregation is typically an arrangement between a buyer and a single seller. Technically, a microtransaction aggregation account could be shared by multiple sellers, but whether this is sensible may depend on the system reporting capabilities rather than anything else. Aggregation systems may report only totals or may have complete transaction detail reporting of the microtransactions themselves. The degree of reporting available is often a function of transaction size. By calculating the equipment and infrastructure costs, the cost of a transaction can be calculated. The data storage necessary to support transaction detail reporting adds significantly to the transaction cost, so detail reporting is only sensible for larger microtransaction amounts.

Payment in the Abstract

Most of the discussion in this chapter has been about systems for the transfer of money in payment of goods or services. However, much commerce in the real world works in an environment substantially separated from payment.

Business to Business

For example, most business-to-business commerce is conducted as follows.

1. Two businesses establish a commercial relationship. The seller agrees to extend credit to the buyer.
2. The buying organization obtains goods and services from the selling organization.
3. Periodically, a bill is sent from seller to buyer.
4. The buyer pays the bills using a check or other funds transfer.

In this model, payment is a function from one finance department to another, and has no direct connection to the actual purchasing. What is really going on here is that many of the real-world and Internet payment systems discussed in this chapter bundle together the notions of authorization and settlement. Credit card systems separate these to some degree, but each authorization matches a settlement. In business-to-business commerce, there is no direct connection between authorization and settlement. Let's reinterpret the events.

- The selling organization makes a decision to extend credit to the buying organization.
- At the point of purchase, the *requisitioner* must authenticate himself as a representative of the buyer. (And sometimes, the buying organization must *approve* the purchase through some other internal mechanism.) This step is equivalent to the credit card authorization.
- Later, the finance departments reconcile and settle the transactions that have occurred.

What has happened here is that the buying organization has delegated authority to the requisitioner. In the abstract, this delegation of authority is very much like money.[6]

---

6. Thanks to Dan Geer for explaining the connection between delegation and money.

Information Commerce

Professional users of information, such as lawyers, bankers, and accountants, frequently engage in information commerce, paying for the knowledge and expertise of others, as codified in writing. For example, lawyers use the Lexis-Nexis or WestLaw online services, or subscribe to CD-ROM distributions of annotated case law.

These information commerce transactions are seldom paid for directly by credit card or cash.

1. A law office sets up a billing relationship with a commercial publisher of case law.
2. On entry to, for example, the online legal information service, an individual lawyer logs in, authenticating himself to the service, and enters an account code. This code will be used for later rebilling of services provided to the lawyer's client.
3. As the lawyer uses the information service, billing events are generated and posted to the law office's account.
4. Periodically, the publisher sends a bill to the law office, and the individual billable items are rebilled, perhaps with a markup, to the clients.
5. The law office pays the publisher.
6. The clients pay the law office.

As in the business-to-business example, the information transaction is not tightly coupled to payment. Instead, authorization and settlement are separated, and there is an initial step of establishing a commercial relationship between buying and selling organizations. During the transaction itself, an authentication or approval step provides an authorization for the transaction and the settlement happens later.

Summary

Many people think that the problems of Internet commerce are all associated with payment. This is hardly true, as the other chapters of this book demonstrate, yet payment is an essential component of many commerce systems. There are a tremendous number of payment systems in use around the globe, with various ways of handling the essential issues of authorization and settlement. In addition, different systems are commonly used for business-to-consumer, business-to-business, and information commerce. Payment is an area of ongoing innovation, as our discussion of microtransactions illustrates, and new technologies will continue to emerge. An Internet commerce architecture must therefore be flexible regarding payment technology, yet the designers must understand both the technology and the business issues of managing trust as well as risk.

CHAPTER 15

Auxiliary Systems

God is in the details.
—Popular saying[1]

The Details Behind the Scenes

This chapter introduces a number of commerce issues—tax, logistics, and inventory management—that need to be addressed in a complete system for Internet commerce. Internet systems for merely accepting orders may be able to avoid these concerns, but if the system objectives include being able to guarantee availability, display an accurate price, and meet legal obligations for payment of taxes, there are few alternatives.

In practice, these issues simply reflect issues in the real world of business. To the extent that Internet commerce grows out of an existing business, such real issues must clearly be part of the system. But even when the business is created because of Internet opportunities, problems such as taxes, logistics, and inventory must still be managed. Indeed, one test of software for Internet commerce is how well it handles these problems.

---

1. This saying was popular with architect Mies van der Rohe and is often attributed to Gustave Flaubert, but the actual origin is unclear.

Taxes

Taxes come in many shapes and sizes, depending on the jurisdiction. Indeed, many governments are currently debating what taxes should be applied to Internet transactions and how they should be collected. While the complexities of tax law are clearly beyond the scope of this book, the following examples illustrate some of the issues in dealing with taxes in Internet commerce systems.

Sales Tax in the United States

In the United States, sales taxes are owed by the purchaser of products to state governments, counties, and localities (cities). In all, there are over 6,000 rules about sales tax, and they change frequently as governments at all levels change the rules and create new laws. As an additional complication, the tax status of digital goods, called *intangible* by tax specialists, is still under active debate.[2]

Sales tax is frequently viewed by consumers as a simple problem in face-to-face commercial situations. The merchant's cash register calculates the tax due and adds it to the bill. The apparent simplicity is because almost all the variables in a face-to-face transaction are fixed. In addition, although the buyer nominally owes the tax, the seller is charged with collecting it.

As shown in Figure 15-1, sales tax calculation is a complex function of information about the seller, the buyer, the product, and the transaction.

Seller Information

- Nexus

  Generally, a merchant is responsible for collecting and paying sales tax to a state if the merchant has a commercial presence, or *nexus*, in that state. A commercial presence is a legal definition; a store or substantial facilities would certainly qualify, a small sales office might not.

- Point of title passage

  The tax calculation works differently depending on where title for the goods purchased passes from seller to buyer. The usual options are that title passes when the goods are shipped (at the seller's warehouse) or when the goods are delivered (at the buyer's address).

---

2. "What Are the Sales Tax Consequences of Retail Marketing on the Internet?" K. Lawrence Gragg and Leonard S. Sosnowski, *Journal of Multistate Taxation*, March/April 1997; see http://www.taxware.com/current/other/JMSTarticle.html.

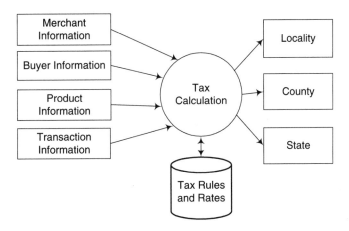

FIGURE 15-1. U.S. Sales Tax Calculation

Buyer Information

- Address

  In an electronic transaction, where does the transaction take place? In the case of mail- or telephone-order transactions, the transaction is usually held to take place at the buyer's location. In the case of credit card payment, the buyer's location is usually held to be the same as the billing address of the credit card. This is not perfect, but it is simple and fairly consistent.

  The buyer's address is then used to determine what jurisdictions may require sales tax payment. Unfortunately, jurisdiction cannot be determined simply from a zip code (postal code), because a zip code can span city and county boundaries. Instead, the complete address must be mapped to a *geo code*, which is a geographic location precise enough to determine the tax jurisdiction.

- Tax-exempt status

  Certain nonprofit and educational institutions are not required to pay sales tax, nor are businesses purchasing items or parts for later resale. The purchaser must typically supply a tax-exempt number for the merchant's records.

Product Information

- Goods classification

  Not all types of goods and services are taxable in all jurisdictions. For example, in the state of Massachusetts, clothing and cranberries have no sales tax. Clothing is held to be a necessity, and cranberries are a mainstay of the state's agricultural economy. For this reason, individual products must be tagged with a product category code with sufficient precision to allow the sales tax engine to determine the applicable rate, if any.

- Price

Sales tax is computed as a percentage of item price.

Transaction Information

- Coupons

Coupons operate in the context of a specific transaction to change the price of an item. The proper computation of sales tax requires such price reductions to be made before tax is calculated.

In order to compute tax, all the necessary source information is fed to a tax rules engine, which produces a total sales tax due for presentation to the customer, and individual tax due amounts to all relevant jurisdictions for inclusion in tax reporting files for the merchant.

Tax computation is a sufficiently complex issue that companies such as Taxware International (http://www.taxware.com/) have come to specialize in this area. They offer tax computation modules and also provide information update services that supply new tax rule databases on a periodic basis.

Alternatives

In very simple situations, small merchants with a commercial presence in just one state may choose to collect sales tax on all transactions, regardless of the actual necessity of doing so. This approach errs on the side of too much tax paid, and has a consequent cost to consumers, but it simplifies the life of the merchant.

Canadian Goods and Services Tax

Canadian sales taxes are not as complex as those in the United States, but they are not too far behind. Most provinces collect a federal governmental sales tax (GST) at a 7 percent rate plus a provincial sales tax (PST) at a rate which varies from province to province. However, in April 1997, some provinces switched to a new harmonized sales tax (HST) which combined the GST and PST into a single 15 percent tax. As in the U.S., tax rates vary for different goods and services.

Special rules apply for goods imported or exported from Canada. As a general rule, whenever taxable goods or services are imported into Canada, GST/PST is incurred. When goods or services are exported from Canada, they are zero-rated and therefore no GST/PST is incurred. The point of title passage is assumed to be the destination, which is the usual case for retail sales. Basically, if the ship-to address is in Canada, then GST/PST/HST must be computed and displayed to the buyer.

The Canadian Department of Finance Web site at http://www.fin.ga.ca/ is a good resource.

Value-Added Tax

In Europe and other parts of the world, value-added tax, or VAT, is a primary source of government revenue. In sales tax, taxes are assessed at the point of consumption—only the final consumer owes tax. In contrast, the model for value-added tax is that goods and services are assessed a tax whenever they change hands. Resellers pay tax on the goods they buy, and are required to collect tax on the goods they sell. Generally, these resellers can get a credit for the tax paid on supplies, so the net effect is to tax the *value added* at each stage in the chain.

As usual, rates vary for different kinds of goods and in different jurisdictions. Cross-border rules are particularly complex. The European Union has decided to tax all transactions in the country of origin. This procedure reduces export and import paperwork significantly, but at the expense of complicating life for those who are not end users. Resellers in Europe apply tax to all sales, but must apply separately to each country from which they purchase to obtain refunds of VAT for items resold.

Proper implementation of VAT in an Internet commerce system requires the following steps.

1. Obtaining necessary input information, including location of buyer, goods classification, and merchant VAT profile.

2. Calculating VAT due for the transaction.

3. Displaying necessary legal invoices to the purchaser. These are necessary if the purchaser is a reseller who will later claim credits or refunds.

4. Preparing necessary records and audit trails for the merchant for submission to the merchant's VAT taxing authority.

Taxware International has a product, WORLDTax, which does much of this work, and supports European Union and other European countries, as well as Canada and some countries in Asia and on the Pacific Rim.

Shipping and Handling

Shipping and handling are parts of the overall area of logistics. Once an order is entered, physical goods must be delivered to the consumer. From the consumer's perspective, this process appears simple, but it contains surprising complexities of pricing, international concerns, and automation of order handoff from merchant to shipping company.

Pricing Shipping and Handling

Shipping costs money. Unless that cost is buried in the seller's overall price structure, it will be visible to the consumer. The seller will want the shipping fees to cover his costs, but beyond that, shipping charges can be a marketing tool and a competitive weapon.

In direct marketing (catalog sales), a variety of pricing models for shipping are used.

- Flat rate

  For merchants selling a small variety of goods of very similar weight and volume—contact lenses, for example—a flat rate for shipping may be appropriate. The flat rate covers per-order processing costs of the seller plus the actual shipping charges. For large items, individual item flat-rate charges may apply.

- Weight based

  For bulk materials, actual shipping charges are usually weight based. This model can simply be passed through to the consumer.

- Value based

  Shipping charges based on the total value of the order, either proportionally or in steps, have the advantage that they are easy for the customer to understand. Steps also serve the marketing function of encouraging the consumer to add items to the order until it is just below a step boundary.

- Distance based

  Actual shipping charges are sometimes linked to the distance shipped. This model can combine with any of the previous three to build a model proportional to both value and distance, for example.

International Transport

One likely effect of Internet commerce will be to create many new international businesses. International commerce has been the province of a few due to its complexity and to the difficulties of international sales and marketing. Because the Internet makes international sales easier, many new organizations will have to face the complexities of international transport. Not least among these difficulties are customs issues and producing the necessary paperwork to ship products internationally.

Customs Duties

Customs tariffs and duties vary widely around the world. One step in simplification has been the adoption of the Harmonized Tariff System Classification, which is a standardized numbering system for traded products. The number assigned to each class of product is used by customs officials around the world to determine the duties, taxes, and regulations that apply to the product. A schedule of these classifications is available on the Internet at http://www.census.gov/foreign-trade/www.

Paperwork

International shipments center around the *commercial invoice*. The commercial invoice identifies the shipper, receiver, and freight companies involved in a shipment, and describes the contents of a shipment. Its purpose is to put in one place all the information needed by customs officials to classify the items shipped in order to correctly assess any taxes and duties required.

Besides the commercial invoice, a wide variety of documents may be necessary for export, shipping, and import. These include:

- Bill of lading
- Consular invoice
- Certificate of origin
- Export license
- Insurance certificate
- Shipper's export declaration
- International letter of credit

A full discussion of export documentation is well outside the scope of this book, but a good place to start (for U.S. companies) is *A Basic Guide to Exporting*, published by the U.S. Department of Commerce.

Transport and Tracking

There is a large national and international infrastructure for freight and shipping. Companies such as Federal Express, United Parcel Service, Airborne, and DHL provide worldwide services. For larger customers, and increasingly for small ones as well, these companies offer automated systems for arranging pickup and shipment of packages. Shipping software creates the appropriate labels, assigns tracking numbers, and schedules pickup and delivery.

Web-based services for tracking shipments are available from each of the four companies just mentioned:

- Fedex: http://www.fedex.com/
- UPS: http://www.ups.com/
- Airborne: http://www.airborne.com/
- DHL: http://www.dhl.com/

Privacy

Several privacy issues arise when logistics are considered. First, is it possible to have an anonymous transaction when physical delivery is needed? Second, what security is offered by package tracking services?

Anonymity

It seems possible that information commerce might be truly anonymous. Payment mechanisms can in principle be anonymous (see Chapter 14), but achieving anonymity in a transaction involving physical delivery of products is more difficult. One approach is that the delivery company might serve as a privacy intermediary between buyer and seller. If the buyer has an account with a delivery company, then the buyer could tell the seller, "deliver via XYZ shipping to customer 12345." The seller would know what was sold, and the shipper would know to whom it was sold, but neither would have complete information.

A second possibility is depot delivery. In depot delivery, the shipper delivers the package to a neighborhood drop-off location such as a grocery store or box company. If the transaction is paid for with electronic cash and the delivery is effectively to "general delivery," then anonymity is possible.

Tracking Numbers

One problem with the current implementation of tracking numbers by shipping companies is that they are not very secure. Frequently, the tracking number is really an account number followed by a sequence number of shipments, together with a simple checksum. Account numbers are easy to obtain—simply buy something from the same company and check the tracking number. After that, sequence numbers can be fairly easily guessed.

Advanced Logistics

In the early stages of commerce, shipping was fairly simple. One ordered from the factory, and the products were shipped from there to the consumer. This model is a good place to start, but does not meet all the requirements for logistics. As examples, we consider the problems of warehouse selection and the virtual corporation.

Warehouse Selection

Large businesses frequently have regional warehouses or warehouses which contain only some products. In these cases, the products ordered or the ship-to address or both may influence the choice of fulfillment center. The choice of fulfillment center may in turn affect the calculation of shipping charges. Designers don't like situations where everything depends on everything, since they make modular design difficult; so in cases like this, a standard shipping charge may be used, calculated to match or exceed actual shipping costs. Occasional feedback can be used to adjust the charges.

The Virtual Corporation

The idea of a virtual corporation predates Internet commerce. A virtual corporation might outsource *everything:* product design, manufacturing, distribution, marketing, accounting, and so forth. Many businesses are not completely virtual, but do depend on partners for substantial components. For example, a distributor of personal computers may manufacture the system unit, but obtain computer monitors from a different manufacturer. If there is no need for a full system test, it makes sense to ship the monitor from one warehouse and the system unit from another warehouse and have the two boxes delivered separately. If this works well, the two boxes will arrive on the same truck at the same time.

Inventory Management

In most commercial transactions, the availability of the product plays a large role in the sale. In face-to-face commerce, the product is on the shelf. In telephone-order commerce, the operator usually has access to inventory information. In sophisticated business-to-business commerce, the concept is *available to promise,* wherein the seller's Enterprise Resource Planning (ERP) system has such complete visibility into inventory, time in transit, previous commitments, manufacturing capacity, and scheduled arrival of parts that precise commitments for current and future delivery can be made.

Inventory management capabilities will become a standard part of Internet commerce—buyers want to know if they can actually get things they order. If products are not immediately available, buyers will switch to alternatives that are. In some cases, buyers will pay a premium for availability.

For large selling organizations, the right way to achieve inventory management is probably to integrate the Internet commerce system with the corporate system which manages all inventory. This can be achieved in two ways.

- Catalog integration

  In this model, the Internet catalog system is updated periodically with inventory-on-hand information. The catalog uses this information to mark or simply not display items which are out of stock. Additionally, items which are in short supply are candidates for promotions or sales to clear remaining inventory.

- Transaction system integration

  In this model, the Internet commerce transaction system is integrated with internal corporate systems. Items on the customer order form are confirmed available and reserved against inventory at the point of sale.

Both techniques may be used to create a fully integrated system in which items found in the catalog are effectively guaranteed to be available.

These techniques can be affordable for large enterprises, but smaller enterprises may not even have computerized inventory systems. One promise of the Internet is that small and medium enterprises can look like larger companies. How can this be achieved in the area of inventory management? One idea is the *virtual warehouse*.

The Virtual Warehouse

The idea of the virtual warehouse is simple. A small or medium enterprise places a portion of its inventory under the management of the virtual warehouse, which can then make commitments to customers against that allocation. Consider the following sequence of events.

1. A small seller of widgets creates a Web-based catalog. Since the market for widgets depends on immediate gratification of buyers, it is important to assure availability.

2. Each business day, the seller uses an administrative Web application to grant control of a certain number of widgets, perhaps 50, to the virtual warehouse.

3. When a buyer browses the widget catalog, the catalog system uses a real-time query to the virtual warehouse to obtain the number of widgets on hand. The catalog uses the quantity obtained to control its behavior, selecting regular or promotional pricing.

4. When a buyer selects a widget for purchase, the catalog system obtains a reservation against inventory from the virtual warehouse. The reservation is good for a fixed time such as 30 minutes. This idea is similar to the way airline reservations work. The reservation is good for a fixed time, and lapses if the tickets are not paid for before the reservation expires.

5. When the transaction commits before the reservation expires, the Internet commerce transaction system records that fact with the virtual warehouse, confirming the reservation and removing the appropriate widget count from the allocation.

6. During the day, or periodically, the seller can add or remove inventory from the virtual warehouse, although inventory cannot be removed if held by an active reservation.

In this way, a small enterprise can obtain the benefits of a fully integrated inventory management system without great expense. The virtual warehouse is merely a debit, credit, and reservation system for paper inventory, but the customer is happy because he can obtain a guarantee of delivery.

The virtual warehouse breaks down only at the margins: if not all inventory is entered in the virtual warehouse, then some customers may not be able to order when in fact supply is available. However, a customer is never promised delivery when inventory is *not* available.

A logical diagram of the virtual warehouse is shown in Figure 15-2.

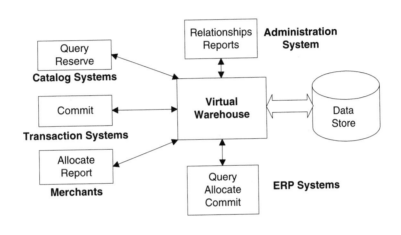

FIGURE 15-2. **The Virtual Warehouse**

The virtual warehouse is built around a database which stores items, inventory, and reservations. Around that database are the applications which interact with it on behalf of catalog systems, transaction systems, merchants, ERP systems, and administrators.

Catalog Interfaces

The catalog system can query the inventory status of items in the virtual warehouse and it can place temporary reservations against inventory. Queries are used by the catalog software to gauge supply levels in order to select an appropriate presentation in the catalog. The catalog system places a reservation when an item is selected for purchase (put into a shopping cart or order form) but the order is not yet confirmed.

Transaction Interfaces

The transaction system, during order processing, checks to see if valid reservations are held for all items being ordered. If they are, then the reservations are confirmed as a component of committing the order. When this happens, the virtual warehouse debits the inventory level.

Merchant Interfaces

Small and medium-size merchants will interact with the virtual warehouse through Web-based interfaces. The merchant can query inventory levels, generate reports, and most important, allocate new inventory to the warehouse.

Enterprise Resource Planning Interfaces

Larger businesses will interact with the virtual warehouse through interfaces with their ERP systems. These systems run the business, and have the ability to query, allocate, and commit changes to inventory due to external transactions.

Administrative Interfaces

In order to make the virtual warehouse work in a shared-services environment across a public network, administrative utilities are necessary to set up new merchant accounts, control security parameters, and report on activity.

Summary

In order to be successful, Internet commerce must provide complete business solutions. If commerce systems are provided as piece parts which must be assembled by each system operator, they will not achieve much market penetration. Complete solutions must supply implementations of all functionality necessary to complete the on-line experience, or must integrate in real time with external components. In this chapter, we have discussed a number of subsystems, taxes, shipping, and inventory, which are necessary to build a fully functional system.

CHAPTER 16

Transaction Processing

> Six thousand years ago, the Sumerians invented writing for transaction processing.
>
> —Jim Gray and Andreas Reuter[1]

Transactions and Internet Commerce

This chapter serves two functions: to introduce the technologies of transaction processing as they relate to Internet commerce, and to discuss a number of issues related to the completeness and integrity of the commerce application, such as backup and disaster recovery.

The purpose of Internet commerce is to facilitate the exchange of payments for goods and services. The purpose of transaction processing, at its most basic, is to assure that if payment has occurred, then goods are delivered, and to assure that goods are never delivered to someone who has not paid. This is substantially more difficult than it seems.

When commerce is conducted face to face, many social and informal mechanisms help perform error recovery. If the change is wrong or goods not delivered, the individuals involved will usually notice and try again. With information systems, getting the software to handle the case where everything flows smoothly is fairly easy. Getting the software to correctly handle all the potential, possibly unlikely, failures is

---

1. Jim Gray and Andreas Reuter, *Transaction Processing: Concepts and Techniques* (Morgan Kaufman, 1993).

very hard. Transaction processing as a discipline provides a framework for building complex systems so that their behavior in the presence of failures is correct.

Overview of Transaction Processing

Functions performed by Internet commerce applications, such as a sale or return, are quite complex. Each is composed of a number of other activities. For example, a sale event might include:

- Debit buyer's account[2]
- Credit seller's account
- Record event for business records
- Transmit order to fulfillment center
- Issue receipt to buyer

Transaction systems make sure that all of these steps happen if any of them do, that the activities of multiple buyers do not interfere with each other, and that records are not lost. From this perspective, transactions have four essential characteristics, known by the acronym ACID.

- Atomicity—In our example, it would be bad if the system debited the buyer without crediting the seller, or if the system charged the buyer without delivering a receipt. In other words, it must not happen that only some steps of the transaction occur. Either all of the steps must be taken, or it must seem to all observers that the transaction never happened at all.

- Consistency—If the state of the environment is represented by account balances, presence of receipts, and so forth, it must never happen that the state is inconsistent. For example, accounts must balance both before and after the transaction.

- Isolation—Because an Internet commerce business transaction takes some period of time, and because there may be multiple transactions underway, it is important that the activities of one buyer do not interfere with those of another buyer. The easiest way to think about this is that even though simultaneous transactions overlap, imagine that they do not overlap, but rather occur in some order or *serialization*—then design the system so that overlapping transactions work as though they were serialized. Figure 16-1 has an example of this concept.

- Durability—Once a transaction is complete or committed, it should be impossible for its effects to come undone due to a system or component failure. In practice, this means that the results of transactions are reliably recorded on a stable storage medium which is resilient to failure, such as duplicate or mirrored disk drives.

---

2. Debit is itself a complex operation, breaking into three steps: reading the old balance, subtracting the debit, and storing back the new balance.

Consider a single credit transaction:

- Step 1—Read old account balance (say, $100)

- Step 2—Add credit and old balance ($100 + $10 = $110)

- Step 3—Store updated balance ($110)

Now suppose that two credits are going on at about the same time, one for $10 and one for $20. With no transaction isolation, it might happen that the steps interleave as follows:

- Transaction A, Step 1, Read old balance ($100)

- Transaction B, Step 1, Read old balance ($100)

- Transaction A, Step 2, Add credit and old balance ($100 + 10 = $110)

- Transaction B, Step 2, Add credit and old balance ($100 + 20 = $120)

- Transaction A, Step 3, Store updated balance ($110)

- Transaction B, Step 3, Store updated balance ($120)

At the end, the account has only $120 instead of the correct $130. With transaction isolation, the correct result is the one obtained as if the transactions were serialized, with Transaction A either completely before or completely after Transaction B:

- Transaction A, Step 1, Read old balance ($100)

- Transaction A, Step 2, Add credit and old balance ($100 + 10 = $110)

- Transaction A, Step 3, Store updated balance ($110)

- Transaction B, Step 1, Read old balance ($110)

- Transaction B, Step 2, Add credit and old balance ($110 + 20 = $130)

- Transaction B, Step 3, Store updated balance ($130)

FIGURE 16-1. Example of Transaction Serialization

Two-Phase Commit

When a transaction affects multiple resources, perhaps distributed across multiple systems on a network, a technique known as *two-phase commit* is used to assure that the total transaction is atomic. In this technique, a central transaction coordinator communicates with the various resource managers and orchestrates the transaction.

- Phase 1a—vote

  The transaction coordinator asks each of the resource managers if they can commit the transaction. If they all vote yes, the transaction will commit.

- Phase 1b—record

  The transaction coordinator records in durable storage that the transaction is committed.

- Phase 2a—commit

  The transaction coordinator informs each of the resource managers that the transaction has committed.

- Phase 2b—complete

    The transaction coordinator records in durable storage that it has received acknowledgments from all resource managers. At this point, no extra work will be necessary to recover from a failure.

Transaction Processing in Internet Commerce

Let's consider a real example: an Internet commerce system in which the following occur.

1. The buyer selects one or several items from a Web-based catalog.
2. The buyer securely enters credit card and shipping information.
3. Product, tax, and shipping charges are computed.
4. The buyer accepts the resulting total amount.
5. A credit card authorization is obtained.
6. An advice of order message is sent to a fulfillment center.
7. The buyer receives a receipt.

The first step is to identify the transaction. Steps 1 and 2 do not need to be "inside the transaction." These are the browsing phase, plus an interactive phase of order completion (entering shipping address and so forth) which may require several attempts to get right. Step 3, in which the order total is computed, does not need to be inside the transaction either, although it is important to disallow any changes to the order which might affect the total (such as adding an additional item to the order). The real transaction is steps 4 through 7. From the point of order acceptance by the buyer, through all activities related to payment and fulfillment, either all steps must be completed successfully, or the system must act as though the order had never been accepted.

The transaction may fail for several reasons.

- Seller's computer crashes or there is a power failure.

    From the buyer's perspective, he clicked on the "OK to buy" button and nothing happened. He may give up or simply click on "OK to buy" again. In either case, he will be unhappy to be charged for goods never received, or to be charged twice for goods received only once.

- Buyer's computer crashes or there is a power failure.

    From the buyer's perspective, he clicked on the "OK to buy" button and then the lights went out. When the power comes back, the buyer would like to try again, and be charged exactly once for one set of goods. Since the buyer's computer failed after the seller's computer received the OK, it is likely that steps 4, 5, and 6 succeeded, leaving only step 7. In this case, the commerce system can simply provide a way for the buyer to get a duplicate receipt.

- The credit card authorization fails.

  If the authorization fails, the system should essentially return to step 2, suggesting to the buyer that the card number may have been entered incorrectly and giving an opportunity to try again.

- The line to the credit card network fails between the time the authorization request was sent and the time the response is received.

  This is a very interesting kind of failure, since the seller's system has no way to tell whether the request message ever got to the credit card network, or whether the reply was lost. It is important that the customer not be charged twice, so the commerce system must employ recovery techniques to figure out whether the authorization succeeded, failed, or never happened.

Integrating External Systems with Transactions

In the previous section, an example was made of the communications channel failing during a credit card authorization message. This is an example of a general issue with transaction systems of communicating with devices and systems outside their control.

For an outside system to participate in a transaction, the functions of the outside system must be *idempotent* or *testable*. Idempotent means that if repeated requests for the same action are made, the action will take place only once (or rather, that repeated requests have no additional effect beyond the first). Testable means that there is a way for the transaction system to test whether the action has taken place, so as not to make a duplicate request.

In the previous example of credit card authorizations, the card protocols have been designed with a reference number as part of the request. If a duplicate request with a known reference number is received, the credit card system merely returns the previous reply, rather than duplicating the request.

Client Software

In an Internet commerce system, the use of Web browsers or other client software requires special analysis.

- Can unanticipated user events cause unwanted effects?

  As in other systems in which an end user operates the terminal, Internet commerce systems which rely on Web browsers for their user interface can expect to receive as input arbitrary sequences of events with arbitrary timing. The user may click on any link or button at any time, enter arbitrary information into forms, click over and over again on the same button, or may simply vanish at any point, only to return hours later. The system must be completely bulletproof against such activities. This problem is much more difficult in Internet commerce than in other systems, because the user terminal—the browser—is a general-purpose device and cannot be easily constrained. In networks of Automatic Teller Machines, for example, the terminal is directly operated by the end user, but the user's behavior is carefully constrained by the terminal software. While the system is considering a request, for example, all keys but "cancel" can be locked. On the Internet, the browser works the same way for all applications and the standard user interface model grants a great deal of power to the user.

- Can unfriendly users generate errors in system behavior?

  Although it sometimes seems as though the desired user population can create the most stressful situations for the system, unfriendly users or "crackers" can also cause havoc. Because the system is available to the open network, an unfriendly user can transmit arbitrary bit strings to the system as though they were valid input. The system must carefully validate all input from any source that is not trusted and should probably carefully check all inputs, trusted or not. Unfriendly users could even reprogram the user terminal or browser to give it completely different behavior.

Sometimes error recovery is a cost-benefit trade-off. System designers will design the system for the common (correct operation) case, and provide rather expensive error-recovery mechanisms. This approach works well when the error cases are unlikely. However, if there is a way for an unfriendly user to force the system to generate errors, or to respond to an apparent error, then even if the system operates correctly, it may perform poorly or invalidate the design assumptions. Again, it is important not to trust any message that could have come from an untrusted party.[3]

Integrating Existing Systems

Many businesses already have information systems for managing their business: order processing, manufacturing, accounting, fulfillment, and so forth. It often makes sense for a new Internet commerce system to integrate with the existing information systems wherever possible, rather than running the Internet part of the business completely separately. Integration must be done very carefully, with special attention to the following issues.

- Real-time requirements

  Existing systems may not have the proper real-time requirements for direct connection to an Internet commerce system intended for interactive use. To some extent, these problems can be handled by buffering, queuing, and caching between the Internet system and the existing system.

---

3. As a particularly egregious example of unwarranted trust, early versions of some Internet commerce systems kept the prices of merchandise in so-called hidden form fields. These fields are not normally visible to the buyer, but an unfriendly user has full access to these fields and could in fact change prices.

- Security requirements

  Existing systems may not be designed with appropriate security mechanisms for Internet commerce. For example, most existing systems are designed for use by specifically trained personnel, who work for the system operator. Internet commerce systems frequently need to be directly accessed and operated by untrained end users, who do not work for the system operator.

- Support for required roles

  Existing systems may not be designed with the roles needed by the Internet system. For example, an existing order entry system for a mail- or telephone-order seller would normally be designed for use by an order entry operator, not for use directly by the customer.

- Trust protections

  Existing systems may not be designed to connect directly with systems operated by different organizations. In these cases, special care must be taken to validate all input from "outside."

Keeping Business Records

Some of the principle outputs of the transaction processing subsystem of an Internet commerce system are business records of various kinds. Some types of records, such as those for orders and payments, are part of the core operation of the business. Others, such as those containing customer data, create a key information asset of the business—the customer database. Still others, such as tax records, are necessary to satisfy regulatory and legal requirements.

Core Business Records

Some records are essential for managing the day-to-day business.

- Orders

  An order is an *offer to buy*, incorporating items, their characteristics, terms and conditions, prices, shipping and billing addresses, and so forth. Each information element is there for a specific purpose. In addition, an order is not created all at once. Instead, an order is built up item by item during an order capture phase, then missing elements are added during the order completion phase: addresses, tax and shipping charges, and so forth. When the buyer and seller are both satisfied, the order is complete and becomes a binding agreement.

- Invoices

  An invoice is a record of fulfillment, recording that goods have been shipped or services rendered. Because the buyer now owes the seller money, the invoice is also a bill, but it is not directly coupled to payments. Normally, an invoice is never changed once created, since it represents a statement of historical fact (something was shipped).

- Payments (receipts)

  A receipt is a record of a payment, usually issued by the seller, but not always (a receipt for a credit would be logically issued by the buyer).

Collateral Records

Some records are kept in order to build a long-term information asset.

- Customer database

  Customer names, addresses, buying history, and preferences help the marketing and sales departments understand their customers better. If the seller's business is distribution, rather than production, then maintaining close customer relationships may be the core value of the business. Customer information is not only useful for reports, but is useful online, for providing personalized services and customized product catalogs.

- Advertising and tracking

  In Internet commerce, as in no other media, it is possible to trace how buyers find sellers. The information generated by advertising not only determines who pays whom how much for the ad placement, but works in an active feedback loop to gauge the effectiveness of advertising and control future efforts.

  Once a buyer locates a seller, Internet-based systems can track buyer behavior and actions at a very detailed level. This information can refine product presentation and provide opportunities for merchandising.

Government Records

Some records are kept pursuant to an external requirement. For example, governments have specific legal requirements for record keeping in support of sales and use taxes. Tax issues for Internet commerce are discussed in Chapter 15.

Record Life Cycle

A typical business record item, such as an order entered by a customer, follows a complex life cycle. Let's follow an order through its life cycle.

- Create

  When a buyer first selects an item for potential purchase, the order is created. This first phase of order building, order capture, can persist for an extended period. During this phase, the order may be a temporary record, perhaps maintained by a Java applet on the buyer's desktop, or it may be a formal database record at the server.

- Store

  During the early life of an order, while the buyer is considering potential items for purchase, it may not be necessary to establish a permanent record. At some point, either because the potential order has reached critical value or merely as a user convenience, the order is stored and given a unique identity. The record may be permanent or it may be erased if the order is never completed, but the order identity or reference number is not reused.

- Process

  The order must pass through several stages of processing as part of the normal order flow. For example, shipping charges and taxes are computed, and credit authorizations obtained. When the order is finalized, it must be communicated to systems responsible for fulfillment.

- Access

  For some period after the order is created, it will be in active use, during order processing the buyer and seller both update the order-in-progress, and after finalization the order will be referenced by the customer service subsystem.

- Report

  The order will likely be the object of a variety of reports during its life. Daily sales reports, open orders, taxable sales, customer billing, and marketing reports all use the order information.

- Archive

  Once the order has completed active processing and a standard span of accessibility for reporting, it will be archived. In practice, archival storage may be the same mechanism as system backup, but their purposes are quite different. Backup systems exist in order to recover from hardware or software failures and for disaster recovery, whereas archives represent a permanent business record.

- Retrieve

  Occasionally, an order which has been moved offline into archival storage will be needed. For example, records are normally kept online for 60 days, but a customer dispute arises after 90 days. In this case, the records involved must be retrieved from the archives. Retrieval can be a very expensive operation, so the period during which records are kept online is chosen long enough to make retrieval requests unlikely.

Design Implications of Record Keeping

The record life cycle has a whole set of implications for the design of transaction processing systems which create and maintain records. First, let's take a look at the characteristics of records.

Mutable and Immutable Records

Some records, once created, are never changed. Invoices and payment receipts are like this. These records represent a factual record of a real event, and therefore are not subject to revision. Such records are called *immutable*. Even when an error is detected later, an immutable record is never revised; instead, another *correction* record is created, referencing the first record. This process is similar to a newspaper. Newspapers, once printed, are not changed. In case of error, a correction may be printed in a later edition. (But there may be different editions of a particular daily, each with different versions of the same story.) Other records are *mutable* and may be freely changed. For example, during order capture, the items and quantities in the order may change frequently before the order is finalized.

Immutable records permit great simplification of transaction processing systems, because they are never modified. As such, the transaction system does not require complex locking of a record to assure that access to a record is consistent. Mutable records require locking, to assure that while one process is reading the record, another process is not in the process of changing it. In addition, copies can be made freely of immutable records; since they are never changed, there is no danger of different copies containing different information.

Failure and Transaction Semantics

Each type of record in the Internet commerce system should be carefully analyzed to establish how it should behave regarding ACID properties. As an example, let's consider the properties that an order should have during the order capture stage, when items are being added or subtracted from the order or when quantities are being changed.

One point of view is that order capture does not need full transaction semantics. Reasoning by analogy with a paper-based order, the order in some sense doesn't even exist until the form is handed to the seller. This analysis might come naturally to a design which implements the order form as a Java applet residing on the buyer's computer. In the normal course of events, the complete order would be submitted to the seller, but if the buyer's computer is turned off before the order is submitted, then the order would be lost.

An alternate point of view is that the Internet permits new capabilities by giving even an order-in-process full transactional semantics. For example, if the order is transactional, then the in-progress order can accurately reserve against available inventory. If the order is durable, then even a crash of the buyer's computer would not result in a loss of information; the partially completed order would still be there when the buyer came back online.

Payments, however, do need full transaction semantics. Sellers are unhappy when payments are lost, and buyers are unhappy when payment is made but no goods arrive.

Access Patterns

The pattern of usage of a type of record is highly relevant to the system design intended to support it. A particular record may pass through several of the following types of access patterns during its life cycle.

- Online records

  Some records are primarily used online. For example, during the order completion phase of processing, an order is primarily used online, as buyer and seller interactively cooperate to build a complete purchase order.

- Offline records

  Audit records (discussed later) and records for reporting are primarily offline records. Audit records may never be accessed and reporting is usually done from a copy of the online master records, so that the processing and queries associated with reporting cannot disturb the performance of the production system. Offline records certainly must be durable, but because they tend to be immutable, they may have little need for isolation.

- Messages

  A message sent from one system to another is a kind of record too. This situation arises, for example, when an order leaves the Internet commerce system and enters a traditional fulfillment system. Typically, the handoff of the order must have transactional semantics—the order must not be lost, and must be entered exactly once into the fulfillment system.

Audit

In normal business terminology, an audit is an independent review which verifies that an enterprise's financial records are accurate and that the enterprise has conformed to sound accounting practices. For the purposes of Internet commerce, two other concepts are relevant.

- Independent verification of design and implementation

  A review is made of the system design and operational practices in order to determine if design objectives are met. For example, in a security audit, a review is
  made of every aspect of system design, implementation, and operations to ensure
  that confidential information is protected and that unauthorized access has not occurred and cannot occur in the future.

- A record trail of an individual transaction

  The audit trail of a transaction is the collection of records which make it possible
  to verify that the particular transaction actually occurred in the way it is supposed
  to have occurred. The audit trail is used for reporting, for customer service inquiries, and for dispute resolutions. It is not part of the main order processing flow.

Backup and Disaster Recovery

Backup and disaster recovery are related. Backup refers to the processes which preserve an application's data in the face of hardware failures such as disk crashes. Disaster recovery is the broader term which includes the procedures and systems which
enable the application to recover from not only hardware failures, but loss of power,
earthquakes, and communications failures.

When business applications were primarily batch oriented, backup and disaster recovery were fairly simple to understand. As transactions occurred, they were written on
tapes. Once a day, the transaction tapes were merged with master files on other tapes.
Maintaining backups meant saving the old tapes, and in the event of a site disaster, the
tapes could be easily run on a similar computer in a different data center.

The situation for online transaction processing is much more complicated, since individual transactions may be occurring on a 24-hour basis, with no downtime to make
backups. In addition, availability requirements may be so stringent that the system as
a whole cannot stop working as a result of a failure (see High-Availability Systems).
Instead, failed components must be automatically replaced with spares, without loss
of data and with minimal downtime. This sort of reliability can be very expensive.

Because Internet commerce systems enable global operations, even small businesses
can have round-the-clock operational requirements for their Internet-based systems.

High-Availability Systems

Internet commerce systems need to be available at the same time that customers want
to use them. Because Internet commerce systems can attract a worldwide customer
base, there is no easy notion of "business hours." As a limit, the system may need to
be available for use 24 hours a day, 7 days a week.

There are many reasons for a system to be unavailable.

- Regular maintenance

    Systems require periodic attention for making backups, configuration changes, and similar efforts. Typically, configuration changes will be tested on a development copy of the system before being rolled into production, so they should be low risk. To the extent that maintenance activities require downtime, the period of unavailability can be scheduled.

- Upgrades

    Periodically, major system components may need to be changed: new software releases, new hardware platforms, facility moves, and the like. These require scheduled downtime, unless extraordinary measures are taken.

- Infrastructure failures

    The commerce system will typically depend on several systems partially or wholly outside one's control: electric power, Internet access service, and other telecommunications services can be disrupted, leading to a loss of service for some or all of the users. Generally, these sources of unavailability can be managed (at a cost!) by providing dedicated backup power and backup communications facilities.

- Environment

    Floods, fires, and other natural or man-made disasters can take a data center offline regardless of the care taken in hardware and software reliability. The usual approach to these sorts of problems is hot or warm backup data centers, typically geographically distant.

- Software failures

    Software, once installed, doesn't change by itself, but latent problems in software are revealed by changes in the environment. The net effect is that software can stop working. In addition, Internet commerce software is exposed to additional risks—if an essential technology such as an encryption method becomes vulnerable due to technical advances, software can become untrustworthy.

- Human error

    Operator error, configuration mistakes, and the like can bring a system down. In some sense, these are controllable factors, and can be improved by additional training and testing. There are also errors outside one's control. On the Internet, for example, routing errors may be introduced into the network by a different service provider, resulting in a loss of service.

- Hardware failures

    Disks, computers, network routers, and other mechanical and electronic components fail. These failures become more rare as the basic reliability of electronics improves, but the probability that something will fail grows as the size of the system increases the sheer number of components.

It is a very good exercise for a system designer and for a system operator to make a list of every source of failure he can think of, explore the consequences of each failure, the appropriate actions to take if it were to occur, and possible ways of preventing the failure or recovering more quickly from the failure.

Approaches to High Availability

There are two ways to make a system highly available as seen by the end user. The mean time between failures can be very long, or the mean time to repair can be very short. In the first case, the system doesn't fail, and in the second, it is fixed very rapidly.

It is also necessary to consider the real goals of availability. There is an enormous difference, for example, between a system which is available for most of the users most of the time, and one which is available for all the users all the time. Finally, what are the transactional requirements? For example, if an application crashes, it is often proper to arrange matters so that the system undoes any partial effects of transactions that were in progress, and depends on the end users to try again. This approach doesn't work when transactions are generated by other applications that lack retry logic.

The two approaches to availability often result in different strategies. Achieving high mean time between failures (MBTF) is often approached through increasing component reliability, whereas achieving short mean time to repair (MTTR) is often approached by making it easy to replace failed components. Often both strategies are pursued at the same time. Redundant arrays of inexpensive disks (RAID), for example, achieve high reliability by internally managing failed components. At the system level, however, server computer systems are sufficiently complex that their availability is usually improved by having a complete spare system ready to resume service should the primary system fail (fail-over).

Fail-over is particularly interesting because replacing a failed component, system, or even data center can also solve problems outside one's own control, such as infrastructure or environmental failures. In addition, if multiple systems are online at once anyway, to help with scaling and load balancing, then a failure need only redistribute the load among those systems which are still operational.

Replication and Scaling

An electronic commerce system has many dimensions of scaling, which admit different strategies for management.

- Growth in catalog content

  Catalog or electronic fulfillment content may grow in richness and volume independent of transaction volume. For example, a business delivering digital movies online might have a small transaction followed by delivery of gigabytes of data. This problem is best addressed by replication and duplication of content servers, which can share a common transaction engine.

- Growth in transaction complexity and volume

  Even with a relatively small online catalog, business may boom, leading to high volumes of transactions. If transactions are largely independent of one another, replicated transaction engines may be possible. If, however, the transactions are complex, then there may be no substitute for scaling of the transaction engine from a single computer, to a multiprocessor, to a cluster of systems working from a common database.

- Growth in customer base

  As the customer base grows in size, and covers ever larger geographies, it may be appropriate to replicate servers in geographic areas close to the customers.

Implementing Transaction Processing Systems

Of course there is more to implementing a business application than assuring ACID semantics, but a careful analysis of the transactional aspects provides a good basis for the system design. In addition, taking this point of view early in the design is much easier than trying to retrofit an existing system to behave better.

Files

It is possible to build a complete transaction processing system on top of an ordinary file system. Indeed, in the early days of online transaction processing, systems were built from a transaction processing (TP) monitor together with a filesystem. Computer filesystems have a set of relatively simple operations: create, delete, open, close, read, write, and seek. Filesystems generally provide no assistance in structuring the contents of files, and no assistance in managing transactions, except that some operating systems provide facilities to lock and unlock files, protecting them from concurrent access. (Locks are a way of providing isolation semantics at the risk of introducing performance problems and deadlocks.)[4] Nevertheless, files are valuable for a number of purposes.

---

4. A deadlock occurs when two or more processes are waiting for resources, and neither can make any progress. For example, suppose two transactions are in progress, and each needs resources A and B. If transaction 1 locks resource A, then attempts to lock resource B, while transaction 2 locks resource B, then attempts to lock resource A, neither transaction can proceed.

- Logs

  Many applications write log files directly to a filesystem. The advantage is that this can be a very high-performance solution and the disadvantage is that the required operation—writing a log record to the end of a file—is surprisingly hard to get right.

  On many filesystems, appending to a file with a single write operation is an atomic operation, but the key word is *single*. One common mistake is to use a buffered input/output package to write log files. This usually works, but under high load, the log records can become mangled. A correct implementation makes sure that each write operation contains an integral number of log records.

  Log files are commonly used for recording application events and errors. For example, most Web servers can be configured to write information about every Web hit to a log file.

- Read-only data

  If data is mostly read-only, then files can be an effective storage medium in a transaction system. Files are highly optimized for read-write operations, but other operations such as locking and unlocking may not be so fast.

Databases

Fundamentally, databases are a way to store structured information, but they are much more than that. Databases have a number of key properties.

- Databases store structured information.

  Online transaction systems work with large numbers of records of many different types. Databases manage all this complexity, leaving the application free to act on the relevant records, rather than worry about, for example, storage allocation.

- Databases are self-describing.

  In modern databases, information describing the structure of the database is stored in the database itself. This makes it possible to write general-purpose tools to work with information stored in databases that may have no specific knowledge of the application at all. For example, general-purpose reporting tools work this way, making it possible to create new and customized reports without traditional programming.[5]

---

5. Using a good user interface to create a solution to a problem really is programming, it just doesn't seem like it. Good tools work at just the right level of abstraction to match the way the application designer thinks about the problem being solved.

- Databases support transactions.

  Databases on the market today typically support the Structured Query Language (SQL), which includes all the mechanisms necessary to support transactions. In addition, databases today are designed to support ACID semantics, which makes it easier to build applications for processing transactions.

- Databases permit rapid information retrieval.

  Database managers provide built-in support for searching and selecting particular records from all those stored.

Transaction Processing Monitors

Transaction processing monitors evolved to solve some of the problems of building online transaction processing systems that go beyond data storage and retrieval. A TP monitor is not a replacement for a database, but it provides an additional set of functionality that makes it easier to assemble and operate complex applications.

- Transaction management

  TP monitors provide two-phase commit transaction management that at first glance duplicates the capabilities of databases. However, the TP monitor transaction services can coordinate a transaction that spans multiple databases and which includes management of other kinds of resources, such as communications systems or remote applications.

- Application management

  TP monitors provide application management. Registered application servers are automatically started whenever the system restarts, and restarted in the event of crashes. TP monitors also provide load sharing and balancing facilities. These sorts of services are sometimes provided by Web servers in the Internet context: Open Market's FastCGI can manage applications, as can Microsoft's IIS version 4.0. Simple Web applications based on the Common Gateway Interface (CGI) may not need management since they are started anew for each request.

- Terminal and communications management

  Traditional online transaction processing (OLTP) applications depend on networks of hardwired or networked terminals. Message queuing and communications services for such terminals are provided by TP monitors, but these functions are not so relevant for Internet applications because they are provided by Web servers.

Object Technology, Middleware, and Application Builders

There are substantial benefits to developing applications by using the most powerful tools available. In this category, we include object technology such as COM and CORBA, middleware such as DCE, and application tools such as Forte.

- Development focus

  Developers are free to think about the application, rather than about details of communications, security, data integrity, or distribution.

- Time to market

  Once development staff is trained, application development tools increase productivity. The old truism is that a programmer can write the same number of lines of code per day regardless of language. Higher-level languages accomplish more useful work per line of code than lower-level languages, leading to increased productivity.

- Application reliability

  If the infrastructure technologies selected are reliable, their use can substantially increase the reliability of the application. Tools make it easier to make sure that all error conditions are handled and can also make an application much easier to test.

Summary

Regardless of whether an Internet commerce system is small or large, transaction processing principles cannot be ignored. Even a very simple commerce application consisting of a Web-based order form which appends orders to a file must carefully use file locking techniques to assure that near simultaneous orders do not cause lost orders or scramble the file. A medium-sized commerce application might use a database management system incorporating transactions, and a very large application might use a transaction processing monitor to route Internet orders into an existing order processing system.

Part Three

Systems for Internet Commerce

CHAPTER 17

Putting It All Together

Three things are to be looked to in a building: that it stand on the right
spot; that it be securely founded; that it be successfully executed.
—Johann Wolfgang von Goethe[1]

Building a Complete System

In the first part of this book, we discussed issues of business, architecture, and implementation. In the second part, we discussed implementation technologies for various
aspects of Internet commerce. In this chapter, we try to assemble the pieces into a
complete system. There are many workable ways to build Internet commerce systems, but the approach we describe here is the one taken in Open Market's products,
since that is the approach we know the most about—we helped design it. In this chapter, we will first review the architecture and its implementation and then describe how
to apply the architecture to some of the business models discussed in Chapter 4.

In Chapter 2, we introduced the commerce value chain. Open Market's approach di-
vides this value chain into three parts:

- Content servers and applications, provided by a number of independent software
  vendors

- Linking the content to transactions, provided by Open Market's SecureLink
  product

---

1. Johann Wolfgang von Goethe, *Elective Affinities* (1808).

- Order management, including order processing, payment, fulfillment, and customer service, provided by Open Market's Transact product

Walking through a Transaction

Before we discuss the system architecture and design issues, we'll walk through a transaction.

Before opening for business, a seller creates an online catalog, containing embedded digital offers. These digital offers encode the product descriptions, price, and so forth as Universal Resource Locators that link the catalog with the Transact order management system. The seller also creates a merchant profile at Transact, describing means of payment accepted and tax and shipping rules, and configures the fulfillment system to route orders.

When the buyer browses the catalog, the purchase process begins, and follows these steps.

1. Buyer locates product of interest in the catalog, and clicks on the associated digital offer. The digital offer is a hypertext link to the order form hosted by Transact, and carries with it the description of the product.

2. The next screen the buyer sees is the order form, shown in Figure 17-1. The screen shown already has some buyer information filled out, as would be the case for a repeat buyer, based on saved member information.

3. Transact calculates sales tax using the buyer's billing address, the seller's tax profile, and the product tax classification code.

4. Transact calculates shipping charges using the buyer's choice of seller-defined shipping methods, together with product price or weight.

5. The buyer clicks on "Buy Now."

6. Transact performs a credit card authorization and address verification check with the seller's choice of card processing network.

7. Transact records the transaction in permanent storage.

8. Transact routes an advice of order received to the seller.

9. Transact returns a digital receipt to the customer, which contains a copy of the invoice and a link to a status page for customer service.

10. The seller ships the product, and informs Transact of the shipment, using the online order status pages.

11. Transact performs credit card settlement, transferring funds from the buyer to the seller's account.

12. Transact updates the buyer's online statement and optionally sends the buyer an e-mail advising of the order shipment.

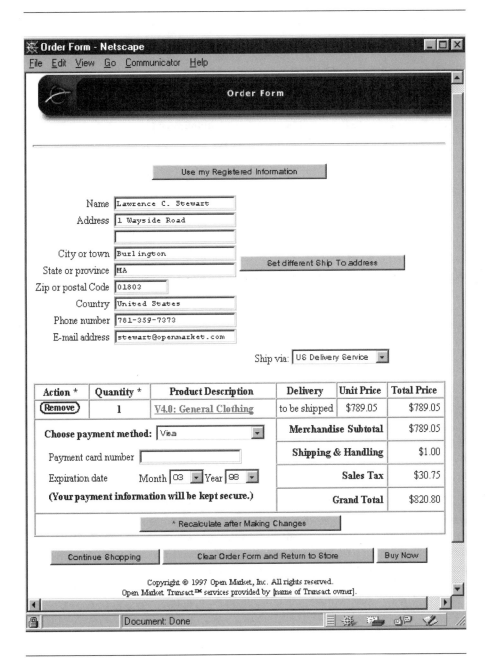

FIGURE 17-1. Transact Order Form

Afterwards, the buyer's digital receipt remains active, bringing the buyer to his online statement of activity. Each item is a hypertext link to a status page for the particular transaction.

Digital Goods

In the case that the product purchased is in electronic form, the digital receipt is a hypertext link directly to the fulfillment area. The digital receipt carries with it security codes granting access by the buyer to specified areas within the fulfillment site for a specified period of time.

Subscriptions

In the case that the product purchased is an ongoing subscription to an electronic publication, Transact makes appropriate entries in its subscription database for the purposes of billing and access control to the fulfillment servers.

When the buyer links to the fulfillment server at a later time, he will be challenged to authenticate himself against the Transact customer database. Then an access control check will be done against the Transact subscription database. If the subscription is current, the buyer will be granted a digital ticket good for access to the content areas. Only when the ticket expires, perhaps weekly, will the buyer be required to reauthenticate himself.

System Architecture

When we introduced various architectures in Chapter 6, we said, "The architecture of a system defines its basic components and important concepts, and it describes the relationships among them."

Figure 17-2 shows a block diagram of a commerce system built from these components. Overall, this is a three-tier architecture with clients using Web browsers connecting over the Internet to content servers of various types. The content servers in turn use shared commerce services provided by Transact. The application is interconnected by SecureLink over the public Internet. Finally, Transact connects to services off the public Internet, such as financial networks and fulfillment systems. We discuss SecureLink and Transact in more detail later in the chapter.

The key architectural ideas are to separate management of content from management of transactions, to support a broad range of applications, to enable scaling of the system, and to accommodate evolution in technology and functionality.

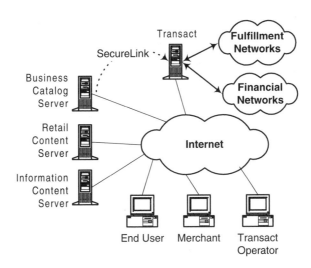

FIGURE 17-2. Open Market Commerce Architecture

Separate Content from Transactions

When we started thinking through the problems of commerce on the Internet, our first observation was that although we usually think of Web content as being on a server somewhere on the network, it only becomes displayable, rendered text and graphics on the screen of the end user's Web browser. Consequently, the buyer's decision to buy will be communicated to the rest of the system as a network event, and we do not have to send that event to the same system that generated the page of content.

Our next observation was on the nature of a business transaction. Typically, information about the buyer, the seller, and the product being purchased must be brought together in one place. Buyer information includes things like means of payment, shipping address, and so forth. Seller information includes items which are not dependent on the particular item sold, but which relate to the seller across multiple products, such as payment methods accepted and means of fulfillment. Product information includes items such as description, price, weight, and taxability.

Our key decision was to treat product information as content, and maintain it on a content server, then to deliver the product information to the transaction server as part of the click-to-buy process, using the standard Web HTTP protocol. This idea enables the separation of the management of content from the management of transactions, and permits a number of benefits.

Reduced Operational Costs

Splitting up content and transaction management can reduce total operational costs.

Content servers have very different operational requirements than transaction servers. Indeed, if content is delivered by e-mail or CD-ROM, there may not be a content server at all.

Placing the transaction and business records in one place minimizes the number of systems which require database management systems and expensive reliability and integrity protections, and minimizes the number of systems which require specialized management and operations skills.

Because many content servers can share the services of a transaction engine, the costs of the transaction engine are amortized over many users. The content server costs are reduced because each system does not need to build in all the common costs of transaction handling.

Enable Service Providers

Multiple content servers can rely on shared commerce services provided by a transaction engine. This enables a new business, that of a commerce service provider, which operates a shared transaction system on behalf of multiple content servers. The transaction server can be shared across multiple divisions of a corporate enterprise or as a business in its own right.

Provide Security Containment

Security systems are as strong as their weakest link. If valuable information is spread around the system, the security properties of the system must be equally strong everywhere. By placing mission-critical business and transaction records in a shared transaction server, the security effort can be focused. The efforts of attackers may be concentrated on the transaction system "because that's where the money is," but the vigilance of security mechanisms is concentrated as well.

It is actually easier to secure the transaction engine, which has limited and stylized connections with the outside world, than it is to secure a content server, which must have access by content creation and management personnel as well as by customers.

Broad Range of Application

A shared commerce services environment enables a very broad range of commerce applications. At the very simple end of the spectrum, small stores can be prepared with desktop publishing tools, and uploaded onto the Net. Offers to sell, encoded in the content, point to a commerce service provider, which manages the resulting orders on a fee basis. There is no need for the content provider to understand or operate a complex transaction system.

In the midrange, dynamic content and rich site development tools can create a compelling commerce experience for the consumer and provide compelling value for the business user.

At the high end, an enterprise may have multiple divisions with different content systems, sharing transaction services provided by the information technology department. The transaction engine may be integrated closely with enterprise financial and logistics systems.

By leveraging a shared infrastructure, small and medium enterprises can access all the services that are available to a large enterprise.

Support System Scaling

Splitting up content and transaction systems allows them to scale independently. Content systems need to grow according to the type and volume of content, which may be unrelated to the volume of transactions. A dynamic content site delivering pages rich in graphics and multimedia will have greater computing and bandwidth requirements than a content system delivering even a large number of simple pages. On the fulfillment side for digital goods, a single transaction may grant very substantial access rights to fulfillment servers over an extended period.

With the shared services design, content servers can be added to the system as the need for them arises due to demand for or volume of content. Content servers representing additional businesses may register for commerce services at any time.

The transaction engine also needs to scale. We designed it as a set of logical servers backed by a relational database management system. The application logic scales through running the component servers on more powerful hardware or by load sharing. The database scales also by more powerful hardware and by exploiting the database vendors' parallel and cluster capabilities.

Support System Evolution

An architecture is needed when you don't know what kinds of problems will arise tomorrow. Internet commerce is changing very rapidly, so systems installed today will need to add new functionality and exploit new technologies as the industry matures.

Functional Evolution

Separating content and transaction systems permits functions to be added to each without affecting or requiring upgrades to the other. For example, a new payment method such as purchase orders can be added in one place at the transaction server, making the new functionality immediately available to all affiliated content servers.

A content server employing dynamically generated pages can replace a server using static pages without any change to the transaction machinery.

Technology Evolution

An important part of an architecture is defining interfaces between the parts of the system which remain stable across multiple releases and technological changes. For example, the Secure Electronic Transaction protocol will replace HTML forms over SSL for credit card payment on the Internet. By adding SET support to the transaction engine, all the affiliated content servers can take immediate advantage of SET without having to upgrade each content system—perhaps using several different content creation and management systems.

SecureLink

SecureLink is really a secure remote procedure call system that works across trust boundaries using standard Web protocols. All of these elements are essential. It is secure because unauthorized parties cannot forge or tamper with messages. It is a remote procedure call because it packages up parameters and delivers them to remotely located systems. It works across trust boundaries—content systems may be operated by different organizations than transaction systems. It is based on HTML and HTTP, the basic protocols of the Web.

SecureLink includes five types of messages, known as SecureLink Commerce Objects shown in Table 17-1. All of these objects are encoded as Universal Resource Locators (URLs). This encoding makes it possible for SecureLink Commerce Objects to be embedded in any kind of Web content where hypertext links can appear.

An example digital offer is:

> http://payment.tscorp.com:80/bin/pay-
> ment.cgi?ac1c7b489d400e4a98a6e9c8b9851a37:kid=196003.190007&valid=81549
> 9241&expire=2592000&goodstype=h&desc=Web%20PCommerce&domain=hardg
> oods&amt=1.00&curl=http%3A%2F%2Fwww.publish1.com%2FProducts%2FFTL
> %2Fbeta.htm&cc=US&ss=env&fmt=get[2]

---

2. The line breaks are inserted for readability.

Commerce Object	Purpose
Digital Offer	Offer products for sale. Contains price, description, tax classification, shipping weight, etc.
Digital Coupon	Discounts and merchandising. Contains discount parameters and product match information.
Digital Ticket	Access control for digital goods subscriptions. Contains user ID of authorized user, group ID denoting content package, and expiration time.
Digital Query	Remote access to customer database. Contains user ID or name for lookup, and returns user information.
Digital Receipt	Access control for digital goods fulfillment. Contains transaction ID for audit, domain of content for which access is granted, and expiration time.

TABLE 17-1. SecureLink Commerce Objects

As a software package SecureLink is shown in Figure 17-3. It consists of four functional blocks, layered on top of a Web server such as Microsoft IIS or Netscape Enterprise Server.

- Key management

  The key management utilities are responsible for creating and maintaining a database of shared secret keys held only by the content server running SecureLink and the associated Transact system. A public key pair is created and the public half exchanged for the Transact key management public key. The utilities then create secret keys and exchange them with Transact using the public keys for privacy, authentication, and message integrity. The secret keys are then used by SecureLink for creating and validating message authentication codes of the actual SecureLink messages.

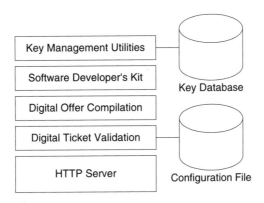

FIGURE 17-3. SecureLink Software Structure

- Software developer's kit

    The software developer's kit (SDK) is a set of runtime libraries and APIs that are integrated with the content management tools on the content server to create and insert the information necessary to create pre-digital offers and pre-digital coupons in the site content. The SDK has been integrated with a variety of content tools, including desktop publishing, database-driven templates, Web authoring environments, and catalog systems.

- Digital offer compilation

    The pre-digital offers and pre-digital coupons are compiled into final URL form statically or dynamically, by a formatting step which attaches a message authentication code using a secret key from the key database. This process is shown in Figure 17-4. The message authentication code is computed using the formula:

    $$MAC(payload)=MD5(Key, Padding, Payload, Key)$$

    The padding consists of blanks to round the size of the payload up to a multiple of 512 bits.

- Digital ticket validation

    For fulfillment of digital goods and subscription content, incoming digital receipts and digital tickets must pass a validation step. This step verifies the message authentication code attached by Transact and verifies that the URL in the receipt or ticket is actually part of the content purchased.

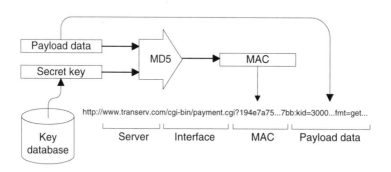

FIGURE 17-4. **Compiling a Digital Offer**

Transact

The best way to think of Transact is as a suite of applications for its different users: buyers, sellers, and operators. This model is shown in Figure 17-5. In more traditional business settings, buyers interact directly with sellers, and both interact directly with operations and support groups. On the Internet, the situation is different because the parties involved are rarely online at the same time. Instead, each group of users interacts with applications that place their retained state in a database where the next group can pick it up and carry on. The database, without loss of generality, can be a set of databases with workflow capabilities.

Transact is organized this way, with application logic and user interface capabilities for buyers, sellers (merchants), and system operators. Transact is a rich application; the following sections are not exhaustive, but are included here to give a flavor for the kinds of functionality and APIs which are included.

Buyer Applications: User Interface and APIs

The buyer experience is primarily with catalog and other content systems. Many buyer interactions with Transact are indirect, through content server user interfaces, supported by application programmer interfaces provided by Transact. At other times, buyers interact directly with Transact user interface software.

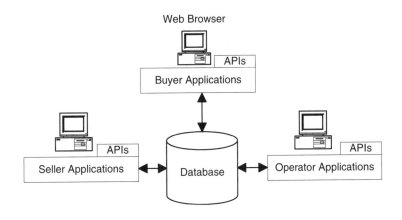

FIGURE 17-5. Internet Application

Buyer Applications with User Interface

- Order capture

  The Transact order capture application has the metaphor of an order form. Buyers populate the order form directly by clicking on digital offers and digital coupons, or the seller may prepopulate the order form through a Transact API. The order form provides the facilities for the buyer to adjust item quantities, choose coupons, enter or edit billing and shipping addresses, and select payment and shipping methods.

  In addition to user interface, the Transact order capture subsystem calculates discounts from coupons, including matching coupons against items, validates addresses, and calculates sales tax and shipping charges, leading to an order total. If a consumer payment method like a credit card is selected, Transact obtains the necessary authorization in real time. The principle is to validate the success of the order to the fullest extent possible while the buyer is online, in order to resolve any problems right away.

  In the case of digital goods and subscriptions, the buyer experience ends with a digital receipt or digital ticket, granting immediate access to the appropriate fulfillment server. For physical goods, the buyer obtains a digital receipt which can be used later for order status and customer service.

- Account registration and management profiles

  Transact supports multiple models of buyers. Walk-in buyers may have no previous relationship with the system. Walk-in buyers must fill out the complete order form—though parts of the process may be automated by buyer software such as an electronic wallet. Transact also supports registered buyers, who have chosen to save an account profile as repeat visitors. Registered buyers get the order form already populated with their stored information, for a faster checkout.

  Registered buyers also have access to account administration applications, for creating and changing user and security profiles, and to register additional means of payment, such as a microtransaction account.

- Customer service

  The goal of the customer service applications on Transact is customer self-service. For registered buyers, Transact provides online statements of all transaction activity in a *smart statement*. Each item is active, and can be clicked through to reach detailed order status information or the catalog page from which the item was originally selected. From the order status screen, the buyer can click through to the package tracking service offered by some logistics companies.

  The subscription capabilities of Transact are also supported by some special customer service applications. For example, if a subscription involves periodic payments, and the associated credit card expires or is cancelled, the system permits the buyer to substitute a different payment instrument without intervention by the operator.

Buyer APIs

Buyers will not use these APIs directly, rather these are APIs that sellers who have relationships with Transact use in order to directly benefit the experience of a buyer.

- Commerce objects

  The SecureLink commerce objects, including digital offers, digital coupons, and digital receipts, are the primary API to Transact. These are the primary mechanisms through which items for sale, merchandising, and fulfillment of digital goods are handled.

- Order injection API

  When a buyer is online, the content server can implement the user interface for the complete buyer experience, and then hand off a complete order for Transact. In effect, the user interface for the order capture phase of commerce can be remotely located at a content server.

- Customer database API

  As was discussed in Chapter 11, in order to deploy sites with personalized content, a site needs to identify users, track sessions, and build pages according to information stored in a user profile. Transact provides user authentication and session tracking to remotely located content servers through its subscription server, and provides remote access to a centrally managed user profile through the Customer Database API. Individual content servers do not need to store authentication information, and do not need to store common profile information, although each content server can extend the profile in a uniform way. Because profile and authentication information is stored in one place, it does not need to be replicated or distributed. A change made to the profile at one content server is immediately available to any other affiliated content server. These services are provided by the SecureLink digital query.

Seller Applications and APIs

In order to run an Internet-based business, sellers need to create content, and to configure and manage a wide variety of business rules and services. In the Open Market model, catalog or site content is prepared and managed with a variety of applications and tools, but commerce facilities are centrally managed by Transact.

Seller Applications

- Merchant profiles

  In order to run his business, the seller or merchant must configure a variety of business rules. Transact provides a merchant administration application organized as a series of profile screens. The seller configures which payment instruments such as credit cards will be accepted from among those offered by the Transact installation, and for each payment instrument, how processing is to be handled. For sales tax or value-added tax, the seller provides information on tax jurisdictions and related business rules. For shipping of physical goods, the seller configures an order delivery mechanism and one or more shipper profiles, which provide the business rules for calculating shipping costs displayed to the buyer.

*   Order management and fulfillment

    Transact can deliver orders to the seller by online or downloaded report, by fax, by regular or secure e-mail, or by use of the Fulfillment API discussed later. The seller has access to tax and transaction statements and reports, and can mark orders as fulfilled and provide an appropriate e-mail message for the buyer.

*   Customer service

    Inevitably, questions and problems arise in handling orders. Transact tries to let the buyer resolve his own questions through online customer service, but also provides means for the seller to process returns and credits.

Seller APIs

Most of the seller-oriented APIs were discussed in Buyer APIs since they relate to buyer activities during browsing and purchasing online. The Order Injection API, however, can also be used in an offline manner.

*   Order Injection API

    Even when order capture takes place in a medium other than the Internet, there is a benefit to using an Internet commerce system for order management and customer service. The Transact Order Injection API permits entry of orders originated off-Net and then applies standard processing and online customer service. This permits both buyers and sellers a unified view of orders.

Operator Applications and APIs

Transact can be operated by a single enterprise on its own behalf, or it can be run by a commerce service provider as a business providing Internet commerce services for other companies. In the first instance, the operator applications and APIs are really seller facilities, whereas in the latter instance, the operator applications and APIs support central services and policies of the commerce service provider.

Operator Applications

- Configuration

  Transact is packaged application software, but it is designed for great flexibility of installation, business rules, and user interface. The operator is responsible for using standard Web tools to create a standard look and feel for the system, even if that customization is only adding a name and logo to the standard templates.

  The operator must also configure the central end of SecureLink in order to establish the cryptographic keys necessary for secure operation and must make a number of policy decisions about trust, security, payment processing, and privacy.

  The operator is responsible for installing support for particular payment mechanisms and payment processing systems, and configuring them for proper operation.

- Administration

  During normal operation, Transact provides application support for ongoing activation and modification of affiliated content servers and central overrides for payment processing and merchant profiles.

- Reporting and logging

  Transact creates log files for error reporting and audit trails, and provides reporting tools for various kinds of system activity and to support auxiliary activities such as fraud control.

Operator APIs

- Customer Database API

  In addition to its use for real-time customer profile access from content servers, the Customer Database API permits individual or bulk loading of customer information. This makes it possible to Internet-enable existing systems.

- Fulfillment API

  In those cases where the Internet order management application must directly connect with existing enterprise order management and fulfillment systems, the Transact Fulfillment API permits programmatic access to pending orders and dynamic update of order status on a per-line-item basis.

- Payment API

  Transact has a variety of Internet-capable payment systems built in, including credit cards, purchase orders, Secure Electronic Transactions, and microtransactions. However, Internet payment technology is changing rapidly, with debit cards, electronic cash, electronic funds transfer, and electronic checks gaining acceptance, and other more innovative systems on the horizon. Transact's Payment API permits new payment systems and additional implementations of old ones to be added. Catalog content uses digital offers to link to Transact, which operates as a payment switch, so new payment systems can be added without the necessity of updating any content servers.

Functionality

Transact is designed with groups of functionality for several Internet commerce market segments: business to consumer, business to business, and information commerce. Many if not most of the differences in required functionality for these markets are addressed by different content systems—catalogs and entertainment sites for business to consumer, catalogs for business to business, and complex search and retrieval engines for information commerce—but the business rules, payment methods, and common services are also distinct.

Business to Consumer

- Order capture

  Transact's order capture subsystem is designed to be easily used with no training by end consumers. The order form metaphor is familiar to users of paper catalogs, and the system tries hard to validate all input in real time to alert the buyer to any difficulties while he is still online.

- Consumer-oriented payment

  Credit cards are the primary payment mechanism for direct marketing to consumers. They offer substantial convenience and ease of use, and in the United States provide very strong consumer protections. Transact supports real-time credit card authorization in support of a transparent consumer experience.

- Personalized content and merchandising

  Merchandising and personalization of content is essential for consumer markets where consumers can choose from a range of suppliers. Transact helps businesses compete on the basis of customer service as well as on price and convenience. Digital coupons provide a means of merchandising even when the buyer is accessible only by advertising and e-mail. The Customer Database API permits sites to create personalized experiences for repeat visitors.

- Support for small and medium merchants

  Through seller profiles and the medium of commerce service providers, Transact can offer complex Internet commerce services to small and midsize merchants who cannot afford to own and operate the entire application themselves. SecureLink lets distributed content servers share the application, so that smaller businesses can use Internet hosting services, while larger ones keep their catalogs in-house.

Business to Business

- Payment mechanisms

  Most business-to-business commerce is not conducted with consumer payment mechanisms such as credit cards. Although procurement cards, the business-to-business version of credit cards, are undergoing substantial growth, the bulk of commerce is done by a business extending credit to another business, issuing purchase orders, and invoicing, and most payments are done by check or electronic funds transfer. At this writing, Transact supports purchase orders for order capture, with approval mechanisms for online creation of business relationships under development, following the Open Buying on the Internet proposed standard.

- Fulfillment

  The Transact Fulfillment API provides a way to integrate orders received over the Internet with the order stream from traditional channels.

- Custom catalogs

  Perhaps the most direct and immediate benefit for business-to-business applications of Internet commerce is the provision of accurate, complete, and timely product information directly to requisitioners in the buying organization. Transact's digital tickets and digital queries (Customer Database API) provide the catalog access to authentication and profile services to permit the display of contract pricing, customized part numbers, reserved inventory, and other characteristics of business relationships. (Open Market's LiveCommerce Catalog is one way to exploit these features but the capabilities are available to any content tools.)

Information Commerce

- Business models

  Transact supports business models that are central to information commerce. SecureLink's digital receipts and digital tickets provide for authenticated, secure distributed access control to fulfillment servers. An information customer can click on a digital offer for an information product or service, and immediately receive the corresponding digital receipt for access to that service. In the case of ongoing subscriptions to electronic content, Transact's subscription server maintains authentication, access control, and payment information on an ongoing basis.

- Payment models

  In addition to credit cards and purchase orders typical of physical goods, Transact supports microtransactions of either parking-meter prepay or taxi-meter postpay styles. These mechanisms permit very lightweight, pay-per-page access to information services.

- Customer service

  In information commerce, or indeed, in any business where item prices are low, it is essential that customer service calls and disputes be held to a minimum. Customer self-service through easy-to-use statements and account administration help to keep customer support costs low.

Block Diagram

As shown in Figure 17-5, Transact is organized as buyer, seller, and operator applications sharing access to a database management system in which long-term state is maintained. This high-level structural view is paralleled by a physical block diagram, as shown in Figure 17-6. The Transact application is normally configured on two computer systems, one facing the Internet and tasked with interactive parts of the application and one more isolated from the Net and tasked with database storage and with connections to other networks. From a security perspective, this structure permits multiple security barriers to be placed between business-critical information in the database and potential attackers on the network.

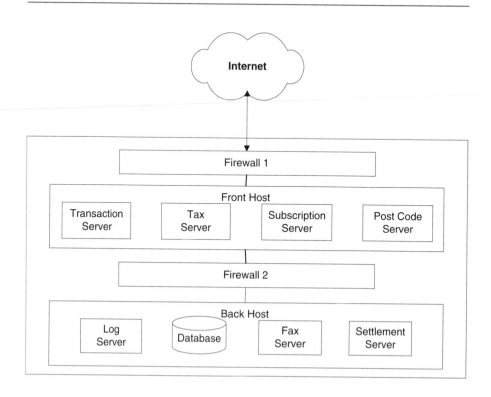

FIGURE 17-6. **Transact Block Diagram**

The application itself is divided into a number of logical servers, which perform separate functions.

- Transaction server

  The transaction server is responsible for the interactive parts of the application, including buyer, seller, and operator user interfaces.

- Subscription server

  The subscription server maintains an access control database of which Transact users have ongoing access to various *content packages* located on remote content servers. Each subscription has various terms and conditions, such as grace and trial periods, installment payments, renewal options, and returns policies. The subscription server performs periodic payment processing as appropriate and provides means for users to replace failed payment instruments with new ones.

- Tax server

  Sales and use taxes in North America are extremely complex. The tax server calculates per-item U.S. sales taxes and Canadian goods and services taxes at the state/province, county, and locality levels according to buyer information, seller profile, and product-specific tax classification. At this writing, the server also supports European-style value-added-tax calculations.

- Postcode server

  The postcode server maps addresses to GEO codes. It is used to help validate addresses entered into the system and to disambiguate some complex sales tax jurisdictions where a postal code is not sufficiently precise.

- Log server

  The log server collects and records log and audit events from all the other servers.

- Settlement server

  The settlement server is responsible for real-time authorization and batch settlement operations for processing credit cards through various financial processors, using a variety of protocols including SET and ISO 8583. The settlement server also implements the Payment API, which permits the addition of new payment systems to Transact.

- Fax server

  The fax server is an optional component which is used to deliver advice of order messages to sellers by fax. These faxes can be triggered on an hourly or daily basis.

- Database management system

  The database management system is a traditional relational database (at this writing, Sybase or Oracle) which is used by the other servers for long-term storage of information. See "More about the Database" for additional information.

Order Pipeline

Figure 17-7 is a process diagram of Transact's order processing flow paralleling the transaction example given earlier in "Walking through a Transaction." The boxes on the main diagonals represent the main functional units of the system, single arrows link functionality to functional units, and double arrows represent APIs or interfaces to other systems.

- Offer and coupon creation

  The seller creates commerce-enabled content using desktop publishing software, Web development tools, Web authoring environments, or a catalog application. The content may be static or dynamic. The content system has access to user authentication and authorization services through digital tickets, and access to the user profile through digital queries. The order items flow from the content system to Transact as digital offers and digital coupons, carrying with them information about item details.

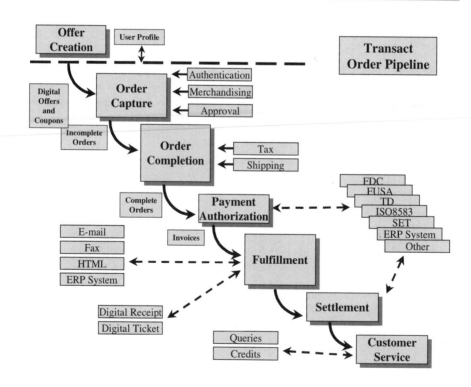

FIGURE 17-7. **Transact Pipeline Diagram**

- Order capture

  The order capture stage was described earlier. This stage of Transact is responsible for gathering customer information—billing address, shipping address, payment method, quantities—and for applying merchandising rules for validation and application of coupons.

- Order completion

  In the order completion stage, order processing that is relevant to the entire order takes place, particularly tax and shipping cost calculation. At this point, the order can still be revised. Once the order leaves the order completion stage, it becomes a purchase order, an agreement between buyer and seller as to the terms of the transaction.

- Payment authorization

  The payment authorization stage is responsible for credit card authorization, which reserves a portion of the buyer's credit, but does not transfer funds. Frequently, other payment mechanisms have a similar function of approving the transaction without actually completing it. Funds movement happens later, in the settlement stage. Transact provides authorization interfaces to a number of different types of external financial networks for this purpose, and provides a Payment API, so that new types of payment systems or processors can be easily added.

- Fulfillment

  In the fulfillment stage, the authorized order is communicated to the seller by online form, downloaded statement, fax, e-mail, or the Fulfillment API. The seller is then responsible for updating the status of the order to indicate complete shipment or cancellation, or by updating the status of individual line items to indicate backorders, partial shipments, and so forth. As the order is fulfilled, the purchase order is translated into one or more invoices, which are effectively bills to be paid. The invoices proceed to settlement.

  In the fulfillment stage, the customer receives a digital receipt. For physical goods, the receipt is really granting access to the interactive order status page for the particular order. For digital goods, the receipt is a URL which actually goes to the fulfillment server and grants access to the product. For subscriptions, the system issues a digital ticket for access to the subscription content.

- Payment settlement

  Settlement processing completes the financial transactions begun in the authorization stage. During settlement, funds transfers actually occur from buyer's account to seller's account. In the case of credit cards, since the authorization request has actually guaranteed credit availability, the settlement processing does not have to be real time, and may in fact proceed on an hourly or daily batch basis.

- Customer service

  Whether orders are in process or completed, the customer service subsystem gives interactive access to current order status and, for registered buyers, to overall account activity statements.

More about the Database

Finally, let's take a look at the organization of the Transact database, as shown in Figure 17-8. All the parts of Transact use a common database engine, but there are really several logical databases, used for different purposes within the system. Each of the following groups represents a set of relational tables.

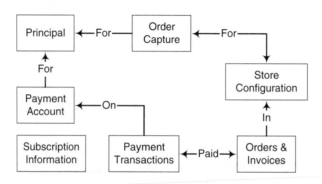

FIGURE 17-8. **Transact Database Schema**

- Principal

  The principal database is responsible for storing information about the users of the system: buyers, sellers, and operators. Each user has authentication information and user profile information. In addition, users may have access to certain roles in Transact. For example, an individual may be a seller with rights to manage the profile of a particular store. Another may be a customer service representative with rights to browse certain parts of the database to resolve customer questions.

- Order capture

  The order capture database is responsible for storing buyer shopping carts or order forms during the interactive phase of their existence in the order capture and order completion stages of Transact. Once an order is completed, it becomes a purchase order and is stored with other orders and invoices.

- Store configuration

  The store configuration tables store information about sellers, particularly business rules and configuration options. For example, if a store wishes to accept certain credit cards but not others, that information is stored in the store configuration.

- Orders and invoices

  The order and invoice database is concerned with fulfillment. As fulfillment events happen, orders become invoices and invoke payment transactions. The primary users of the order and invoice databases are the fulfillment and customer service modules.

- Payment transactions

  The payment transaction database stores information about the status of authorization and settlement activity. This part of the system is also responsible for payment processing of recurring and installment payments for the subscription subsystem. Payment transactions are subtle because frequently the financial networks responsible for executing them are not transaction oriented (see Chapter 16) so Transact must make special efforts to assure that transactions are executed exactly once, and not duplicated or omitted.

- Payment accounts

  The payment accounts database permits registered buyers to store payment credentials in Transact both for ease of use and for customer-not-present transactions such as subscription installment payments and renewals.

- Subscriptions

  The subscription database contains access control and authorization information so that Transact can manage authentication and authorization of users to remotely located subscription content packages. Information from subscription digital offers is entered here, and Transact issues temporary-use digital tickets for day-to-day access to subscription content.

Summary

In this chapter, we have put together application knowledge and technology and described the architecture and implementation of the Open Market suite of Internet commerce products. Of course, there are many other approaches to commerce applications, but we hope this example has provided some insight into one way that ideas about Internet commerce can be turned into real systems. The Transact architecture was designed to provide a foundation for a wide range of commerce applications, and it addresses many of the problems we have examined in this book.

CHAPTER 18

The Future of Internet Commerce

It's difficult to make predictions, especially about the future.
—Yogi Berra[1]

For all the excitement and hype about Internet commerce in the past few years, we are really just at the beginning of a business revolution. Some businesses will change radically and quickly. For others, the revolution may be less dramatic, but it will happen nonetheless. The choice now is not whether to embrace the Internet, but how to do it and how fast to do it. The customers will demand it, and the competition will stake out the new territory if you do not.

In this chapter, we take a look at some of the predictable changes and trends, as well as the problem of unpredictable or discontinuous changes. Because we expect Internet technologies to continue to evolve rapidly, we discuss some ideas for keeping an Internet commerce system up to date. Finally, we return to the strategic imperatives of the Internet.

Accepting that change will come is the first step. Turning the Internet to your advantage is the next.

---

1. Folklore attributed to Yogi Berra.

Trends

It is always difficult to forecast the future, but we can try to examine some of the forces that will shape it. We are enmeshed in those forces, so they are hard to recognize. Instead, we can look at trends, and try to discern an historical pattern that may extend into the future.

Hardware Technology Trends

Computing is unlike any other activity in history in its sustained progress. Computer metrics such as processor performance and storage capacity have been experiencing exponential growth for the past 20 years and the trend is expected to continue for at least another 10 to 20 years. Gordon Moore, one of the founders of Intel, predicted in 1965 that the density of transistors on semiconductor chips would double roughly every 18 months. This prediction has been so accurate that it is called Moore's Law. Moore's Law isn't really a law, and staying on the curve has required the inspired creative efforts of an entire industry. As a result, however, we face some nearly certain changes in the Internet environment.

- Computer performance

  We can look forward to 10 to 15 years of steadily improving performance and declining prices of computer equipment, both personal computers and servers. Between 1982 and 1997, the performance of a $2,000 personal computer increased 1,000-fold. *Between 1997 and 2012 there will likely be another 1,000-fold improvement.*

- Storage capacity

  In 1985, 5 MB hard drives were common elements of personal computers. Today, 5 GB drives are commonplace. It is more difficult to predict how the next 1,000-fold improvement in storage will be achieved, but it will happen.

- Communications capability

  In 1985, modems that ran at 1,200 bits per second were common. In 1997, we had modems operating at 56,000 bits per second over conventional (albeit high-quality) telephone lines. Internet access by satellite, cable network, and corporate LAN delivers multimegabit performance. It is easy to foresee corporations with gigabit connections to the Internet, and it is certainly plausible to expect individual homes to have multimegabit connections.

In addition to these "nearly certain" trends, two other technological trends seem very likely.

- Portable equipment

  Laptops are already approaching the capabilities of desktops, and many people (including the authors) now use portable computers as their primary computing platforms. Smaller *palmtops* will become more common as well.

- Wireless communications

  Wireless data communications will become so sufficiently common and inexpensive to use that portable devices will be connected to the network at almost all times.

All of these trends are driven by improvements in hardware of one sort or another, and our conclusions are simply extrapolations based on historical data. Stated simply, they seem almost obvious. But the business implications of these order-of-magnitude changes may be tremendous.

Software Technology Trends

There are many clear trends in software technology as well. These include the following.

- Security and authentication

  All of the technological pieces are in place for a global security and authentication infrastructure that should make it possible for businesses and individuals to identify one another and communicate securely over public networks. However, that infrastructure has not yet emerged. Cryptography, smart cards, and digital signatures are all available today, and we expect the necessary supporting systems and environments to be developed and deployed over the next five to ten years. In the meantime, Internet commerce will grow most rapidly in communities of interest, in segments where some infrastructure exists, and in situations where off-Net relationships can be moved online.

- Component software

  The current trend toward object and component software will accelerate. The next steps in this transformation will be software that can assist in its own testing and assembly—extensions of design-time behavior—and a rapid expansion of translation capabilities that can make software objects more adaptable to communications in different formats.

- Business objects

  The great lesson from the slow growth of EDI over the past 20 years is that standard *formats* for data are not enough. What is necessary for interoperability of business messages without costly configuration and development is standardization of *meaning*. In other words, we must move from *syntax* to *semantics*. The beginnings of this trend are visible in the use of new standards such as XML to define standard sets of business messages, as well as the development of *business objects* that encapsulate behavior as well as information.

Software Development and Standardization Trends

- Greater interoperability

  The industry trend toward standard, interoperable interfaces between systems will continue. This means that it will be more possible to assemble complete systems using components and packages from multiple vendors.

- More software reuse

  To date, software engineering has been a cottage industry, with hundreds of thousands of skilled workers painfully creating software one line at a time. Mainly through class libraries and other forms of object technology, developers will begin to create new applications by standing on the shoulders of their predecessors, rather than rebuilding every element from scratch.

In combination, these effects mean that the rate of change of software will increase. New functionality will take less time to develop. There will be a countervailing effect that greater complexity of applications will take longer to test, but that effect will be abated by improved understanding of automated testing and software quality assurance. Historically, most bugs are in new code, not in reused components.

Infrastructure Trends

- Commercial environment

  There is very nearly a worldwide common commercial environment for individual consumers, namely credit cards backed by global brands such as Visa, Mastercard, and American Express. Business-to-business commerce, on the other hand, does not have the same level of service. Services such as Dun & Bradstreet can help create trading relationships, and electronic funds transfer networks such as ACH can be used for payments. Today, however, these systems are not global, they are not real time, and they are not integrated. It seems likely that highly integrated systems specializing in trust and payment for businesses will evolve to support global Internet commerce.

- Government environment

  Today, the government environment is incredibly complex. Taxes, customs, and regulations vary both in space and time, across political boundaries, and as countless regulators and legislators change the rules. It is possible that international unity and concord, driven by commercial demands for a consistent operating environment, will simplify and regularize all the rules. This seems unlikely. Far more likely is the development of sophisticated, knowledge-intensive software that automates the complexity. As we saw in Chapter 15, once software can fully implement the tax system, its complexity becomes more of an irritation than a hindrance to commerce.

- Legal environment

  Today's business environment is the result of centuries of accumulated experience and practice, codified in law and interpreted by the courts. The Internet brings new questions, such as the exact standing of a digital signature or the liability of a certification authority. These questions are currently being tested, jurisdiction by jurisdiction, according to the usual progression of the legal system. Over the long term, however, uniform standards and definitions for commercial practice are essential. At first, these standards will evolve by mapping electronic situations to their closest physical analogies, but occasionally new situations will arise and new precedents will be needed.

Application Trends

In the early days of business computing, enterprises employed staffs of developers and maintained their own business software for applications such as accounting. As the functionality of these applications became standardized, platform vendors began to supply software for applications, and not merely development tools. As the complexity of applications grew, software product companies evolved to deliver packaged application software for business applications. Today, very few companies write their own accounting software.

These trends seem likely to repeat in Internet commerce. In the early days, enterprises develop their own Internet commerce applications using whatever expertise they have. This period will be followed by one characterized by development tools and applications supplied by software vendors. As the complexity of commerce applications grows, the likely successor stage will be characterized by specialized packaged applications for Internet commerce.

The Internet is growing so rapidly that these phases overlap, and it is easy to point to examples of all three stages coexisting. In developing a strategy for Internet commerce, it is worth considering how your own systems will develop over time, and what "build or buy" decisions are most appropriate for your own company.

Discontinuities

Evolutionary trends can be amazing to contemplate, especially exponential trends. But what about the changes wrought by new ideas? These are potential discontinuities in society and in commerce. It may be fun to invent a slightly better printing press, but what happens when someone creates television?

In software engineering, there is a rule of thumb that every factor of ten in *quantity* creates a *qualitative* difference. Earlier we suggested that processing power, storage capacity, and communications bandwidth will each improve by a factor of 1,000 over the next 15 years. These changes will create new kinds of experiences, not merely evolutionary changes in current modes of operation. In addition to these sorts of changes, there will be innovations we cannot guess. In the current heady explosion of the Internet, we frequently make the error of thinking that the World Wide Web is the final innovation in networking, and we forget that the Web is only a few years old. Five years from now, the Web may seem like a quaint idea.

Some potentially discontinuous changes seem very plausible, because they have been demonstrated in limited settings. These include speech interfaces, natural language understanding, and virtual reality. Other ideas, such as direct neural control of computers, still seem to be figments of the science fiction writer's imagination. All we can suggest is that if an idea does not violate physical laws, it will probably be built.

One fascinating possibility is the use of nanotechnology to construct physical objects at the other end of a network connection. This will probably not happen by 2005, but within our children's lifetimes it seems entirely possible.

Staying Up to Date

When you buy a new car, the resale value drops precipitously the moment you drive it off the lot. Even so, a new car can last for years, and in ten years the new models are not one hundred times better. By contrast, the PC you buy today is technologically obsolete by the time you get it installed, and that trend shows no sign of abating.

How do you keep your system up to date in this environment? In part, this is the role of architecture in an Internet commerce system. An extensible architecture allows the addition of new components on top of the old ones. A scalable architecture can handle growth smoothly, without disrupting the system for customers.

Architecture also provides some guidance on what technology changes make sense, and which can be left aside. With that kind of assistance, it becomes much easier to sort through both the hype and the reality of new technologies and new products. Some can contribute to your system, and others will not. In a few years, the system may have replaced all the important components, even though the fundamental architecture has not changed much.

Strategic Imperatives

As we suggested in Chapter 3, the Internet introduces two factors into business thinking: the Internet can transform customer relationships, and the Internet can displace traditional sources of business value.

- Transform customer relationships

  Traditionally, a customer has few points of contact with a business. The Internet allows a complete *outside-in* reengineering of the relationship of a business to its customers, transforming the business from an internal focus to a customer focus.

- Displace traditional sources of business value

  The Internet transforms business from dealing with physical artifacts to dealing primarily with information. Economies of scale in the physical world transform into economies of scope. Distribution becomes an opportunity rather than a constraint. The net effect is to upset the basis of competition.

These factors require nothing less than a fundamental review of business strategy based on a sober assessment of the strength of the business' relationships with its customers and its core value proposition.

Closing Remarks

Ultimately, customers will determine the fate of Internet commerce, not business. If the Internet is effective for customers, businesses will find ways to deliver value with it. In the process, new businesses will succeed and others will fail. Some existing businesses may negotiate the transition and others will not.

Returning to our railroad analogy of Chapter 3, we close with a letter from Martin Van Buren (then governor of New York) to President Andrew Jackson in 1829.

Dear President Jackson,

The canal system in this country is being threatened by the spread of a new form of transportation known as "railroads"...

If the canal boats are supplanted by "railroads"...boat builders would suffer, and towline, whip, and harness makers would be left destitute...

The Almighty never intended that people should travel at such breakneck speed.

Sincerely,

Martin Van Buren, Governor
State of New York
The thirty-first of January, 1829

Resources and Further Reading

What follows is a list of some resources and readings that we have found useful in our own work on Internet commerce. We have not listed many that deal with particular software packages, since those details change quickly as new versions and new products become available. Rather, we have chosen some that (for the most part) have more lasting relevance to thinking about the design of systems for Internet commerce.

Introduction

In *Frontiers of Electronic Commerce* (Addison Wesley Longman, 1996), Ravi Kalakota and Andrew B. Whinston examine a wide range of technologies that affect the development and deployment of Internet commerce systems. It provides an excellent overview for business professionals. They have also written *Electronic Commerce: A Manager's Guide* (Addison Wesley Longman, 1997). David Kosiur's *Understanding Electronic Commerce* (Microsoft Press, 1997) is another good overview of what is happening in the Internet commerce market, including some interesting case studies.

The Commerce Value Chain

Many of the important legal issues for Internet commerce are discussed in *Law and the Information Superhighway* by Henry H. Perrit, Jr. (John Wiley & Sons, 1996), as well as in *The Law of Electronic Commerce* by Benjamin Wright (Aspen Law & Business, 1995). Note, however, that the law is changing quickly in these areas, though not as fast as the technology.

Internet Business Strategy

This book does not examine marketing strategies on the Internet. Kim M. Bayne's *The Internet Marketing Plan* (John Wiley & Sons, 1997) and *Marketing on the Internet,* 2nd edition, by Jill H. Ellsworth and Matthew V. Ellsworth (John Wiley & Sons, 1997) both look at Internet commerce from a marketing point of view, with some high-level descriptions of the technologies used on the Web.

In *The 1:1 Future: Building Relationships One Customer at a Time* (Currency Doubleday, 1993), Don Peppers and Martha Rogers examine the business implications of relationships with individual customers. Although the book was published before the Internet came to be used for much commerce, the development of Internet commerce only reinforces the central concepts they describe.

net.gain by John Hagel III and Arthur G. Armstrong (Harvard Business School Press, 1997) examines the business opportunities offered by the Internet in building virtual communities.

Geoffrey A. Moore has written two classic marketing books about high-technology markets. The first, *Crossing the Chasm* (Harper Business, 1991), introduces a model of the adoption of new technologies. The second, *Inside the Tornado* (Harper Business, 1995), is about the market explosion that occurs when new technologies become accessible to mainstream customers. Arguably, the Internet is just beginning a tornado phase.

Functional Architecture

For additional information on OBI, see the SupplyWorks Web site (http://www.supplyworks.com).

Introduction to Part 2: Technology

One of the classic introductions to computer networking technologies is *Computer Networks,* 3rd edition, by Andrew S. Tanenbaum (Prentice Hall, 1996). The book *Internetworking Technologies Handbook* by Merilee Ford et al. (Cisco Press, 1997) describes many current technologies in networking.

Richard H. Baker's *Extranets: The Complete Sourcebook* (McGraw-Hill, 1997) focuses on creating extranets to link multiple organizations.

An interesting history of the Internet and its predecessor, the ARPAnet, can be found in *Casting the Net: From ARPAnet to Internet and Beyond* by Peter H. Salus (Addison Wesley Longman, 1995).

For those interested in the deep details of TCP/IP implementations and how the protocols really work, we recommend *TCP/IP Illustrated, Volume 1: The Protocols* by

W. Richard Stevens (Addison Wesley Longman, 1994) and its successors *TCP/IP Illustrated, Volume 2: The Implementation* by Gary R. Wright and W. Richard Stevens (Addison Wesley Longman, 1995) and *TCP/IP Illustrated, Volume 3: TCP for Transactions, HTTP, NNTP, and the UNIX® Domain Protocols* by W. Richard Stevens (Addison Wesley Longman, 1996). Christian Huitema's book *Routing in the Internet* (Prentice-Hall, 1995) discusses in great detail how IP routing works in the Internet.

For a preview of the changes in IP version 6, see *IPng: Internet Protocol Next Generation,* edited by Scott O. Bradner and Allison Mankin (Addison Wesley Longman, 1996).

Much more information about the Web and its applications can be found in Lincoln Stein's *How to Set Up and Maintain a Web Site,* 2nd edition (Addison Wesley Longman, 1997).

Finally, the Web site of the Internet Engineering Task Force (http://www.ietf.org) is a good source of information about standards for Internet protocols as well as for getting a view about work in progress for future standards.

Building Blocks for Internet Commerce

There are many books about Web browsers and servers, as well as about programming environments such as Java, JavaScript, and ActiveX. All of these are changing fast, so we suggest seeing what is available about the specific topics of interest when you need the information. The Web sites of the vendors, such as Netscape (http://www.netscape.com), JavaSoft (http://www.javasoft.com), and Microsoft (http://www.microsoft.com) provide a great deal of technical information on their products as well.

One emerging approach to identifying and finding information online is digital object identifiers, described in more detail at http://www.doi.org.

System Design

For an in-depth discussion of how high-reliability systems are constructed, see *Reliable Computer Systems: Design and Evaluation,* 2nd edition by Daniel P. Siewiorek and Robert S. Swarz (Digital Press, 1992).

Ivar Jacobson's *Object-Oriented Software Engineering: A Use Case Driven Approach* (Addison Wesley Longman, 1992) advocates a style in which scenarios for how the software will be used are the basis for design. Jacobson, Griss, and Jonsson's *Software Reuse: Architecture, Process, and Organization for Business Success* (Addison Wesley Longman, 1997) introduces the current best word in design languages, the Uniform Modeling Language (UML).

Steve McConnell has written some very good books about software development and project management: *Code Complete* (Microsoft Press, 1993), *Rapid Development* (Microsoft Press, 1996), and *Software Project Survival Guide* (Microsoft Press, 1997).

David Taylor has written an excellent introduction to object technology for managers, *Object Technology: A Manager's Guide,* 2nd edition (Addison Wesley Longman, 1998).

Many other books about object technology are listed at http://www.paul-harmon.com/html/oo_books.html.

Creating and Managing Content

As with browsers and servers, there is a plethora of books about HTML and its variants. For some things, the Web itself is the best reference. For example, more information about cascading style sheets (CSS) can be found at the Web site of the World Wide Web Consortium (http://www.w3.org/pub/WWW/Style).

Adobe's Web site (http://www.adobe.com) contains information about PDF along with free software for viewing PDF files on various systems.

Martin Nemzow's book, *Building CyberStores* (McGraw-Hill, 1997) focuses on examples and content development for Internet commerce sites.

Cryptography

For a comprehensive discussion of cryptographic algorithms and protocols, there is no better reference than Bruce Schneier's *Applied Cryptography,* 2nd edition (John Wiley & Sons, 1997). Richard E. Smith's *Internet Cryptography* (Addison Wesley Longman, 1997) is an accessible discussion of the uses of cryptography for building secure systems on the Internet. David Kahn's *The Codebreakers: The Story of Secret Writing,* 2nd edition (Macmillan, 1997) is a fascinating history of cryptography.

Security

Web Security & Commerce by Simson Garfinkel with Gene Spafford (O'Reilly & Associates, 1997) is a useful reference on security issues in the World Wide Web. The classic work on firewalls is *Firewalls and Internet Security: Repelling the Wily Hacker* by William R. Cheswick and Steven M. Bellovin (Addison Wesley Longman, 1994).

The particular security issues involved with database systems are described in detail in *Database Security* by Silvana Castano et al. (Addison Wesley Longman, 1995).

Warwick Ford and Michael S. Baum's *Secure Electronic Commerce* (Prentice Hall, 1997) focuses on the technical and legal aspects of public key technology.

Payment Systems

Peter Wayner's book *Digital Cash: Commerce on the Net* (Academic Press, 1996) discusses many payment systems that have been developed on the Internet, along with the underlying concepts of security and cryptography. At a somewhat higher level, *Digital Money* by Daniel C. Lynch and Leslie Lundquist (John Wiley & Sons, 1996) is a useful executive briefing on payment systems for Internet transactions.

Details about SET and its specifications can be found at the Web sites of Visa (http://www.visa.com) and Mastercard (http://www.mastercard.com). Mondex is described in more detail on its Web site (http://www.mondex.com).

Transaction Processing

C. J. Date's *An Introduction to Database Systems,* 6th edition (Addison Wesley Longman, 1995) is a classic book about database systems from a technical point of view. An authoritative reference on transaction systems is *Transaction Processing: Concepts and Techniques* by Jim Gray and Andreas Reuter (Morgan Kaufmann, 1993). *Principles of Transaction Processing* by Philip A. Bernstein and Eric Newcomer (Morgan Kaufmann, 1997) is a somewhat more accessible introduction to transaction systems.

The Future of Internet Commerce

There are many books that look forward to the future of computing, communications, and business. Two in particular that touch on the uses of the Internet for commerce are *What Will Be: How the New World of Information Will Change Our Lives* by Michael Dertouzos (Harper-Collins, 1997) and *Release 2.0* by Esther Dyson (Broadway Books, 1997).

Index

Numerics
3DES (Triple DES) 218
7x24 116–118

A
Access control 335
Accountants 90
ACH (Automated Clearinghouse)
       network 58, 274
ACID properties 308, 316, 321
Active Server Pages (Microsoft) 150, 190
ActiveX controls 150–153, 159, 188, 191
   basic description of 147, 152–153
   bots and 189
   client technology and 161
   Java Beans and 160
   security and 251
Adaptability 8
Address Verification Service 272
Adobe Acrobat 198
Advertising
   See also Marketing
   business models and 43, 45, 47, 55, 60
   commerce value chain and 16–18, 25
   documenting 314
   printing hyperlinks on 47
Affinity programs 275
Agents 136–137
Aggregation 58, 64, 291
Airlines 24
Algorithms 210–214
   See also specific algorithms

Alice 209, 216, 220
Amazon.com 31, 33, 202
American Express 50, 267
   See also Credit cards
Anchors 133, 182
Anonymity 302
ANSI (American National Standards
       Institute) 115, 223
Apache server 149
APIs (Application Programming
       Interfaces) 149, 154, 281
   encapsulation and 157
   Transact and 336, 339
Applets 151–152, 156, 199
   See also Java
   basic description of 132–133, 146
   multimedia and 199
   security and 251
   shopping carts and 163
Application(s)
   buyer 337–339
   choosing 194
   development, custom 106–107
   development, rapid 160
   distributed 160
   future trends in 355
   operator 340–342
   relay 257
   reliability of 324
   security and 255–257
   seller 339–340
   sessions and 154

Approvals 56, 87
Architecture 111, 132
  basic description of 83–101, 330–334
  components of 90–92
  CORBA (Common Object Request
      Broker Architecture) 158, 160, 192,
      323
  core ideas for 84–86
  developing 83–101, 171
  examples of 92–100
  OBI (Open Buying on the Internet) 204
  system design and 171–177
Archiving 198, 315
ARP (Address Resolution Protocol) 128
ARPA (Advanced Research Projects
      Agency) 124
ARPAnet 124
Artificial intelligence 136
ASP (Active Server Pages) 150, 190
Atomicity 174–175, 308
Attacks 239, 243–247, 249–251, 253–254
Audio 113, 115, 199
Auditing 166, 243, 257, 317
Authentication 98, 200–201, 247
  basic description of 155, 178, 210, 257–
      263
  business models and 63
  client 260–262
  cookies and 78
  credit card 79–82, 269–271, 285, 310,
      328
  cryptography and 210, 217
  World Wide Web and 260–262
Automatic user recognition 78
Available to promise 303
AVI format 199

B

Back office 92
Backup systems 256, 318
Bandwidth 60, 63, 109, 206, 352
Banking 5, 63, 79, 80–81
Basic authentication 260
Beans (Java) 159
Benefits, measuring 112
Bill of lading 301
Bill presentment 284
Biometric 258
Block ciphers 217
Blowfish algorithm 219
Bluestone 192
Bob 209, 216, 220
Bonus payments 273
Bots 189, 191

See also Robots
Bottlenecks 33, 119
Briasco-Stewart, Samantha Marie iii, xiii
Brochureware 4
Brokerages 5, 39, 63
Browser(s)
  See also Web browser(s)
Brute force attacks 213
Bugs 36, 247–248, 254
  See also Debugging
Business rules 339
Business-to-business commerce 41, 53–59,
      62, 200, 293, 343
Buyer(s)
  anonymous 87
  applications 337–339
  goals of 70–71
  system architecture and 85, 87
  use of the term 70–71

C

CAs (Certificate Authorities) 232–233,
      261, 262
Caching 142–143
Cash 48, 64, 266–267, 287
CAST algorithm 219
Catalog(s) 35–51, 310, 321
  business models and 41, 46, 53–59, 62
  business-to-business 41, 53–59, 62, 200
  caching and 143
  cost of 4, 43
  custom 55–56, 204, 343
  inventory management and 303
  LiveCommerce and 192
  printing hyperlinks on 47
  system architecture and 93–100
CBC (cipher block chaining) 218
CD-ROMs 18, 61, 163, 207, 294, 332
Census Bureau 300
Centralization 104–105
CERN (Center for European Nuclear
      Research) 124, 132
Certificate(s) 227, 232–233, 261
  of origin 301
CGI (Common Gateway Interface) 148–
      150, 154, 191, 263, 323
Change, reactions to 115
Channel master strategy 34, 35, 38–39
Channels 144–145
  See also Push content delivery
Charge cards 50
  See also Credit cards
Charge-up transaction aggregation 292
Checks 49, 273

Chip cards 279
CHIPS 274
Ciphertext 210, 217
Clearinghouses, financial 61, 269, 274
Client(s)
  See also Servers
  authentication 260–262
  certificates 261
  programming 151–153
  security issues 249–252
  -side user profiles 78
  software 147–148, 311
  state mechanisms 155, 176–177
  system architecture and 90–93
  technology 160–163
  universal 151
  use of the term 91
COGS (cost of goods and services) 41
Cold Fusion (Allaire) 192
COM (Component Object Model) 159, 323
Commerce Suite (iCat) 192, 194
Commerce value chain 15–21, 30, 40, 43–
  67, 359
Commercial invoice 301
Commodities 72, 105
Competition 5, 38, 244
Complexity 82, 247, 321
Compression 224
Consistency 174, 308
Consular invoice 301
Consumer Credit Protection Act 50, 80, 271
Containers 61
Contamination, data 246
Contracts 27
Cookies 77–78, 153–156, 200, 202, 263
"Cool Notify" service 38
Copy protection, for digital goods 66–67
Copyright law 28, 167
CORBA (Common Object Request Broker
  Architecture) 158, 160, 192, 323
Core competency 105
Corporate purchasing cards 277
Coupons 45, 162, 278, 298, 335
Crackers 244
Creation phase 195
Credentials 252, 255
Credit, extending, to customers 49
Credit card(s) 19, 94, 267–273, 281
  See also Payment systems
  authorization 79–82, 269–271, 310, 328
  business models and 44, 50, 57, 63
  Consumer Credit Protection Act and 80,
    271
  payment online 284–287

processors 72, 269–271
  SET protocol and 79–82, 92, 95, 162,
    272, 284–287, 334, 345
  transaction costs 50, 63, 268
Criminals 244
Cross selling 47
Cryptography 29, 91, 209–233, 362
  See also Cryptosystems
  algorithms 212
  data compression and 224
  how to evaluate 212
  key management 212
  protocols 212
  strength 213–214
Cryptoki API 281
Cryptolopes (IBM) 166
Cryptosystems 211
  See also Cryptography
  public key 221–223
  secret key 218–219
CSPs (commerce service providers) 108,
  111, 118
CSS (Cascading Style Sheets) 184
Custom
  application development 106–107
  catalogs 55–56, 204, 343
Customer magnet strategy 34, 36, 38–39
Customer service 20–21, 43, 89, 201, 269
  basic description of 52
  business models and 44, 52, 59, 62, 66
  commerce value chain and 16–17
  cost of 2, 21, 53
  Transact and 338, 344, 348
Customs duties/tariffs 300, 354
CyberCash 162, 194, 283
CyberCoin (CyberCash) 283

D
Data
  compression 224
  contamination 246
Database(s) 62, 154, 298, 322
  access control 163
  administrators (DBAs) 88
  connectors 190–191
  -driven templates 150
  Transact and 341, 345, 348
DCE (Distributed Computing
  Environment) 323
  RPC (Remote Procedure Call) 159
DCOM (Distributed COM) 159
Debit cards 49, 281
Debugging 119, 254
  See also Bugs

Delegation 56
Demographics 22, 24, 60, 201
Denial of service attacks 245, 255
    See also Attacks
Department of Commerce (United
        States) 301
Department of Defense (United States) 124
Deployment phase 103–104
Depot delivery 302
DES (Data Encryption Standard) 213, 216–
        219, 223
Desktop publishing tools 189–190
Development focus 324
Diagnostics 119
    See also Debugging
Dialup connections 127
Diffie-Hellman algorithm 227
Digest authentication 261, 263
DigiBoxes (InterTrust) 166
Digicash 288
Digital coupons (Open Market) 335
Digital distributor strategy 37, 38–39
Digital Equipment Corporation 213, 289
Digital goods 20, 65–67, 89
    technology for 163–167
    Transact and 330, 338
Digital offers (Open Market) 335
Digital queries (Open Market) 335
Digital receipts (Open Market) 164, 335
Digital signatures 28, 211, 227
Digital tickets (Open Market) 156, 335
Disaster recovery 318
Dispute resolution 165
Distance based pricing model 300
Distinguished names 227
Distributed object computing 157
DNS (Domain Name Service) 109, 124,
        126, 129, 134
    basic description of 130–132
    security and 246, 262
Document(s)
    electronic filing for 62
    sales 61
DOI (Digital Object Identifier) 29
Domain names 109, 130–132
    See also DNS (Domain Name Service)
Dotted quad form 126
Downloading 20–21, 65
Draw down transaction aggregation 292
Durability 174, 308
DVD (digital video disk) 207
Dynamic HTML 184, 188

E
Ease of use 71
Eavesdropping 246
Economies of scale/scope 33, 35, 357
EDI (Electronic Data Exchange) 6, 20, 41,
        353
Editing phase 195–196
Editorial review 198
EFT (Electronic Funds Transfer) 57–58, 274
Electronic cash 64, 266–267, 287
Electronic purses 281
Elliptic curve algorithms 222
E-mail 45, 206, 207, 332
    ISPs and 109
    security and 251
Encapsulation 157
End-to-end protocols 127
Enigma 209
ERP (Enterprise Resource Planning) 45, 52,
        303, 305
Ethernet 33, 127–128
Europe 272, 299
European Union 299
Evolution 170, 334, 355
Exclusive OR operation 217
Exhaustive search 213
Export license 301
Extension mechanisms 145–147
Extranets 137

F
Failure 175–176, 316
    recovery 164
FAQs (Frequently Asked Questions) 53
FastCGI (Open Market) 149, 154, 323
Fax servers 345
FDDI (Fiber Distributed Data
        Interconnect) 127
Federal Reserve 274
FEDWIRE 274
Fields 185
    hidden 143, 156, 312
Filesystem(s) 321
Filtering, packet-level 256
Fingerprints 67, 167, 258
FIPS (Federal Information Processing
        Standard) 218
Firewalls 111, 128, 248, 256–257
First Virtual 194, 283
Flash crowd phenomenon 113, 173
Flat rate pricing model 300
Flexibility 160, 171, 248
Folio 192, 193–194

Foreign countries, domain names for 130
Forms 156, 162, 185
Forums 63
Frame relay 127
FrameMaker (Adobe) 190
Frames, for Web pages 183
Fraud 237, 245
Frequent buyer programs 46
Front office 92
FrontPage (Microsoft) 189–190, 191
FTP (File Transfer Protocol) 189
Functional
    architecture 360
    evolution 334
    units/interfaces 85
Functionality 162, 342

G
GEO codes 297
GET command 134
GIF format 134, 145, 185, 188, 198
    See also Images
GNFS (General Number Field Sieve) 222
Goals 6–7, 69–82
Government
    See also Legal issues; Taxes
    environment, future of 354
    interests, overview of 73
    records 314
    security and 244
GST (governmental sales tax) 48, 298
    See also Taxes

H
Hardware 319, 352
Harmonized Tariff System
        Classification 300
Hash functions 225–226
High-availability systems 318
Hits 262
HMAC algorithm 226
Hosting services 110–111
    See also ISPs (Internet Service Providers)
Hostnames 109
Hot spots 184, 187–188
    See also Hyperlinks
HST (harmonized sales tax) 298
HTML (Hypertext Markup Language) 7,
        139, 148
    basic description of 132, 182–185
    editors 94, 108, 189–190
    MIME type 145
    server-side scripting and 150

tables and 147
URLs and 134
HTTP (HyperText Transfer Protocol) 126,
        132, 148, 185, 331, 334
    Active Server Pages and 191
    basic description of 134–135
    keepalive option 142
    MIME types and 145
    pull content and 142–144
    security and 260, 261
    sessions and 153
Humor, translating 26
Hyperlinks
    See also URLs (Uniform Resource
        Locators)
    basic description of 133–134, 182
    image maps and 184, 187–188
    testing 197

I
IBM (International Business
        Machines) 162, 226
IDEA (International Data Encryption
        Algorithm) 214, 218
Idempotent systems 311
IDL (Interface Definition Language) 158
IETF (Internet Engineering Task
        Force) 115, 127, 129, 135
IIOP (Internet Inter-ORB Protocol) 159
Image(s)
    field 185
    GIF format 134, 145, 185, 188, 198
    HTML for 183
    JPEG format 134, 145, 185, 198
    maps 184, 187–188
    MIME type 183
Immutable records 316
Implementation 103–120
Implementors 88
Import/export laws 25, 73
Indexing 197
Infobases 193–194
    See also Databases
Infrastructure trends 354
Input syntax 254
Insurance 268, 277
    certificate 301
Integrated systems 107–108
Integrity, data 210, 217, 224, 324
Intellectual property 28, 61
    See also Copyright law
Intelligent agents 35
Interactivity 161
Internalization 104–105

International letter of credit 301
International operations
    credit cards and 272
    domain names and 130
    international software 26
    transportation and 300
Internet commerce 1–363
Internet Explorer browser 146, 147, 261
    See also Web browsers
Internet malls 111
Interop conference 125
Interoperability 125, 157, 354
Interruption of service 245
Intranets 137
Inventory 85, 302
Invoices 301, 314, 349
IP (Internet Protocol) 77, 109, 126, 128–
        129, 138, 249
IPv6 (Internet Protocol, Version 6) 138
ISAPI 149, 154
ISO (International Standards
        Organization) 223, 271, 345
ISO 8583 271
Isolation 174, 308
ISPs (Internet Service Providers) 7, 92,
        108–111, 118
IT departments 8, 72, 104, 114
ITU (International Telecommunications
        Union) 115
IUWC (Informix Universal Web
        Connect) 191
IV (Initialization Vector) 217

J
Japan 273
Java 113, 115, 138, 150–153, 157, 161, 188,
        192
    See also Applets
    basic description of 152
    Beans 159
    Card API 281
    Electronic Commerce Framework 152
    write once, run anywhere feature 159
JavaScript 146, 150, 188, 191
JavaSoft 162
JPEG format 134, 145, 185, 198
    See also Images
Just-in-time delivery 33

K
Key(s)
    basic description of 210
    destruction 231

distribution 231
exchange 227
generation 228
length 214–215
lifetime 215
management 211, 212, 228–232, 335
sessions 224
storage 229–230

L
Language binding 157
Language support, multiple 53
Laptop computers 353
Latency 173
Layering 126
Legacy systems 108
Legal issues 73, 239
    commerce value chain and 26–29
    consumer protection 50, 80, 271
    copyright laws 28, 61, 167
    in the future 355
Licensing 30, 65, 67, 163
Links
    See also Hyperlinks
Lists 183
LiveCommerce (Open Market) 192, 343
LiveWire 150
Log servers 345
Logging 322
Logistics 299–306
Logos 26
Long-term operation phase 103–104

M
MAC (message authentication code) 226–
        227, 336
Magazines 23, 42, 62
Managing state 172, 176–177
Marketing
    See also Advertising
    basic description of 22–25, 42–46
    business models and 42–46, 55
    commerce value chain and 16–18, 22–25
    one-to-one 24–25, 44, 46
    system architecture and 89
Masquerade 246
    See also Security
MasterCard 50, 267, 276
    See also Credit cards
MBTF (mean time between failures) 320
MD5 (Message Digest) algorithm 225, 226,
        336
MDC-2 algorithm 226

MDC-4 algorithm 226
Merchandising 44–46, 77–78, 205–206, 342
Merchant servers 93–95
Message(s)
    as records 317
    authentication codes (MAC) 226–227,
        336
    digests 225–226
    integrity code (MIC) 226
Metcalfe's law 33
Micropayments 268, 288–292
Microsoft Active Server Pages 150, 190
Microsoft Component Object Model
        (COM) 159, 323
Microsoft FrontPage 189–190, 191
Microsoft Powerpoint 198
Microsoft Visual C++ 159
Microsoft Windows 147
Microsoft Windows NT 253
Microtransactions 63, 64
Millicent (Digital Equipment
        Corporation) 289
MIME (Multimedia Internet Mail
        Extensions) 145–147
MIS departments
    See IT departments
Misappropriation 246
Modem speeds 206
    See also Bandwidth
Mondex 281, 288
Money orders 277
Monitoring 119, 243
Moore's Law 213, 352
MOTO (Mail or Telephone Order) 50, 272
MPEG format 145, 199
MRO (maintenance, repair, and
        operations) 41, 53–59
MTTR (mean time to repair) 320
Multimedia 63, 144–145, 182, 188
    audio 113, 115, 199
    presentation 198–199
    video 113, 115, 145, 199
    Web fundamentals and 132–133
Multiorganization operation 118
Multiple-language support 53

N
Naming 158
Nanopayments 289
Narrowcasting 44
National Security Agency 225
Natural disasters 318
NetBill 290

Netscape Communications Corporation 34,
        76, 135, 146, 261
Netscape Communicator 189
Netscape Composer 189
Netscape Navigator browser 146, 261
    See also Web browsers
Network(s)
    computers 138
    Ethernet 33, 127–128
    filesystems 116, 129
    security and 250
Newspapers 23, 62
Nexus (commercial presence) 296
NFS (Network File System) 116, 129
Niche markets 43
NIST (National Institute of Standards and
        Technology) 225
Non-repudiation 210, 217
Notational money 266
NSAPI 149, 154

O
OBI (Open Buying on the Internet) 97–100,
        204
Object Management Group 158
Object Request Brokers 158
Object technology 156–160
ODBC (Open Database Connectivity) 191,
        193
OLE (Object Linking and Embedding) 146,
        152, 159
OLTP (online transaction processing) 323
One-time pad systems 215–216
One-to-one marketing 46
OOP (object-oriented programming) 157
Open Market xiii, 288, 327
    FastCGI 149, 154, 323
    LiveCommerce 192, 343
    SecureLink 334
    SecurePublish 193
    Transact 192, 337–349
Open Profiling Standard (Firefly) 76
Operations managers 89
Operator applications 340–342
Order forms 93–100, 328
Order fulfillment 20, 107–108
    agents 89
    business models and 42, 51, 58, 65
    Transact and 338, 341, 343, 347
Order processing
    See also Payment systems
    business models and 43–44, 47, 52, 56–
        58, 63
    commerce value chain and 16–20

documenting 312
OBI architecture and 97–100
packaged applications and 107–108
Outsourcing 104–106
Overloaded Web sites 113

P

Packaged applications 107–108
Packets 128
Palmtop computers 353
Parametric search capability 193
Parking meter aggregation 64, 292
Pass phrases 229
Passwords 163, 229, 257–263
See also Security
for single sites 200, 202
guessing 253
Patent licensing 30
Payment system(s) 162
See also Transactions
basic description of 48–51, 57–58, 265–294
billing 293
business models and 42, 48–51, 57–58, 63–64, 67
business-to-business commerce and 293
CSPs and 112–113
in the abstract 293–294
information commerce and 294
Internet 282–294
multiorganization operation and 118
packaging 268–269
real-world 266–279
resources for 363
system architecture and 92, 93, 100
Transact and 341, 342, 343, 347, 349
PayNow electronic check system 283
PCMCIA (Personal Computer Memory Card Industry Association) cards 279
PDF (Portable Document Format) 145, 188
Performance
problems, troubleshooting 119
system design and 172, 172–173
PERL 254
Personal digital certificates 201
Personal newspaper site example 203–204
Personalization 71, 193, 203
PGP (Pretty Good Privacy) 218
Physical goods (hard goods) 20, 48
Physical layer 127–128
PINs (Personal Identification Numbers) 238, 260, 267, 281
PKCS (Public-Key Cryptography Standards) 222, 281

Plaintext 210
Plug-ins 146, 198
Point of title passage 296
Point-to-point data circuits 127
Polymorphism 157
Port numbers 129
Portable storage 280
POST command 134
Postcode servers 345
Powerpoint (Microsoft) 198
Pricing 46, 55, 71, 300
Privacy 26, 70, 156, 161
See also Security
cryptography and 29, 210, 217
merchandising versus 77–78
physical delivery and 301
Private-label cards 276
Problem-solving procedures 119
Processors 173
Procurement cards 57
Product displays 45
Profiles 201–203
Project design phase 103–104
Project management 112–113
Promotions 46
Proof of purchase 21
Protocol(s)
See also specific protocols
as key to the Internet 2
attacks 251
core network 127–132
cryptography and 211, 219, 223–228
customer service and 53
designation, in URLs 133–134
evolution/future of 8, 138–139
layering of 126
packet-switched 53
smart cards and 282
system architecture and 85
PST (provincial sales tax) 48, 298
See also Taxes
Public key (asymmetric) systems 164, 211, 214, 219–223
Pull content 142–144
delivery 141
Purchase orders 57, 94, 274
Push content 144–145
delivery 62, 66, 141

Q

QuickTime (Apple) 145, 199

R

RAID (redundant arrays of inexpensive
        disks) 320
Railroad system xi, 31, 34, 357
Randomness pool 229
Rate of change 106
RC4 algorithm 214, 219
RC5 algorithm 214
Read-only data 322
RealAudio MIME type 145
Real-time requirements 312
Receipts 21, 162, 164, 330, 335
Records 269, 313–317
   theft of 246
Registration 200–203, 338
Reliability 161, 172, 174
Replay, protection against 224
Replication 320
Reporting 57, 62
Requirements 69–82
Requisitioners 56, 98–100, 293
Researchers 244
Reverse lookups 131
Revolutions 31–32
Rights management 61, 66–67, 166–167
RIPEMD algorithm 226
Risk 73, 239, 243–247, 271–272, 292
RMI (Remote Method Invocation) 159
Robots 135–136
   See also Bots
Roles 86–90
Round-the-clock operation 116–118
RSA
   algorithm 221–223
   Laboratories 214, 221–223, 281
   Secret-Key Challenge 214
Rules, business 339

S

Sales tax 44, 73, 345, 354
   basic description of 296–299
   computing 27, 48
Sandboxes 152
Sapphire/Web (Bluestone) 192
Scaling 172, 172–173, 320, 333
Scripting 146, 150–151, 199
Search engines 47, 135–136, 197
Secret key (symmetric) systems 211, 216–
      219
Secret sharing 228, 230
Secure storage 280
SecureLink system 96, 97, 327, 334
SecurePublish (Open Market) 193

Security
   See also Passwords
   attacks 239, 243–247, 249–251, 253–254
   basic description of 235–263
   client technology and 161
   communications 178
   containment 332
   design 241–243
   digital goods and 163–167
   firewalls 111, 128, 248, 256–257
   future of 138, 353
   implementation and 111, 118
   IP (Internet Protocol) and 128–129, 138
   ISPs and 111
   object technology and 158
   policies 240
   requirements 313
   resources for 362
   routers and 128
   secure container technology and 166
   system design and 172, 177–179
Seller applications 339–340
Serialization 309
Server(s) 131, 253–255, 262
   See also Clients
   APIs 149
   components, basic description of 148–
      150
   HTTP and 135
   implementation and 112–113, 116
   managing state and 176–177
   name designation, in URLs 133–134
   offline browsers and 144
   push 133
   -side includes 150
   -side scripting 150
   systems, sizing 112–113
   Transact and 344
Sessions 153–156, 224, 262–263
SET (Secure Electronic Transactions)
        protocol 79–82, 92, 95, 162, 272,
        284–287
Settlement servers 345
SHA-1 (Secure Hash Algorithm) 225
Shipper's export declaration 301
Shipping and handling 48, 51, 58, 299–306
Shockwave (Macromedia) 199
Shopping carts 18–19, 47, 85, 162
S-HTTP (Secure HTTP) 135, 261, 284
Signatures, digital 28, 211, 227
siteDirector (Folio) 192, 193–194
Skimming 247
SKUs (stock keeping units) 44
Smart cards 258, 279–282

Smart statement 338
SNFS (Special Number Field Sieve) 222
Software
    Developer's Kit (SDK) 336
    development 103–107, 336
    failures 319
    installation 256, 319
    reuse 354
    sales 20, 42, 118–119
    technology trends 353
    upgrades 249, 256, 319
Source control tools 196
Specifiers 87
SQL (Structured Query Language) 150, 323
SSL (Secure Sockets Layer) 135, 219, 261,
        262, 263, 284
Staging phase 197
Standards 74–75, 115–116, 127, 353
State 154–156
Storage systems 202–203, 229–230
StoryServer (Vignette) 192
Strategy 4, 5, 7, 31–40, 355, 360
Stream ciphers 217
Subscriptions 60, 66, 330, 338, 345, 349
Sun Microsystems 116, 129, 281
Superdistribution 61
Supplier-centered relationship 34
Support systems 333
SWIFT 274
System administrators 89
System architecture 111, 132
    basic description of 83–101, 330–334
    components of 90–92
    core ideas for 84–86
    developing 83–101, 171
    examples of 92–100
    OBI (Open Buying on the Internet) 204
    system design and 171–177
System configuration 248, 256
System design 169–179, 361
System integrators 118–119
System supervisors 89

T
T1 connections 109
Tables 147, 183
Tariffs 25, 300, 354
Tax(es) 44, 73, 345, 354
    basic description of 296–299
    computing 27, 48
Taxi meter aggregation 64, 292
TCL (Tool Command Language) 254

TCP/IP (Transmission Control Protocol/
        Internet Protocol) 74, 115, 116,
        124, 126, 129, 150, 174, 249
    sequence number attack 253
Technical support 16–17, 59, 110
Technologists 73
Telephone(s)
    calls, over the Internet 63
    cards 281
    customer service by 44
    invention of xi
    marketing 23
Templates, database-driven 150
Testing 197, 311
Text MIME type 145
Theft 67, 245, 252
Threats, analyzing 245–247
Throughput 173
Timestamps 150, 227
Time to market 324
TLS (Transport Layer Security) working
        group 135
Tokens 64, 258, 266
TP (transaction processing) monitor 321
Tracking
    buyer behavior 314
    cookies 78
    packages 301
Trademarks 26
Traffic analysis 246
Training customers 59
Transact (Open Market) 192, 337–349
Transaction(s)
    aggregation 58, 64, 291
    basic description of 307–324
    inventory management and 303, 304
    OBI architecture and 97–100
    resources for 363
    separate content from 331
    system architecture and 85, 91–93, 97–
        100
    system design and 172, 174–176
    volume, financial processors and 72
    walking through 328
Treese, Erica Briasco iii, xiii
Triple DES 218
Trust 86, 232–233, 269, 312
    boundaries 334
Trusted execution environment 281
Two-phase commit 309

U
UDP (Unreliable Datagram Protocol) 126,
        129

Uncertainty, problem of 30
Uniform addressing/naming 126
Unique ID numbers 205–206
Universal identifiers 127
Universality 161
Unix 147, 253
Upgrades 113, 249, 319
URLs (Uniform Resource Locator) 25, 133,
        164, 206, 334
    See also Hyperlinks
    basic description of 133–134, 182
    CGI and 148
    custom 263
    DNS and 130–132
    dynamic 156
Usage-based charging 61
User IDs 156
User profiles 162, 201–203

V
Value
    based pricing model 300
    chain pirate strategy 34, 37, 38–39
    proposition 34–35, 43, 54, 60
VAN (Value-Added Network) services 6
VAT (value-added tax) 48, 299
    See also Taxes
VBScript 146, 150, 191
Venona 216
Video 113, 115, 145, 199
Virtual
    corporation 302
    inventory 302
    machines 152
    warehouse 302, 304
    worlds 63, 188, 199
VirtualPIN 283
Viruses 250, 252
Visa 50, 79–82, 267, 276
    See also Credit cards
Visa Cash 281, 287
Visual C++ (Microsoft) 159
VRML (Virtual Reality Markup
        Language) 188, 199

W
W3C (World Wide Web Consortium) 76
Wallet applications 91, 95, 162, 203, 290
Warehouses 302
Watermarks 67, 167
Web browser(s)
    client software requirements and 147–148
    extensible 135

implementation and 116
Internet Explorer browser 146, 147, 261
Java and 152
Netscape Navigator 146, 261
Netscape Navigator browser 146, 261
offline 144
plug-ins and 146
scripting and 146, 151–153
system architecture and 91–93, 96, 98
tables and 147
testing Web pages with 197
user-specific state and 176
XML and 139
WebTV 138
Weight based pricing model 300
Windows (Microsoft) 147
Windows NT (Microsoft) 253
WIPO (World Intellectual Property
        Organization) 29
Wire protocols 158
Word for Windows (Microsoft) 190
WordPerfect (Corel) 190
Workflows 56
World Wide Web
    See also HTML (Hypertext Markup
        Language)
    authentication on 260–262
    basic description of 123–139
    fundamentals 132–133
    payment systems and 284–287
    sessions 262–263
    technology issues and 7–8
WORLDTax 299

X
X.509 certificates 164, 233, 261
XML (Extensible Markup Language) 139,
        184